William Y. Adams

Defining Peasants

Defining Peasants

Essays concerning Rural Societies, Expolary Economies, and Learning from them in the Contemporary World

Teodor Shanin

Basil Blackwell

British Library Cataloguing in Publication Data

A CIP catalogue record for this book is available from the British Library.

Library of Congress Cataloging in Publication Data
Shanin, Teodor.
Defining peasants: essays concerning rural societies, expolary economies, and learning from them in the contemporary world / Teodor Shanin.
    p. cm.
ISBN 0–631–15037–4
1. Peasantry. 2. Peasantry—Soviet Union. I. Title.
HD 1521.S448 1990
305.5′633′0947—dc20   89–17537
                                                    CIP

Typeset in 10 on 12 pt
by Vera Reyes
Printed in Great Britain by
TJ Press Ltd., Padstow

Contents

Acknowledgements

The author and publisher are grateful to the following for permission to reproduce previously published articles by Teodor Shanin:

Journal of Historical Sociology for chapter 6; *Race and Class* for chapter 8; Routledge for chapter 12; Cambridge University Press for chapter 14; *ZWAN* for chapter 16; University of Wisconsin Press for chapter 19.

1

Agendas of Peasant Studies and the Perception of Parallel Realities

In Place of a Preface (1989)

1 Assumptions and Meanings

There are three fundamental ways to approach contemporary peasantry as a social phenomenon. The first is to assume that we do not encounter in it a distinguishable set of related characteristics, which can be analytically treated as a type of social structure. It would therefore be a notion of no conceptual significance, just a word, possibly a linguistic reminder of a historical past. Consequently there could also be no place for a theory concerning peasants' particularities, be it one of economy, patterns of political behaviour, collective perceptions and so on. The second approach is to assume that peasants differ consistently from non-peasants in ways which are socially significant, but that this diversity can and should be fully explicated within the existing body of general theory, by extending its application. Lastly, one can assume that peasant distinctiveness exists, as well as that conceptual particularity must follow from it, i.e. that the most effective way to analyse peasants is to establish and use to that purpose discrete theoretical structures. This would mean consideration of peasant economies with the help of a Peasant Economics as a distinct section of the discipline of Economics, and a similar procedure for some other dimensions of social structure and action. To avoid misunderstanding let me state at once that no totally separate conceptualization and no total division of all and sundry along peasant/non-peasant categorical boundaries are being claimed within this third view (or are even possible to perceive for contemporary societies). The price of any taxonomy is abstraction from the shades and riches of actuality. It makes some characteristics stand out more clearly while others turn opaque. This advances perception but only in so far as its relative nature is understood and accepted.

One can present the suggested three fundamental categories of approach graphically as shown in table 1.1.

Table 1.1 Categories of analysis of contemporary peasantry

	1	2	3
Social distinctiveness of peasants	No (−)	Yes (+)	Yes (+)
Theoretical distinctiveness of peasanthood	No (−)	No (−)	Yes (+)

The categories suggested crosscut many accepted ideological divides and bridge over different schools of thought and intellectual generations. Up to a point they also defy explicit self-presentations by the analysts themselves, who are not always aware of or ready to admit to the epistemological structures which underpin their particular views and, even more, to the strange bedfellows these can land them with. To exemplify, the very young Lenin of *The Development of Capitalism in Russia* (1899) would share category 1 and its two 'nos' with McNamara in his World Bank Director's Statement of 1973. The first was still putting the term 'peasants' in quotation marks in the times when his book was written, while the second avoided the word altogether, talking instead of 'the poor . . . in the rural areas . . . not significantly contributing to growth'.[1] Likewise, Kautsky's *The Agrarian Question* (1899) would share epistemological design with Schultz's *Transforming Traditional Agriculture* (1964).[2] Similarly to McNamara, Schultz did not even use the term in question (for reasons related to the tacit semantic messages inbuilt into the language of English and US academic culture, an issue to which we shall return). Kautsky did use the term; and he aimed at a strategy for the creation of a socialist commonwealth, while Schultz was offering plans for a healthier capitalism all around the globe. Yet, for analysing peasants and rural social environments, the similarities in general approach of Kautsky and Schultz are in this view more basic and significant than their divide. Finally, since the late 1960s, in category 3 the most influential impact and symbol in Western rural-directed social sciences proved to be *The Theory of Peasant Economy* by Chayanov.[3] But Chayanov's way of reasoning in approaching peasantry can be found in a variety of authors, traditions and disciplines.[4]

1 V.I. Lenin, *Collected Works* (Moscow, 1960–9), vol. 3; R. McNamara, *Address to the Board of Governors* (International Bank for Reconstructional Development, Nairobi, 1973).

2 K. Kautsky, *The Agrarian Question* (London, 1988); T.W. Schultz, *Transforming Traditional Agriculture* (Chicago, 1964).

3 A. Chayanov, *The Theory of Peasant Economy* (Manchester, 1986).

4 For a broad sample see M. Bloch, *Les Caractères Originaux de l'Histoire Rurale Française* (Paris 1952/56); H. Alavi, 'Peasant Classes and Primordial Loyalties', *Journal of Peasant Studies*, 1(1973); J.C. Scott, *Moral Economy of the Peasant* (London, 1976); W.I.

The suggested diversity being usually implicit, i.e. present as a subterranean logic which defines methods and plausibilities rather than in manifest declarations, meant that much of the argument about contemporary peasantry's characteristics and definitions ran at cross purposes. Only too often the blows and the fighters did not even connect as different questions were unwittingly being addressed and/or different assumptions and rules of analysis taken for granted. The piling up of 'data' did nothing to resolve such arguments and, indeed, often made the puzzlement worse. To explore the choice of pre-assumptions and epistemological designs we must move in a different direction.

At the roots of the divisions in the fundamental approach to peasantry lies a more general issue of perception of parallel realities. Existentially, all of us know the diversity of human phenomena. On the other hand, the effort and the achievements of all sciences have centred on bringing complexity to its simplest (most 'elegant') common denominators, in what can be seen as a monumental exercise in application of the analytical logic of Occam's razor. Somewhat greater relativity and 'softer' propositions as to the determinants of action were usually accepted within *social* sciences, but their principal goals and standards of success were as extensively linked to the teasing out and/or explanation of the uniformities. Into this context linked the Theory of Progress, as the most influential and seductive model of social sciences. It assumed a necessary sequence of social advance from multiplicity of inadequacies towards uniformity of social forms and arrangements, a uniformity which is at once more rational, more satisfying of material needs, better on ethical grounds and historically necessary. The high plausibility of and the preference for the assumption of universally human and social characteristics (at least, in the making), an operational uni-logic and a single epistemological design follow as a matter of course.

A major particularity of peasant studies, especially in their 'category 3' interpretations, lies in the challenge they offered to the assumptions of social uniformity and of a uni-logic of social analysis. Hence the 'natural' attraction of these studies for some and their disregard and hostility towards others. For, from the inception of the contemporary social sciences, peasantry's generalized image was extensively used as a yardstick of 'otherness' – of social arrangements different from our own, yet with discrete consistency and logic. In particular, sociology began with a number of binary typologies: the 'community' versus 'society' of Toennies, the 'collectivism' versus 'individualism' of the de Coulangues,

---

Thomas and F. Znaniecki, *The Polish Peasant in Europe and America*, first published in 1918 (New York, 1958); G. Esteva, *The Struggle for Rural Mexico* (New York, 1983); etc.

the 'primary' versus 'secondary' relations of Cooley, etc. If we look more closely at the substantive underpinning of the empty boxes of these taxonomies, we can recognize it usually as a division between 'modernity' (which included 'us') and, at the other pole, an abstract description of what was mostly the known or assumed life of the peasant communities of the day. Durkheim acted likewise in his use of the categorization of 'mechanical' versus 'organic' solidarity, but added a third box of a future and better society due to combine the positive qualities of the earlier two types within a system of neo-guilds.[5] Marx, the major classical theorist who avoided dual or triple taxonomies and gave particular attention to historiography, still put peasantry to a similar use. In his *Capital*, vol. 1, and in the *Grundrisse* the generalizations of peasantry played a major role in establishing the starting point of the history of pre-class societies, their pre-capitalist transformation and/or the eventual formation of capitalism.[6] Peasanthood as the type of existence the authors could then see through every window, or, at least, at the local market and in the foreign travels of the literati, entered the perception of the social scientists of the day mostly as the synonym of otherness and of the past which is 'still' in the present.

2 'Peasantology's' History: Silences and Agendas[7]

While indirectly evident in the very fabric of social sciences, the direct perception and analysis of peasantry was often suspended and ever uneven in its flow. A short social history of 'peasantology' would help to put the current agendas of peasant studies in context.

In the pre-industrial world the literate attitude to peasants combined hostility with silence. This massive majority of all people produced the wealth of the wealthy and provided for the culture of the cultured, while their numbers, when under control, defined the might of the powerful. To deliver the goods peasants had to be subjugated. It seems that they had also to be dehumanized in the consciousness of those who ruled, administered and wrote. The carnel of binarities of latter-day sociology was already there, for peasant brutishness was being treated as a counterpoint to the civilized society. It was also used as the justification of the privileges of the civilized. Peasant resistance was seen as but an irrational mob violence to no purpose, for it is easier to grind humans

5 E. Durkheim, *Socialism* (New York, 1962).

6 See in particular *Capital*, vol. 1, chs 1, 27–30, and the *Grundrisse* part presented as *Pre-Capitalist Economic Formations* (London, 1964).

7 Section 2 is based on the argument offered in T. Shanin, 'Short Historical Outline of Peasant Studies', in *Peasants and Peasant Societies*, second edition (Oxford, 1987).

into dust and see this as natural and eternal if we do not admit that it is the enslavement of beings like ourselves that lies at the root of our good fortune. It was even better to forget 'them' altogether. Medieval writings are full of kings and wars, of philosophy and poetry, of law and astrology, with some lives of saints and sages thrown in for good measure. They are mostly silent about peasants.

When peasants were recognized, usually in connection with some human-induced disaster (be it a new tax, a law of enserfment or a rebellion of the brutalized), hostility and contempt for the peasants burst through. The *Declinatio Rustica* of the thirteenth century defined 'the six declensions of the word peasant' as 'villain, rustic, devil, robber, brigand and looter; and in the plural – wretches, beggars, liars, rogues, trash and infidels'.[8] The usages of language tell us much the same. In early Russian the term peasant was *smerd*, from the verb *smerdet'*, 'to stink'. The Polish term 'cham' indicated crudity and was mythically rooted in different tribal origins from those of the nobles' 'nation'. In eighteenth-century English a peasant meant a brute and an illiterate, while the verb 'to peasant' was still used to mean to subjugate and to enslave.[9]

Modernity and capitalism came to Europe with the triple revolution of industrialization, of citizenship within a nation state, and of the spread of a secular, mathematics-bound science of practical application. In its most fundamental self-images this was a world without peasants; indeed, depeasantization became a major index of modernization. The past hostility towards peasants by those who drew their living from peasant sweat was now being exchanged for detached pity, a shrug of the shoulders over the irrationalities and the brutalities of the past and a cheerful assumption of its all rapidly coming to an end. It was less vicious but as dismissive. Peasants were now treated as an anachronism and therefore as an irrelevance

Anachronistic or not in the face of growing manufacturing industries, in the nineteenth and still in the first half of the twentieth century peasants were the majority of Europeans, let alone of humanity at large. The way the peasants were approached in scholarly endeavour differed deeply and to make that clear three global regions must be singled out, even though, of course, no absolute matching of geography and intellectual tendencies was the case.

First, the popular and the scholarly consciousness of the industrial West (of which those who wrote in English provided a major component) was dominated by the historiography-cum-typology dividing the

8 J. Le Goff in C. Cipolla, *The Fontana Economic History of Europe: The Middle Ages* (London, 1977), p. 71.
9 *The Oxford English Dictionary* vol. vii, (Oxford, 1933), p. 594.

social world into 'modern' and 'backward'. The assumption of the decomposition and necessary disappearance of all things backward was part of it. On such an intellectual map the actual (rather than the abstracted) peasants disappeared even more effectively than in the olden days by falling under an unspecific heading of the 'remainders of the past' (together with slaves and feudals, caravans and pirates, astrology and witchcraft). The one unifying characteristic of that category was its necessarily declining significance. When at the turn of the century rural sociology emerged as a subdiscipline in its own right (first in the USA), it focused on farming as an occupation, disregarding peasants as a social entity. The word 'peasant' was assigned in the English language to its medieval context. Seemingly offensive to modern eyes and to the people so called, it was excluded from modern scholarly discourse, from policy making and from expert advice.

The polar opposite of the West, with its modernity, power and plenty were, in those days the colonies and the 'Orient'. There life seems to have trickled more slowly, the hand of the state to have been heavier and modern science more sparse, imported or imposed as it was from the West. The fact that very often nine-tenths of the population was peasant mattered little to the local literati. To the extent that this was discussed at all it was done under the direct impact of the European theories of progress and was as dismissive of the issue. There were some honourable exceptions to it, both foreign and native. But exceptions they were.

It was the third region, Eastern and Central Europe, where studies of peasantry as such blossomed at the turn of the century. In those countries a highly sophisticated 'intelligentsia', politically committed to nationalism and/or modernization in its liberal, populist or socialist forms, faced massive peasantries – the poorest and most oppressed segment of their people. Ideologies and policies turned attention to the peasant majorities as the major object, the possible carrier or the main bottle-neck of the necessary advance. By the eve of the First World War and later, the intellectuals' political attempts to look at and to activate peasantries were being increasingly matched by the peasants' own efforts to establish viable political movements (referred to then as 'Green') in defence of their own interest in Poland, Rumania, Bulgaria, Russia, etc. Farther to the west, the German academic culture offered a possible case of marginality-induced analytical advance which was West European in its impetus, East European in much of its rural experience. It produced some inspired writing about peasants and the rural scene, present and past: Marx and Weber, Sombert and Kautsky, Buchner and David. And it was Denmark which became for a time the prime example of an autonomous and very successful rural cooperative movement and of self-generated innovations by peasant smallholders. From the German Sea to the Black Sea and to the Urals, studies of peasantry flourished on both the empirical and the theoretical plain. Much of the analytical work done then is still unsurpassed in quality and insight.

The blossoming of peasant studies in Eastern and Central Europe and some measure of their cross-fertilizing impact elsewhere came to an end in the 1920s–30s. Rapidly spreading dictatorships destroyed or crippled most of the peasant parties which initiated the Green International. Nazism and similar pests demolished also the academic heritage which played a central role in the advancement of the studies of peasant societies. Stalin's collectivization and 'purge' brought a great silence into the USSR, as both its Marxist and non-Marxist analysts of peasantry went under. The build-up towards the World War, and the War itself, focused intellectual and political attentions elsewhere. With a few significant exceptions like Fei and Warriner,[10] peasant studies passed into an oblivion which lasted for thirty years.

They were to re-emerge *en masse* into a very different world. The World War followed by rapid decolonization changed the global map and its power balance. The United Nations provided a major international scene where the case of the global underdogs came to be presented in international terms, as an issue of 'underdevelopment'. For a time, a global theory of progress, the Modernization Theory, defined the prevailing images, self-images, predictions and plans. Independence, the education and the world markets, with a dash of economic planning, were to ensure that the 'Backward Societies' of the world, especially its ex-colonies, would rapidly catch up with the industrial West. The failure of this prediction and these strategies, the 'growing gap' of wealth and power, came eventually to be theorized by new images and models which were well represented by the simultaneity of appearance of Myrdal's concept of 'comulation of advancement and backwardness' and Paul Baran's 'the political economy of backwardness'.[11] The 'developing societies' became synonymous with 'dependence' and a world's slum. Social scientists, politicians and planners were made to turn their attention from the purely economic indices and curves of 'up and up' to the particularities of the social structure of the 'developing societies'. A majority there were peasants. Simultaneously, a 'critique by arms' – an assault against the corrupt regimes of the Third World – was increasingly being mounted by guerilla movements, taught by Mao that their success was subject to their link with the common

10 C.N. Arensleag, *The Irish Countrymen* (Macmillan, 1937). Fei Hsiao Tung, *Peasant Life in China* (Duton, 1939); D. Warriner, *Economics of Peasant Farms* (Oxford, 1939).

11 For further discussion see H. Alavi and T. Shanin, *Introduction to Sociology of the 'Developing Societies'* (London, 1982).

people. A majority of them were peasants. Right and left, scholars, politicians and revolutionaries, were turning their attention towards peasants and peasant societies. A virtual explosion of peasant studies in the late 1960s was as much part of a new political situation as of a major conceptual refocusing which reached its symbolic peak in the heady days of 1968.

When this came, the general knowledge of the (re)discovered subject matter and, especially, its analytical and theoretical components was remarkably thin. Yet the appetite for it broke all bonds. A new theoretical armoury was rapidly set up consisting of some of the old and partly forgotten texts by Znaniecki, Marx, Lenin, Sorokin, Kroeber (via Redfield, who expanded it considerably), and a few more. These were now supplemented by and integrated with a number of major classical works, which were 'new'; that is, freshly translated and introduced into the Anglo-Saxon academic tradition. Of those, particularly dramatic was the impact of Chayanov's *Theory of Peasant Economy* and of Marx's newly discovered *Grundrisse*, first published in 1966 and 1964 respectively. A number of integrative works, especially those by Wolf, Shanin and Galeski, mapped out anew the subject matter, establishing the basic parameters of contemporary peasant studies.[12] A number of other important works probed particular aspects of peasanthood, with their results being incorporated into the general conceptual debate.[13] Defining peasants became a matter of major significance, circumscribing a field of study and setting its agendas. While approaches differed, all of the definitions offered by those who did not now accept peasantry as a legitimate and useful concept carried two characteristics in common. They assumed that contemporary peasants represented a social system 'embedded in' and/or linked to broader social system(s), yet differently structured. They suggested also some institutional characteristics of peasantry which make for its social reproduction, explicating the paradox of its non-disappearance contrary to most of the nineteenth-century predictions. My own definition offered then can exemplify this. It suggested, in 1971, the distinguishing of the peasants as 'small agricultural producers who, with the help of simple equipment and the labour

12 In particular E.R. Wolf, *Peasants* (Englewood Clifts NJ, 1966); T. Shanin, *Peasants and Peasant Societies* (Harmondsworth, 1971); B. Galeski, *Basic Concepts of Rural Sociology* (Manchester, 1972).

13 To exemplify from a rich field of new ideas explored and of old assumptions challenged: Alavi, 'Peasant Classes and Primordial Loyalties', G.M. Foster 'The Peasants and the Image of Limited Good', *American Anthropologist*, 62(1965), no. 2; A. Pearce, *The Latin American Peasant* (London, 1970); T. Shanin, *The Awkward Class* (Oxford, 1972); G.H. Skinner, 'Marketing and Social Structure of Rural China', *Journal of Asian Studies*, 24(1964); R. Stavenhagen, 'Capitalism and Peasantry in Mexico', *Latin American Perspectives*, 5(1979), no. 3; etc.

of their families, produce mainly for their own consumption and for the fulfilment of obligations to the holders of political and economic power'. The more developed general type of this approximation defined peasants through four interdependent facets: the family farm, agriculture, the village and its culture as well as a plebian slot within the systems of social domination.[14]

The continuous debate of three decades and a variety of applications within social planning made the field of peasant studies gather extensive evidence and grow in sophistication. It became factionalized as well along lines representing a diversity of goals, different disciplinary perspectives and diverse regional traditions but, also, the deeper epistemological divides discussed above. For a time the subject matter became a vogue, with the particular dynamics of academic fashions taking over – the term was being overused and made less clear by excessive application while the actual intellectual product was becoming thinner in content and more repetitious. At times, the old orthodoxies which made peasants disappear were substituted by new oversimplifications in which peasants were treated as a new key to all things, unrelated to broader society and/or unchanging.

We are now at a post-peak period of peasant studies. The dynamics of fashion have eased off as the intellectual treasure-hunters have moved elsewhere in pursuit of more easily saleable commodities. A substantive group of specialists has been established and continues its work. On the base of the achievements of the 1960s–70s, excellent new studies relating evidence and theory proceeded to emerge in the 1980s. At the epistemological level the fundamental debate about peasantry's existence or otherwise has come back as yet another turn of the intellectual spiral – the issue of defining peasants is clearly with us to stay. Up to a point this return of an argument represents the logical consequence of swings in intellectual fashion – an overuse of a phrase and of a concept followed by dismay and by a move to drop (and to demystify) old pets. It must be read also within the context of the current general disarray within the field of 'development theories'. But the issue itself goes to the root of the social sciences; it is a matter of what they are or are not. The substantive answer to it when peasantry is concerned cannot come solely within logical elaboration but must lie in the appreciation of the usefulness or otherwise of the concept, as to the questions, plausibilities, values and methodologies it facilitates in our perceptions and political choices. (For further discussion of this see item 4 below.)

Another way to look at this is to consider agendas of peasant studies,

---

14 Shanin, *Peasants and Peasant Societies*, Introduction (and for its expanded version see item 3 below).

their development and their further heuristic potentials where perception of parallel but combined realities is concerned.

3 Agendas and Achievements

The initial agenda of the contemporary peasant studies of *the late 1960s and the 1970s* addressed four major puzzles, the very recognition of which was dependent on both the (re-)emergence of peasantry in the public eye and the way in which the concept and the field of studies were being constructed. Firstly, there was the issue of peasantry's *non-disappearance* (or of a decline too slow to meet the prescriptions of the prevailing theories). Secondly, there was the issue of particularities of peasant *response* to market economies and to agricultural state policies (e.g. peasants' non-bankruptcies). In the background there was surprise and new insights in the face of the inventive responses of peasants to crisis and change. Thirdly, there was the issue of peasantry's evident *power* to bend the policies of the state and the dictates of the market, and to do so in their own way, as much through a variety of 'weapons of the weak' as by taking sides in political confrontations and armed struggles. The power of the seemingly amorphous, the pressure of the manifestly atomized, politics where political parties did not matter, have challenged and stimulated the perceptions of social scientists. Lastly, combining all of the issues, there was the matter of the social reproduction and functioning of peasanthood as a particular system within which many contemporary humans live – the considering of its actual character rather than of deductions about it from global theoretical schemes.

Extensive work on peasant family farms as social and economic entities, i.e. basic units of living as well as of budgeting and combining families' potentials and needs, was central to the 1960s/1970s agendas of contemporary peasant studies. This was being undertaken for widely different regions and at different levels of sophistication. The flexible use of family labour (*vis-à-vis* wage labour) explained much of the inexplicable in peasantry's survival and its competitive capacities in relation to larger and better equipped production units. Increasing attention was given to family strategies of combination in the use of family labour, especially to the peasant-workers phenomenon. Studies of rural–urban re-emigration and of cases of repeasantization were uncovered and studied on a par with depeasantization and out-migration. Cases of the 'peasantization' of African tribal economies were also considered. The picture was proving more complex and more interesting than the earlier visions of it. Images of rural stability were giving way to the appreciation of its inherent dynamics, transforming as well as reproductive.

Particularities of peasant markets and marketing networks *vis-à-vis* impersonal market relations were looked at anew. So was the political economy of rural patronage. Villages and personalized market networks were explicated as institutions of socialization, communication, mutual dependency and support, providing better understanding of the social economy of rural life. Images of complexity and of conflict when rural communities were concerned supplemented those of unproblematic simplicity. Ecological and social particularities of agricultural husbandry compared to manufacturing, and of peasant characteristic choices compared to those made by farmers with high capital investment, were also increasingly recognized. Quantitative methods were being designed or adopted to act as tools for the empirical investigation of characteristically peasant economies: the budget studies of family-farms, time budgets, the family histories studies exploring flows of resources and land-ownership, the rural dynamic censuses, etc.

The drawing of attention to the removal of 'obstacles to progress' gave the initial inducement and impetus to contemporary studies of peasant culture. From descriptive studies of 'folk cultures' (or of their 'survivals'), interest has moved to policy advice concerning resistances to development and to matters of political mobilization. To that purpose scholars shaped new analytical concepts such as the 'peasant view of a bad life'. Sympathetic response to the peasant cultures of survival and resistance found its own language when Jim Scott spoke of the 'moral economy' of the peasant.[15] It was the study of the daily lives of *rural* communities, mostly peasant, which offered major explanations of the particularity of peasant culture, its social reproduction and its patterns of change.

Mao's victory in China and the war in Vietnam with its aftermath underlay an extensive effort aiming to grasp the particularities of peasants' revolutionary wars in the twentieth century. The outstanding significance of peasants in established regimes led by Marxists was unexpected to friend and foe, and the surprise dramatized the research effort to follow. It linked to the search by militants of the day for political agencies of change capable to challenge and to outface the Third World's corrupt regimes and the imperial armies there. Parallel research has been conducted by those who looked for ways to reform rural communities into secure, conservative preserves supporting the existing political systems. Important beginnings were made also in the study of local dimensions of power: issues of faction, patronage and outsider–

15 Scott, *Moral Economy of the Peasant.*

insider relations in village communities were looked at in this light.

The outsider–insider relations of peasants were studied also in their broader sense, i.e. that of policies by governments and international bodies towards peasantries. These studies closely followed the turns and twists of ideological fashion: the Land Reform advocated as the solution to rural poverty in the 1960s, the Communal Development pro-grammes, the Green Revolution hopes of a technological end to all problems, and their equivalent in state-socialist societies – Collectiviza-tion and Decollectivization. While the results of all these efforts proved remarkably far off their goals as set, the insight gained was to play a major role in the analytical work of the 1980s, contributing particularly to its critical edge.[16]

General extension in the available data and the growing sophisti-cation of its analysis led to reconsideration of some methodological and epistemological issues of relevance. Units of analysis were considered *vis-à-vis* actual social networks and communities of living; models of economic response were looked at in the light of the multiplicity of actual responses by the family-farms. Advancing realism linked to the advancing acceptance of a general complexity of forms, and to the growing recognition that the historical paths of societies lead from complexity to new complexities (rather than from a social complexity to some final simplicity – massive, uniform, clean and dull).

Further advances of peasant studies *in the 1980s* linked to the broadening of their focus and the expanding impact of the insights gained. Peasants were being put increasingly in the context of broader analysis of social structures, national and international. At the same time many of those who studied peasants moved on from peasant studies to related topics of which peasantries were but a component. New approaches to social history and historiography followed, such as the studies of 'non-historical' people, of 'scripts' of actual interclass interaction, of revolutions as 'moments of truth' and of the social roots of Islam.[17] While exploration of peasantry was becoming more of a study of peasants within society, some of the analysts were now giving more attention to what we can learn from the peasants as to their own lives and trade as well as to the nature of the broader society and of the orthodox social sciences.[18]

16 For example, the assessment of the results of the Green Revolution by the team set up by the UN research establishment in Geneva and directed by Andrew Pearce.

17 The examples are taken from the 1980s work and/or publications by Eric R. Wolf, Jim C. Scott, Teodor Shanin and Hamza Alavi respectively.

18 For example, P. Richards, *Indigenous Agricultural Revolution* (London, 1985); Esteva, *Struggle for Rural Mexico* and 'A New Call for Celebration', *Development*, 1986; etc.

Much of the 1980s work advanced the topics established in the 1970s. Peasant households, i.e. family-based units of production and management, remained the major focus of peasant studies. New lessons of the combination and linkages of family functions and production activities, of marketed goods and unmarketable yet necessary tasks and services, were learned. The place of women in peasant economies was explored anew. Determinants which could be treated as 'objective' and quantifiable, such as a maximization of profit, were considered as against skills, loyalty, prestige or applied ethics. Studies of the combination of sources of income in contemporary peasantry have shown how much this capacity to combine, rather than the agriculture *sensu strictu*, defines the nature of 'peasant economy'. Peasant strategies and choices in the use of resources and the selection of goals proceeded to stimulate the type of analytical approach which was more flexible (and realistic) in not accepting narrow economic determinisms or mistaking government-adopted policies for what actually happens in the countryside. It is not, of course, that peasant family-farms were being discovered as free from external impacts, controls and exploitation, or to be *sui generis* in their existence. To the contrary, it was the better understanding of peasantry's involvement with 'external' forces and agencies which permitted more realistic assessment of its actual results: no possibility to opt out but no consequent conclusion that a smallholder is but a puppet and a prey of outsiders, without the capacity to make some choices and to play his own games in 'using' some of those who use him. At the same time, matching actual trends, a major dimension of the advance of peasant studies was that of increasing attention to the peasants' economic and political incorporation into ('subsumption' under) national and international systems. The 'embedment' of peasants in the larger structures of power and exchange was ever assumed by those who studied contemporary peasantry, but its understanding became more elaborate and informed.

The economic impact of the state (on a par with that of market relations) increasingly became a focus of attention through the recognition of the exceptional significance of state institutions and personnel in the rural areas where peasantry plays a major role. The ways local informal structures, formal bureaucracies and global networks interlink were also looked at more closely, offering better understanding of the actual social fabric of 'incorporation'. It all gave an additional dimension to studies of rural populations in the context of 'external' and 'internal' social inequalities, massive state interventions, World Bank strategies and extensive 'aid programmes' as well as natural and human-induced disasters. The issue of the starvation of the food producers in major parts of an exceedingly rich world came to the fore, to be considered as one of social power, privilege and 'entitlement' rather than of capacity to produce.[19] The way peasants survive the unsurvivable and manage those who manage them, with the help of social and material resources unrecognizable in most policies and formal analytical schemes, attracted new attention as a major element without the understanding of which the existence of major parts of humanity remains a mystery.

The better understanding of flexibility of responses, combinations of 'economic' and 'non-economic', multiple systems and resistance to external pressures was reflected also in new studies of localities in which peasants dwell. Studies proceeded of the local power, the cooperation and the confrontations, offering a more realistic picture of worlds of direct encounter and the politics of daily life. Issues of applied ecology and farming tradition were increasingly linked to the rural social life. A tacit element of the changing analytical scene was offered by the slow growth in the perception of peasant good sense and realistic appreciation of experience. These understandings advanced as specific knowledge of actual relations, processes and institutions was being put in place of abstractions, be they methodological individualism, universal class war or belief in the natural unity and goodness of the rural communities. Actual studies of community life helped to define further the social roots of collective cognitions at the core of what was usually considered under the general heading of the peasant culture. Scott's concept of 'weapons of the weak', to follow that of 'moral economy', both at the point of juncture of culture and politics, helped to make less abstract the institutional structure on which popular resistance to dependency and oppression rests. It facilitated a wave of specific studies and helped to explicate ways of peasant/non-peasant interdependence and of ruralities' place *vis-à-vis* national bureaucratic structures. So did a number of excellent studies in modern rural history.[20]

A conceptual gap has been being filled between the analysis of the peasantries of the Third World, and the phenomena of the highly capitalized family farmers of the 'First' World and the collectivized ruralities of the 'Second' one. Djurfeldt and others documented and explicated the extent to which family farmers out-competed the 'food factories' in the Western world, as capital fled agriculture into agribusiness which skims farmers' incomes 'from the outside'.[21] In agriculture, a calculus of capitalist profit making was clearly winning through as

19 For example, K. Griffin and A.R. Khan, *Poverty and Landlessness in Rural Asia* (ILO, 1976); A. Sen, *Poverty and Famine* (Oxford, 1982).

20 For example, T. Ranger, *Peasant Consciousness and Guerilla Warfare in Zimbabwe* (1985) or H. Bix, *Peasant Protest in China* (Harvard, 1986).

21 See G. Djurfeldt in Shanin, *Peasants and Peasant Societies*.

against the 'classical' capitalist forms of production. Further work of definition was being done on the similarities and dissimilarities between the peasant and the farmers' wing of the broader category of 'family farming'.[22] The crisis of agriculture in the state-socialist countries led to a wave of studies of patterns of collectivization and decollectivization, while major attention was being given to the interdependence between the narrowly economic and the broadly social aspect of it. The analytical and political borderlines between the categories of collective farming and of peasanthood were being explored. There are major ironies and some important insights in the calls of the Soviet press of Gorbachev's era to repeasantize the countryside of the USSR as part of the country's 'second socialist revolution'.

This is the background to which the latest round of rediscovering peasantry's nonexistence as a viable concept should be related.[23] It was presented as 'defence of Marxism', and returned to views as early as those of the Erfurt Programme of German Social Democracy in 1891, in which peasantry was but a specific case of the petite bourgeoisie.[24] This 'category 1' approach (in the taxonomy suggested above) was reinforced once again by the term 'populism', used to disqualify as anti-Marxist (and, thereby, untrue) other views of the matter. This is where the irony of the Soviet 1987 return to Chayanov, as the one realistic view of their collectivization experience and the mainstay of the current programme to rectify the situation in agricuture (as well as the Marxist outlook on it), becomes particularly evident. So does the increasing recognition in the USSR and elsewhere that the Russian Populist theory and political creed were part and parcel of a socialist – indeed, a Marxist – tradition, the dismissal of which by Plekhanov was dearly paid for by the Soviet regime. The use on the left of the term 'populism' as a leftover category (neither 'us' nor 'them'), with no relation to the actual populism's characteristics, has been for long analytically misleading and politically harmful. All in all, be what may one's *Weltanschauung*, deduction from axioms is no way to shed light on society. This is true when 'populism' is

22 For example, V. Danilov as reviewed by O. Figes in Shanin, *Peasants and Peasant Societies*.

23 P. Gibbons and M. Neocosmos, 'Some Problems in the Political Economy of African Socialism' in H. Bernstein and H. Campbell, *Contradictions of Accumulation in Africa* (Sage, 1985), and H. Bernstein, 'Agrarian Crisis in Africa and Neoclassical Populism' unpublished MS (London, 1986). It is interesting to see how a much different line of argument based on similar epistemological assumptions and restrictions resulted in similar, one could say pre-set, conclusions; e.g. compare to that offered in J. Ennew, P. Hirst and K. Tribe, 'Peasantry as an Economic Category', *Journal of Peasant Studies*, 4(1977), no. 4, to which the source in footnote 24 responds. One could add to it T. Shanin, *Late Marx and the Russian Road* (Monthly Review Press, 1983).

24 See the discussion of Kautsky in item 16 below.

considered proves particularly true when peasanthood, the concept and the reality, is concerned. As to the substance of this debate there is no need to add to what was already said in an earlier round of it.[25]

Contemporary peasant studies have offered not only a yardstick of 'otherness' but also an antidote to deductive and/or uni-logical systems of social analysis, which tend to act as blinkers promoting oversimplification. Put otherwise, the up-to-date process of defining and studying peasants as a sociological concept and a field of study facilitated recognition of the parallel realities, i.e. diverse social systems, linkage between which does not lead to their uniformity. It has also focused attention on the combinations of forms with often contradictory logic, rather than on elegant but unrealistic simplicities. In my view the resulting theories and models, necessarily more complex but the more effective for it, have been the most significant general illumination and input of contemporary peasant studies into social sciences at large. This characteristic will also last in the future.

Predictions of the future have often been a fools' paradise, especially so when peasants were concerned. Yet there is little doubt as to the momentum of this field of studies, moving farther still in following the main parameters of its contemporary advance: the social economy anchored in family economic units, its interrelations with the market and the state economies, the particularities of rural communities and their collective perceptions, issues of peasant politics and peasant resistance and the way peasant behaviour amends policies and programmes coming from elsewhere. Also, the 'peasants aren't stupid, but differ' message will find new adherents.

The focus of peasant studies will most likely proceed to expand, reflecting the increasing interdependencies within the global society as well as the internal logic of an analytical paradigm. Of the directions of expansions one can already sense at least three. The first is the growingly significant consideration of social economies which are neither market-and-capitalism nor state-and-plan defined, nor a simple combination of both. Such expolary economies have been usually dismissed as marginal and transitory by the predominant theoretical paradigms (see item 6). We are rapidly learning the non-marginality of such forms and about the increasing significance and expansion of what is clearly not just a flash in the pan. Second, there is the growing significance of the

---

25 T. Shanin, 'Defining Peasants: Conceptualizations and Deconceptualizations', *Peasant Studies* 8(1979), no. 4 (item 4 below).

general issue of combinations of different forms and social organizations which reinforce rather than devour each other. Thirdly, there is the growing interest in the studies of the old and new forms of survival, of initiative and of resistance 'from below' in the face of the processes and pressures which C. Tilly once described as 'capitalisation and state-making'.[26] The consideration of the contemporary importance and definition of ways in which analysis and policies from below may supplement and transform future models of and movements for social justice and efforts to generate a socialism with a human face may prove one of the most significant of the contributions of peasant studies to what scholarship can offer to the twenty-first century.

26 C. Tilly, 'Proletarianization and Rural Collective Action in East Anglia and Elsewhere, 1500–1900', *Peasant Studies*, 10(1982).

Part I

Conceptualizing Peasants:
Reconsidering Others

2

A Generalization: Peasantry as a Social Entity (1965)

This paper was written by a 'mature' (i.e. belated in academic career) graduate student at Birmingham University, UK. It was first discussed at a seminar in the Centre of Russian and East European Studies there and first published as 'Peasantry as a Political Factor' in 1966 in The Sociological Review, *vol. 14. It represents a first effort to make sense of peasantry theoretically and comparatively, on the basis of the accepted authorities of the day and of evidence drawn from preliminary studies of peasantries of Russia/ the USSR, Poland, China and Mexico. The article reflected also the deepening feeling of dissatisfaction with much of what was available then. Ex post factum one can see that the article, its many reprints and its mood formed part of the remarkable turn-of-the-1960s outburst of peasant studies which was to establish much of their contemporary analytical parameters and* problematique.

In its content the article was somewhat reminiscent of what it said about peasanthood as an occupation. It ranged over a multiplicity of goals and tasks and did it at a very varied level of proficiency. It was initially delivered in atrocious English, which Professor Charles Medge charitably described as 'using the English tongue the way a caveman wields his axe – crudely but effectively'. This text was improved by friends who tried, bless them, to English it, while preserving its barbarian challenge. Warts and all it stands for a period of my own development, made socially relevant by the fact that it represents an intellectual generation at the origins of the current 'peasantology'.

It is more than a piece of intellectual nostalgia, however. Much of its questioning and discourse is still at the centre of contemporary debate, e.g. the particularities of family economy as a political factor as much as peasant passive resistance. Even the turning of the noun 'class' into a 'quantifiable' adjective 'classness' was the type of terminological cheek which is useful fun – its relevance to current debate is clear, at least to me. The part devoted to peasantry and history was the article's weakest spot –

I had not yet shed or even thought through the evolutionist historiography, with its unilinear images, of those from whom I had learned the intellectual craft. Looking at it now I find the idea that pastoral economy must be more lowly than a pre-stage of sedentary farming (and not a parallel, highly effective and often symbiotic form of the use of nature) particularly outrageous. But it took a visit to the Zagros Mountains of Iran with Professor Nader Afshar-Naderi to see it all with a different eye and, later, to relate this to a general historiography arguing consistently for the 'multiplicity of roads' and alternativity of histories, as in my Marx and the Russian Road *(New York, 1983) and* The Roots of Otherness *(New Haven, 1985, 1986).*

The text offered a point of departure for two of this book's parts – the one devoted to peasantry's definitions and the one devoted to its particular institutional dimensions, in this case focusing on the social structure of political action. The paper was dismantled accordingly. What follows is its first part, devoted to generalization of peasantries as a social syndrome. Its final part appears below as item 10.

Peasants are the majority of mankind. For all but comparatively few countries, 'the people' (as opposed to 'the nation') still denotes peasants, the notion of a specific 'ethnic culture' closely corresponds to the local peasant culture, 'the army' means peasant sons in uniform, officered by men different from themselves. And yet one has to be reminded of this.

'It is commonplace to say that agrarian history, as such, is neglected – the fact is too obvious to be denied':[1] this holds true for many branches of social science as far as the countryside is concerned. The decade which has elapsed since this passage was written has not much improved the situation, apart from several notable exceptions in the fields of anthropology and history in the last years. Indeed, in the growing flood of social science publications, the few existing rural studies have almost been submerged. But reality seems to confute this solipsism of the 'civilized' mind. Day by day, the peasants make the economists sigh, the politicians sweat and the strategists swear, defeating their plans and prophecies all over the world – Moscow and Washington, Peking and Delhi, Cuba and Algeria, the Congo and Vietnam.

Even more striking than neglect are the emotional undertones and diversities of opinion which shroud this subject. Writers, scientists and politicians have all contributed to discussion in which the image of the peasant has swung from that of an angelic rustic humanist to a greedy, pig-headed brute. For example, in Russia, in one and the same period, the peasantry was held to be 'the real autocrat of Russia' and 'non-

---

1 F. Davring, *Land and Labour in Europe, 1900–1950* (The Hague, 1956).

existent, historically speaking'.[2] This kind of verbal contest did not make reality much clearer while peasantry went its own way, quite oblivious of being an intellectual nuisance.

The emotional tension underpinning ambiguous contempt or utopian praise, the replacement of definition by allegory and other acute short-comings in the conceptual grasp of the peasantry, are strongly felt in the Western intellectual tradition. The neglect of the subject is but a symptom of this. It calls for a sociology of knowledge of the intellectual image-makers as they deal with the 'class that represents the barbarism within civilization'.[3] The treatment of peasantry's action, especially of its politics as an 'undecipherable hieroglyphic to the understanding of the civilized',[4] has been determined by a conglomeration of factors, of which one stands out as crucial. The peasantry does not fit well into any of our concepts of contemporary society. This 'maddening' peasant quality seems to lie at the roots of the problems of research in this field.

In this paper, we shall start by an attempt to define the *differentia specifica* of the peasantry – the uniqueness by which the peasantry may be defined and selected. The analytical definition will then be used as a reference point in historical context. We shall proceed to the problem of the peasantry as a part of society, and then to the patterns of political action particular to this entity. In dealing with this subject, other lines of approach are feasible and, indeed, needed. The translation of complex reality into a verbal form of fewer dimensions makes many approaches possible and valid, subject to the clear recognition of the methodological and epistemological problems involved.

1 Peasantry: an Analytical Definition

'Peasant society and culture has something generic about it. It is a kind of arrangement of humanity with some similarities all over the world.'[5] In this way Redfield summarizes a wide comparison made of peasants in different periods and countries. The peasantry appears to be a 'type without localization – not a typical anthropologist's community'.[6]

As to the nature of this 'type', I suggest the following characterization of it. *Peasantry consists of small agricultural producers who, with the help of simple equipment and the labour of their families, produce mainly*

---

2 Quotations taken from V. Chernov and G. Plekhanov respectively.
3 K. Marx and F. Engels, *Selected Works* (London, 1950), vol. 1, p. 159.
4 ibid., p. 159.
5 R. Redfield, *Peasant Society and Culture* (Chicago, 1956), p. 25.
6 ibid., p. 23.

for their own consumption and for the fulfilment of obligations to the holders of political and economic power. This definition implies a specific relation to land, the peasant family farm and the peasant village community as the basic units of social interaction, a specific occupational structure and particular patterns of past history and contemporary development. This leads, furthermore, to some particularities of peasants' position in society and of political action typical of it. To specify:

(1) The relationship to land and the character of agricultural production lie at the root of some of the particular features of the peasant economy. The produce of the farm meets the basic consumption needs of the peasant family and gives the peasant some relative independence from other producers and from the market. This makes for some extra stability of peasant households which, in crises challenging their survival, are able to maintain their existence by increasing efforts, lowering consumption and partially withdrawing from market relations.

Agricultural production puts limits on the density and concentration of population and determines patterns of social intercourse, notably those characteristic of peasant labour and household life as well as the village. Nature introduces here a strong element of chance, i.e. factors beyond human control, which the whole of the peasant community faces.

The use of land is 'a necessary and generally sufficient condition to enter the occupation',[7] and acts therefore as an entrance ticket into the peasantry. Moreover, position in the hierarchy of peasant subgroups is, to a large extent, defined by the amount of land held or owned.[8]

I define land property as a socially accepted, enforceable and exclusive right to hold and utilize the land concerned, a right which is separate from the rights acquired by the investment of labour and the use of equipment. This right finds expression and definite test in the holder's competence to transfer it, at least temporarily. Property in land may take the form of, on the one hand, land-holding defined by custom and communal interaction, and on the other of state-formalized legal ownership. In peasant households, land often appears as the object of traditionally defined holdings which do not necessarily constitute the

7 B. Galeski, *Chlopi i zawod rolnika* (Warsaw, 1963), p. 48.

8 'A rise within the professional group of farmers is traditionally achieved by enlargement of the land holding, by a rise from the position of owner of a small farm to the position of an owner of a bigger one, and the description "good farmer" is generally attached in the view of the village to all owners of the biggest farms without exception and is not linked to the real professional skill or effectiveness of their work' (Galeski, *Chlopi i zawod rolnika*, p. 47).

object as of personalized or legal ownership. The legal ownership of peasant land may actually lie with the peasant himself or the commune, a landlord or the state; the land being correspondingly a private plot, communal property or a leaseholding. That is why 'landlords are not needed to establish the fact of a peasantry'.[9] Their appropriation of part of the peasants' produce, and even their political and administrative domination, has generally failed to break the characteristic features of the direct and particular peasant–land relationship.

(2) The family-farm is the basic unit of peasant ownership, production, consumption and social life. The individual, the family and the farm appear as an indivisible whole. Identification of the interests of family and farmholding seems typical of the traditional peasant family. The farm is a production-consumption unit. The balance of consumption-needs, of available family labour and of the farm's productive potential strongly influence peasants' activities. The profit and accumulation motives rarely appear in their pure and simple form. This makes the conceptual models of maximization of income, extensively used in a market economy, of lesser applicability to a peasant economy. The new, rapidly developing, social patterns of industrial society are mostly to be found outside agriculture in which the family farms proceed to prevail.

Peasant property, inclusive of land, is, at least *de facto*, family property. The head of the family appears as 'the manager rather than proprietor of family land',[10] and his function 'has rather the character of management of common family property'.[11] These two descriptions, given by different scholars about peasantries of two different countries and a generation apart, show striking similarity.

The family's social structure determines the division of labour, and the hierarchy of status and social prestige. The prestige and position of an individual in peasant society is determined by two factors, as is his image of himself. These factors are, firstly, the status of the family he belongs to and, secondly, his position within his family. His position within the family depends primarily on his progression through certain basic ascribed positions – i.e. childhood, partial maturity before marriage, the period after marriage but before full independence, independence (which is gained either by leaving the family farm and establishing his own, or by becoming head of the family farm on his parents' death or retirement) and, finally, the period of retirement. Family labour, both

9 Redfield, *Peasant Society and Culture*, p. 28.

10 W.I. Thomas and F. Znaniecki, *The Polish Peasant in Europe and America* (New York, 1958), p. 92.

11 V. Mukhin, *Obychnyi poryadok nasledovaniya krest'yan* (St Petersburg, 1888), p. 62.

male and female, is an essential requirement for conducting a farm adequately. Therefore marriage is 'an absolute postulate'.[12] Family interest directs the marital choice. An unmarried man (even a farm-owner) 'arouses unfavourable astonishment' and 'does not count',[13] since he cannot fully conform to the norms of the way of life of his fellow villagers. This is so because 'the family is the production-team of the farm and position in the family determines duties on the farm, functions and rights attached. The rhythm of the farm defines the rhythm of family life.'[14]

The defining feature of family membership lies in full participation in the life of the farm unit, the core of which consists of a married couple or a polygamous group and their offspring. The family to the Russian peasant at the beginning of the twentieth century was described as 'the people who eat from the same pot' and, for the French peasant of the same period, 'the people who are locked behind the same lock'. Family solidarity provides the basic framework for mutual aid, control and socialization. The individual's personal feelings are markedly subordinated to the formalized restraints of accepted family role behaviour. The life of a family-farm determines the pattern of peasants' everyday actions, relationships and values.

(3) The fundamental importance of occupation in defining men's social position, role and personality is well known, if little studied. The ambiguity residing in the definition of peasant farming seems to stem from its unique character as an occupation. Apart from its family base, necessary connexion with landholding and a degree of independence from the market, its uniqueness lies in its consisting of a peculiarly wide set of interrelated functions carried out at a rather unspecialized level. Although many of the jobs undertaken by the peasant are also the domain of other occupational groups, the particularity of the peasant's work lies in their unique combination. This leads to some special features characterizing everyday peasant life, in the way it changes as well as in its resistance to industrialization. Growing specialization in the countryside leads to the expansion of the rural non-farming population while farming is progressively narrowed and professionalized, as peripheral jobs and jobs requiring other specialist skills are unloaded onto specialists. The farm begins to develop into an enterprise. The peasant becomes a farmer.

However, the tasks which cannot easily be broken down into a few

---

12 Thomas and Znaniecki, *The Polish Peasant in Europe and America*, p. 107.
13 ibid., p. 107.
14 Galeski, *Chlopi i zawod rolnika*, p. 140.

repetitive actions and mechanized (for example, livestock husbandry) remain largely his special province.

The features of peasant farming also influence the character of the socialization and occupational training of the young peasants as one which is highly diffused, personal, informal and taking place mainly within the framework of the family.

(4) To an extent greater than that of the family-farm, villages present us with features unique to a specific country and period. In the village community or peasant commune, the peasantry reaches the highest potential for autonomy and social self-sufficiency. A common interest in services, safety and productive activity requiring the participation of more than one family generates cooperation, usually coupled with some type of grass-roots democracy. Marriage, social and religious needs can be taken care of at the village level. Its members being born into a single community, undergoing similar life experiences, are necessarily involved in face-to-face interaction – with the consequent absence of anonymity. This facilitates the highly traditional and conformist culture peculiar to a rural community. All this made the word *mir* (meaning 'the world' as well as 'peace'), used by the Russian peasants to refer to their village community/commune, a significant description of its functions. The village has been the peasant's world. The society of small producers consists of innumerable village segments which are generally dominated and exploited by alien hierarchies.

(5) The peasantry is a pre-industrial social entity which carries over into the contemporary society many specific elements of a different and older social structure, economy and culture. This point will be elaborated in the following section but, at this stage, it should be noted that I am not just referring to the 'relics of the way of production which already belongs to the past';[15] that is, I speak not only of delayed development, but also of specific features of the social transformation which is taking place.

2 Peasantry: the Historical Context

The peasantry manifests itself not only as a distinctive social group, but as a dominant pattern of social life which defines a stage in the development of human society. 'The peasantry . . . is a way of living', says Fei[16]

15 Marx and Engels, *Selected Works*, vol. 2, p. 303.
16 'The peasantry, the key towards understanding of China, is a way of living, a complex of formal organization, individual behavior and social attitudes, closely knit

in his classical description of Chinese society. This way of living makes its appearance as a growing sector of earlier, mainly nomadic, society becomes decisive and typifies a historically distinct period of a 'society of small producers', and then gradually sinks to become a decreasing sector within industrial society. The appearance of the small-producer pattern of life is marked by that major change which has been referred to as the 'agricultural revolution'.[17] This stage of development lays the base for stable settlement, land division and the rise in productivity which brings with it the possibility of a comparatively stable surplus. Production comes to be determined, to an increasing extent, by labour utilized.

The transformation of property relations and of the nuclear units of social interaction may be treated as a dual major indicator of these stages of rural history. The concept of property relations over land barely exists in nomadic society except for that of tribal hunting and grazing territories, defended from strangers. It appears in the sense discussed above, in the small producers' society, and becomes fully formalized in a capitalist, industrial one. The kinship group is the basis of social relationships in tribal-nomadic society, and remains so but is more narrowly defined by the familialism of the small producers' society. The individual 'doesn't count': he is but a part of the lineage and later of the family. The town-and-market-centred industrializing society breaks down this system of relationships. The individual becomes the nuclear unit of society, free to interact with any others in the huge new complex of social hierarchies and structures. The combination of the 'broad' concept of property with social conditions in which family is the most substantive social unit, i.e. the prevalence of family property and family farm, may serve to identify and delimit 'societies of small producers' and the historical periods characterized by their predominance.

The 'societies of small producers' show distinctive cultural patterns the features of which persist at least partly among the peasantry of industrializing societies.[18] A 'social' rather than 'economic' way of reasoning has been widely documented by students of contemporary peasant life. A great deal has been said about the irrational behaviour of peasants as far as land, loans, prices and income are concerned.[19]

---

together for the purpose of husbanding land with simple tools and human labor' (Fei Hsiao Tung, 'Peasantry and Gentry', *American Journal of Sociology*, 52 [1976], no. 1).

17 V.G. Childe, *Social Evolution* (1963).

18 A cultural pattern being seen for this purpose as 'the lens of mankind through which men see; the medium by which they interpret and report what they see' (C. Wright Mills, *Power, Politics and People* [1962], p. 406).

19 For example, Thomas and Znaniecki, *The Polish Peasant in Europe and America*, pp. 173, 161, 169, 166.

Peasant thinking often seemed to the outsiders capricious or subjective,[20] containing large elements of what may be called pre-Socratic thought, in which two contradictory opinions may be held simultaneously. What often remained overlooked was the fact that the alleged 'stupidity' of peasants was not necessarily evidence of absence of thought, but rather of a frame of reference and patterns of thought peculiar to the group, and serving well their needs.[21]

This point is borne out increasingly in recent studies. R.E.F. Smith has pointed out the cyclical rather than linear concept of time held by Russian peasants, which is clearly linked to their productive life.[22] Pitt-Rivers notes the main features of a closed community to be habitual personal contact, widespread endogamy, homogeneity of values, emphasis on strict conformity, intense group solidarity and marked egalitarianism,[23] and this may serve as a fair generalization of much recent anthropological research into specific peasant cultures. The clash of this particular culture and its gradual giving way to a new, foreign, *Weltanschauung* of the industrializing 'civilized' world is an important part of modern social history.

The 'small producers' society' falls historically in the intermediate period between tribal-nomadic and industrializing societies. The word 'intermediate' is often used interchangeably with 'transitional', 'unstable' and even 'not important to look at'. However, this pattern of society proved as lasting as other historical types of social structure. In fact, the types of society based on a non-structural dynamism, with the family-farm as the nuclear unit, has demonstrated exceptional stability all over the world. Indeed, one does not need Wittfogel's hydraulic eastern despotism to explain the striking examples of arrested structural change collected in his book.[24] For the 'stagnant societies' considered by Wittfogel, the basic social nuclei of family subsistence farm and peasant village community, and their cyclical stability, seem to constitute much more of a common element than do any 'hydraulic' features. As to the

20 See, for example, Mukhin (*Obychnyi poryadok nasledovaniya krest'yan*, p. 311), who states that the peasants' court or meeting tends to decide about property disagreements 'according to men' – i.e. according to the personalities of the people involved rather than general principles or formal precedences.

21 See, for example, the Polish sociologists' studies of the prestige determinants of peasant economic action, or Chayanov's demonstrations of the 'economically irrational' renting of land when the cost of letting is higher than the additional income gained, and which is yet a sensible thing in conditions of an otherwise unemployable labour surplus.

22 R.E.F. Smith, 'A Model of Production and Consumption on the Russian Farm', *Discussion Papers*, University of Birmingham, CREES, RC/D (1964), no. 1, p. 11.

23 J. Pitt-Rivers, 'The Closed Community and its Friends', *Kroeber Anthropological Society Papers* (1957), no. 16. For a summary of anthropological research into peasant communities, see *Biennial Review of Anthropology*, 1961, 1963, and 1965.

24 K. Wittfogel, *Oriental Despotism* (1963).

surplus-appropriating highly centralized state, it may actually bear the main potentialities for structural change through the introduction of powerful external economic pressures into a world of natural economy and cyclical stability.

The peasant backbone in the 'small producers' society' dissolves under the influence of the rise of a market-and-town-centred money economy and consequent industrialization. Capital formation is necessary to understand this process. Yet while agriculture provides a basis for industrialization, the family-farms themselves remain, to a great extent, a part of the new social framework which emerges.

The producing and trading town introduces social patterns alien to the old world of small producers. In it, impersonal, warfare-like, profit-centred market relations underlie human relations. A man freed from the bonds and the protection of his family becomes here an individual participant in a mass society, structured by huge bureaucratic hierarchies. Accumulation of anonymous capital determines economic growth. The pursuit of profit, efficiency and individual achievement provides the core of the social value system.

The advantages of capital concentration, population growth, high productivity and widespread education, as well as its political weight, make the urban sector of society likely to overtake rapidly the rural one and to become the determinant of social and economic change. The small producers' world becomes a mere segment of a world very differently structured. Moreover, whilst still preserving some elements of uniqueness, the peasant countryside develops a closer relationship with the town – one which becomes increasingly decisive for its own development. The town's lead is felt through the increasing influence of market relations, the draining-off of 'surplus' labour and of capital, the professionalization of agriculture, and the spread of mass producers, of mass culture and of the related anomie and 'social disorganization'.

The view that the development of the peasant sector of a town-centred society is one which simply lags behind, rather than is different in kind, has proved wrong but persistent. In fact, three parallel patterns of spontaneous development for the countryside can be clearly distinguished.

(1) Competition from large-scale, capital-intensive, mechanized agriculture gradually destroys the small farms. Concentration of landownership is followed by concentration of production. Agriculture, fully taken over by industrial methods of production, becomes 'merely a branch of industry'.[25] The development is apparent in the large farms of

25 V.I. Lenin, *Collected Works*, fifth edition, vol. 3, p. 58.

the United States, North Italy and Central France, as well as in some of the Soviet *sovkhozy*. Yet the special features in the techniques of farming occupation create obstacles to breaking them down into simple, repetitive actions – i.e. to its full automation. This, together with the resilience of the family-farm unit and the fact that synthetic foods still remain relatively unimportant, has prevented 'food factories' becoming the main form of food-production.

(2) A town-centred society makes for the development of the peasants into a professional stratum of farmers. The poorer villagers are increasingly sucked in from the countryside by the expanding urban areas. The same happens to peasant entrepreneurs – and to part of the economic surplus in agriculture. At the same time the middle peasants, relying on the advantages of the family production unit and an increasing cooperative movement, fight successfully for a place in market society. These unique features of the development of the farmer stratum were pointed out as early as Marx[26] and were seen as the only way for the peasantry to develop by Bauer.[27] The latest studies of Polish and German sociologists have shown, furthermore, the growth of a new stratum of worker-peasants, who supplement their agricultural, mainly subsistence, production by hiring out their labour.

This pattern-transformation of the peasantry into a cohesive, increasingly narrow and professionalized occupation group of farmers can be clearly seen in most parts of North-Western Europe. Although becoming ever more tied to industrial society, farming still retains some of its peculiar elements. The socialist states which permit the activity of small producers in the countryside and provide them with necessary aid, though curbing capitalist development (the USSR in the New Economic Policy period, contemporary Poland and Yugoslavia), bring this pattern to its clearest expression.

(3) The third pattern of development appears mainly in the so-called underdeveloped societies and is characterized by cumulative pauperization of the peasantry.[28] A population explosion, developing market

26 'The moral of this story, which may also be deduced from other observations in agriculture, is that the capitalist system works against a rational agriculture, or that a rational agriculture is irreconcilable with the capitalist system – even though technical improvements in agriculture are promoted by capitalism. But under this system, agriculture needs either the hands of the self-employed small farmer, or the control of associated producers' (K. Marx and F. Engels, *Sochineniya*, 2nd Russian edn., vol. 25, part 1, p. 135).

27 O. Bauer, *Bor'ba za zemlyu* (Moscow, 1926), p. 203.

28 G. Myrdal, *Economic Theory and Underdeveloped Regions* (London, 1957), chapters 2, 3, 10.

relations and the industrial competition with traditional peasant handicrafts break up the cyclical equilibrium of society. A relatively slow industrialization is able neither to drain the countryside of its excess labour nor to provide sufficient capital accumulation. The potential surplus is swept away by growing consumption needs. In the small-producer world, this is expressed not by increasing unemployment, but by 'hidden' underemployment, 'agrarian over-population', falling per capita income and increasing misery.[29]

(4) As distinct from the three spontaneous trends of development, the increasing strength of the modern state and the wish of the revolutionary elites to tackle the problem of development within the framework of socialist, collectivistic thinking made for the appearance of state-organized collectivization of agriculture. This pattern differs qualitatively from the spontaneous trends by being a conscious plan put into operation by a political hierarchy. Long-period evaluation of its success, in any of the different forms it has taken, would seem premature; in the Soviet Union, where the earliest attempts were made, the capacity of the elements of specifically peasant life, especially the strong base of the peasant family plot and the unique ability of farming, to defeat town-designed plans was demonstrated to quite a remarkable extent.

3 Peasantry and Society

The difficulties involved in obtaining an overall conceptual grasp of the nature of a peasantry have been clearly felt in debates about the place of the peasantry in society. Even people starting from similar theoretical assumptions have reached opposite conclusions. Among the Russian Marxists peasantry was 'a class' to Stalin,[30] a 'petit bourgeois mass' to Kritsman[31] and 'not a class but a notion' to Plekhanov.

This has been partly due to differences in definition. Ossowski has distinguished at least three different ways in which the concept of social

---

29 See, for example, United Nations, *Pourquoi les travailleurs abandonnent la terre* (1960), pp. 138, 144, which reports, on India, that during the years 1941–51 the natural growth of the labour-force in the countryside was absorbed as follows: into agriculture (70.3 per cent), into services (28.3 per cent), into industry (1.4 per cent). During the years 1931–51, the share of workers engaged in agriculture rose from 71 per cent to 74 per cent of the working population; in 1952, 74 per cent of peasant families held less than 2 hectares of land and one-third was reported as landless. For an elaboration of such social processes, see I.H. Boeke, *Economies and Economic Policy in Dual Societies* (New York, 1953).

30 J. Stalin, *Problems of Leninism* (Moscow, 1945), p. 510.

31. A. Gaister, *Rassloenie sovetskoi derevni* (Moscow, 1928), p. xiii.

class was used by Marx;[32] many more conceptual subdivisions of society have been used by other writers. The different definitions have, in fact, often reflected different analytical aims and different concepts of society.

The main European sociological tradition of conceptual subdivision of modern society stems from Marxist class analysis. Social class is here approached as a unity of interest, expressed in group subcultures, group consciousness and group action, shaped in turn by the conflict-relationships with other classes. Society is structured by class domination and the working out of the dialectics of inter-class conflict and unity.

If we take the criteria for defining class as being relationships to the means of production,[33] or locuses of power[34] or capacity to organize production, the peasantry in an industrializing society will fall either into a huge amorphous group of 'the ruled', or into an even more amorphous group of 'middle classes'. The peasantry, as a qualitatively distinct entity, disappears. This led the majority of Marxist social scientists to approach the peasantry as a fading remnant of pre-capitalist society – as 'non-existent, historically speaking'. Yet, when a major part of the population remains outside the concept of society as a whole, the definition in use does seem to be sadly inadequate, even if the consolation of a glimpse into the future is offered in exchange. Unfulfilled predictions would seem to be the inevitable result of working to such a model.

Max Weber's modification of the Marxist concept of class puts market relationships at the heart of the definition, with the issue of class domination retreating into the background. 'Class situation is, in this sense, ultimately market situation.'[35] 'Class situations are further differentiated, on the one hand, according to the kind of property that is usable for returns, and, on the other hand, according to the kind of services which can be offered in the market.'[36] For Weber, therefore, 'owners of warehouses' and 'owners of shares', for example, constitute social classes, as much as do industrial workers and peasants. The shortcomings of an unlimited analytical division of society into small sub-groups when approaching social reality had already been pointed out by Marx in his unfinished manuscript on social class.[37]

32 S. Ossowski, *Class Structure in the Social Consciousness* (London, 1963).
33 Lenin, *Collected Works*, vol. 39, p. 15; Marx and Engels, *Selected Works*, p. 33.
34 R. Dahrendorf, *Class and Class Conflict in Industrial Society* (London, 1959).
35 G.H. Gerth and C. Wright Mills, *From Max Weber* (London, 1961), p. 182.
36 R. Bendix and S.M. Lipset (eds), *Class, Status and Power: A Reader in Social Stratification*, (London, 1953, revised edn. 1966), p. 64.
37 K. Marx, *Capital* (Moscow, 1967), pp. 1,031–2.

In history, the peasantry many times has acted politically as a class-like social entity. Moreover, the peasantry in industrial societies has shown an ability for cohesive political action – and not only when facing traditional land-owners in belated battles of a pre-capitalist type; their common interests have also driven peasants into political conflicts with large capitalist land-owners, with various groups of townspeople and with the modern state.

The polarization of the countryside in an industrializing society – into capitalist owners and a rural proletariat (as predicted by Marxists) – was checked by the draining-off of capital and labour into the towns, as well as by the specific features of a peasant family-farm economy. The widely accepted picture of the countryside as being rapidly sundered by an inevitable economic polarization proved oversimplified. Economic counter-trends seem to have acted in the opposite direction and greatly influenced the final result. Furthermore, the significance of specific culture, consciousness and the meaning attached to the class position proved to be the most important. All this made peasant cohesiveness as a potential basis for political class formation much stronger than the predictions of the Russian Marxists or of the American strategists would have led us to believe.

On the other hand, the inescapable fragmentation of a peasantry into small local segments and the diversity and vagueness of their political aims considerably undermine its potential political impact. Hence, how far a peasantry may be regarded as a class is not a clearcut problem, but should be seen rather as a question of degree and historical period. If we posit an imaginary scale or continuum, we could say that the peasantry would appear as a social entity of comparatively low 'classness', which rises in crisis situations.

But the peasantry's specific features as a socio-political group are not to be seen as merely quantitative. Marx's classical description of the duality in the social character of the peasantry (on the one hand, it is a class; on the other, it is not)[38] leaves the riddle unsolved. In so far as the peasantry is not a class, what is it – granting its qualitative existence?

A class position is basically a social interrelationship – a conflict interrelationship with other classes and groups. Outside these inter-relations, a class ceases to exist. Yet 'because the farmer's produce is essential and, at the lowest level, sufficient for human existence, the

---

38 'In so far as millions of families live under economic conditions of existence that separate their mode of life, their interests and their culture from those of other classes, and put them in hostile opposition to the latter, they form a class. In so far as there is merely a local interconnection among these small-holding peasants, and the identity of their interests begets no community, no national bond and no political organisation among them, they do not form a class' (Marx and Engels, *Selected Works*, vol. 1, p. 303).

labour of the farmer is necessary for the existence of society; but the existence of society as a whole is not to the same extent necessary for the existence of the farmer.'[39] Peasants prove this by withdrawing from the market in crisis situations and, indeed, sometimes consciously use this ability as a means of exercising political pressure.

The main duality in the peasants' position in society consists in their being, on the one hand, a social class (one of low 'classness' and on the whole dominated by other classes) and, on the other, 'a different world' – a highly self-sufficient 'society in itself', bearing the elements of a separate, distinctive and closed pattern of social relations. The peasantry is the social phenomenon in which the Marxist approach to class analysis meets the main conceptual dichotomies of non-Marxist sociological thinking; Maine's brotherhood versus economic competition; de Coulangue's familistic versus individualistic; Toennies's *Gemeinschaft* versus *Gesellschaft* or Durkheim's mechanic (segmentary) versus organic societies.[40] This unique duality ('class' and 'society') leads to conceptual difficulties, yet may well serve as a qualitative definition of the peasantry – especially when differentiating this entity from wider, more amorphous groupings such as 'middle classes', 'exploited masses' or 'remnants of feudalism'.

As has already been mentioned, A.L. Kroeber advanced a definition of peasants as those who 'constituting part societies with part cultures, definitely rural, yet live in a relation to a market town . . . [those who] lack the isolation, political autonomy and self-sufficiency of a tribal population, yet their local units maintain much of their old identity, integration and attachment to the soil'.[41] Redfield elaborates Kroeber's point and concludes 'there is no peasantry before the first city.'[42]

The anthropological approach, under which the extent of cultural self-sufficiency is used as an index of social development, is no doubt valid. Moreover, research centring on the problem of development from tribal to small-producer society will, necessarily, stress different factors to research centring round the problem of development from small-producer to industrial society. However, Redfield's definition of the peasantry seems to be too narrow and his definition of tribal society too wide. Groups of settlers in many parts of the world, cut off from towns, far from the nobility and out of reach of the state and its tax-collectors, can hardly *ipso facto* be labelled tribal. These groups share the main features of a peasantry. They seem to demonstrate peasantry's self-sufficiency, its ability to exist out of the thrall of nobility and town. It

39 Galeski, *Chlopi i zawod rolnika*, p. 49.
40 R. Redfield, *The Little Community* (Chicago, 1955), pp. 139–43.
41 A.L. Kroeber, *Anthropology* (London, 1923), p. 284.
42 R. Redfield, *The Primitive World and its Transformation* (New York, 1953), p. 31.

was the socio-political significance of these features which gave rise to the characteristic structure of power relations found in pre-capitalist society – it was this very self-sufficiency which made political control a necessity for the rulers.[43]

The main stream of contemporary sociology has bypassed the traditional peasantry. Rural sociology has been localized in and financed by rich industrial societies and has consequently been centred upon the problem of how to promote members of farming minorities into fully productive and prosperous members of 'civilized society'. Few sociologists have so far elevated the peasantry from the footnote to the page. Yet, were historical and social significance the criteria for the choice of objects of study, we should be almost overwhelmed by the flood of publications on the peasantry. Innumerable problems of our world's political and economic development lead us back to the subject of the peasantry and to the understanding and misunderstanding of it by the policy makers. To take but one example, the history of the Soviet Union was time and time again (in 1918, 1920, 1927–9, etc. – up to the 1960s) largely shaped by unexpected responses to the ruling party's policies, based on such evaluation and prediction. Countless other examples could be cited from Africa, Asia, Latin America, etc.

Only a cross-disciplinary combination of both conceptual and factual studies may overcome the astonishing shortcomings in our knowledge of the peasantry, in spite of the methodological difficulties involved. Limping along main roads achieves more than strolling along side roads.

43 For the argument on the political characteristics of peasantry, see item 9.

3

Peasantry: Delineation of a Sociological Concept

An Extract (1970)

Following on generalization came the need to delimit more strictly the concept involved and to consider its relations to social reality and especially the definition of 'edges' and the half-shadows, the categories of social transformations and the strategies of change. The resulting 'delimitation of peasantry as a field of study' was first published in European Journal of Sociology, *1971, vol. XII. What made it more urgent was the need to define, choose and commission relevant texts for* Peasants and Peasant Societies *(Harmondsworth, 1971) which was to become a sociological bestseller of a sort.*

Contemplation of analytical doubts and queries related to this task, together with the deliberations of a multidisciplinary discussion group at Sheffield, led to another publication that was devoted to conceptual models, i.e. T. Shanin (ed.), The Rules of the Game *(London, 1982).*

The existence of peasantry as a real and not purely semantic concept can be claimed for both empirical and conceptual reasons. Firstly, it is sufficient to read concurrently a sequence of peasant studies originating in countries as far removed in their physical and social conditions as Russia, Hungary, Turkey, China, Japan, India, Colombia and so on to note numerous similarities. In Redfield's words, there is 'something generic about it'.[1] There are, of course, important differences, but what is striking is, in Erasmus' words, 'the persistence of certain peasant attributes'[2] in societies so far removed.

Conceptually, a tendency to treat 'peasantry' as a bodiless notion can be countered on grounds related to the essence of sociology – to the trivial but often forgotten truth that *a sociological generalization does not imply a claim of homogeneity, or an attempt at uniformity.* Quite to

1 R. Redfield, *Peasant Society and Culture* (Chicago, 1956), p. 25.
2 C. Erasmus, 'Upper limits of peasantry and agrarian reform: Bolivia, Venezuela and Mexico compared', *Ethnology*, XI (1967), p. 350.

the contrary, a comparative study implies the existence of both similarities and differences, without which a generalization would be, of course, pointless. In pursuing 'a generalizing science' a sociologist lays himself open to the outrage of the adherents of those disciplines in which the study of uniqueness is central, and easily develops into a canon of faith. Many such complaints are based on misunderstanding. Some of them illustrate the limitations of the sociologist's trade, and of any conceptualization of an unlimitedly unique reality. In Max Weber's words: 'The science of sociology seeks to formulate type concepts and generalized uniformities of empirical process.' In such study 'sociological analysis both abstracts from reality and at the same time helps us to understand it, in that it shows with what degree of approximation a concrete historical phenomenon can be subsumed under one or more of these concepts.' Consequently, 'the abstract character of sociology is responsible for the fact that, compared with actual historical reality, they [i.e. sociological concepts] are relatively lacking in fullness of concrete content.'[3]

1 The Main Traditions of Thought

In the framework of thought which accepts both the brief of sociology, as 'a generalizing science' and the existence of peasantry as a specific, worldwide type of social structure, we can discern four major conceptual traditions: the Marxist class theory, 'the specific economy' typology, the ethnographic cultural tradition, and the Durkheimian tradition as developed by Kroeber and allied to functionalist sociology. Each of the traditions tends to stress a particular aspect of peasant livelihood (with a frequent tendency to view this aspect monistically, as the determinant of all others) and adopts a closely related approach to the analysis of social change and of disintegration of peasantry in the 'modern world'.

The Marxist tradition of class analysis, in particular when presenting two-class models of society (i.e. in the tradition of the 'Communist Manifesto' rather than of the '18th Brumaire'[4]), has approached peasantry in terms of power relationships. Peasants were viewed as the suppressed and exploited producers of pre-capitalist society. Contemporary peasantry appears as a leftover from an earlier social formation, its original characteristics reinforced by remaining at the bottom of the social power

3 Max Weber, *The Theory of Social and Economic Organisation* (London, 1964), pp. 109–10.
4 For an elaboration of the differences see S. Ossowski, *Class Structure in the Social Consciousness* (London, 1963).

structure. Powerlessness and productivity are the essential features of peasants under such a definition. They account for peasant domination by powerful minorities and for the expropriation of agricultural surpluses which secure the conspicuous consumption of the ruling class and lead to the repeated attempts at peasant revolt. The process of expropriation of agricultural surpluses from peasantry leads on the other hand to accumulation of capital and creation of new class structures, culminating in the disappearance of both the *ancien régime* and peasantry as such.[5] The influence of such analyses can be traced in much of the current work on South East Asia, on Latin America and to an extent on Africa.

The second tradition has viewed peasant social structure as being determined by a specific type of economy, the crux of which lies in the way a family-farm operates. The roots of this approach, too, can be traced to Marx, once his '18th Brumaire' is linked with the *Grundrisse*, but it was explicitly formulated by Vasilichakov in 1881.[6] The familistic nature, the highly autonomous and consumption-based character of the small farm enterprise, determine a specific peasant economy which, in turn, generates a typical peasant social structure and a peasant–nonpeasant dualism on the national level.[7] The extension of market economy, money exchange, wage labour, cheap mass production, etc., make for the disintegration of peasantry. A number of Western economic anthropologists such as R. Firth or M. Nash, the recently rejuvenated Chayanov and many current East European scholars follow this line of thinking.[8] Andrew Pierce's stress on land communities can be understood as developing the same theme.[9]

The third tradition, which stems from East European ethnography as well as from traditional Western anthropology, tends to approach peasants as the representatives of an earlier national tradition, preserved through 'cultural lag', by the inertia typical of peasant societies. Such an analysis focuses on the traditional obstacles to industrialization and 'modernization' and on the gradual acculturation to 'Western' and urban standards of rationality which operate as the major mechanisms of peasant dissolution. In G.M. Foster's words: 'It is the relationship between city and village – the cultural lag that we always find, which

5 For an excellent presentation of the case see E. Mandel, *Marxist Economic Theory* (London, 1968).

6 Karl Marx, *Pre-capitalist Economic Formation* (London, 1965), also vol. iii of *Capital*; A. Vasilichakov, *Sel'skii Byt i Sel'skoe Khozyaistvo v Rosii* (St Petersburg, 1881).

7 For amplification see J.H. Boeke, *Economics and Economic Policy of Dual Society* (New York, 1953).

8 R. Firth, *Human Types* (London, 1960); M. Nash, *Primitive and Peasant Economic Systems* (San Francisco, 1966); A.V. Chayanov, *The Theory of Peasant Economy* (Homewood, 1966).

9 A. Pierce, *The Latin American Peasant* (London, 1971).

keeps peasants backward and old-fashioned – that is static. Once this cultural lag disappeared, as it increasingly does in an industrial world, peasants disappear.'[10]

The fourth tradition, originating with Durkheim, has followed a rather devious path. The basic dualism accepted by Durkheim and his generation (Toennies, Maine, etc.), divides societies into traditional and modern. Those traditional are made up of social segments – autonomous, closed, uniform, informal and cohesive. Those modern are based upon division of labour and necessary, 'organic' and formalized interaction of their units.[11] Kroeber later referred to peasants as 'definitely rural part societies with part cultures', i.e. partly open segments of a town centred society.[12] Such a definition places peasantry in an intermediate position between self-sufficient segments of the 'folk' societies and the modern societies of 'organic' interaction. Peasant part-segments were subsequently made by Redfield the cornerstone of a conceptualization accepted by the majority of American anthropologists, with the consequent effect of recurrent reification as self-evident truth by the sheer volume of monotonous repetition. An increase in societal complexity, multiplication of institutions and the functionally necessary reintegration of social structure are accepted in this tradition as the mechanisms of social change. This was an essential tenet of Durkheimian theory, put in a more sophisticated form in the contemporary functionalist theories of change.[13]

The most interesting theoretical developments of the last decade are related to attempts to broaden the analysis and conceptualization of peasantry, incorporating a wider variety of aspects considered. E. Wolf, whose work is particularly noteworthy in that sense, has transcended in the USA the initial 'Redfieldian' approach by turning attention from 'culture' to the power and economic aspects of the peasant v. non-peasant social duality.[14] Galeski has integrated and developed further the 'specific economy' and the Marxian class analysis in his approach.[15] Barrington Moore Jr explored the impact of different histories of landlord–peasant relations on the character of the modern state. Recent works of historians and economists, such as those of E. Hobsbawm, D. Thorner and D. Warriner, have facilitated a broadening of the outlook of contemporary sociologists and anthropologists.[16]

10 J. Potter, M.N. Diaz and G.M. Foster, *Peasant Society* (Boston, 1967), p. 17.

11 E. Durkheim, *The Division of Labour in Society* (first published in 1893).

12 A.L. Kroeber, *Anthropology* (New York, 1948), p. 248.

13 N.J. Smelser, *Theory of Collective Behaviour* (London, 1962); S.N. Eisenstadt, *Modernization: Protest and Change* (Englewood Cliffs, NJ, 1966).

14 E. Wolf, *Peasants* (Englewood Cliffs, NJ, 1966).

15 B. Galeski, *Rural Sociology* (Manchester, 1971).

16 Barrington Moore Jr, *Social Origins of Dictatorship and Democracy* (Boston, 1966);

2 The Field of Study: a General Type

Sociological definitions and models resemble two-dimensional sketches of a multi-dimensional reality. Each contains a partial truth, each reflects only part of the characterized phenomenon. The reality is richer than any conceptualization, and that holds true particularly for peasant societies – highly complex social structures with little formal organization. Yet, without conceptual delineation of peasants and peasant societies as a type of social structure, a sociological study of peasantry would turn into a ghost story. A consistent definition of peasantry is necessary if only for the purpose of having it rejected in the process of further analysis.

I shall attempt to delimit peasant societies by establishing a general type with four basic facets. A definition of peasantry by a single determining factor would be neater but too limiting for my purpose. No doubt a definition incorporating only some of the facets suggested may frequently be sufficient for an analysis of specific aspects of peasant social life. The general type proposed would include:

(1) The peasant family-farm as the basic unit of multi-dimensional social organization. The family, and nearly only the family, provides the labour on the farm. The farm, and nearly only the farm, provides for the consumption needs of the family and the payment of its duties to the holder of political and economic power. The economic action is closely interwoven with family relations and the motive of profit maximization in money terms seldom appears in its explicit form. Family membership is based on total participation in the life of the family-farm. The division of labour is family-based and ascribed. The self-perpetuating family-farm operates as the major unit of peasant property, status, socialization, sociability and welfare, with the individual tending to submit to formalized family-role behaviour. The head of the family organizes production as the patriarchal manager of family property rather than as owner, with his rights grossly restricted by customary duties towards his family. Of these the approach to repetition of life cycles by the marriage of his children and the possibility of having to provide them with a farm of their own may be the most crucial.

A peasant family unit usually consists of two to three generations

---

E. Hobsbawm, *Primitive Rebels* (Manchester, 1959); D. Thorner, 'Peasant Economy as a Category of Economic History' *IIe Conférence internationale d'histoire économique* [Aix-en-Provence], II (1962), repr. in *Economic Weekly* [Bombay] (1963), special issue: D. Warriner, *Economics of Peasant Farming* (London, 1964), as well as her studies of agrarian reform.

living together. A son who was 'partitioned out' and set up an independent family-farm becomes an outsider while a son-in-law or adoptee who joined the farm shares in the membership rights. In a number of peasant societies some of the described family functions were taken over by larger kinship networks, e.g. the Serbian 'Zadruga', or to a lesser degree the Arab 'hamula' and the old South Chinese clan or lineage.

(2) Land husbandry as the main means of livelihood directly providing the major part of the consumption needs. Traditional farming includes a specific combination of tasks on a relatively low level of specialization. Many of these tasks may develop into specialist occupations (e.g. carpenter or smith), yet their specific combination defines the occupation of a peasant and is necessary for the performance of farming in a given set of social conditions. Such occupation necessitates, in turn, the family-bound and traditional vocational training of the young. Food production renders the family-farm comparatively autonomous. The impact of nature is particularly important for the livelihood of a small production unit of such limited resources. It restricts the density of population and makes for the interdependency of the deep-rooted rhythm of family life and of production on the peasant family-farm. The mainly agricultural economy with low capital investment accounts for the crucial importance of landholding and makes it a decisive factor of social stratification in terms of wealth, power and prestige.

(3) Specific traditional culture related to the way of life of small communities.[17] Specific cultural features (in the sense of socially determined norms and cognitions) of peasants have been noted by a variety of scholars. To use Redfield's somewhat flamboyant expression, the peasants form a 'psycho-physiological race', i.e. they display specific cognitive paradigms, the manifest irrationality of some of which, in the framework of a capitalist society, makes them neither less acceptable nor necessarily less functional to members of a peasant community.[18] The predominance of traditional and conventional attitudes, i.e. the justification of individual action in terms of past experience and the will of the community, may be here used as an example.

Much of the cultural patterns typical of peasant communities may be

17 Culture is here used not in its fullest anthropological sense (i.e. as the opposite of Nature), but as 'the lens . . . through which men see; the medium by which they interpret and report what they see'. Cf. Wright Mills, *Power, Politics and People* (New York, 1962).

18 See, for example, G.F. Foster, 'Peasant Society and the Image of Limited Good', *American Anthropologist*, LXVII (1965), F.G. Bailey, 'The Peasant View a Bad Life', *Advancement of Science*, XII (1966). For a different view see S. Ortiz, 'The Structure of Decision Making', in *Themes in Economic Anthropology*, ed. R. Firth (London, 1967).

deduced from the character of any *small village community*. The latter can be treated as an additional basic characteristic of peasantry. Within the village community peasants reach levels of self-sufficiency unobtainable in the individual household. Activities such as the exchange of marriage partners and at least rudimentary economic cooperation at tasks too big to be handled by one family are in many cases carried out at the community level. A small community in a relatively stable society is generally characterized by habitual personal contact, a lack of anonymity, a high level of homogeneity and a tendency towards endogamy. Such conditions are reflected both in the typical personalities of village members and in the accepted 'world view' in which communal identification, ideological solidarity and egalitarianism form an important part. The agro-towns of Southern Italy or of Yaruba should be approached here as an analytically marginal case (see below).

(4) The 'underdog' position; the domination of peasantry by outsiders. Peasants, as a rule, have been kept at arm's length from the social sources of power. Political organization, educational superiority, and mastery of the means of suppression and communication give to powerful outsiders an almost unchallenged hold over the village communities. Political subjection interlinks with economic exploitation and cultural subordination. Land tenure, political power and market cartelization operate here as the major mechanisms of exploitation. The political economy of peasant society has been, generally speaking, based on expropriation of its 'surpluses' by powerful outsiders, through corvée, tax, rent, interest and terms of trade. The doctrinal and bureaucratic centres of the basic networks of socialization which penetrate rural areas (e.g. the church, the state education, the mass media, etc.) generally lie in the town.

The social structure of peasantry is reflected in a number of characteristics specific to its political life. 'Vertical segments' (e.g. households, villages, patron–client pyramidal networks) are most important in the political sociology of such societies and the outsider/insider division in such segments *may* prove politically much more meaningful than national socio-economic stratification. The characteristics of peasant society render *mediating* outsiders, which operate on the borderlines between peasant society and its social counterparts, particularly important. The broadly accepted term of *power-brokers* is suggestive of such social groups but may give an incorrect image of neutral intermediaries operating between those in power and those without it. *Plenipotentiaries* of the powerful national bureaucracies may be a more realistic term. Finally, all this explains the critical significance of those conditions in which peasantry (usually under the influence of specific external 'catalyst' groups) unites, or is united, into a political force which sweeps the countryside, shaking societies and regimes.[19]

3 The Analytically Marginal Groups of Peasantry

The suggested general type incorporates the major characteristics of peasantry and pinpoints the most significant units of peasant interaction: the peasant family-farms and the peasant village community, while taking account of the broader power structures in which peasantry operates. This general type also makes clear the low degree of institutional differentiation and the close overlapping of family, polity, economy, culture and socialization patterns in peasantry. Having defined such a general type must lead to a further delineation of *analytically marginal groups* which share with the 'hard core' of peasants most, but not all, of their characteristics.[20] (In general, such differences can be presented on quantitative scales of more/less.) Analytical marginality so defined does not in any sense imply numerical insignificance or some particular lack of stability.

The major marginal groups can be classified consistently in reference to the proposed general type by the basic characteristics which they *do not* share with it:

1 *Agricultural labourers* who lack a family-farm (though who in many cases may hold a small plot of land) and who draw their main means of livelihood from working on a large estate, e.g. a Latin American peon.
2 Rural inhabitants who draw their main means of livelihood from *crafts and trades*, but who live in peasant environments and often work some land, e.g. rural craftsmen.
3 Some of the *frontier squatters* and Latin American gauchos with a specific non-village individualist culture, at times showing common characteristics with the next marginal group. The inhabitants of agro-towns, already mentioned, may be also for a number of reasons meaningfully classified into this category.
4 The *free armed peasantry* who managed to hold its own (and its land) and to escape, especially along frontiers and in the mountains, centuries of domination and oppression by 'outsiders', e.g. the Swiss, the

19 For elaboration see E. Wolf, 'On Peasant Rebellions', *International Social Science Journal*, XXI (1969); Also T. Shanin, 'Peasantry as a Political Factor', *Sociological Review*, XIV (1966). See also item 9.

20 Redfield *Peasant Society and Culture*, (p. 20) seemed to refer to some of such groups as 'edges' of the peasantry.

Cossacks or the Kurds. Many *tribesmen*, who match in all other ways the general type of the peasantry suggested, but who participate more fully in such political organizations as their tribes provide (especially in Africa), may be in many ways considered under this heading.

Analytically marginal groups may also be either a product of different stages of economic development or, alternatively, of contemporary state policies towards agriculture. (Such categories would partly overlap with those above.) The most significant of these groups are:

5 *Pastoral tribal peoples* who may combine some peasant characteristics with a nomadic type of life and appear to be a transitional form somewhere on the borderline between the pre-peasant and the peasant types of social organization. At the other end of the historical scale:
6 *Peasant-workers* – commuters who represent one form of industrial penetration from the cities into the countryside (at times they may represent their mutual interpenetration). The peasant-worker increasingly keeps his farm merely for consumption purposes and as a place to live while drawing the greater part of his income from town-based wages.
7 *Members of Kolkhozes and communes*. The large-scale production units created under the impact of urban socialist political elites are usually combined with small family plots. In spite of the large-scale changes involved, these societies retain many typically peasant characteristics.

4 Peasantry as a Process

Analytical typologies come, at times, to be regarded statically, i.e. as an implicit declaration of social stability/stagnation. In actual fact, such typologies present but an analytical dimension of reality, 'a history of the present' in Sweeze's celebrated phrase. Typologies must be interlinked with the study of the basic processes involved. But while historical analysis will concentrate on unique sequences of events, a sociologist will *ex officio* come to explore the general patterns of change.

Comprehensive discussion of the dynamics of peasant societies would have to include non-structural changes which, on the whole, get a poor hearing from social scientists. In such processes quantitative changes and changes in personnel leave the basic patterns of social interaction and interdependence essentially intact. For example, the cycles of nature and family life form an important part of peasant social existence, and seem to be reflected in patterns of social mobility in which changes in the position of family units involved *do not* lead to change in the character of the social structure and may even support its stability. Geographical mobility, in which the most active members of the community emigrate, may act likewise.

The attention of analysts was understandably focused on structural change. Such changes in peasantry usually have been determined (or at least triggered off) by the impact of non-peasant sections of society, a situation which can be explained both by the character of the peasant social structure discussed above and by the very fact of peasant domination by powerful outsiders. The spread of industrialization, urbanization, market economy, mass media, etc. play their role in the gradual disintegration of the peasant society as a specific social structure and in the integration of its members into new and nationwide networks of social interaction. Delineation and classification of the major factors of structural change based on the four-facet typology suggested above may prove, once again, useful:

1 The spread of *market relations*, the advent of a money economy and new technology, gradually transforming the *peasant family-farm* into an enterprise of a capitalist nature. Increase in exchange, introduction of planning of farm production in generalized terms of money and profit, and the growing importance of capital formation in agriculture lead to the integration of farms into an all-embracing national capitalist economy and to the 'individualization' of their members. Introduction of specific 'cash crops' or wage labour is an important stage in such development. The spread of market relations may lead to proletarianization of peasantry and growth of agricultural estates. At times, however, the major processes of concentration and accumulation of capital taking place in towns seem to influence agriculture through the market of goods and capital rather than through production. (Such development does not exclude possibilities of extensive exploitation of farming by merchant capital.) At the same time some technical advantages of small-scale farming (e.g. breeding), as well as the draining of the countryside of the richest and the poorest of its inhabitants in the process of urbanization, may lead to the establishment and stabilization of middle-sized capitalist family-farms within the contemporary industrial society.

2 Some division of labour has existed in every peasant community and was generally made rigid by tradition, reaching its climax and sanctification in the Indian caste. The rapid increase in division of labour, interrelated with the spread of a market economy, has lead to rapid development in *professional specialization* in the villages. More and more tasks are taken over by specialized agencies which also undertake responsibility for professional training. On the other hand,

the functions of the farmer have become narrowly agricultural and increasingly skilled. Peasantry as a specific social class and a way of life develops into farming as an occupation.[21]

3 The word *acculturation*, formerly used to depict the cultural impact of the colonizers on the colonial population, can be validly applied to the process of disintegration of traditional and specific peasant cultures under the impact of *mass communication*. The mass media, the national educational system, military service and the temporary migration of labour, all exercise powerful influences by spreading new cultural patterns into the countryside. Improvement of the means of communication and increasing geographical mobility facilitate and gradually establish a town–village continuum. Peasant workers as a new social stratum come to symbolize this process.

4 *Radical political change* by non-peasant power-holders and occasionally by a successful peasant revolution may lead to some basic changes in the structure of peasant society. The two major instances of such change in our century are *agricultural reform* and *collectivization*. Egalitarian agrarian reform has aimed at land redivision and improvement in agriculture within typical peasant social structures. Collectivization has attempted to replace peasant agriculture by modernized and state controlled big enterprises manned by semi-cottagers. The establishment of agricultural cooperatives was the declared aim of both those developments.[22]

The discussion of patterns of change should not result in a, so to speak, 'dynamist' bias in which the existence or even the accomplishment of social processes are assumed on the sheer strength of evidence of causes or even of the processes themselves. A tendency or a trend may after all be blocked by culturally reinforced inertia or by powerful groups interested in maintaining the status quo. Moreover, the impact of factors of change may be limited to, or even reversed by, social mechanisms sustaining the existing structure. Peasant societies, especially at early stages of development, display a variety of such social mechanisms, e.g. social mobility and selective emigration of the most active members, mentioned above. Some structural changes may reestablish, at least in part, typical peasant patterns of social structure, e.g. an egalitarian agrarian reform. However, all this being said, there is little doubt that the major patterns of change in the contemporary world lead it away from encompassing typical peasant social structures. In this

---

21 For discussion see B. Galeski, 'Sociological Problems of the Occupation of a Farmer', in T. Shanin (ed.), *Peasants and Peasant Societies* (Oxford, 1987).

22 For discussion see T. Shanin, 'Cooperation and Collectivization', in *Two Blades of Grass*, ed. P. Worsley (Manchester, 1971).

sense, the definitions of peasantry which view it as representing an aspect of the past surviving in the modern world, seem, on the whole, valid. Yet to discard peasantry as a social group and a specific social structure remains manifestly wrong. Even in our 'dynamic' times we live not in the future but in a present rooted in the past, and that is where our future is shaped. And in the present as in the past, peasants are the majority of mankind.

4

Defining Peasants: Conceptualizations and Deconceptualizations (1980)

The *Declinatio Rustica* from thirteenth century Germany had six declensions for the word peasant – villain, rustic, devil, robber, brigand and looter, and in the plural – wretches, beggars, liars, rogues, trash and infidels.

J. Le Goff

Peasantry is not a class but a notion.

G. Plekhanov

. . . as though it were a question of dialectical reconciliation of concepts and not of the understanding of the real relations.

K. Marx

A decade which bridged the 1960s and the 1970s, and reached its peak in the events and ideas of the extraordinary year 1968, has seen a multiplicity of challenges to accepted world views. It brought forth extensive analytical experimentation with new answers as much as questions newly perceived. The explosion of peasant studies, which increased in this period from few and far between to hundreds and then thousands, shared these origins with a variety of radicalisms and rediscoveries. It carried also some of their birthmarks: imagination and flair, but also excessive speed in theorizing which made some of the claims less than thoughtful. The new evidence, analytical insights and queries concerning peasantry were considerable, but once the heady days were over doubts surfaced as to the actual relevance and validity of studying it at all. At the core of this new turn of an old debate stood the issue of peasant particularity and of the utility of the concept 'peasant' as an analytical tool. In its substance it was the evolutionist credo – unilinearist, scientist, teleological – which formed the base of this challenge. It was formulated at its clearest (and speediest) by a fashionable Marxist wing of the evolutionist species, armed with Althusserian statements of what legitimate Marxism is or is not (and claiming the monopoly of it). Its significance was considerable because of its influence with radicals of the 'developing societies', and because, in a Marxist garb, it raised issues cross-cutting ideological divides and relevant to all and sundry within 'Development Studies'.

This article (first published in Peasant Studies *14 [1980], no. 4) was written as a polemic against attempts to redefine social sciences in a way which would take us back into a world where peasants did not exist, conceptually speaking. A Marxist challenge was answered in Marxist terms. Also, the end of the first decade of Anglo-Saxon peasant studies called for a review of the conceptual structure advanced at the turn of the 1960s mostly by the works of Eric Wolf, Boguslaw Galeski and myself, and in the two 'classics' then published: Chayanov's* Theory of Peasant Economy *(1966) and Marx's* Grundrisse *in Eric Hobsbawm's edition (1964). (For discussion see item 1 above.)*

My major personal conclusion then was that while further use of peasantry as an analytical concept is well justified, the way to advance is to treat it in its broader societal context (i.e. to move from a comparative sociology of peasantries towards a historical sociology of societies, in which peasantry is given its legitimate place), and to consider broader analytical categories to which the achievements of 'peasantology' can contribute. The two volumes of The Roots of Otherness, *both written in the 1980s, are a proof that this conclusion was followed through. So are 'Expolary Economies' and 'Four Models' (items 6 and 13 of this volume). In a number of ways the preface of this volume (item 1) takes up and proceeds with issues raised in the article to follow, explicating its last section from a ten-years-after perspective.*

There are reasons to define 'peasants', and reasons to leave the word vague, a figure of speech but not a judicious category of scholarship. Such a decision is never inconsequential, for this concept, if accepted as such, reflects in conclusions of immediate analytical and political concern. Ways in which such words are put to use matter.

One can, no doubt, overdo concern with terminologies and sink into deadening discourse where long words are used only to spin more words, still longer. Once in a while a test of concept and a look at its epistemological roots are indicated, however. The time seems ripe for that, because, for reasons we shall return to presently, the intellectual fashion of 'peasant studies' seems to be approaching a new stage and a turning point.

1 Peasants as a Mystification

To test a concept it is probably best to commence by considering its content in the way sanctified by the 'null hypothesis' of conventional statistics, i.e. to begin from reasons why it should be ruled out altogether. In that light claims of validity, links to reality, internal consistency, theoretical setting and the possible illuminations of the concept can be examined at their harshest. Let us begin at those beginnings, and state them.

Peasants are a mystification. To begin with, 'a peasant' does not exist in any immediate and strictly specific sense. Over no end of continents, states and regions those so designated differ in ways as rich in content as the world itself. Within the same village the rich and the poor, a landowner and a tenant, a householder and a hired 'hand' will usually break any continuity of smooth gradations. History adds its dimension of diversity, for even 'the same' would not be the same in different years, decades and centuries. A stricter conceptualization of the social context will make it all stand out even more, for, to take a few examples, we may ask whether similar meanings can attach to 'a peasant' within different periods and societies, be it feudal Burgundy, slash-and-burn bushland of Tanzania, the mercantalized Punjab of today or the cotton-for-industry-producing Gezira. Finally, general cross-historical and acontextual terms have a nasty habit of turning into reifications of reality, if not, worse still, conscious manipulations by smart politicians and prestige-hunting academics. That is why and how peasants become a mystification.

All that is factually true for every one of the four points made. (1) The heterogeneity of the peasants is doubtless. (2) Peasants cannot be understood or even properly described without the more general societal setting, and (3) the same holds true for the historical context. (Indeed, only analytically can we divide 'the diachronic' and 'the synchronic' within social phenomena.) (4) The term 'peasants' can be and has been used in mystification. Yet to stipulate all that is no more than to clear ground for the discussion. What is at issue is the way this concept operates within the process of knowledge about societies. In those terms a 'null hypothesis' will be to state that the usage of the concept 'peasants' turns social reality opaque to our eyes, or at least does not contribute at all to its illumination. If so, the conclusion at its most consistent would be to get rid of the awkward term, to avoid afflictions it may lead us into. The alternative, i.e. retaining 'peasants' in conceptual usage, will have to be clarified and defended.

A major and increasingly significant role in such considerations has been played by the 1970s surge of Marxism. Its impact in the 'developing societies' defines its significance. Some of the arguments have restated, and to an extent repositioned, the case against peasants as a legitimate concept. Others declared the opposite. Within the Marxist conceptual framework a problematic was being explored, the relevance of which will be easily recognized also far outside that camp. Many of the positions taken, conclusions offered and doubts proffered cross-cut Marxist/non-Marxist frontiers and battle-lines.

The paper will proceed from the meaning within which the concept is used, through the ways it becomes problematic within a recent Marxist debate, to pose the general issue of deconceptualization in sections 6 and 7. It will follow roughly the case against peasants as a meaningful concept as set out above.

2 Peasants as a Generalization

Even to argue the term 'peasants' into the ground, one has to say first what it is all about. More so, if one would like to put that concept to analytical use. So what do we mean by 'peasants'? Redfield's statement that 'peasant society and culture has something generic about it . . . [that it is] an arrangement of humanity with some similarities all over the world' and Fei's description of peasanthood as a 'way of living'[1] represent well a widespread feeling of most of those who have studied peasants in a systematic and comparative way. Their claims of peasant specificity can be presented under six categories of characteristics by which peasants have been delineated from 'others'.

Firstly, the economy of peasants has been said to differ by a distinctive blend of extensive self-employment (i.e. family labour), control of own means of production, self-consumption of produce and multi-dimensional occupational expertise.[2] Another way to present it is to show how much peasant conditions of productive life necessitate and are shaped by the establishment of an eco-system and a particular balance of agriculture, animal production, gathering and crafts with a particular stress on growing rather than manufacturing.[3] A different yet structurally similar scheme will appear within nomadic economies, some fishermen groups, etc.[4]

A variety of economically relevant characteristics follows. For example, planning of production and calculation of performance differ consistently from those of a capitalist enterprise. Kautsky's notion of peasants' under-consumption and Chayanov's of 'self-exploitation' refer to the problem of poverty and oppression, but also to their specific resolutions in forms which do not operate outside the scope of the peasant

1 R. Redfield, *Peasant Society and Culture* (Chicago, 1956), p. 25; Fei Hsiao Tung, 'Peasants and gentry', *American Journal of Sociology*, LII (1946).

2 See, for example, B. Galeski, *Basic Concepts of Rural Sociology* (Manchester, 1972).

3 For example, E. Wolf, *Peasants* (New York, 1966); N. Malita, 'Agriculture in 2000', *Sociologia Ruralis*, L (1971).

4 For example, N. Afshar Naderi, *The Settlement of Nomads: Its Social and Economic Implications* (Tehran, 1971).

economy.[5] The actual pattern of land control expressed in family property and 'rights of domain' differs from the legal ownership of the
contemporary non-peasants.[6] A broad range of occupational tasks is
'telescoped' into peasanthood as an occupation. Typical methods of
expropriation of peasant surplus by the holders of political and economic power differ from those used against the wage labourers. Inter-
peasant and inter-village exploitation show once again specific forms
and direction of development. The links of supply/demand/price movements within market-centred societies differ within massively peasant
populations, e.g. the movement of wages which is often inversely
proportionate to the price of bread. By the accepted standards of
calculation, many peasant farms are 'working at a loss' and should 'go
bankrupt', yet proceed to operate and even to invest.[7]

Secondly, the patterns and tendencies of political organization of
peasants have often shown considerable similarity in different regions
and countries of the world. Systems of brokers and patronage, the
tendency for 'vertical segmentation' and factionalism, the place of
banditry and guerilla struggle, even the typical atmosphere of peasant
politics and peasant rebellion can be, and indeed have been, meaningfully compared in societies thousands of miles apart in both geography
and social space.[8] The same holds true for the patterns and problems of
political interactions between peasants and both the landlords and the
outsiders, the representatives of national bureaucracies.

Thirdly, typical and closely similar norms and cognitions have been
singled out in peasantries far enough removed to preclude claims of
simple dispersion. These patterns both reflect and influence in turn the
ways of social life and production. The pre-eminence of traditional and
conformist rationalization, the role of oral tradition, specific 'cognitive
maps' (e.g. a circular perception of time) were used as examples.[9]
Specific patterns of socialization and training into peasant occupation
were also traced and related here.[10] The same can be said about peasant

5 A.V. Chayanov, *The Theory of Peasant Economy* (Homewood, Illinois, 1966);
J. Banarjee, 'Summary of Selected Parts of Kautsky: The Agrarian Question', *Economy
and Society*, 6 (1976) no. 5, pp. 26–8, 35. Marx had already spoken about the peasant's
ability to 'Irish himself': K. Marx, *Capital*, vol. I (Harmondsworth, 1976), p. 1068.

6 Wolf, *Peasants*, chapter 2.

7 For discussion see T. Shanin, 'The Nature and Logic of Peasant Economy', *Journal of
Peasant Studies*, I (1973) nos. 1 and 2.

8 E. Wolf, *Peasant Wars in the 20th Century* (London, 1969); R. Stavenhagen, *Agrarian
Problems and Peasant Movements in Latin America* (New York, 1970); etc.

9 For example, F.G. Bailey, 'The Peasant View of the Bad Life', *Advancement of
Science* (December 1966); K. Dobrowolski, *Peasant Traditional Culture* (for an English
translation, see T. Shanin (ed.), *Peasants and Peasant Societies*, [Harmondsworth, 1971]).

10 Galeski, *Basic Concepts of Rural Sociology*, chapter 2.

ideological tendencies and the related patterns of political cooperation, confrontation and leadership.

Fourthly, the basic and characteristic units of social organization and their significance and functioning have shown considerable similarity all round the globe. In particular, the peasant household, but also the village and the broader still networks of social interaction, like a market centre and the localized lowest ring of the state authority, are easily recognizable in their specificity to peasants, scholars and political leaders far afield. The typical patterns of interaction and/or exploitation within the communities that peasants share with rural labourers, craftsmen and possibly petty bureaucrats and petty capitalists, are distinctive and highly repetitive. So is the general subservient position of peasant social units within societal networks of political, economic and cultural domination.

Fifthly, one can analytically single out specific repetitive social dynamics of the peasant society (in reality the statics and dynamics would, of course, be indivisible). In particular, social reproduction, i.e. the production of the material necessities, the reproduction of the human actors and of the system of social relations, show patterns specific and generic to the peasants. For example, typical patterns of family property and inheritance customs, referred to above, are central to the reproduction of peasant family-farms. The in-family occupational training, as mentioned, is relevant here. The rhythm of life of the peasant household and village reflect powerfully major 'natural' cycles, e.g. the agricultural year. And so on.

Finally, fundamental patterns and causes of structural change have been seen as both generic and specific to the peasants. Theories of structural transformation have been rightly expressed in a broader-than-peasantry framework of national societies or of international systems. At the same time peasant specificity has been claimed in the ways those general processes are reflected within, and reacted to by, the peasant communities. For example, commercialization has usually resulted at first in a stage of 'agriculturalization' of the peasants, their earlier non-agricultural tasks taken over by industrial mass production (often with the villagers boxed into exploitive networks of agro-business of various types). On the other side of the fence, collectivization has also led to a variety of specifically peasant patterns of reaction, e.g. the differential patterns of production on the house plot as against the collective field, and their impact on the actual social operation of agriculture.[11] The often-repeated surprise at the tenacity of peasant

11 For example, Pham Cuong and Nguyen Van Ba, *Revolution in the Village; Nam Hong, 1945–1975* (Hanoi, 1976).

social forms (the 'problem of non-disappearance'), and even contemporary 'repeasantization' of some areas, would also belong here.

There can be no place here to discuss the scope of comparative evidence presented often enough in support of those generalizations. Let us proceed directly to what such generalizations imply. To begin with the negatives, the consequent use of the concept does not, of course, imply homogeneity of peasants. Nor does it assume a clear-cut separation of actual categories, of the 1:0 variety. Any such generalization assumes heterogeneity as well as 'margins' or 'hedges' of conceptual ambivalence. The number one charge against peasants as a conceptual entity in the list above is either beside the point or else doubts essentials of social science and not simply one of its terms. The status of 'peasants' as a generalization was well expressed in a recent lecture as that of a 'recurrent syndrome' – it assumes, and indeed necessitates, diversity.[12] The existence of repetitive, massive and strategic similarities is a point well worth making, and that is what this generalization based on comparison came to signify. It helped to focus study, to elicit insights and employ methods of enquiry tested elsewhere, as well as to lay out a field for analysis. It did not provide a substitute for it.

The flourishing of 'peasant studies' in the 1960s was linked to new attempts to define peasants by exploring the structural logic behind their 'peasantness'. In that debate the wing of Western anthropology which interpreted Redfield's and Fei's intuitions in terms of political economy met and blended with the parts of West European rural history and the extension of East European tradition of peasant studies, both Marxist and non-Marxist. The results of those encounters led to much more than simple generalizations from the empirical, yet they did not usually offer a fully developed structural analysis either.[13]

A hierarchy of significance must bring out into the open what was previously often left implicit, eclectic or unclear.[14] Peasant specificity reflects interdependence between the basic elements mentioned and cannot be simply reduced to any one of them. At the same time, the core of the determining characteristics seems to lie with the nature and dynamics of the family-farm as a basic unit of production and social

12 E. Wolf, 'Is the Peasant a Class Category Separate from Bourgeois and Proletarian?', notes for a talk, 2 March 1977 (Binghampton, 1977).

13 For a relevant critical comment on the tendency, see G. Claus, 'Toward a Structural Definition of Peasant Society', *Peasant Studies Newsletter* II (1973) no. 2. That criticism implicitly involves also my own early work (Shanin, *Peasants and Peasant Societies*, introduction).

14 For the epistemology involved, see, for example, E. Hobsbawm, 'Karl Marx's contribution to historiography', in *Ideology and Social Sciences*, ed. R. Blackburn (London, 1972).

livelihood. The very existence of peasants as a specific social entity is contingent on the presence of family-farms as the basic unit of economy and society. A point to remember, especially within the diverse 'Western' experience, is that the essence of such a unit lies not in kinship but in production. The worldwide repetition of economic, political and cultural traits as well as of the typical patterns of dynamics would have to do with the *modus operandi* of the peasant family-farms and the specific ways they link and transform. That is essentially the approach to characterization of the peasantry which was at the core of the mainstream of Central and East European research and political debate during the last century. While presumptions, questions and conclusions differed, the way the concept was singled out and assumed has cross-cut ideological camps and academic schools of thought. In particular, while a debate raged over the issue of peasants' differentiation and stability, nobody seemed to doubt where the root of peasanthood lay. Nor was there much argument about the criteria by which we might judge when and if that social entity comes to an end. It was the peasant family unit of production and its structural metamorphosis or disappearance which has delineated both. Three generations later this tradition is still fully reflected by the leading students of peasants in Eastern Europe.[15]

3 Peasant Differentiation, or Multilinearity of the Capitalist Transformation of Agriculture

Contradictory and often remarkably far-fetched interpretations of Marx rapidly became a major academic industry of the post-1968 period. It is within this type of debate that a call to deconceptualize peasants has been recently heard, claiming Marx's authority. A quick look at his actual views may be not amiss, therefore. Marx's early insights and assumptions concerning peasants are very much those of a Central European (with a knowledge of East European languages and tradition), who was placed within the English milieu of depeasantized capitalism. In the study in which Marx tackled peasants of his own times most directly, he characterized and delineated 'the most numerous class of French society' through the concept of '*parzellen* holding'. What is *parzelle* if not the peasant family-farm, duly described in the sentences of his text which follow the phrase? It is indeed easily placed also as the 'individual workshop [which] contains an entire economy, forming as it does an independent centre of production' of an earlier period, subsequently commercialized and partly transformed by the early capitalist

15 For example, the works of B. Galeski, V.P. Danilov, A.M. Anfimov.

development of France. Or, to decode metaphorical language, the ultimate 'potato' within 'the sack of potatoes' – Marx's characterization of the French peasants – is no doubt a peasant family-farm. The anticipated direction of further development was also clear. It was to be the 'dissolution of private property based on labour of its owner', i.e. the advance of capitalist development due to restructure society into two fundamental classes, dissolving peasant family production units and thereby peasantry in the process. To wit, 'the production of capital and wage workers is therefore the major product of the process by which capital turns itself into value.'[16] The main stream of Marxist social theorizing has consequently approached the contemporary peasantry via the problematic of its capitalist transformation, expressed in two major conceptual debates concerning: (1) differentiation, and (2) modes of production. The issue of peasants' location within history and society was set accordingly.

Capitalist transformation provided the major direction and mechanism of structural change within the contemporary peasant societies. Capitalism means depeasantization – in the nineteenth century that view had been generally adopted by 'the educated public' with the fairly few exceptions of the reactionary romantics, extreme populists and some 'revisionists' within the German Social Democracy.

The major work which dominated Marxist thought of those times was *The Agrarian Problem* by K. Kautsky. It was (and still is) rich in content and insight into the peasant problematic. It accepted the possibility of some difference in the way capital penetrates agriculture as against the other branches of economy. It stressed that the reported lack of concentration of land ownership within German agriculture did not mean failure of capitalism to take hold there. The prime mover of capitalist transformation of the rural society was the capital accumulation within industry, which outstripped, subordinated and was finally to destroy peasant agriculture. Kautsky's position closely followed Marx's presentation of the English/Irish example in *Capital*, suitably generalized, elaborated and advanced.[17]

Lenin's political success eventually made for the decisive influence of his contribution to this debate, in so far as the following generations of Marxists were concerned. In the earliest of his books Lenin was still very much 'a Kautskian', but the stress clearly differed. To him it was the *inter-peasant* dynamics of 'deepening' market relations, division of labour and class differentiation which provide the central point of

16 The quotations come from K. Marx, 'Eighteenth Brumaire of Louis Bonaparte', *Selected Writings* (Moscow, 1973), vol. I, pp. 478–9, *Pre-Capitalist Economic Formations* (London, 1964), pp. 79, 118; *Capital*, vol. I, p. 926.
17 Last chapter of Marx, *Capital*, vol. I, part 8.

capitalist transformation.[18] The stress moved from production to market relations. The polemics were aimed at that wing within Russian populism which believed that broad autarky, homogeneity and stability of peasant society would abort capitalist development in Russia. To Lenin, the logic of commodity relations and exploitive capacity of the richer peasants indicated a necessary polarization of the peasants into rich and poor, rapidly transforming into rural capitalists and proletarians. The problem of differentiation, its character, speed and political results, subsequently dominated the analysis of peasant societies within the Third International and the communist movements of 'the East'. Long stretches of Lenin's 1899 book, *The Development of Capitalism in Russia*, still appear practically verbatim within many of the studies of diverse societies today.

A thin line divides the appreciation of a masterly analytical achievement from religious self-stupefication by it. The best way to tell the difference is simply to ask: was anything substantively new learned during the eighty years which have passed since Lenin's book was published? Indeed, did Lenin himself learn anything new from the twenty-five years of his own revolutionary experience which followed the publication of his treatise?

To begin with the second of those questions, Lenin's own approach to peasantry underwent a consistent change. Already by 1907 he declared that his earlier conclusions about the capitalist nature of Russian agriculture were clearly overstated. Lenin's further move in the acceptance of persisting peasant traits underlay the changes in his party's policies and programmes in 1917, in 1921 and at its strongest in 1923 on Lenin's deathbed.[19] Indeed, already the fact of the cancellation of the first 'agrarian programme' of his party meant that the 1897 book's analysis, directly related to it, could not be sustained. Yet the book which resulted was never rewritten, and drifted into canonization together with the man himself.

In the last decade attempts to consider anew the differentiation debate were made. Massive amendments of analysis were suggested by contemporary Soviet historians looking anew at Russian data. Critical work was done in 'the West'. Fresh attempts to put to use Lenin's methodology concerning differentiation of peasantry presented new insights and new opportunities. Yet in most of those studies the basic pre-assumptions of Lenin concerning peasant differentiation have been

18 V.I. Lenin, 'The Problem of Markets', in *Collected Writings*, vol. I (Moscow, 1968); and *Development of Capitalism in Russia* (Moscow, 1974); but also later works, e.g. *Polnoe Sobranie Sochinenii*, vol. 17 (Moscow, 1968), pp. 120, 127.

19 In particular, 'On Cooperation', 'Better Fewer but Better' and the December 1923 letter to Congress, in *Selected Works*, V.I. Lenin, vol. 32 (Moscow, 1971), pp. 681–713.

treated very much as akin to laws of nature by many Marxists, with a clear nod of approval from neoclassical economists. Critical comments and/or amendments, if any, centred only on the speed of polarization and possible countervailing influences. Yet one must look also at the fundamental model at the root of the differentiation analysis. How satisfactory is Lenin's theoretical preamble to his 1898 book for the contemporary scene?

The picture emerging from the bits and pieces of international comparison seems much more complex and multi-directional than the early differentiation model would grant it to be. In the case of capitalist transformation of agriculture, not one but three major types of change seem to occur, often simultaneously, in different regions and, indeed, within the same society. Each of them has major analytical significance. Those processes will be referred to as differentiation, pauperization and marginalization.

Without doubt *differentiation* has played an important role in the capitalist transformation of peasant agriculture, and has often represented the most significant structural change of it. The theoretical and factual claims in support of that are valid. It is the interpretation of it as the axiomatically necessary and exclusive pattern of development which is not.

To begin with that model, exploitation plus what Myrdal has termed 'circular causation' in 'cumulation of advantages and disadvantages'[20] should lead to an increasing capital accumulation at 'the top', i.e. in the hands of the rural and urban rich and/or capitalists. A free market economy is on the whole implicitly pre-assumed. Such a process would also, it is assumed, produce jobs for the newly pauperized, turning them into proletarians and extending capitalism in its classical sense. Let us vary one of the components: the surplus value is accumulated neither in the villages nor in the towns of the country itself, but in a metropolis 5,000 miles away. What will follow is a twisted 'polarization' in which the downward trend is not matched by an upward one, i.e. not differentiation and proletarianization of the majority, but a process of *pauperization*, an aggregate downward shift producing 'surplus' rural population and shanty towns. It is not a 'labour reserve army' which will come into being, for nobody is to call on those reserves within the decades to come. Nor are those 'deviants', 'marginals' or other such words assuming exceptionality, for the social grouping referred to is constant and central to such a society.

Is such a variation of the 'differentiation model' realistic? Of course, it happens in every colonial society and often typifies what is today

20 G. Myrdal, *Economic Theory and Underdeveloped Regions* (London, 1957).

referred to as 'neocolonialism' and 'peripheralization' in, say, Java.[21] Does it call for specific conceptual and analytical effort? No doubt, for those peasants will neither remain structurally 'as before' nor turn rural proletarians in terms of the classical theory of capitalism. Even the ethnography of the scene will differ, and so would the political conclusions and anticipations, i.e. the stuff which makes social analysis relevant.

To proceed, the optimistic, 'youngish' capitalism of the nineteenth century has very much influenced the Marxist view of it. It was seen as aggressive, constructive, overwhelming and supra-energetic in its capacity to spread. Like the finger of Midas which turns everything it touches into gold, so also capitalism turns everything it touches into capitalism. The earth was the limit. Today, all that seems an overstatement by far. The capacity of capitalist centres to milk everybody and everything around is doubtless; it is their capacity or their need (in terms of optimization of profits) to transform everything around into the likes of itself which is not. Peasants are often a case in point. In the doubtlessly capitalist Mexico the relative share of the peasants within the population has been decreasing, but their numbers have kept remarkably steady between 1910 and 1970. In the no less certainly capitalist Brazil, an absolute increase in the numbers of peasantry, i.e. actual repeasantization, has been taking place.[22] Even the World Bank's chief, after a considerable change of mind, has recently spoken about hundreds of millions of small producers on the land by the end of the century.[23] What does it all mean in terms of the assumptions of capitalist transformation of peasant agriculture?

It seems to mean that under some conditions peasants do not dissolve, differentiate and/or pauperize. They may persist, while gradually transforming and linking into the encapsulating capitalist economy, which pierces through their lives. Peasants then continue to exist, often coinciding with agricultural units different in structure and size from the classical peasant family-farm in ways partly explored already by Kautsky. Peasants are *marginalized*, the significance of the peasant agriculture within the national economy decreases, while slower production growth often turns it into a backwater. Peasants came to serve capitalist development as a type of permanent 'primitive accumulation', offering cheap labour, cheap food and markets for profit-making goods. They produce also healthy and stupid soldiers, policemen, servants,

---

21 For example, H. Geertz, *Agricultural Involution* (Berkeley, 1963).

22 J.R.B. Lopez, *Capitalist Development and Agrarian Structure in Brazil* (Sao Paulo, 1976).

23 See McNamara, 1974 address to the Board of Governors (Washington).

cooks and prostitutes; the system can always do with more of those. And, of course, they, i.e. peasants, produce tasks and troubles to scholars and officials who puzzle over 'the problem of their non-disappearance'.

To accept marginalization as one of the patterns of *peasants'* change under the impact of capitalism is conditional on the resolution of a conceptual query. When, if at all, does a peasant stop being a peasant while retaining a family-farm unit of production? To put it specifically, is a West European farmer, using family labour to drive and supervise a couple of self-owned tractors, a few cars and a super-mechanised farm, based on massive capital investment but with no wage labourers, to be defined as a peasant? If not, where does the divide lie? A current study by Danilov et al. suggests a neat conceptual solution here. It divides the forces of production of the family-farm into 'natural' (e.g. land or labour) and those which are man-produced (e.g. machinery and equipment) and suggests that we define as peasant only those farms in which production is decisively determined by the 'natural' means of production.[24]

The same work, an original 'Eastern' Marxist contribution to the conceptualization of peasants, has also sounded a powerful reminder about the basic limitations of the classical differentiation theories, which pre-assume a free market economy and one very much abstract from the nature of state intervention. Even in medieval China the imperial agrarian reforms successfully removed large land-ownership, reversing differentiation processes back to square one. The Soviet NEP represented a different dimension of regeneration of peasants by the state and the revolution. On the other hand, in a number of 'developing societies' the state transformed peasant economy through the imposition of monopolistic centralization of rural trade into a 'gigantic dispersed manufacture', exploitive in its nature, e.g. the position of the small coffee farmers of Ghana. State-induced transformation defined anew the peasants' 'place and role within the social structure'. All of it well said and no need to spoil it by a superfluous comment.

4 Modes and Peasants: Peasants as a Mode of Production

The second road along which the peasant problematic was approached in Marxist terms was via the elaboration of the properties of modes of production. The problems of specificity, i.e. of the 'existence' of peasants,

24 V.P. Danilov, L.V. Danilov and V.G. Restyanikov, *Osnovyne Etapy Razvitiya Krest'yanaskogo Khozyaistva* (Moscow, 1977). For a broadly similar approach in 'Western' writing see S. Amin, *Capitalism and Ground Rent*, (Dakar, 1974).

have been presented accordingly. Particular significance lies here in the fact of focusing analytical attention on what seems to be the kernel of the conceptual awkwardness of the whole problematic, i.e. on the issue of peasants fitting into the broader society and history.

Part of the current debate concerning modes of production has been no more than fashionable verbiage, a bid for a place on a platform or for a Marxist badge, within communities where such things matter. It often resembled the worst examples of functionalism: logical manipulation of elaborated abstractions, cruelly verbose in neologisms and essentially sterile in advancing understanding of social reality. Yet beside all that we find some of the most serious theoretical concerns and opportunities. Identification of fundamental units of analysis, their character, flexibility and changing usage play a crucial role in the way our intellectual maps are shaped and in turn shape social reality. Modes of production are such fundamental units of analysis within Marxist theoretical thought.

Marx's authority still very much designates what 'mode of production' is assumed to be. His own usage of the concept was changeable and often implicit, to be distilled from working papers which find their internal coherence elsewhere. 'Mode of production' represents the general (in the sense of abstract) and the specific (in the sense of a particular historical setting) way the material needs of society are provided for at a given stage of its development. This makes it crucial for the analysis of the whole nature of society's existence and of the characterization of its specificity. It also explains why the exposition of the concept usually begins with the interdependence of the relations of production and the forces of production, i.e. 'appears equally as the relationship of individuals to one another and the specific daily behaviour towards inorganic nature, their specific mode of labour.'[25] A system of political economy centred on the creation, appropriation and control of surpluses through the domination of men by men, i.e. an 'essential relationship or appropriation [which is] the relationship of domination'[26] provides a central and distinguishing element of a mode of production. A typically patterned dynamics is part and parcel of the concept and is specific to every mode of production. In structuralist terminology a mode of production has therefore both a synchronic and a dyachronic dimension, i.e. it represents not only a social system but also a historical epoch. It incorporates reproductive processes of material goods, labour and the system of social relations, as well as distinctive patterns of structural change, i.e. of its transformation.

---

25 Marx, *Pre-Capitalist Economic Formations*, p. 94.
26 ibid., p. 102.

The concept of mode of production as defined provides the core and/or determinant of a number of further characteristics. The character and extent of such determinations is never simple and is usually mutual in character. The legal systems of ownership reflect it well (much of Marx's attention was devoted to it). It defines a political economy, yet it represents also a patterned consciousness of a type. It reflects the actual relations of production and control, but at the same time shows partial autonomy and capacity to feed back (with its own determining capacity) into the economy *sensu strictu*. The same can be said about a number of basic structures of social control, interaction, and consciousness, of which the modern state is probably the most crucial.

Marxist analysis in the 1970s was for a time influenced with particular strength by the work of Althusser and his disciples, in which Marxism interacted with French structuralism.[27] The analytical focus moved towards the hidden beneath the observable, the non-subjective, with the logic of modes of production overshadowing any other units of analysis. The attraction of such a preference clearly related to the intellectual's quest for the more certain and deterministic, expressed as deeper, more objective and more theoretical. That has been terminologically reflected in the way 'science', 'scientific' and 'rigorous' came thereby to be used as major badges of Marxist scholarship (with Marx's *Capital* becoming more 'scientific' than his *Eighteenth Brumaire*).

In that light the above scope of the problematic concerning conceptualization of the peasants can be restated in the following sequence of questions:

1 Is peasantry as such to be constituted as a *mode of production* and, if so, how does it 'articulate' with the society at large? (and if not . . .)
2 Is peasantry to be seen as a *component* of a specific (and exclusive) mode of production? (and if not . . .)
3 Is peasantry to be understood as a social entity autonomous enough to relate to, and to transfer between, different modes of production? (and if not . . .)
4 Is peasantry an 'empty word' exposed and nullified by the satisfactory usage of the concept of 'mode of production'?

Are peasants a mode of production? Evidently the answer relates to the way mode of production is defined and the way peasants are. In the terms suggested above, peasants are not a mode of production because they lack a relatively self-contained structure of political economy, i.e.

27 For example, L. Althusser and E. Balibar, *Reading Capital* (London, 1970). Initial presentation of it in English. For recent discussion see A. Foster-Carter, 'The Modes of Production Debate', *New Left Review* (1978), p. 107.

the most significant systems of exploitation and surplus appropriation have been on the whole external to them. It goes without saying that all peasants are not 'equal' and that every peasant community displays structures of 'neighbourly' exploitation often linked within complex networks of 'patronage'. Yet to most of the peasants, inter-peasant inequality and exploitation is secondary to extra-peasant, both in terms of the share extracted and in the way structural dynamics and class structure bear upon them. Indeed, a turning towards decisive predominance of inter-peasant structures of inequality and exploitation could spell the end of peasantry as such, i.e. as a specific social grouping.

There are two alternatives which may lead to the categorization of peasantry as a mode of production. The first is to stipulate two sub-types of 'mode of production', one along lines suggested above and another one differently defined. A number of recent studies designate a 'secondary mode of production' which differs from a primary one by appearing only in articulation with other modes of production but never on its own.[28] A society (socio-economic formation?) therefore provides the framework within which an exploitive political economy acts as a determining link between the dominant (exploitive) and secondary (exploited) mode of production. 'Secondary mode of production' would represent a linked structure of forces and relations of production, a necessarily incomplete political economy in which the dominant societal conflict and determinations lie at its boundaries. The 'rules of the game' of the dominant mode of production would dominate such a formation as a whole.

The origins (and legitimation) of the concept of 'secondary mode of production' and its present usage are in the discussion of the smallholders – the 'immediate producers' referred to by Marx as 'a mode of production . . . [which] also exists under slavery, serfdom and other situations of dependency . . . but . . . flourishes where the worker is the free proprietor of the conditions of his labour and sets them in motion himself'.[29] The interpretations of this text varied from the treatment of the concept as an essentially pedagogic device (i.e an abstract 'point of beginning' set to clarify the dynamics of capitalism), to the assumption of a fully-fledged ('primary') mode of production of independent commodity producers, e.g. an epoch in USA history in which it would have offered a temporary barrier to the development of capitalism there.[30] The idea of a peasant secondary mode of production falls somewhat in between those polarities. Peasant economy is approached as a sub-

28 C.F.S. Cardoso, 'On the Colonial Modes of Production of the Americas', *Critique of Anthropology* (Autumn 1975) nos. 4 and 5, pp. 1–36 (first published in 1975 in Spanish).
29 Marx, *Capital*, p. 926; Marx, *Pre-Capitalist Economic Formations*, p. 94.
30 See the debate of J. O'Connor and R. Sherry, *Monthly Review*, 28 (1976).

category of a broader family of 'petty commodity modes of production', their position within society caught well by the term 'a tributary society'.

The second alternative is to redesign the term 'mode of production' in an even more radical fashion. Once more, Marx's own text has been used as support. Mode of production is seen here in its most direct and descriptive sense, i.e. as a way of producing, a labour process, a general technological stage of development – a concept greatly reduced in scope, as, for example, in Marx's designation of *agriculture* as a 'mode of production *sui generis*'.

What are the heuristic gains and limitations of such an analytical strategy? The presentation of peasant specificity through the concept of 'peasant mode of production' provides a possible way of theorizing a number of issues in question, e.g. peasants' societal setting. Yet the cutting edge of the concept of mode of production has been very much subject to its designation as a system/dynamics in which production and exploitation are central and linked. (The same can probably be said about the very contribution of Marxism to social sciences.) A mode of production as a unit of analysis which does not carry these essential characteristics seems to categorize out of existence its most important analytical insights. That is why, on balance, the concept of 'peasant mode of production' has probably too many heuristic limitations to be sustained.

5 Peasants and Modes: Totalities and Units

To proceed to the second question of the sequence concerning modes and peasants, is peasantry a component of an exclusive mode of production? The most likely candidate here would be feudalism, appropriating peasant labour and produce within a mainly agricultural and decentralized economy and society, with landowners-cum-local-rulers-cum-knights at its top. However, a number of 'progressive epochs in the economic formation of the society'[31] of Marx's contain the 'something' which he himself and those others who study peasants delimit as the core of peasant specificity. Peasant households as basic units of production and social living, peasants as a social entity of considerable structural similarities and even with established political self-identity can be found within differently structured socio-economic systems: the 'Asiatic' (if there is such a 'thing'), in antiquity, within the (early?) capitalism of Germany and France, in the colonial and post-colonial 'developing societies' and as far as the Soviet NEP and Poland of

31 Marx, *Selected Writings*, p. 504.

today.[32] The only way to insist on peasants as exclusively embedded in the feudal mode of production is to do it by a tautology, i.e. by arbitrarily defining (1) all modes of production containing peasants or share-croppers as feudal (or semi-feudal, whatever that means), (2) all family production units outside feudalism as not peasants (or else as aconceptual remainders which share societal space with those who legitimately occupy it, e.g. the wage workers under capitalism). Such procedures blind us to social reality in its complexity and contradictions.

The diversity of actual approaches to the way family-farms fit into modes of production can be presented on a continuum between two poles, both represented within the works published during the last decade. On the one hand, it is the characteristics of the dominant production units which exclusively define the broader structure (mode of production? formation? society?); on the other hand, the essential characteristics of family-farms have been treated as exclusively determined by the broader socio-economic system, i.e./or by the (dominant) mode of production.

To exemplify the first approach, 'the household is to the tribal economy as the manor to medieval economy or the corporation to modern capitalism; each is the dominant production institution of its times.'[33] While Sahlin's designation of a household as tribal (with peasant farms dropping out of sight) may mislead, the logic of a position is spelt out admirably. It has also been explicitly and rightly related to the comparative taxonomy of economic systems by Chayanov and as manifestly put in contradiction with the structuralism of Terray. The fully developed conclusion of such an approach has been expressed already in Thorner's category of 'peasant economy' defined as a 'whole economy of sizeable countries . . . a widespread form of organization of human society' to be delimited by the percentages of distinctly peasant social units within its population. Consequently, the spread of the peasant units of production defines also an epoch of considerable length and heterogeneity, for peasant economies existed 'long before feudalism, alongside feudalism and long after it'. The drop in the share of the peasant family-farm will eventually make the term 'peasant' inapplicable.[34]

On the other hand, different modes of production would mean a totally different social essence of family-farms (and of 'peasantry' generally) even if formal similarities can be traced. Marx's comment that

---

32 To remind ourselves, Marx himself never doubted the propriety of the usage of the concept 'peasant' in capitalist France.

33 M. Sahlin, *Stone Age Economics* (London, 1974), p. 76.

34 D. Thorner, 'Peasant Economy as a Category in Economic History', in *Peasants and Peasant Society*, Shanin, pp. 202–8, 216–17.

'even economic categories appropriate to earlier modes of production acquire a new and specific historical character under the impact of capitalist production'[35] is consequently interpreted to mean that 'there is no "peasantry" in general, only specific forms of agricultural production, worked and managed to a greater or lesser degree by 'household units . . . specific to the mode of production in which they exist. Typologies based upon technique, agronomic and cultural conditions are at best misleading.' Or, in the more rounded-up form of the same text, 'Peasantry as a theoretical economic category does not exist in Marxism' and should be treated but as a 'specific agrarian detachment of petty bourgeoisie'.[36] The same would necessarily go for specific peasant history or for any of its assumed characteristics. At its crudest such a position can be proceeded with by certification of orthodoxy-cum-truth, through the simple dividing of the conceptual field between Marxist structuralism and a camp of unit-directed 'non-Marxist approaches'.

The actual answer seems to lie, at least initially, on the epistemological plane. The underlying question is that of the relation between 'totality' and its sub-units. Does a general structure exclusively determine and define its component units, or is it that the sum total of sub-units defines the whole? Are there any other possibilities? Also, can peasants be seen as 'inter-mode' transferable entities or is such a notion absurd?

Marxist analysis has been structuralist in its refusal to accept reduction of any totality to the sum total of its sub-units (as is also, by the way, sophisticated non-Marxist scholarship of today).[37] The conclusion which cannot be drawn from it, however, is a reduction 'the opposite way round', i.e. an attempt to deduce sub-units from the characteristics of the whole. It is the interaction of the whole and its parts in all of their different and related characteristics, the often contradictory dynamics and logic of both totality and its units which must be grasped at once. Complex as it is, there is no way around it. The often over-employed words 'dialectical relationship' will be here, for once, not out of place. To exemplify, social classes reflect the contradictions and laws of motion of modes of production, but no deduction of the first from the second (or vice versa) can substitute for the specific analysis. Turning back to the peasants, what must be rejected is a misleading question, assuming a fake duality of possibilities. One cannot understand the operation of

35 Marx, *Capital*, p. 950.
36 P. Hirst, 'Can There Be a Peasant Mode of Production?' (ms), p. 7. The final version of it appears as J. Ennew, P. Hirst and K. Tribe, 'Peasants as an Economic Category', *Journal of Peasant Studies*, 4 (1977) no. 4. The quote comes from pp. 295–6.
37 For example, L. Von Bertlanffy, *Problems of Life* (New York, 1952); A. Koestler and J.R. Smithies, *Beyond Reductionism* (London, 1969). Also see T. Shanin, (ed.), *The Rules of the Game* (London, 1972).

peasant units of production without their societal context. Nor can one deduce them or reduce them or conceptually dissolve them simply because of that. Deductionism is not a satisfactory answer to empiricism or eclecticism.

That is why acceptance of 'inter-mode' existence of the peasants brings us closer to the 'richness' of reality. To say so is not to claim that peasants under capitalism equal peasants under feudalism, for that is not at issue (and the opposite is, of course, assumed). What it does mean is that peasants represent a social and economic specificity of characteristics which will reflect on every societal system they operate within. It means also that peasant history relates to broader societal histories, not as their simple reflection, but with important degrees of autonomy. At its simplest, it means that a capital-dominated social formation encompassing peasants differs from those in which peasants do not exist, and cannot be understood without a specific analytical expression of it. Once again, the issue cross-cuts the Marxist/non-Marxist frontiers for, as the once leading exponent of the structural functionalist school has it, the conceptual crisis of that school was followed by the new 'strong emphasis laid on the autonomy of any subsetting, subgroup or subsystem' thereby 'problematised'[38] – a comment which would fit the Marxist structuralisms as well. Most importantly, these conclusions are not simply an exercise in logic but central to strategies of research and political action. They mean that peasants and their dynamics must be considered both as such and also within broader societal contexts to further understanding of themselves and the society they live in.

To give relief to those who like the authority of Marxian textual references, all that has been methodologically implicit also in Marx's own work. For example, his consideration of merchant capital and merchants related them to different modes of production and gave them a part-autonomous history of their own. Merchant capital is neither totally independent of capitalism nor simply reflecting it, nor else only a stage within it. Nor are merchants ahistorical in terms of the society they operate in. While stating that it is production and not circulation where 'true political economy begins', merchant capital is singled out for study in its relative independence and undeducible specificity as a clearly necessary part of the process of understanding of the whole.[39]

So, what are peasants, conceptually speaking? Generalizations and

38 S. Eisenstadt, 'Sociological Theory and an Analysis of the Dynamics of Civilizations and of Revolutions', *Daedalus*, 106 (1977) no. 4, p. 66.

39 For example, Marx, *Capital*, vol. 3, chapters XIX and XX. See also the relevant letter of Engels to C. Schmidt in K. Marx and F. Engels, *Collected Writings*, vol. 3 (Moscow, 1973), pp. 483–5.

models are not reality, which is ever richer. The question is what the concepts illuminate and what they conceal. That makes a generalized question like 'Are peasants a mode of production, *or* an economy, *or* a class?' nonsensical, for those concepts are neither mutually exclusive nor interchangeable; their illumination may be added up. None of such conceptualizations can be total except for those which are tautological and/or trivial. Concepts are tools of analysis, their usefulness and usage subject to the questions asked, the ways those relate into more general theoretical schemes of questioning. Such a statement does not offer a defence of principled eclecticism, for hierarchies of significance are presumed and central in any effective analysis, and different concepts show different measures of illumination (or none whatever). It is the way of usage of the concept and its heuristic results which must be looked at in our case.

Peasants have initially entered the Marxist parley as the analytical prehistory of capitalism and its passive fodder within 'primitive accumulation', but in particular as a historical class of, so to say, low 'classness', explainable in turn within terms of peasant specificity.[40] In Marx's writings peasants belong to ancient or medieval times in the *Grundrisse*, to the more immediate past of England in *Capital*, to become politically central in his analysis of actual history in France. They are not only an analytical construct, not only 'bearers' of characteristics of a general 'matrix', but a social group which exists in the collective consciousness and political deed of its members. Only such a conceptualization of a class 'for itself' – an actor and subject within social history – allows of posing questions like those of class crystallization and decrystallization, class coalitions, retreats, victories and defeats. Class struggle means on this level not only an objective contradiction of interest, but actual confrontation of specific organizations, slogans and men. That is why the historically actual peasants gradually took over from their nominal-only brethren 'in themselves' as Lenin's writings and deeds grew more mature and delved deeper into the making of history. A similar story for Mao and Tito will some time be written. As immediately relevant political analysis took the pride of place, peasants transformed from derivations or deductions to armies and actors; and simultaneously the relative autonomy of class from the (dominant?) modes and/or society it links into was increasingly granted.

---

40 For an explanation of a somewhat different view see Wolf, 'Is the Peasant a Class Category Separate from Bourgeois and Proletarian?', pp. 2–4: 'Marx . . . still worked with a homogeneous model of the hypothetical society . . . The reason this seems to me important is that peasantries are always localised. They inhabit peripheries and semi-peripheries by definition and peripheries within peripheries. And this is perhaps why it is difficult or impossible to speak of the peasantry as a class.'

Peasants became a class while placed within a substantively capitalist country in the eyes of the post-1906 Lenin.[41]

That is no happy end, with all doubts resolved and peasants found out for what they truly are within Marxism, i.e. a class within a given historical context. Peasants 'are' a class, a sub-economy and some other 'things' we have not yet conceptualized besides. No social reality can be neatly divided into one, deductively chosen, type of units of analysis with all conclusions derived from it. Reality is not neat, nor can relevant analysis of it ever be. Indeed, to dispose of inelegancies is to rid us of the very points where puzzlement breeds discovery within social sciences.

6 Peasants as a Fashion

To understand what peasants 'are', one must understand what and how we think about them. A history of peasants as a concept or fashion would be a major task in itself. We shall limit it to a few aspects relevant to the issue in hand. The political significance of the concept provided for a periodicity of its usage, reflecting social history in its broadest sense, but also specific dynamics of academic thought. An upsurge of interest in the topic was taking place in what can roughly be termed the early stages of industrialization and capitalist transformation of Central and Eastern Europe. It commenced in the second half of the nineteenth century and produced by the beginning of the twentieth most of the relevant conceptual and ideological tools of today. Most of it has come into properly 'Western' thought through the mediation of the Central and East Europeans who knew how to write English (e.g. Marx, Znaniecki and Sorokin) or else through translations (e.g. Weber, Lenin and Chayanov).

The upsurge came to an abrupt and dramatic end during the 1920s and 1930s. It was flattened by repressions as much as by the advance of the ideologies and policies of militant nationalism and rapid industrialization which placed peasants where witchcraft and homespun dress belonged, i.e. outside the scope of progressive political and intellectual concerns. East and Central Europe have thereby caught up with an earlier dominant West European/United States tendency. A basic taxonomy of modern/traditional turned peasants terminologically invisible within a general bag of 'traditionals' and of other exotics. During the 1930s, the 1940s and later, in the fool's paradise of 'the post-colonial' modernization theories of 1950–60, peasants proceeded not to exist, conceptually speaking.

41 e.g., V.I. Lenin, 'Agrarian Programme of Social Democracy etc.' (1908), in *Polnoe Sobranie Sochinenii*, vol. 17, pp. 170–2.

A building up of crises in the so-called 'developing societies' and world agriculture, the collapse of simple-and-quick modernizing prescriptions, China's decision 'to walk on both feet', the World Bank's discovery of peasant tenacity, and the way Vietnam stood up to the most industrialized country of the world have brought peasants sharply into focus. A virtual explosion of studies, publications and debate followed. The structure of the publishing business and academia as business have rapidly turned it all into fashion with the laws of motion of fashion-mongering increasingly taking over. It meant a rapid increase in the use of the word 'peasant' as a publishing gimmick (together with naked females and shirts with the pictures of Che). It meant scrambling to say something new and career-promoting in a rapidly overcrowding field, much before any actual advance in knowledge would justify it. The stage to follow can be easily enough predicted within the rationale of such academic dynamics: disenchantment, signs of annoyance with the over-used and trivialized term, discoveries of its 'actual non-existence', a rush to new gimmicks and often enough an attempt to cash in academically on the demystifying of old pets (a couple of books can be always squeezed out of that). We are now rapidly approaching this stage within the peasants' fashion cycle.

It goes without saying that to see pursuers of fashions go to graze elsewhere should delight those seriously engaged in study. That may be, also, the right moment to retire the trivialized concept altogether. Words like 'peasant' are not holy scripture, and the less complex the terminology the better. How about 'the agricultural detachment of petty bourgeoisie' instead, to have it all fresh, neat and clear?

7 Retiring Concepts: Some Rules of Thumb

To answer the last question, let us proceed from some rules of thumb for deconceptualization before turning for the last time to the issue of defining peasants. To begin once more with negations, the following can be said in a general way:

1 No concept should be retired simply on the grounds of its representing only some aspects of reality. Every concept is systematically selective and therefore carries necessary blinds and limitations. To pitch the demands on our concepts too high is to dualize research into, on the one hand, totally empirical facts and, on the other hand, totally theoretical and thereby absolute constructs. Both are of little use.

2 No concept should be retired on purely deductive and/or logical grounds without a thorough investigation of the insights into reality which may be lost through such a deconceptualization and/or the

adequacy of alternative ways to handle those insights.

3 No concept should be retired to suit a simple division of concepts into 'ours' and 'theirs', with 'ours' placed in an aseptic world free from any alien admixtures. Marxist concerns and findings must be recognizable both in fact and problematic to genuine non-Marxist analysts and vice versa, deep differences assumed and excepted. Deductive purism destroys links with reality, which is necessarily richer than any of its conceptualizations. One must guard in particular against the swings of fashion, and those trying too hard to be Marxist (or something else) in accordance with the last compilation of it. As with sex, the less hard the trying, the better the performance.

Deconceptualization is justified for concepts which are misleading or devoid of illumination because of misrepresentation of social reality and/or irrelevance and/or faulty logical structure. All those may exist from the outset, or else come as the result of changes in reality or new theoretical grasp. How do peasants fare in all those senses?

To recollect first the position stated, the term peasantry does not imply peasants' total similitude all around the world and/or their existence out of the context of the not-only-peasant society or their extra-historicity. Those are scarecrows, which juveniles take delight in knocking down. Peasants necessarily differ from one society to another and within any one society too; the question is that of their generic and specific characteristics. Peasants necessarily reflect, relate to and interact with non-peasants; the question is of the part-autonomy of their social being. Peasantry is a process and necessarily a part of a broader social history; the question is of the extent of specificity of the patterns of its development, the significant epochs and strategic breaks where peasants are concerned. The concept peasant is selective; the question is what do we learn by using it. Peasants are mystification; the problem is when, how and when not.

A major example can pinpoint the issue and give substance to an answer. The defeat of US armed intervention in Vietnam is still fresh in the mind and doubtlessly a social event of most central political significance in contemporary history. It also constitutes the type of 'data' against which both understanding and attempts to shape social reality have been and will be tested all around the globe. Can one satisfactorily explain the defeat of the largest/richest/techonologically most advanced military-industrial complex without singling out the specifically peasant social structure of 90 per cent of the Vietnamese? A complexity of factors operates in such struggles, but that is not at issue. Can one understand what happened considering *only* the international economic system, the capitalist mode of production, Johnson's neurosis and/or the inter-US contradictions and protest? Or was it the jungle terrain, brainwashing, military tactics and/or the qualities of the AK47 carbine? Or is it simply the superiority of socialist *Weltanschauung* and the personal devotion of the party cadres? All those played their role, but it is probably enough to compare Vietnam to other areas where a challenge to imperialist military might was attempted, to admit the crucial analytical importance of the singling out of peasant specificity in this case.[42] Further examples of heuristic gain were quoted or footnoted under the headings 'Peasants as a generalization.' It is by the day-to-day work of actual research or political action that the uses of a concept must be judged. And it is in that light that the generalization about peasant specificity is neither devoid of illumination nor irrelevant to the major questions of the world we live in, nor incoherent in the structure of its logic. It is without doubt insufficient on its own, but so is, of course, any other concept, differences in scope excepted – which should explain why the last of the basic charges against peasantry as a valid concept, that of its mystifying quality, should be answered along the following lines.

'Peasant' is not an empty word reflecting the prejudices of the *populus*, the linguistic frivolities of the intellectuals, or else the plots of ideological henchmen, even though each of those may be true at times. If retired, this concept cannot yet be easily substituted by something else of similar ilk. It carries together with concepts like 'capitalism', 'proletariat' and, of course, 'mode of production' potentials for reification, i.e. can be misleading and can be used to mislead, especially when used naively. That is why it was right to say that 'the price of using models is eternal vigilance.'[43] It is also true that without such theoretical constructs no advance in social sciences would be possible at all.

Peasants have been a mystification mainly to those who are prone to become mystified. Typically, it was the brilliant theorist and the indifferent politician Plekhanov between whose fingers Russian peasants conceptually disappeared, only to reappear within Lenin's political grasp and deed since the 1905 revolution, but especially in the civil war and after. (Some time later Li-Li San and Mao seemed to re-enact this duality.) It is the grand deductionists with little contact to reality who fell most easily into the reification trap and, at the other end, those to whom only the empirical counts. The conceptualization of peasant specificity rests on the admission of the complexity and degrees of ambivalence of social reality, and expresses an attempt to grapple with it on a theoretical level. It is not an answer but a working hypothesis and a tool which help to elicit answers.

42 For a major example of such analysis, see E. Hobsbawm, 'Vietnam and the Dynamics of Guerilla War', *New Left Review* (1965) no. 17.
43 R.B. Braithwaite, *Scientific Explanation* (Cambridge, 1953), p. 93.

Fundamental issues of social reality can be understood at a fair level of epistemological sophistication or not at all. At the same time, even the strictest rigour of deduction cannot on its own resolve basic issues, any more than the correct use of syllogism can prove to us the existence of the world around us. It is in the final resort not 'a question of dialectical reconciliation of concepts' but 'the understanding of the relations'[44] which concepts are to serve. Within the socialist tradition one must add the commitment to define dimensions of oppression of men by men and the ways to struggle against them. Mystification and ideological usages accepted, the concept of peasantry has performed all these services often enough. This capacity is not yet spent.

44 K. Marx, *Grundrisse* (Harmondsworth, 1973), p. 90. The translation has been changed to bring it somewhat closer to the original text.

5

Shanin's Law of Mythodynamic Drift

In Place of an Epistemological Discourse (1981, first published 1989)

A science which restricted itself to stating that everything happened according to expectations would hardly be either profitable or amusing.

Mark Bloch

What follows is a comment on Soviet mainstream historians' interpretations of peasantry in pre-Gorbachevian times. Looked at with hindsight, it indicates how far Russian historians have travelled in the few years since it was written. Yet, in my view, the relevance of the paper has not disappeared. Nor will it, for 'them' any more than for 'us'.

While I was working my way through what was to become the two volumes of The Roots of Otherness, *many related ideas and queries buzzed around in my head. I tried to treat them the way one treats mosquitoes, as a bother which should not sidetrack us and must be disregarded. But much of it persisted as such breeds do. A variety of notes on scraps of paper went into files for further work. Some of it became a spin-off book,* Late Marx and the Russian Road *(New York, 1983). Two more pieces were written up. The first was about blinkers scholars wear, about knowledge and about applied ethics. It became 'Matter of Choice', the postface of* Russia 1905–7: Revolution as a Moment of Truth *(New Haven, 1987). The second was about the way some choose to analyse peasants in a revolution. It followed through their logic, which was total, objective, deductive, mathematized and wrong. This made it, one must admit, less serious. But then, in science as in politics and in life a sense of humour is a serious matter.*

1 Introduction: the Art of Lawmongering

The origins of the term 'law' are legal and theological; it assumes normative propriety and the punishment of offenders, or even the damnation of sinners. The conceptual foundations of this usage within the social sciences lie in the early advances of mechanics and chemistry, treated as the supreme model for the exploration and prediction of truth. The concept is consequently loaded with the assumptions of goodness and formal logic as well as of the uniformity of matter, the detachment of the observers, the inevitability of the results and mathematical precision; while anything else and anything less is dismissed as metaphysical, moralistic, subjective or poetic – all known as crimes or at least as major indiscretions in the lexicon of positive sciences.

With well-justified alarm we encounter the contemporary sharp regression, one may even call it extinction, of the genus of immutable social laws. The trend is dangerous to the social scientists because such laws are their major collective property and marketable produce. Fearful of the consequences of such retrogression and aware of our responsibilities, we leap into the breach by offering our own modest contribution in law-procreation. It is in that spirit that a new social law is being offered to illuminate the fundamental process of mythodynamic drift. We mean by this the ways in which scholarly understanding of social reality gradually transforms under the impacts of the ideological needs of the state, the structure of the academic environment, the minds of scholars and the distance from the datum in question. With courage, determination and the characteristic modesty typical of academic environments we have called it Shanin's Law of Mythodynamics.

Our law is rooted in the empirical observation that no scholar worth his salt, unless in peril, would stoop to lies in the sense of simple and systematic defiance of evidence open to inspection. He leaves that to politicians, generals, journalists or policemen, and tends to despise those in his own community who are incapable of doing better than that. On the other hand, only few bring their attachment to truth to the levels of extremism which alienate them from polite society and its resources or may even lead to crucifixion, both figuratively and physically. Such things do happen and benefit the clergy with their trade, the novelists with their words and the psychopathologists with their exploration of the possible therapies. But normal science – that is, the way the majority of its practitioners resolve the complex formula of relating the demands of the state, budgetary dispositions, public moods, scholarly prejudices and the incoming evidence – is an interpretation which is at any stage honest, logical, satisfying, profitable and safe. The law of mythodynamics is the explication of the way this is done.

Ever true to the proprieties of form, order and mathematization, without which science would look like a waiter without black pants, we shall present our law by formulating its axioms, and then specify the way mythodynamic principles are deduced and put to operational use. We shall commence by a statement of goals and round up our discourse by setting up a hypothetical-deductive model to test our conclusions scientifically and to illuminate the future; that is, to do what social laws are substantively for. It goes without saying that should the results prove negative we shall proceed at once to establish a Shanin Law of Non-Mythodynamics (with a mathematical expression of the non-drift appendixed to it).

2 Statement of Goals and Principles

Before turning to the issue at hand, we must establish the goals and the values which will guide our investigation. Its immediate task is to relate the changing views of three generations of the rural historians of Russia, described in chapter 4 of *Russia 1905–7: Revolution as a Moment of Truth* (New Haven, 1986), to a more general explanation of truth-production by scholars. But, firstly, we must reject most vigorously the constant Soviet claims of primacy in this field of scholarly endeavour. Our own tradition of mythodynamics is altogether as good as theirs and contrary claims are an outrage. All we may grant (to show prudent impartiality) is that its more advanced academic planning and state guidance give the Soviet scholarly establishment a slight edge and improve there the visibility of the characteristics in question. Yet, guided by the unceasing efforts of our own leaders, to whom President Reagan and the British prime minister offer magnificent examples, we are now rapidly closing our gaps with the Reds. Indeed, Shanin's Law of Mythodynamics finds a most significant proof in the universal and absolute support it will doubtlessly gain with the authorities on both sides of the great West/East divide – a most satisfactory unanimity which we modestly suggest must eventually contribute to global understanding and world peace.

As for the values which guide us, those are simple. We are scientists and therefore absolutely value-free. As the fountainhead of our epistemology we adopted G. Flaubert's philosophical study *Dictionnaire des idées recues*, to which thoughtful readers should address further queries.

3 Axioms and Derivations

Shanin's Law of Mythodynamics finds its universality and its uncontroversial nature in two fundamental axioms from which all further principles derive. The axioms are intuitively felt to be true and can be analytically abstracted from the self-evident preferences of scholars' minds; that is the actual substance of science. Those axioms and their most immediate derivations are:

1 *Truth is absolute, logical and final.*
   1.1 *Absoluteness* is supreme in the hierarchy of knowledge-attributes and thereby the contradictory, the controversial, the relative and the transitory are an inferior type of truth or no truth at all.
   1.2 The *transitory*, that is the historical, is logically unstable and therefore only partly true, i.e. untrue *vis-à-vis* the absolute. It may carry an element of (still-unfolding) truth if it at least accords with an absolute law of change; that is, with the Theory of Progress.
   1.3 Truth is moral and thereby *ethics* is the service of the absolute truth (as defined) and the invariable future (given to us by the Law of Progress). All those luckily coincide with the institutional goals of the most supreme human achievement; that is, the state. The relation of ethics to the contemporary state makes it patriotic, while its relation to a future state makes it revolutionary. To be patriotic and revolutionary is good.
      Ethics is ever deduced from a higher form of human endeavour, i.e. from scientific or political truth produced by geniuses.

2 *Geniuses produce truth; that is, all of what is absolute, logical and final; that is, the laws of science and the maxims of ethics.*
   2.1 We *identify* a genius by his/her success; that is the fact that he/she is not contradicted, be the reason for this what it may.
   2.2 A genius cannot err, and therefore cannot change his/her views but only develop what is already in them. To ask 'when did a genius err?' is not only bad form but also *ex definitione* illogical.
   2.3 The relation of a genius to the rest of mankind is five-fold. All of the others are co-geniuses, comrades-in-arms (*soratniki* in Russian), followers, traitors, or fools.
      2.3.1 Co-geniuses agree with dead geniuses and interpret them.
      2.3.2 Comrades-in-arms agree but do not interpret. Their task is to offer the faceless background of the genius. Any sign of originality disqualifies them from being what they are.
      2.3.3 Followers follow.
      2.3.4/5 There can be only two possible reasons for failing to follow a genius. The first is being false and wicked and thereby destined for damnation (2.3.4). The second is being a fool (2.3.5).
         Enemies and fools are naturally transitory. Also they cannot be right in any element of their thoughts or deeds,

under any form or at any stage. One must be careful, however, in dividing between fools, to be educated, and enemies of the truth, to be condemned and rendered incapable of doing further harm. For a true truth is not only good but charitable as well.

4 The Dynamics: The Drift of Truization

The axioms of science make the eternal self-evidently supreme to the changeable; the understanding of the latter is thereby less profound. However, before arriving at the top of the scholarly ladder where he/she will devote himself/herself to the eternal, the social scientist must pass through the inferior stage of involvement with the dynamic. The essential dynamics of scholarship is the eradication of any ambiguities; that is, the closing of the gaps between truth as expressed in the laws laid down by the geniuses and any experience which does not fit them. We call this scholarly endeavour *truization*. The term is particularly apt because it relates the words 'truth' and 'truism' to make them one, as they must be within any orderly society and in a respectable social science. Simultaneously, the term *drift* is introduced to accentuate the dynamic nature of the stage-by-stage truization. Progress is built into science, because as time passes and the actual events are forgotten our knowledge becomes spontaneously more absolute, more logical and more final. Yet we cannot leave matters of such significance to spontaneity only, because this would make social sciences obsolete and thereby impoverish their practitioners and mankind.

Truth as defined is good and therefore the process of truization is morally good, and any impediment to it morally bad.

5 Truization Step by Step

The following *Rules of Truization* operationalize the steps by which the evidence and its analysis are being scientifically improved to fit the truths. These rules concern logic, evidence, time, context, canonicity, and safety. Consequent on Adam Smith's Law of Social Division of Labour, their usage is hierarchically structured in terms of administration and the personnel in charge.

(5.1) Truization of *logic* is a skilful operation and should be restricted to senior scholars only. The clear supremacy of the patron-genius helps to select the necessary interpretations and citations also for the lesser authorities. But how about the allegedly diverse views expressed by a genius? On such an occasion the mental drill is as follows: (1) such allegations are to be rejected as delusions; (2) one of the quotations is treated as true while the others as transitional, and thereby unrepresentative and best forgotten; (3) of the interpretations available, the most abstract, the most logical, and the least disturbed by empirical evidence stands naturally higher in its truth-value.

The choice of the truest truth is made accordingly.

For our case study the move by Soviet interpreters from Lenin's writings of 1905–7 concerning Russia of 1905–7, to his views of 1893–9 concerning the same, exemplifies this procedure. Generally, the Kautskian Marxism adhered to by the very young Lenin fits orderly logic better, for it is less disturbed by the social facts and political experience, and hence more true.

(5.2) The processing of *evidence* is made through the system of *cenlection* (a term relating 'censorship' and 'selection'). This is the simplest of truizations and can be executed by junior scholars, aspiring graduates and such-like sub-academics. One simply forgets evidence which does not fit ones superiors' preferences. This technique can be improved by *sneerization*. Sneerization, a more sophisticated form of cenlection, consists of the dramatizing of the text by introducing into it some selected elements of data and views contrary to those known to be true, and then sneering at them by the use of words like 'allegedly', 'typically', and 'as one would expect', while any substantial argument is avoided.

For our case study, most of the regional discussions which appeared as part of the '70 Years Since . . . 1905' celebrations followed cenlact sneerization, which greatly advanced (that is, standardized) their truth-content. For example, the one point of agreement of all the Russian Marxists in SDP – that separate organizations of the rural proletariat were to be set up in 1905–7 and again in 1917 as their most important party task – is quoted, the criticism of it is sneered at, and then comes silence (which, as the maxim has it, 'is better than gold') as to what happened. (Nothing did.)

(5.3) The *time dimension* enters truization through the *problematique* of evidence-distance. As the period in question retreats in time, direct witnesses die out and documents and faces are forgotten, the truth-content of scholarship tends to improve, that is to become more absolute, logical and final. With some skill (say in the middle ranks of scholars or above), one can promote it through the utilization as

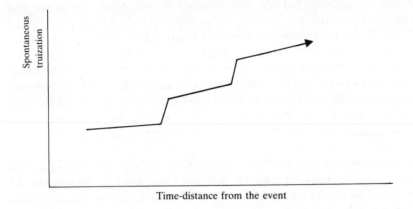

Figure 5.1 Time, evidence and truth

stepping stones of the cenlections of past generations. Truth already truized by them is treated as prime and uncontroversial evidence on which to build new supra-truization, remembering Newton's maxim that even if we are dwarfish we can cringe on the shoulders of giants. To advance the scientific nature of our conclusion, we shall present this conclusion diagramatically (see figure 5.1).

To exemplify, in our case the KGB Beria's presentation of what really happened in rural Georgia in 1903–7 and 1917–25 is stripped of the name of the author and repeated as prime evidence in a study by the 1970s Rector of Moscow University, who then proceeds to deepen this analysis.

(5.4/5) Contextualization and canonization are two sides of a single methodological coin. They differ mostly in the degree of eternality, that is of truth, and thereby by the related ranks of the academic staff which may be authorized to handle those methodologies.

(5.4) To avoid elitism, true science must stay in constant touch with the needs and the will of the people. These (needs and will) are best expressed in the government's circulars and newspapers. *Contextualization* is the ongoing process by which the conclusions of the social scientists, especially the narratives of the History of Motherland, are kept in constant touch with the needs of the people, as defined by those who govern them. Lists of ideas, people, organizations, countries, continents and planets which are eternally and absolutely hostile to the people are the major tools of contextualization. Their daily adjustment is time-consuming, but can also be handled, fortunately, by junior staff (under supervision).

The 1930s proclamation of the All-Russian Peasant Union of 1905–6 as a 'kulak-assembly', and the simultaneous discovery of the long-term sabotage of Russian agriculture by all its major analysts, e.g. Chayanov, offer an example of effective contextualization. The excellent and final solution of all problems of the agricultural needs of the USSR past, present and future (and many other problems besides) during the Collectivization of the 1930s offers the context of the case.

(5.5) *Canonization* of texts is the way to secure orthodoxy, and to advance continuity. It thereby promotes the truth by bestowing the grace of eternality on some assumptions. This increases understanding and puts the mind at ease. (The marginal problem of some of the canonizers snoring while undertaking such mental treatment can be rectified by the medical staff in any elite hospital.) Established long since in the maxims of the ancients is the fact that 'Science which is not boring is suspect.'

It is the task of scholarship to extend canonization and to enrich thereby the truth-in-reality, as well as the reality-in-truth. The first is the satisfying feeling that truth-anticipation by the geniuses extended to all of what has already happened, leaving nothing to chance. The second is the exciting fact that the primary canon of knowledge – the Supreme Texts – carries in itself all that needs to be known. One can consequently advance knowledge by the hermeneutics of citations dealing with essences, and leave to lesser minds the concern with the contradictory, the relative, the factual, and the transitional; that is, with appearances only.

In our case, the exploration of Lenin's 1903–6 attitude to the peasantization of Russia's land can be used as an example. The dilemmas are: (1) Lenin himself claimed change in his own views; but that is clearly wrong, for geniuses do not err. (2) Lenin adopted (and in 1917 decreed) the division of all lands via an equalizing redistribution by the peasant communes, while the sale of land and permanent employment of non-family labour were prohibited. This was what the Russian peasants did when able to follow their collective will and, precisely, the Russian SRs' idea of 'land socialization', and therefore evidently utopian. (3) Lenin spoke in 1905 of land nationalization and 'the American road' of small-farming in Russian agriculture as possible elements of the bourgeois revolution. This proved annoyingly irrelevant in 1917 and after, for it was not a bourgeois revolution. Yet land was seized, divided by peasant communes and declared societal property.

The resolution of these dilemmas is simple, once you know how to proceed. What Lenin (and the Russian peasantry) demanded is defined as 'land nationalization' – the SRs got the word wrong when talking of 'socialization'. Some problems are still to be ironed out, like the one concerning the 'American road' of Russian peasants in 1921–8 towards collectivization; that is, socialism. This will be resolved: do not fret.

(5.5) The rules of *safety* aim to defend research personnel from the harm they may come to through careless use of the poisons and explosives related to their trade. Our point of departure must be the observation that unexpected knowledge is dangerous to those who hold it, and that the impudence of claiming it directly may make things considerably worse. The computer analysis of the relevant data (e.g. the files of Amnesty International) makes these conclusions positive. A second point is that social scientists, being of the highest value to themselves, their families, and to scholarship as such, should not come to harm. Third and last, we must remember that considerable societal resources have been invested in scholars' training and their wastage would be socially wrong.

(The current price value of scholars can be established with scientific exactitude by the formula:

$$Vs = \Delta y \frac{v}{z} \left(\text{ß}x \frac{w}{z} \right)$$

where:

Vs = value of a social scientist
y = monies spent on his/her tuition (in dollars)
v = weight of studies produced (in kg)
z = coffee input (in cups)
ß = academic rank (in kiloergs)
x = number of committees sat on
w = number of conferences slept at.)

Pure logical deduction leads us to conclude that to optimize individual and social gain, we must minimize social scientists' exposure to evidence and/or their involvement in doubtful speculations. Looked at from the point of view of experience, the same conclusion must be drawn. This surprising and exciting coincidence of theory and *empeiria*, of truth and of the interest of the truth-producers, makes those conclusions outstandingly valuable. To sum it up in a maxim: 'Tautology is the safest expression of scientific truth.'

Conceptualizing Peasants

6 In Conclusion: the Hypothetical-Deductive Test

To finalize our discourse, we should, as promised, set up a hypothesis predicting future truization to test our Law. To go to the core of the matter, in our field of exemplification the major issue lies with the obvious fact that there can be no peasants in the societies involved in socialist revolution, while, as uncontroversially, Soviet Russia underwent a socialist revolution. (To sustain our objection to the idea of total Soviet predominance in the field of mythodynamics we can set up here some similarly self-evident assumptions in the West, e.g. one concerning the advance of USA parliamentary democracy to the point where nobody in his/her right mind runs for the presidency without $250 millions or so.) In our case, to conclude the process of truization, we must proceed to lay the ghost of the utopian idea of the existence of a peasantry in Russia in 1917. This is not easy for a population 82 per cent of which was bona fide peasants, but then, scholarship is not for those who look for easy tasks.

Our hypothesis is that within a couple of decades of further mythodynamic drift the following will be proven:

1 The Russian peasantry disappeared completely at the end of the Russian feudal epoch; that is, on the morning of 11 March 1763.
2 Capitalism became established in Russia in the second week of February of 1827 (with a variability factor of 152 years, 3 weeks, 2 days and 11 minutes).
3 In 1917 the Russian rural and urban proletariat was 99.9 per cent of the population. As to the rest, 12.4 per cent were the bourgeoisie, 0.000001 per cent the social scientists, and 0.0000001 per cent the tsar. The class composition of the rest is yet unknown but actively studied.
4 These figures were maliciously withheld from us for a time, but with the help of scientific vigilantes, the culprits are being apprehended.

6

Expolary Economies: A Political Economy of Margins

An Agenda (1988)

Peasants do not exist singly nor is their particularity absolute. Many characteristics of peasants overlap with those of other social groups and categories. This means also that the insights gained during the century of systematic peasant studies as well as during their 1960s–80s upswing can be utilized in the study of other aspects of contemporary social being. Of such cross-analyses or cross-intuitions in which peasant studies can shed light the most important seems to me the issue of 'informal'-cum-'marginal' economies, which for reasons to be explained I shall prefer to call expolary *economies. The significance of the informal, under-monetized, family-rooted, personalized and community-bound charac-teristics of such economies makes such social forms particularly recogniz-able to students of peasant economies and societies. Growing relevance and recognition of these forms of social living make them increasingly important for a realistic appreciation of the world we live in. The end part of the paper devoted to Chayanov (item 19) points to the paradox of his work's growing significance in an environment where peasants disappear. What follows represents the next step along this line of thought.*

The text was prepared as a discussion document for a conference concerning expolary economies which took place in Toronto in 1988. It was first published in Journal of Historical Sociology *1 (1988) no. 1.*[1]

1 The Image of Margins: the Poles and the Pendulum

All images of political economy carry an assumption of margins. As against systemic models of full consistency stands social reality which is

1 The initial text was prepared in Ann Arbor with the help of Akos Rona-Tas, to whom it owes some of its elements, e.g. the risk and information aspect of expoliar economies etc. Thanks are due to Margaret Carey for help with the semantics of the term introduced.

invariably less pure. Images and explanatory logic tend to dismiss such impurities from the picture as irrelevant, accidental or unsubstantiated. When the massive nature of impurities and the more subtle minds begin to militate against such simplification, the impurities are admitted but then, usually, categorized out of the centre of the analytical field through some form of conceptualization which defines them as 'marginal'. Two fundamental scholarly traditions of the nineteenth-century social sciences, that of political economy and that of evolutionist historiography, meet at this point. 'At margins' lay forms of political economy which are structured differently from the prevailing system, its general dynamics and its assumed logic (to a Marxist, the dominant mode of production). Once Evolutionism is injected (or taken for granted), the status of the margins becomes that of the not-yet-dissolved 'past in present' and/or a cul-de-sac with no autonomous dynamic and no long-term future. Their survival is due to social inertia and/or to the transitional service they may offer to the core/mainstream of power and economy, dynamics and forms. The margins' subsumption to core must result in their eventual demise.

The experiential root of this overarching epistemology of contemporary societies and economies seems clear enough. It lies in a romanticized history of industrialization. This fundamental social experience established the basic plausibility and the taken-for-granted assumptions of endlessly ascending material demands matched by their unrestricted fulfilment through the tapping of unlimited riches, where more and more combines with the technological larger and larger. All these together with scientific endeavour, popular welfare, mass education, and individual liberty have been treated as necessarily related to each other. This endless multiple ascent, entitled Progress, means also rapid unification, universalization and standardization of the world around us. All societies are seen as moving from the heterogeneity of inadequacies and irrationalities to the true, the logical and the uniform, while anything else is pushed to the margin, with its natural oblivion to follow.

This fundamental outlook entered the dualized post-war world of power blocks, systems of political economy, ideological images and propaganda. The category of margins and the dismissive reading of their characteristics was built consequently into the two broad ideologies-cum-historiographies-cum-programmes on offer, linked to the two superpowers. Both views/programmes carry the unmistakable birthmarks of nineteenth-century evolutionism and share its optimistic postulate – that the inevitable, the rational, the good and the programmatic are the same. Both of the paradigms reinforced each other by adopting a logical 'either/or' stand expressed as the socialist 'state plan' as against the liberal-cum-capitalist 'free market', the 'East' v. the 'West'. On the one hand was the planned economy, executed by the rational state in a scenario by which it was bound to devour and transform after its own image any societal diversities and inconsistencies in its own society. Strengthened accordingly, it was also to out-compete its sole alternative, i.e. the 'free market' economy of capitalism, and to emerge triumphantly as the new, uniform and total world of riches and of humans made free. On the other side, the same was being claimed for the 'free market' economy making short shrift of anything else within its direct reach, and then 'rolling back' the statist monsters outside its own political frontiers (followed by another inevitable crescendo of the future better world of a universal Texas).

The assumption of either/or, i.e. either state plan or free market, with nothing else on offer, meant also that the inevitable logical conclusion from the harsh self-criticism and partial reversal of the rules of the game in the state socialist societies of the 1980s (be it China's de-collectivization or Gorbachev's reforms) is being treated as the self-evident proof of the superiority of the capitalist economy and/or of a move toward it. The state socialisms are becoming (sensibly) 'like us'. Alternatively we have a scale between the two exclusive possibilities. One cures state-planned economies by injecting more of a capitalist market or, vice versa, cures capitalisms by some increase in state intervention. And the pendulum is now swinging against the state planners equated with socialism.

The unrealistic nature of the logical scheme which sustains all these views, i.e. the assumption of the exclusivity of two socio-economic forms – the capitalist free market and the socialist state plan – is not even usually considered. Nor is the highly relevant experience of the 1970s/80s *parallel* structural crisis of both of the supersystems of political economy taken into account. Inability to reassume the 1950s/60s rates of growth, to eradicate poverty, unemployment or underemployment, to overcome global diversities and local slums, to make one's system 'work' – i.e. to fulfil its earlier declared promise – has been as true of the USA as of the USSR. To include the lesser powers and, especially, the so-called 'developing societies' would accentuate the more this message of contemporary experience. Ours has been a period of massive reductions downwards of the ambitious long-term plans and of the assumptions of rapidly and constantly improving social welfare. It is also manifest that 'margins' are not being reduced; indeed, the extent of actual economic action taking place outside the dominant systems and logics of the political economy has been growing.

By now evidence which contradicts the available analytical devices and axioms has matured to the point where re-analysis of the whole paradigm of explanation seems necessary. A way to consider it anew is

to bring into focus and to study actual evidence concerning 'margins' of
the existing political economies and to review our representations of
them. Let us name this social syndrome and order the related pieces of
evidence which do not fit the poles-and-pendulum view of contemporary
societies and economies, before trying to make better sense of them.
For reasons to be spelt out presently we shall call the syndrome *expolary
economics*.

2 An Inventory of Analytical Dissonances

(1) There is less and less reason to assume the Evolutionist model which
was accepted by the mainstream of the social sciences and presented
anew in the 1950s/60s by the Modernization Theories of the day.
Neither can endless economic ascent and global unlimited resources be
simply postulated, nor the growth of rationality and of human liberty (or
even the tides of struggle for them) be seen as in necessary ascent.
Unilinear schemes of history linked to taken-for-granted optimism are
unrealistic.

Changes have occurred and the global linkages of units and types of
economy have grown, but social and economic forms have not moved
from the heterogeneous to the uniform, but rather from one internally
contradictory complexity to another. Much of it was totally unexpected.

(2) The conflict between the two basic types of political economy,
backed by the prevailing political superpowers, has been anything but a
1:0 game. The failure of one of the forms did not necessarily imply the
success or the advance of the other. The eulogists of free markets and of
planned economies who engaged in criticism of the mote in the others'
eye were both right in their criticism; neither system 'worked' by its own
standards. Also, none of the initial master-theories offers a satisfactory
working plan to set this right on its own terms, i.e. to secure limitless
and rapid 'economic growth' resolving all social ills. Furthermore, both
of the poles together or a mixture of their characteristics do not exhaust
social reality and its potentials. The parallel crisis of both super-
projects, and the growing disbelief in its transitional nature, call for
thorough consideration of evidence on alternative economic forms.

(3) In this context one must also refuse the status of self-evident truth to
what I shall call the Midas Finger Principle. Whatever this king of
legend touched turned to gold, and likewise, to some analysts, the
prevalent political economy necessarily transforms after its own image
any economic forms within its reach and impact. In fact, not only have

the expolary economics at systemic 'margins' failed to decline, but they have often shown high vitality and the capacity to 'deliver the goods' in so far as human welfare and the creativity of social and productive forms of survival are concerned. Nor is there reason to believe that their functioning is only a reflection of the 'needs' or the dictat of a dominant 'core' economy. Looked at outwardly, the core economies failed to colonize fully their 'margins'. Looked at from the opposite aspect, the expolary forms show autonomy, logic, dynamics and the capacity to manipulate their own environment (while, of course, responding at the same time to the broader social context). They also show the capacity for social reproduction. The actual structures and forms which hide under such anti-concepts as the 'second economy', 'petty bourgeoisie' or 'informal economy' must be cognized and considered on their own terms.

(4) There is growing evidence that societal systems of political economy which are more complex and contradictory – one may also say logically paradoxical in their composition (i.e. less advanced by the usually adopted historiographic standards of Progress and less pure when logical models are concerned) – prove more effective in so far as the wellbeing of the population, the functioning of the national economies and their 'growth' are concerned; that is, by the standards of excellence formally assumed by economic planners of today.

Expolary economies often seem to act as the necessary admixture, lubricant or catalyst for the effective functioning of the existing socio-economic systems. A society's index of non-incorporation, i.e. extent of non-purity, of mixing 'state plan' or 'free market' with economies which cannot be so defined, corresponds well enough with its place in the success league of comparable countries: the economy of Hungary is 'healthier' than that of the USSR, Japan is more 'dynamic' than the USA, Italy has seen in the last two decades faster economic and welfare advance than the UK. It goes without saying that all this is relative; in all of the examples chosen most of the long-term predictions by social scientists were, in the 1980s, full of gloom.

(5) The demystification of parallel economic forms must be taken through a number of stages to reach the point at which the issue of our concern can be made fully apparent. First and easiest to accept, there is deliberate falsity built into both the 'free market' and the 'planned economy' assumptions – reality is not like that, models caricature it through overstatement. No market economy was ever free of state intervention nor was there ever a planned economy totally structured by a plan (which would apply also, naturally, to any theoretical model of the expolary economies).

More important and controversial, we must take on board that actual economies are not a set of diverse mixtures of two polar principles, i.e. not something in between (and therefore too much planning cannot be cured by a judicious injection of the market and vice versa). The scale itself is a falsity, for it obscures economic forms which do not fit its 'either/or' analytical and ideological message. Nor can one save this analytical scale by admitting to 'other things', but then promptly labelling them 'the survivors of the past' (why do they survive?) or assuming them to be simple reflections of the 'needs' of the big boys on the scene, and thereby in no need of farther explanation. To repeat, the social economy of the off-scene, its capacity to survive, its internal logic and its overall impact must be brought into the field of vision.

The expression *expolary* economies stresses two characteristics of the phenomenon in question. First is its being external to *polis* when, as in ancient Greece, the *polis* stands for the state as well as for the origins of the market society (particularly true of Athens).[2] Second, it stands *outside* the two *poles* of the enshrined analytical scale of either 'plan' or 'market', indeed defies the scale itself. This still misses some important characteristics, e.g. the deeper social embedment of such economies, but no term would have it all in a single word. I assume also the reader's understanding that no total isolation of forms is envisaged, but a system combining diversities. One should not rush into production of neologisms, but a term which helps to circumscribe a social syndrome and a field of study can serve the good purpose of advancing clarification.

A final comment: the blossoming of the expolary economies cannot be deproblematized as just the result of the contemporary economic crisis. Crises of the dominant systems did indeed correspond with the expansion of the 'marginal' economies, but the crisis of the 1970s/80s unfolded not as a temporary down-turn but as the condition of contemporary human existence. It is realistic to assume that the end-of-the-millennium socio-economic history will be one of permanent crises. The economic forms of our time should be considered in this given framework.

3 Expolary Economies: the Categories of the Species

My initial definitions of 'margins'-cum-expolary-economies have been relational and negative in delimiting mostly what these are not. We face, consequently, a number of overlapping forms and characteristics. Their

2 K. Polanyi, C.M. Arensberg and H.W. Pearson, *Trade and Market in the Early Empires* (Glencoe, Minn., 1957).

specification must form a step of the analysis. Actual economic forms which come under the category of expolarity can be listed as follows:

(1) The *family production unit*, when the absence (or limited use) of wage labour, family-centred consumption, the mutual, non-contractual, long-term support and loyalty anticipation, as well as the inheritance patterns, result in a different operational logic from that of the two supra-systems discussed (and, the more so, of the theoretical models of 'free market' or of 'state plan').

(2) The *specialized (monopolizing) small unit*, the separate 'free-lance' existence of which *vis-à-vis* the large-scale bureaucratic-industrial complexes is based on its monopoly of some skills, higher flexibility of response, personalized contact or privileged access to some capacities or resources. Alternatively, the vitality of the small unit may be based on the diseconomies of scale operating in a particular field.

(3) The inter-family reproduction of labour, i.e. the form of labour-use which shares with form (1) the family production units, their non-monetary characteristics, the lack of simple transfer into alternatives which are market-related, the gender structuration and 'informality'. On the other hand, its aims are consumption- and welfare-directed and socially reproductive of family rather than productive of marketable goods. It may be therefore treated, historically, as a family production unit stripped by 'modernization' of its major productive functions and refocused to handle the expanding task of children's socialization and new needs, rooted in the bureaucratization of and emotional upheaval in a rapidly 'atomizing' and anomic society which increasingly depends on educational certification.

Chauffeuring middle-class children between the ballet and the music schools of a large city becomes a mother's role, as time-consuming and as socially necessary as a part-time job, while there have been no economically feasible, state- or capitalism-produced alternatives which are as effective.

(4) The *'second' economy*, as defined by the Hungarian social scientists, i.e. the part-time employment or contractual work outside the mainstream of waged labour (in Hungary, outside the state-owned or cooperative enterprises and organization). Looked at from the vantage point of those engaged in it, the second economy operates as supernumerary source of income through the use of one's 'free time'. The social scientists of Hungary accentuated in their designation the particularities of the operational rules of the game and of the social

organization of this phenomenon when compared to the 'first' (i.e. large-scale and official) economy, to its functioning, regulation and structure.

(5) The *black economy* (described by the Hungarians as 'third'); that is, the manufacturing and the services outside of those legally permissible – operations which if uncovered would lead to criminal charges. While *vis-à-vis* the 'planned economy' such activity usually represents the illicit use of scarce resources monopolized by the state (possibly blending into the 'second economy'), the open market economies find their own extensive terrain of 'shoddy deals', in the tax-evasion industry as much as smuggling, pimping and organized crime.

This review has accentuated the expolary economies' diversity as much as their relational nature, i.e. the existence of a powerful system and of a logic of 'core' or 'mainstream' *with which expolary forms link, by which they are influenced, but from which they structurally differ.* Nobody would argue that, for instance, the role of a shoe-maker or of the farmer of contemporary Punjab is identical with that of the shoe-makers or farmers of pre-colonial India (or with those occupations in the Hungary or Italy of today). They differ because they have to fit into different environments; to all of them, coexistence with the dominant social system or mode of production is a matter of necessity. But the concept carries also the assumption of substantive particularities, as against the operational logic of the rules of the game and of the bureaucratic structures at the core of the contemporary 'free market' as well as 'state planned' economies. The 'margins' of the contemporary political economy are not purely epiphenomenal, lacking their own sources of causality. The consequent image of nationwide political economies is complex and shot through with contradictions, but the more realistic and dynamic for it.

The next major step must be to define the common characteristics, if any, of the 'margins' which could justify their analytical generalization expressed in the term the 'expolary economies'. Let us begin with generalization, i.e. the characteristics in which the above mentioned actual forms tend to overlap. What stands out is the informal and personalized (rather than bureaucratic, legalistic and stereotyped) format of arrangements which guide production, services, exchange, financing and renumeration. There are also the particular and usually extra-legal (not thereby necessarily illegal!) methods of securing and enforcing agreements, tasks and payments. The same is true insofar as employer/employee relations are concerned. Painted with a thick brush, all this is expressed in the tendency of expolary types of economic action to be more deeply 'embedded' or 'dissolved' within the broader patterns of human interaction, i.e. to be seldom purely profit-oriented or orders-execution directed (and narrowly 'rational' in this sense). They are thereby more explicitly 'social', i.e. defined by norms of primary communities and individualized choices by families or the individual participants.[3]

One should add here, secondly, the specific types of budgetary arrangement which go with the more socialized economy, inclusive of the extent of 'family purse' arrangements, the lesser significance given to the money-and-wages nexus *vis-à-vis* barter, inter-family and intra-family informal cooperation, self-consumption and such considerations as patronage and clientalism, kinship loyalties and factional hostilities. There is no means of full quantification and accounting in this field. As significant is that while the participants try to optimize the result of their effort they see this in terms of survival, welfare, social reproduction and of 'being', rather than of limitless capital accumulation aiming to overturn (through 'shooting up' in social power and rank) their existing social and economic status. These relationships must not be romanticized, for personalized interdependence can be at times highly exploitative. The point is that, be this as it may, it will always differ in form and results from bureaucratic procedure or depersonalized, limitless competition.

Third, the way such economies operate shows often particularly high levels of flexibility and adjustability in the use of labour, especially when effective use of unsupervised labour is concerned. This as well as the other reasons already discussed makes many of the major socioeconomic functions impossible to carry out as effectively through the use of state-directed or market-defined institutions and monetary networks.

The tendency of the characteristics discussed to combine (and the structural reasons for this) explains why we should speak here of a type rather than of an eclectic 'shopping list' of behavioural items or an epiphenomenon of something else. Moreover, the particularities of the expolary economies are represented not only in the way they function but also in the patterns of their social reproduction and structural transformation – they are particular not only in the way they operate and survive but also in the ways they transform. We are talking of a particular and consistent and self-reproducing set of social institutions and of related operational logics (anti-logics, i.e. areas of irrationality, if looked at from the point of view of the dominant system).

---

3 See especially K. Polanyi, *The Great Transformation*, (Boston, 1957).

4 Agenda for the Study of Modes of Non-Incorporation as Parallel Forms of Social Economy

The term 'expolary' was used to circumscribe a territory which tends to escape systematic viewing but is central for the realistic study of the economic and social forms of our time. One can speak of it alternatively as the modes of non-incorporation into the dominant political economy, always remembering the relative and partial nature of such 'non-incorporations'. Social and functional characteristics which are particular, which combine and which consistently differ from the assumed logic of 'the poles' of state economy and market economy *sensu strictu*, define it positively. To test its significance and to specify its characteristics is to establish analytically and empirically the alternative ways expolary economies operate *vis-à-vis* the dominant political economies of state plan or free market, and especially the industrial/bureaucratic complexes at their centre. The basic operational dimensions for such farther analysis and study – i.e. its agenda are, in this view:

1 labour-use and the family budget strategies
2 information and uncertainty
3 operational goals (especially consumption *vis-à-vis* expansion)
4 technology, resources and skills (and economic segmentation)
5 drudgery and boredom *vis-à-vis* the existential and social goals.

The significance of the thesis stands or falls on farther work along these lines.

Part II

Analysing Peasants: The General and the Particular

7

The Nature and Logic of the Peasant Economy (1972/3)

In its initial form this text was written as a 'source paper', 'The Social Structure of Peasant Economy', for the World Congress of Rural Sociology which met in the summer of 1972 in Baton Rouge. The primary task of the paper defined its form, i.e. the accentuation of taxonomy and of generalized description, an extensive list of references, etc. It was the first international congress of 'Western' rural sociologists which set out, somewhat ambivalently, to discuss peasant economies as a generic phenomenon. The presence of participants from some 'developing societies' and from Eastern Europe provided for an interested and well-informed audience of diverse experience. This, as well as the general atmosphere of ideological upheaval reflecting the after-effects of the exceptional year 1968, and the new theoretical input and impact of Chayanov's Theory of Peasant Economy *and Marx's* Grundrisse, *made for a remarkably sophisticated debate. A particular field of peasant studies was rapidly being recognized and established as part of Sociology and also as an interdisciplinary project. The particular social content and context of the agricultural family economy was increasingly being adopted as the most significant particularity of peasantry and the 'cutting edge' of the analysis by which it was being defined.*

The paper was published first under a somewhat different title in the initial issues (1 [1972/3], nos 1 and 2) of Journal of Peasant Studies, *coinitiated and coedited by me in those days, while a shorter version was published in* Sociologia Ruralis XIII (1973), no. 2.

1 Introduction: Peasants and Disciplines

I aim to consider the social structure of the peasant economy. This topic relates three concepts of exceptional complexity and scope. *Economy* depicts patterned human interaction in the production, distribution and consumption of material goods and services as well as a broad variety of affiliated issues of domination, technology, social differentiation and government policies. Reference to *social structure* broadens the range still more, relating economy to social systems and giving it a historical dimension. Focusing on *peasantry* tames somewhat the overwhelming richness of the subject matter, but then, the characteristics and even the definition of this 'oldest and most universal mode of production known in history'[1] are anything but self-evident and provide for additional conceptual queries.

Scholars often stumble over words to become enslaved by some of them. We must therefore spell out first what we mean by peasantry. This cannot be done comprehensibly in an introductory paragraph; the reader must be referred to a paper published elsewhere,[2] and to other contributions to our discussion. To sum it up in a telegraphic style, I here delimit peasantry as a social entity with four essential and inter-linked facets: the family-farm as the basic multi-functional unit of social organization; land husbandry, usually combined with animal rearing, as the main means of livelihood; a specific traditional culture closely inter-linked with the way of life of small rural communities; and multi-directional social subjugation to powerful outsiders. Such a 'general type' depicts also a number of analytically marginal groups which share with the 'hard core' of the peasantry most but not all of its major characteristics (e.g. the Latin American peons who share all but the first of the characteristics mentioned, the rural craftsmen who fall short only of the second, etc.). This typology can then be used also as a yardstick to define peasantry as a process, treating it as a historical entity within the broader framework of societies, yet with a structure, consistency and momentum of its own: emerging, representing at some stage the pre-vailing mode of social organization, disintegrating, re-emerging at times.[3]

There are at least four disciplines which deal directly with peasant economy: Economics, Sociology, History and Anthropology. The main-stream of contemporary Economics has centred on economizing, i.e. on the optimal resolution of the problems of limitless scarcity of goods, services and resources in terms of utility and/or profit. The majority of its theorists have focused on the universal *modus operandi* of economy,

---

1 B. Galeski, *Basic Concepts of Rural Sociology* (Manchester, 1972), p. 23.

2 T. Shanin (ed.), 'Peasantry: Delineation of a Concept and a Field of Study', *European Journal of Sociology*, XII (1971) see item 3 above.

3 See D. Thorner, 'Peasant Economy as a Category in Economic History', *Deuxième Conférence Internationale d'Histoire Economique*, vol. 2 (The Hague, 1962); B. Galeski, 'Social Organization and Rural Social Change', *Sociologia Ruralis*, 8 (1972), nos 3–4.

approached as an autonomous sphere and illuminated by more or less perfect market models.[4] An important minority in this discipline has stressed and brought into systematic analysis institutional and/or culturally relative aspects of economic theory.[5] This basic division into a more narrow and a broader conception of Economics has been reflected also in the analysis of peasant economies. Peasants have been identified by a major section of economists as 'efficient but poor', i.e. within the limits of meagre resources, as acting and economizing in the universal way explained by neoclassical economics.[6] On the other hand conceptualizations specific to peasant economy have been tried, be it a fully fledged theory of peasant economics,[7] or but an extension of conventional economics or econometrics to handle some specifically peasant issues like fluctuations in yield, high innovation risk, etc.[8]

The disciplinary tradition of contemporary Social Anthropology has been very much the opposite of that of economics. It has grown out of participant observation and multi-facet description of small tribes and communities. Through this Social Anthropology has accumulated extensive data relevant to economics and a growing awareness of the fact that processes of production and distribution in the 'uncivilized lands' are not necessarily governed by economizing concerns only, but have to do with 'non-economic' determinants like kinship, ritual, mythology, and so on.[9] The severe plight of the so-called 'developing societies' and the repeated failure of economic policies there have drawn economists specializing in economizing and anthropologists specializing in exotic lands into cooperation as well as confrontation in policy-makers' advisory bodies and on the campuses. In this process a specific brand of economic anthropology was both established (since Herskovits)[10] and ideologically split. On one side are those of its practitioners who have

---

4 e.g. P.A. Samuelson, *Economics – An Introductory Analysis* (New York, 1948), the textbook on which a generation of Western students was trained.

5 e.g. G. Myrdal, *Economic Theory and Underdeveloped Regions* (London, 1957); J. Robinson, *Economic Philosophy* (New York, 1962).

6 D. Edwards, *An Economic Study of Small Farming in Jamaica* (MacLehose, 1961); T.V. Schultz, *Transforming Traditional Agriculture* (New Haven, 1964).

7 A.V. Chayanov, *The Theory of Peasant Economy*, eds D. Thorner, R.E.F. Smith and B. Kerblay (Homewood, Ill., 1966); N. Makarov, *Krest'yanskoe khozyaistvo i ego evolyutsiya*, vol. 1 (Moscow, 1920); in part H.H. Mann, *The Social Framework of Agriculture* (London, 1968); J.H. Boeke, *Economics and Economic Policies in a Dual Society* (Vancouver, 1953).

8 M. Lipton, 'The Theory of Optimising Peasant', *The Journal of Development Studies*, IV (1968), pp. 327–51; E. Jay, in *Themes in Economic Anthropology*, ed. R. Firth (London, 1970).

9 e.g. the turn-of-the-century study of the 'institutionalized gift' in M. Mauss, *The Gift* (New York, 1954).

10 J.M. Herskovits, *Economic Anthropology* (New York, 1952).

accepted in principle or *in toto* the universal usefulness of neoclassical economic theory.[11] On the other side stand those who have claimed the need of a different theoretical framework for studies outside the scope of industrial society.[12]

The economics/anthropology intersection has offered in recent Anglo-Saxon literature the main field of interdisciplinary debate about the 'primitive and peasant' economies.[13] In this argument some of the veteran disciplines were either forgotten or discarded with a curt nod. To recall, the issue of peasant society and economy was first analysed in terms of contemporary concerns at the borderlands of history and sociology, illuminated by the powerful figures of Karl Marx and Max Weber.[14] Nor is this a mere prehistory, for much of this work is unsurpassed and forms a major element of the conceptual apparatus of contemporary social sciences. Social and economic history, both general and specifically rural in their concerns, have proceeded since then to accumulate a host of relevant data and also to present much material of theoretical content – Bloch, Pirenne, Robinson, and Tawney, to mention but a few.[15] Indeed the early presentation of the argument about particular versus non-specific in peasant economy can be related to the famous *Oikos* debate by Bucher, Meyer, Weber, Rostovtzeff, etc. about the economy of Ancient Greece.[16] Further analysis of change in peasant societies, specific as well as generalizing, can be found within the work of other historians.

Finally, rural sociology developed along two paths separated by different experiences and problems as much as by ideological and linguistic barriers. Since its beginnings in the United States the 'Western' rural sociology has been studying 'advanced' capitalist farming and has concerned itself with the further improvement of it, mainly in terms of efficient use of resources and of profitability. Traditional peasantry was very much out of sight and out of mind; the more so because the anthropologists seemed to be already busy in the 'backward lands'

11 e.g. Firth, *Themes in Economic Anthropology*; and in an extreme form L. Pospisil, *Kapanka Papua Economy* (Yale University Publications in Anthropology, no. 67, 1963).

12 e.g. K. Polanyi, C.A. Arensberg and H.W. Pearson, *Trade and Market in the Early Empires* (New York, 1957); G. Dalton, 'Theoretical Issues in Economic Anthropology', *Current Anthropology*, 10 (1969), no. 1, February.

13 R. Firth and B.S. Yamey (eds), *Capital, Saving and Credit in Peasant Societies* (Chicago, 1964); Firth, *Themes in Economic Anthropology*; etc.

14 Karl Marx, *Precapitalist Economic Formation* (London, 1964); Max Weber, *General Economic History* (New York, 1961).

15 M. Bloch, *French Rural History* (London, 1966); H. Pirenne, *Economic and Social History of Medieval Europe* (London, 1936); G.T. Robinson, *Russia under the Old Regime* (London, 1949); R.H. Tawney, *Land and Labour in China* (London, 1932).

16 For a review see Polanyi et al., *Trade and Market in the Early Empires*, pp. 3–11.

while, as accepted by the majority of sociologists, the sociology/ anthropology similarities 'vastly outweigh the differences' and 'are frequently matters of shading' only.[17] On the other hand, the interrelated issues of 'modernization' along Western lines – industrialization, national renewal, democracy – and of the poverty of the majority of the population brought the peasantry sharply into focus in Eastern Europe. Within the voluminous and illuminating work of East European rural sociologists and agrarian economists the studies relevant to specifically peasant economy run into hundreds.[18] Very little of that tradition has been brought to the English-speaking audience.[19] After the long, forced silence of the thirties and forties it is only now that East European rural studies are beginning to make once again their appearance in the West.[20]

Superficially, the simultaneous concern of a number of scholarly disciplines should have been highly beneficial to the analysis of peasant societies. Different aspects of social structure and economy could be simultaneously tackled: the general and the specific, the national scale and the small production unit, etc.[21] In fact, the academic disciplines provide major foci of systematized but also solidified conceptual thought. Disciplinary boundaries and reifications create major communication problems, producing numerous rediscoveries of things well known outside one's own discipline as well as mutual ignorance and disregard, if not hostility. Furthermore, in all of the disciplines reviewed, contemporary peasant economies are somewhat outside the main focus of the old-established paradigms of questions and thought, be it the economizing in a modern capitalist state, the primitive tribesmen, the irreversible past, or the successful semi-industrial farmer, for economics, anthropology, history and sociology respectively. These disciplinary theoretical frameworks must be somewhat 'strained' or

17 N. Smelser, *The Sociology of Economic Life* (Englewood Cliffs, NJ, 1963), p. 31.

18 Galeski, *Basic Concepts of Rural Sociology*, introduction; Chayanov, *Theory of Peasant Economy*, introduction.

19 W.I. Thomas and F. Znaniecki, *The Polish Peasant in Europe and America* (New York, 1958); P.A. Sorokin, F.F. Zimmerman and C.J. Golpin, *Systematic Source Book in Rural Sociology* (New York, 1965).

20 e.g. Galeski, *Basic Concepts of Rural Sociology*; and, in economics, Chayanov, *Theory of Peasant Economy*.

21 One could, for example, decree a disciplinary division of labour by which economics would deal with the general (universal) and one-dimensional, i.e. economizing; anthropology with the unique and multi-dimensional, i.e. specific social structure; history with the unique in the past; and sociology with the general and multi-dimensional in the present. That would be neat, but not very helpful (a good scholar will ever surpass such disciplinary divisions, as will a rapidly developing discipline itself) and would make sociology into the epitome of all, which makes me suspect it. I was after all trained mainly by sociologists.

adjusted if not reshaped altogether to accommodate what concerns us here. What is missing is a fully formed theoretical system transcending current disciplinary boundaries and centred on peasant economy, its structure, dynamics and change, its broader societal frameworks – all treated as a unity – a 'peasantology' of a type, something like Marx's *Grundrisse* updated and transformed,[22] or else what, despite the differences of schools and prejudices, a major part of the Russian scholars were jointly attempting before collectivization struck in 1929–37.

Nothing like that exists, yet one can detect a powerful undercurrent unifying the four disciplines, not least from the fact that their practitioners divide into conceptual camps which cross-cut disciplinary boundaries and traditionally defined schools of thought where peasant economy is concerned. A fundamental division more relevant than a disciplinary one lies between those who treat peasantry as a qualitatively specific social entity and those to whom it is but a semantic notion covering a 'mixed bag' of social forms, or else an arbitrarily chosen quantitative range on a scale. Actual conceptual differences appear, of course, on a continuum between these two extreme types or take the form of an argument about 'the actual current stage of historical development' (more 'advanced' to those who doubt peasant specificity), but the very existence of an interdisciplinary division seems plain enough. My own paper is firmly placed within the trend of thought which concludes that peasantries have a conceptual particularity, i.e. accepts peasantry as 'a kind of arrangement of humanity with some similarities all over the world'.[23]

I shall begin in section 2 with a general type of peasant economy – a purposely oversimplified picture presented to establish the starting point for further analysis. In sections 3 and 4 I shall specify it, consider the patterns of change and transformation of the peasant economies and look at policies of rural reform.

2 Peasant Economy as a Generalization

Comparative studies have consistently pointed to some startling similarities between peasant societies – startling in view of the diversity in history, political structure, production technology, culture and so on. A particular economy forms a central component of and reason for these generic characteristics. Typically, the low level of institutional specialization is expressed in the fact that essential units of social action – the

22 Marx, *Precapitalist Economic Formation*.
23 R. Redfield, *Peasant Society and Culture* (Chicago, 1956), p. 25.

family-farm, the village and some broader networks of interaction and domination – appear in the peasantry also as basic units of economic life. The peasant family-farm forms the primary and basic unit of both society and economy. The village community operates to a great extent as an autonomous society composed of family-farms and providing both economic and other services which family-farms cannot or do not perform singly (e.g. as much the mostly endogamous marriages as common pastures etc.). The relative and historical character of such autonomy must be remembered. The separateness of the villages is usually broken in at least two ways. Firstly, there are some relations between different villages, e.g. the market places, the kinship networks and so on.[24] Secondly, there are the more or less centralized networks of domination which penetrate the countryside linking political and cultural hegemony with exploitation by the landlords, the state and the town. 'Embedment' of peasant economy within the more general social structure forms a key issue of analysis of contemporary peasant economies. A major historical watershed lies here between the peasantries of pre-industrial societies and the rapidly 'socializing' peasantries of the later stage.

2.1 The Family-Farm

The peasant farm forms a small production/consumption unit which finds its main livelihood in agriculture and is 'manned' chiefly by family labour. The basic needs and rhythms of peasant family life and the agriculture cycles closely mesh and are mutually determining. Family consumption needs and its dues to the holders of political-economic power define to a major degree the strategies of production. Both outsiders and its members treat the peasant family-farm as the basic focus of social identification, loyalty, property and economic cooperation.

The basic character of peasant family consumption was well expressed by the common-sense nineteenth-century definition of the Russian peasant family as 'those who eat from the same bowl'. Furthermore, the consumption rights of its members correspond here to the customary peasant understanding of property rights. Even though land, cattle and equipment may be formally defined as belonging to the man who heads the household, in actual fact he acts rather as a holder and manager of the common family property, with his rights to sell or give it away

24 M.N. Srinivas and A.M. Shah, 'The Myth of Self-Sufficiency of the Indian Village', *The Economic Weekly*, Bombay (1960), 10 September; M. Nash, *Primitive and Peasant Economic Systems* (San Francisco, 1966).

heavily restricted or made altogether absent, by peasant custom and/or communal pressures.[25]

The way in which means of production customarily revert from generation to generation reflects peasant social and economic organization and has often stood in contradiction to the inheritance laws of industrial societies.[26] Contrary to the contractual arrangements by which property reverts to new owners on the death of the original owner and in accordance with his wish, the major part of the means of production tends to pass into the hands of the young peasant family, as a part of its being set up as a new family-farm at the customarily defined time of social maturing of every married son.

The usual division of labour on the farm is closely related to family structure and runs according to gender and age. Functions are rigidly allotted, with powerful pressures operating against the crossing of the dividing lines. Reflecting once more the essential oneness of social and economic structure, the farm's chief supervisor and formal owner is on the whole the father of the family, who holds extensive rights over its members. These are curtailed, however, by traditionally defined duties, a highly 'patriarchal' relationship. Each peasant is expected to proceed along a predefined life-path. For example, a male begins as a boy helping with the cattle. As a young man he becomes increasingly involved in farming. He is to become then an independent head of a family-farm, and finally a semi-retired man fulfilling functions specific to an old man. The rigidity of the gender division of roles makes *both* male and female labour on each farm obligatory and turns marriage into a necessary condition of fully-fledged peasanthood.[27] The farms of single males, widows etc. are notoriously dogged by economic troubles and in many cases are frowned on by the rural community.

The productive *occupation* of a peasant consists of a wide range of interrelated tasks at a relatively low level of specialization. The occupational skills are defined very much by experience transferred directly or else formalized in an oral tradition of numerous proverbs and tales. Training for the occupation of a peasant is carried out mainly within the family: a young peasant boy learns his job by following his father and helping him at work while a peasant girl learns it from her mother. Such socialization procedures both strengthen the family ties and add to the traditional character of peasant agriculture and day-to-day life. Many of

25 e.g. S. Ortiz in Firth, *Themes in Economic Anthropology*, pp. 201, 210–13; H. Mendras, 'Un Schème d'Analyse de la Paysannerie Occidentale' (ms, 1971); T. Shanin, *The Awkward Class* (London, 1972), appendix B.

26 H.R.J. Habakkuk, 'Family Structure and Economic Change in Nineteenth Century Europe', *Journal of Economic History*, XV (1955); Shanin, *The Awkward Class*, appendix B.

27 Thomas and Znaniecki, *The Polish Peasant in Europe and America*.

the typical tasks 'telescoped' into peasant agriculture constitute a nucleus of occupations which became gradually separated, specialized and professionalized with the advance of the social division of labour, e.g. carpentry, production of linen, construction of agricultural implements etc.[28]

Peasant production includes at least three out of the four stages in the classification of production forms suggested by Malita (i.e. gathering, husbanding, manufacturing and creativity).[29] Non-peasant observers of peasant economy tend to underestimate the extent of gathering in it; that is to say, living on what nature provides without being prompted, such as fruits, nuts, mushrooms, wood for building or fuel, natural fodder for livestock and dung as the main natural fertilizer. At the other end of this scale peasant crafts and trades to which wage labour must be added represent the 'manufacturing' aspect in Malita's terms, i.e. acquiring goods in a way more independent of nature. However, it is husbandry (both arable farming and livestock rearing) which is central to peasant economy.

Agriculture has been defined as 'supplying mankind with food and those raw materials which are of animal or vegetable origin'.[30] Nature, while essentially parasitized on by gathering and to a fair extent controlled in industrial processes of production, operates in agriculture as a powerful corrective to the input/output relations. Agriculture means utilitarian intervention against nature without, however, fully bending it to human goals or needs and with no ability to predict fully an outcome. It represented a tremendous step forward which laid the foundations of our civilization,[31] but also some of its limits, i.e. the 'conservatism inherent in agriculture production',[32] at least in its peasant forms. The partial character of the control over the results of one's own labour exposed peasant agriculture to constant ups and downs, with famines forming part of peasant life. It also meant uneven distribution of labour through the agricultural year and often 'hidden unemployment'. On the other hand, agriculture supplemented by crafts catered directly for a major part of the physical needs of those engaged in it. In times of crisis and war, family-farms have been able to expand these capacities,

28 Galeski, *Basic Concepts of Rural Sociology*; H. Franklin, *European Peasantry – The Final Phase* (London, 1969).
29 M. Malita, 'Agriculture in the Year 2000', *Sociologia Ruralis*, XI (1971). Translators of Malita in this presentation have used 'growing' for the second category/stage and 'production' for the third one. Both terms seem inexact. The first wrongly excludes animal husbandry, the second does not stress sufficiently the organizational and technological nature of the process in question.
30 R. Dumont, *Types of Rural Economy* (London, 1957), p. 1.
31 G.V. Childe, *Man Makes Himself* (New York, 1952).
32 Malita, 'Agriculture in the Year 2000', p. 303.

making peasants autonomous of the larger socio-economic framework in decline.

There are two more forms of significant qualitative diversity within peasant agriculture. Firstly, the traditional division of labour between the genders resulted in specific 'female economies' (which may include gathering, vegetables, hens ect.), with their products and incomes usually well guarded from male control and the outsider's eye. Such niches of female prerogative in the male-owned world may develop into independent 'female trades' (for example, the female traders of West Africa or the Caribbean).[33] Secondly, the increasing need for cash, introduced by taxes and rent and further developed by the advance of the market, creates a necessity for cash earnings. To a considerable if decreasing extent, peasant family-farms tend to solve that problem by a physical division of their resources into land and labour assigned to consumption-directed as opposed to cash-directed crops or crafts, and seasonal wage work aimed at cash earnings.

We may now turn to the *modus operandi* of the peasant family-farm, relating the analysed elements within the single socio-economic unit. Comparison with the basic models of the economics of a capitalist enterprise may illuminate the specific characteristics of the peasant one. Classical economics assumed for each 'firm' a free market interplay and the use of three basic factors/inputs of production: land, labour and capital (their costs expressed by rents, wages and interest respectively) aimed at maximization of profit and/or utility. The category of entrepreneurial innovation, risk and profit was added at the later 'neoclassical' phase. The flow of goods and profits is controlled by book-keeping, expressed by the balance sheet and planned in terms of profits per investment.

A discussion of such a balance in the peasant family-farm must begin by stating its essentially imaginary nature. Firstly, the personal supervision of a small enterprise makes strict control and planning less necessary, while the owner's limited education would make their execution difficult. Stumbling blocks are inherent also in the very character of peasant economy. A major part of the production is consumed while labour is utilized directly. The pricing of both of these is therefore to a considerable degree arbitrary.[34] Survival rather than accumulation as the aim of family-farms finds expression in the fact that use-value repeatedly takes precedence over exchange-value in peasant

---

33 P. Bohannan, *African Outline* (Harmondsworth, 1966); S.W. Mintz, 'The Question of Caribbean Peasantries: A Comment', *Caribbean Studies*, 1 (1961), no. 3.

34 For a discussion of the resulting errors in surveys of peasant agriculture see, for example, Mann, *The Social Framework of Agriculture*.

considerations.[35] The often-noticed tendency to reduce risks by 'unprofitable' diversification of crops[36] illuminates the rationale of such planning in peasant conditions.[37]

The three basic 'factors of production' referred to above are, to the peasant planner, anything but similar in essence, easily inter-convertible, 'value-neutral' and definable in money terms. To begin with, landholding is a necessary (and often sufficient) condition to enter the occupation and, accordingly, carries particular prestige. At the same time, the supply of land on the market is either limited, i.e. 'inflexible', or altogether absent. Opportunities for wage labour are also limited and the use of family labour within the farm is extendable. An increase in consumption pressures would usually lead to an intensification of family labour. When rest forms the main alternative to labour within his farm, a peasant tends to consider his own labour as 'of no cost' and to use it even when the small amount of the additional output achieved makes the additional 'labour input' incredibly 'unprofitable'. This seems to underlie the paradoxical fact that the majority of farms in India's Farm Management Survey proved to be consistently unprofitable by commercial standards and yet nevertheless proceeded to operate and even to show 'net investment'.[38] In peasant economy such 'irrationalities' result not in bankruptcy but in the tightening of the belt and harsher 'self-exploitation' of the family.[39]

As to the peasants' capital, it is limited. The entire property of the family-farm, apart from land, often consists of a house, some simple equipment, a few head of livestock and the personal belongings. Land, if it can be bought, livestock and in some areas female jewellery provide the major forms of saving. Investment plays in those conditions a relatively small role.[40] This is not to say that the peasant would not like to save or would refuse to invest in ventures which are profitable *in his eyes*. However, surpluses are meagre and largely appropriated by the extra-peasant economy. Also credit is expensive and ceremonial duties such as dowry and marriage eat into possible extra resources.[41] A number of powerful levelling mechanisms, discussed in section 3, limit

35 e.g. M.N. Diaz in *Peasant Society*, eds J.M. Potter, M.N. Diaz and G.M. Foster (Boston, 1967), p. 51; Galeski, *Basic Concepts of Rural Sociology*, p. 11.

36 Firth, *Themes in Economic Anthropology*, p. 222.

37 The primitive monoculture of staple food evident in some of the peasant agricultural systems (especially rice in densely populated areas of South-East Asia) needs further study and would probably modify the above statement.

38 B. Hoselitz in Firth and Yamey, *Capital, Saving and Credit in Peasant Societies*, p. 372.

39 Chayanov, *Theory of Peasant Economy*.

40 Firth and Yamey, *Capital, Saving and Credit in Peasant Societies*.

41 E.R. Wolf, *Peasants* (Englewood Cliffs, NJ, 1966); Nash, *Primitive and Peasant Economic Systems*.

capital formation. All this signifies, of course, a basically limited potential for expansion of typically peasant economy *in toto* ('stagnation' if
one feels strongly about it). It means also economic choices typical of
credit-limited small producers, such as the paradox (in terms of a
capitalist economy) of the price of meat falling in strict correlation with
the rise in the price of fodder.[42] It means also that swift growth in
population produces in such conditions 'vicious circles' of deepening
backwardness and poverty.[43]

Finally, the issue of 'entrepreneurial' innovation, profit and risk once
more makes clear major differences between the operation of the
peasant family-farm and that of a typically capitalist economy. The
peasant production unit of small resources and limited credit is exposed
to the powerful vagaries of nature, of market and of state policies, while
the risk of actual starvation and danger of losing even the means of
possible recovery (e.g. land, equipment and livestock) is part of the
bargain. The stock-exchange type of speculation is barely possible here.
In terms of the neoclassical analysis, the extent of the risk would call for
exceptional profits to make it worthwhile, i.e. the 'survival algorithm is
not necessarily the maximising one'.[44] Also, the repeated mistakes of
Western advisers and specialists, who time and again applied administrative pressures against traditions to end up with a crisis of land
erosion, cattle starvation, etc., are today part of what is referred to as
the peasant's traditional suspicion of innovations – not so irrational as
all that.

To recapitulate, the specific *modus operandi* of the peasant family-
farm places in doubt the usefulness of purely economic models rooted in
the reality or the assumptions of a free market. Even in 'purely economic' terms, Economics as an academic discipline when applied to
peasantry necessitates conceptual rearmament. But it cannot be realistically applied without also taking account of the particular character of
the peasant society in a broad sense. One has to move, in the language
of Economics, to the causes of the 'constraints and rigidities' of the
economic models. For example, partition of a farm between a peasant's
sons can be economically 'unprofitable', yet generally accepted as
providing the only way to the social position of head of a household.
Which brings us directly to the point where the structure of family-farms
interrelates with culture, i.e. the norms and cognitions typical of the
peasant society.

That is why, indeed, 'peasant conservatism is out',[45] as a satisfactory

42 Chayanov, *Theory of Peasant Economy*, p. 171.
43 G. Myrdal, *Asian Drama* (New York, 1968).
44 Lipton, 'The Theory of Optimising Peasant', p. 331.
45 ibid., p. 327.

explanation of peasant economy. But not quite. The differences between peasant economy and the 'normal' economic behaviour of a Weber-wise, rational, capitalist entrepreneur cannot be explained merely by peasant traditionalism, for traditionalism itself must also be explained. Investigation of the rationale underlying peasant beliefs and choices in terms of the specific economic conditions has constituted, therefore, a fruitful and important stage in the analysis of peasantry.[46] That accepted, a peasant family-farm operator does not act simply as a rustic economist of the conventional type, wise to his own specific 'production algorithm'. It is both the extent to which peasant villagers, members of the family-farms, are bound to take into account 'non-pure-profit' considerations and the type of consideration they do take into account which set them apart from the contemporary urbanites.

2.2 The Village as an Economic Unit

To claim the crucial importance of the family-farm unit does not, of course, imply that all of the peasant's production takes place there. In his search for supplementary wages the peasant may find himself hundreds of miles from home and in the different economic environments of a plantation, a mine or a factory. He may also work on the local estate, working for wages or as part of various sharing-crop arrangements. Also, peasants join trade partnerships, craftsmen's teams, etc. However, it is the village and neighbourhood which provide the most immediate framework outside the family-farm for peasants' traditional cooperation in production. Many of the large jobs for which the labour of a single family is not sufficient are taken care of on that level. This is often done without waged labour involved, through the aid of neighbours or via an institutionalized 'party' where the help of a large group is obtained (e.g. for the building of a new house), while the benefiting family provides food and drink. The provision of some economic services (for example, the mill, or a craftsman supplying village needs)[47] as well as the welfare of those who do not have the support of a family-farm (e.g. orphans) are often met by the village community. Various forms of cooperation of neighbours have been used by different peasantries for clearing ground, gathering, looking after the cattle and so on. In the agricultural ecotype based on rice, transplantation will be often done by village teams and irrigation handled by the village as an entity, while in the three-fields system of grain production the village

---

46 Chayanov, *Theory of Peasant Economy*; S. Ortiz in Firth, *Themes in Economic Anthropology*; Lipton, 'The Theory of Optimising Peasant'.
47 O. Lewis and V. Barnoun in Potter et al., *Peasant Society*.

will form the framework which sets the farming calendar, allocates the grazing rights, etc. Finally, the peasant community may lay claim to much of the peasants' land (for example, the common land or the forest) or to appear as the legal owner of all of it, present or past (e.g. when demanding on behalf of the peasants' lands grabbed by landlords three centuries before).[48] Indeed, community membership and the right of land-use have been traditionally understood as one.[49] Village economic units are on the whole supervised by a conclave or an oligarchy of the heads of the family-farms – a major form of peasant 'grass-roots democracy'.

2.3 Exchange, Market and Money

Exchange of goods and services is related to the social division of labour transcending the internal cooperation of the family production-consumption unit. Market relations have provided the basic archetype and the categories of exchange within which those born in contemporary industrial societies tend to view such phenomena. Discussion of the issue with reference to peasant society must begin with a double clarification of concepts, delimiting 'exchange' from the 'market' and 'market place' from 'market relations'.

We owe thanks to Polanyi and his associates for a new, more sophisticated taxonomy of exchange with a powerful reminder of its non-market forms.[50] Their division consists of three types: (1) institutionalized reciprocal gift, (2) centralized redistribution following traditionally prescribed taxation by a centralized ruler, and (3) market relations. Peasant societies displayed the full scale of this form of exchange, while the stress moved slowly from the first to the last.

The term 'market' means two different things. On the one hand it is the place where people meet off-and-on at predefined times to exchange goods by bargaining. On the other hand, it is an institutionalized system of organizing the economy by a more or less free interplay of supply, demand and prices of goods. These two meanings of the term represent two social realities which are not simply different but contradict each other.

Market places are typically related to conditions in which a major part of the goods never reaches the market but is consumed within the family units. In this sense markets form a typical component of the peasant

48 E. Feder, *The Rape of Peasantry* (New York, 1971).

49 Marx, *Precapitalist Economic Formation*; Robinson, *Russian under the Old Regime*; O. Lewis, *Life in a Mexican Village* (Urbana, 1963); A. Pearse, 'The Latin American Peasant' (forthcoming).

50 Polanyi et al., *Trade and Market in the Early Empires*.

system of economic organization, providing a place where primary producers sell part of their produce to obtain cash and to supplement self-consumption by outside supplies. Market places also fulfil a variety of 'non-economic' functions, as centres of inter-village contact, information, gossip, sociability and fun.[51] Each market place draws its attendance from a circle of neighbouring villages, providing them with a natural meeting and exchange centre as well as a link with the urban economy.[52] Skinner has pointed out the essential significance and stability of such networks of trade and considered a group of villages with its market centre (rather than a village) the most natural unit of peasant communal life. Local markets held on different days provide for a measure of specialization (livestock markets, crop markets, etc.) and enable their specialized participants (e.g. peddlers or performers) to tour the markets of a region. In contemporary peasant societies the local markets are, furthermore, linked with regional and national ones into a multi-tier system in which the central markets draw rural produce from the local ones and supply these with industrial goods. It is through the development and the contradictions of this structure that the peasant market gradually becomes part of the market system of economy.

The market network is serviced, and to a large extent controlled, by a variety of petty merchants of distinctive characteristics. Their numbers are vast and the fierceness of competition produces systems of non-economic control of the mainly peasant clients through debts, personal relations, and so on.[53] The merchant ethnic minorities (Jews in Eastern Europe, Indians in Africa, Chinese in South-East Asia, etc.) have been particularly prominent here, their social marginality and close 'clannish' links facilitating their operations.[54] Under some conditions, e.g. in West Africa, they are supplemented or even supplanted by professional female traders.[55]

As against market places, *market relations* provide the major system of economic organization of the capitalist industrial societies and are closely linked with their prevailing political organization, as well as with the ethic of individualism, competition, and utilitarian rationalism. The major characteristics of market relations – universality, anonymity, abstract profit aims and eventual bureaucratization – are very much the opposites of the typical way of life of the peasant society. Competition,

51 Nash, *Primitive and Peasant Economic Systems*; Bohannan, *African Outline*.

52 Chayanov, *Theory of Peasant Economy*; G.W. Skinner, 'Marketing and Social Structure in Rural China', *The Journal of Asian Studies*, XXIV (1964), nos 1 and 2.

53 Boeke, *Economics and Economic Policies in a Dual Society*; Firth and Yamey, *Capital, Saving and Credit in Peasant Societies*, pp. 233–9.

54 B.E. Ward in Potter et al., *Peasant Society*.

55 Bohannan, *African Outline*.

the profit motive and capital accumulation give typical market economies a powerful tendency towards expansion and growth. All this makes for conditions in which the juxtaposition of the two different modes of exchange (i.e. the marginal exchange at the market places by primary producers and a universal system of production for exchange governed by the more or less free interplay of price, supply and demand) leads to the gradual transfiguration and 'swallowing up' of the first by the second. Such developments do, however, take a relatively long time, for reasons which will be discussed in section 3.

Money constitutes the main medium of exchange, pricing, saving, investment and credit. In peasant economy its uses are restricted by the extent of direct consumption and family labour and by limited resources. In the early stages some peasant societies developed a variety of particular 'moneys' for different types of socio-economic interrelations; for example, the use of cattle as bride money in Africa.[56] The establishment of universal money and the universalization of money relations proceed hand in hand with the advance of market exchange. The need for money, produced first by the demands of rents and taxes, is later increased by market exchange and the development of new needs. Agricultural cycles, rent and tax demands, the expenses of large, socially prescribed ceremonies such as weddings, the vicissitudes of nature and the general shortage of resources make for a frequent need for credit, which ordinarily is limited and expensive. Worse still, a major part of the loans obtained is not invested in production and does not secure additional income in the future.[57] Banks are often inaccessible to the majority of peasants. This explains the power of the rural moneylenders, the difficulty peasants face in repaying, and the ability of moneylenders to make control of land slip sometimes from the hands of the peasants into their own, creating a new group of landlords.[58] Yet the flexibility and informal relations underlying the deal between the moneylender and the peasant may be preferred by the peasant, a fact which hinders attempts at state control or reform of rural credit.[59]

2.4 The Political Economy

Political economy deals with the control of economic resources and the redistribution of goods determined by that control. Peasant political economy closely links the network of social relations with land tenure, a

---

56 ibid.; G. Dalton (ed.), *Tribal and Peasant Economics* (New York, 1967).

57 e.g. B. Hoselitz in Firth, *Themes in Economic Anthropology*.

58 e.g. Mann, *The Social Framework of Agriculture*, pp. 318–19.

59 B.E. Ward in Potter et al., *Peasant Society*; Mann, *The Social Framework of Agriculture*.

crucial determinant of the peasant's wellbeing and the family's social standing. The peasant land tenure represents a map of human relations rather than of impersonal slices of real estate along 'Western' lines.[60] This map of social relations is structured by diverse hierarchies of societal control. Land rights do not appear as clear-cut, absolute and exclusive divisions of legal ownership: a variety of rights with different degrees of formalization intermingle. While a peasant holds his land, which implies customary rights of use, its legal ownership may be vested in him but also, alternatively, in his village, in the state or in a landlord. Side by side with the peasant family-farm, large agricultural under-takings may exist (haciendas, manors), related in a variety of ways with peasant land use. The systems of land-ownership and political organiz-ation give the non-peasant landlords large slices of peasant income and extensive political control over the peasant communities.[61] The social system of power organization deeply influences the way in which the peasant economy operates. The land held carries exceptional character-istics which cannot be expressed in purely economic terms. Land means power, and, vice versa, power is often translated into land and a land-owner's position.

Large parts of the peasants' produce are taken away by rent and various types of sharecropping arrangements. However, the exploi-tation of the peasantry is not limited to the landlords; other social groups share in peasant production through rent, interest on loans, tax, etc. Terms of trade unfavourable to peasant producers turn market exchange into yet another channel of exploitation of the peasantry by urban society at large. Capital generated in agriculture is in many cases absorbed into the urban tertiary sector, with a new urban bourgeoisie taking over much of the controlling function of traditional land-owners.[62]

A large number of middlemen play a major role in the political economy of peasant societies.[63] They represent landlords (overseers, etc.) or large bureaucratic organizations (buyers, tax collectors). At times these are 'free entrepreneurs'. They are, however, not simple mediators, i.e. the even-handed brokers between the different social groups and powers. Their social position, between the powerful and the

---

60 Bohannan, *African Outline*.

61 Feder, *The Rape of Peasantry*.

62 See, for example, R. Stavenhagen, 'Social Aspects of Agrarian Structure in Mexico', *Social Research*, XXXIII (1966), no. 3; as against Fei Hsiao-tung, 'Peasants and Gentry', *American Journal of Sociology*, 52 (1946).

63 E.R. Wolf, 'Aspects of Group Relations in a Complex Society: Mexico', *American Anthropologist*, 58 (1956), no. 6.

powerless, makes their exploitive tendencies turn against the peasants as a matter of course.

Within the peasantry, socio-economic differentiation often inter-relates with and is transfigured by demographic factors and political hierarchies. Peasants often form 'vertical' patron–client segments, with the 'clients' led, controlled, aided and exploited by the leading family unit. Such patron–client relations may link in turn with the network of plenipotentiaries of central bureaucratic organizations, becoming its lowest ladder. These two types of political structure may, however, clash, reflecting the differences between the centrally imposed policies and the interests of the local peasant elites.

Over a large stretch of human history peasants formed the productive and exploited majority of humanity. The 'surpluses' extorted from the peasantry have provided the most substantive 'material base' of prein-dustrial civilization as we know it, and formed a necessary component of the industrial revolution. With the advance of urbanization and indus-trialization peasantry's social significance changes. It loses its position as the main producer within the national economy and develops into a backwater of economic action. But political submission to and exploi-tation by outsiders remain an essential characteristic of peasant political economy in most of the countries in which peasantry forms a major part of the population.

2.5 *The Conceptual Divisions in the Field of Studies*

The issue of whether a specific peasant economy should be assumed and, if so, what it is, can now be approached in more general terms. Various characteristics of it closely interlink, yet the simple listing of them has not satisfied most of the analysts. Differing hierarchies and assumptions as to what constitutes the *differentia specifica* of peasant economy have played a major role in dividing different schools of thought. Nor has this quarrel over definitions been mere methodological pedantry. It has a bearing on conceptualizations employed, conclusions drawn and predictions offered.

The delineation of a specific peasant economy has been variously based on three approaches, i.e. seen as rooted in either feudal subjec-tion, or normative conservatism, or else some particular characteristics of production and exchange. The first of the approaches views the peasantry as the productive and exploited (farming) majority within a feudal system of domination. The second depicts the specific qualities of peasant economy as cultural inertia expressed by rural part-societies lagging behind their urban, commercialized and dominating 'other part'. The fact that the first approach excludes a major part of contemporary peasants, while the second is by far over-inclusive and qualitatively vague, seems to account for the decreasing popularity of both. It is the third view, in its different variants, which is by now clearly the most popular.

If we focus on this general view the current discussion of specific peasant economy assumes, in turn, one of three possible views as to the mainspring of a particular peasant economy. The division lies here between definitions focused on the characteristics of exchange as against those of production, with one more dividing line drawn between the 'Janus-faced' and the 'organic unity' images of the economy of peasant family-farms.

The first of these trends, powerfully expressed in contemporary economic anthropology,[64] defines specific peasant economy in terms of a limited exchange relations. A basic dualism of non-commercialized versus commercialized economies is assumed, clearly linked to the classical conceptual dualism of 'primitive' versus 'modern' society (i.e. Toennies, Maine, Durkheim, etc.). Furthermore, some analysts equate market economy with capitalist economy for 'once a product can be sold, the producer can be bought.'[65] Within such a theoretical framework, peasant economy presents 'something in between' (between, that is, the primitive, i.e. non-commercial, and the 'modern', i.e. commercialized); i.e. it is the partly commercialized type of economic organization.[66]

Defining peasant economy as a specific type of production by productions/consumption units based on family labour makes for such unlikely bedfellows as Marx (not necessarily the Marxists!), Chayanov, Firth and so on. Marx drew a sharp distinction between the well-developed money and market economy of ancient Rome and the nineteenth-century capitalism based on waged 'free labour', following the separation of the peasant producer from the 'natural laboratory'.[67] His basic image of an 'individual household containing the entire economy'[68] as a precapitalist social formation is very much one with those of the later analysts who defined peasant economy through particular characteristics of production. They divide further, however. On the one hand are some of the orthodox followers of Marx (e.g. Lenin) regarding

64 e.g. Dalton, 'Theoretical Issues in Economic Anthropology'; G.W. Skinner in Potter et al., *Peasant Society*.

65 C. Meillassoux, 'The Social Organization of Peasantry', *Journal of Peasant Studies*, 1 (1973), no. 1, October, p. 88.

66 Dalton, 'Theoretical Issues in Economic Anthropology'.

67 Marx, *Precapitalist Economic Formation*, pp. 67, 118–19; E. Laclau, 'Feudalism and Capitalism in Latin America', *New Left Review*, 67 (1971).

68 Marx, *Precapitalist Economic Formation*, p. 79.

the typical contemporary peasant as a Janus-faced producer, a capitalist and a proletarian rolled into one. On the other side are followers of Sombart, Rosa Luxemburg or Chayanov, who dismiss such a double-faced peasant economy as 'an empty abstraction', stressing the specific, organically indivisible unity and analytical particularity of the basic peasant enterprise-family.[69] To the latter group peasant economy is a specific type of organization of production, capable of existing within different broad societal systems or formations.

3 Peasant Economy – Diversity and Change

Generalizations about peasant economy necessarily limit discussion of the specific, the unique and particular contexts. They also make for a somewhat static picture of reality. While helpful as a yardstick to measure processes, such typologies may be misconstrued as a declaration of or even as a support for lack of change. The differential impact on peasant economic units of the other economies present within the wider society to which peasants belong has been only touched upon above. This is why it may be in order to stress again at this stage that the 'type' presented above is not a deductive construct but a generalization based on comparison. The bulk of contemporary peasant societies display most of the characteristics presented in section 2.

Furthermore, while the impact of the societal systems and modes of organization (feudalism, absolutism, 'oriental despotism', capitalism, and so on) on peasant family-farms has been unmistakable, yet it has not destroyed certain 'generic' similarities of peasant economy and social structure in different periods and parts of the world. Peasant economies have shown a remarkable degree of structural persistence under different external impacts, their essential characteristics outliving, as they were, most of the social and economic systems in which they appeared. Boeke's notion of dual economy and society seems to document, in a somewhat overstated form, such a case.[70] While structural specificity, persistence and relative autonomy make it valid to analyse peasant economy on its own terms, the differing mutual impact of various social and economic systems on their peasant sectors provided a major parallel issue for contemporary studies and debate.[71]

At the local level, i.e. within the rural communities, typical peasant

---

69 Chayanov, *Theory of Peasant Economy*, introduction.
70 Boeke, *Economics and Economic Policies in a Dual Society*.
71 Mendras, 'Un Schème d'Analyse de la Paysannerie Occidentale'; Barrington Moore Jr, *Social Origins of Dictatorship and Democracy* (Harmondsworth, 1969); E.R. Wolf, *Peasant Wars of the Twentieth Century* (New York, 1969).

economies are often the neighbours of and are interlinked with large agricultural enterprises. A number of recent studies explore such large enterprises, as well as their interaction with peasant family-farms.[72] It should be remembered that a number of similarities in the 'logic of management' of traditional large-scale land-holdings and peasant family-farms[73] have often facilitated their symbiotic (if exploitive of the peasants) coexistence, in which the basic characteristics of peasant economy persisted or even were strengthened.

The heterogeneity of peasant societies is expressed in part as regional diversity. The differences between 'regional peasantries' have their roots in disparities of ecology, past history and the broader societal framework.[74] It is, however, the heterogeneity indicating general patterns and sequences of structural change of the countryside which has been particularly interesting.[75] In our times these were, for the most part, related to the impact of industrialization, commercialization, urbanization and political centralization, at times resulting from colonization by an industrially advanced foreign power. (Heterogeneity reflects, then, a major discontinuity arising from the dominant impact of expanding and structurally different economies upon peasant economies.) It is to this axis combining capitalist growth and modern state formation that I shall mainly restrict myself in what follows when referring to rural social 'change'.

3.1 Heterogeneity and Change: Production, Market and Power

The diversities among the family-farms most relevant to the issue of peasant economy relate to the structure and size of their memberships, their place within the broader societal groups and their position in terms of property and output. For the majority of contemporary peasants, a family-farm consists of one-and-a-half to two-and-a-half generations and centres on a married couple and their offspring. It has been known, however, to include a broader group of kin, or else to be polygamous (possibly divided into sub-units, each consisting of one of the wives and her children, e.g. in contemporary Africa). A broader lineage group (clan, *khamula*) may at times play an important role, taking over aspects of what is elsewhere the function of a village community. The socio-

---

72 Feder, *The Rape of Peasantry*; Galeski, *Basic Concepts of Rural Sociology*; Stavenhagen, 'Social Aspects of Agrarian Structure in Mexico'.
73 Mendras 'Un Schème d'Analyse de la Paysannerie Occidentale'.
74 D. Warriner, *Economics of Peasant Farming* (London, 1939); Wolf, *Peasants*; H. Stahl, *Les Anciennes Communautés Villageoises Roumaines* (Paris, 1969).
75 e.g. Makarov, *Krest'yanskoe khozyaistvo i ego evolyutsiya*; Galeski, 'Social Organization and Rural Social Change'.

economic differentiation and the related ranking within the rural communities make for a major dimension of hierarchial structuring of peasant communal life.

Sequential patterns of rural social change may take a number of forms. Sociologists referred to 'individualisation,'[76] with individuals liberating themselves from the compulsory and total framework of the membership in a family-farm, becoming independent parties to diversified arrangements as far as their work, property, family life and place of living are concerned. Consumption claims on family property are being replaced in parallel by individual legal ownership or a contractual share, while competition and universality take the place of family-bound ascription of social roles. The processes of socio-economic polarization and levelling present another major axis of societal change which will be amplified below. Major demographic processes (intermarriage, natural growth, extinction, migration) play an important role in shaping socio-economic diversity and underlie many of the basic economic processes in peasant society.[77]

Many peasants and, even more so, peasants' sons, emigrate or leave temporarily and consequently find themselves in towns, possibly in the enterprises of an urban industrial society. Peasant involvement in the non-peasant modes of production begins typically with labour,[78] specific peasant-worker groups developing as part of this process.[79] However, the family-farms of those who stay put are also deeply influenced by such developments. The growing social division of labour and increasing peasant 'fit' into commercialized wider society are reflected in the specialization of peasant agriculture, its 'agriculturalization', while an increasing number of non-agricultural tasks are taken over by specialized occupations and industries. Within farming in its narrower sense further specialization takes place (for example, animal rearing or a few specific crops), while professionalized services come into being to provide farming communities with seeds, fertilizers, and so on. Farming is on the whole restricted to peasants by birth, but within this group whether to enter the occupation becomes more of a question of individual choice. Occupational training becomes specialized and subject to extra-family institutions. The type of production and the agriculture/wage-work division of labour is increasingly determined by profitability checks and 'economizing', rather than by the use-value of production.

Peasant societies and communities differ markedly in wealth and in

76 Thomas and Znaniecki, *The Polish Peasant in Europe and America.*

77 Wolf, *Peasant Wars of the Twentieth Century*; Shanin, *The Awkward Class.*

78 Nash, *Primitive and Peasant Economic Systems.*

79 Franklin, *European Peasantry – The Final Phase*; M. Dziewicka, *Chlopi-Robotnicy* (Warsaw: 1963).

their prospects for economic growth. Their socio-economic changes have taken, in the contemporary world, two clearly distinguishable directions, very much in accord with Myrdal's model of 'cumulation of advantages and disadvantages'.[80] In countries where industrialization and investment in agriculture draw out part of the rural labour power while simultaneously intensifying and mechanizing farming,[81] peasant agriculture and economy become increasingly integrated within the broader societal framework. Consequently the family-farm becomes increasingly run as an enterprise aimed at maximizing profits. Any problems of natural population growth are solved by emigration and/or intensification of production through investment. (A symbiosis of both takes the form of 'educating out' a 'surplus' son into a non-agricultural profession.) Such an agriculture also becomes increasingly industrialized in terms of massive capital investment, growing interchangeability of production factors, market and profit aims and determination of output by input.[82] The vicissitudes of nature are more and more subject to control. (Mann has commented that 80 per cent of usual production is considered a bad agricultural year in England, while in India annual production fall to less than 10 per cent of the ordinary has been reported more than once.)[83] With the rapid extension of the urban labour market, the unemployable villagers leave for town or become wage-earning rural commuters. Rural/urban differences in income, character of work, economic planning and way of living gradually narrow. The peasant becomes a farmer.

An increase in the size of the agricultural unit through the establishment of factory-like capitalist enterprises or anti-capitalist collectives and state farms may take place in the conditions described. However, a number of the economic preferences of a family-operated farm in agriculture[84] may lead to coexistence and even to the further development within the industrial, capitalist or state-controlled economy of capital-intensive and commercialized family-farms, much as these will differ from the typical family units of a traditional peasant economy. Increasingly dependent on the 'upstream' supplies and the 'downstream' demand, a farmer on such a commercialized farm may reach a stage where he resembles a specialized assembly-line worker or a technician-entrepreneur rather more than his peasant predecessors.

On the other hand, in many countries, the above changes have been prevented by delay in industrialization related to a colonial past and/or

---

80 Myrdal, *Economic Theory and Underdeveloped Regions*.
81 Dumont, *Types of Rural Economy*; Malita, 'Agriculture in the Year 2000'.
82 Malita, 'Agriculture in the Year 2000'.
83 Mann, *The Social Framework of Agriculture*.
84 Warriner, *Economics of Peasant Farming*; Chayanov, *Theory of Peasant Economy*.

neocolonial present. Population increases rapidly while traditional crafts and trades are destroyed by cheap industrial goods, with a resulting forced 'agriculturalization' of an increasing proportion of ruralites.[85] Large-scale investment in agriculture which could increase productivity is lacking; the opposite in fact takes place, as wealth is drained out of agriculture by the ruling groups. Sources of alternative wage income are limited and may even decrease. The land of family-farms is often being fragmented by inheritance while ability to feed its workers lessens. Worse still, destruction of agricultural potential takes place through land erosion triggered off by over-use of the land and overgrazing. A variety of 'vicious circles' result, with poverty and stagnation of resources linked in mutual determination.[86] Growing poverty and lack of prospects for the majority make the rigidity of agricultural methods increase, while peasant communal life disinte-grates in 'agricultural involution'.[87] The village becomes 'an agricultural slum'.[88] The peasant becomes a pauper.[89]

The Green Revolution, with its rapid growth of investment, increas-ing agricultural productivity and rural differentiation between those who can and cannot participate in it, without industrialization capable to secure employment for the 'excess' ruralites, provides a major contem-porary testing-ground for 'betting on the strong' agricultural develop-ment policies.[90] The poor strata of peasantry lose ground and find themselves caught between, on the one hand, farms which are rapidly mechanizing, increasing in size and being intensively run but do not need much permanent wage labour, and, on the other hand, the limited labour market in towns.

As to the market exchange, peasant communities and farms vary in the extent of their involvement in it and in the types of produce they offer. The main direction of change has been subject to the two major patterns of development referred to above. In the peasantries which

85 Mann, *The Social Framework of Agriculture*, pp. 300–1.

86 Myrdal, *Asian Drama*; Mann, *The Social Framework of Agriculture*; Feder, *The Rape of Peasantry*.

87 C. Geertz, *Agricultural Involution* (Berkeley, Cal., 1968).

88 Mann, *The Social Framework of Agriculture*, p. 301.

89 The annual growth of the agricultural production per capita during the 1957–68 period was, for example, 0.1 per cent in the 'developing societies' as against 1.6 per cent in the 'developed' ones (FAO, *The State of Food and Agriculture* [Rome: FAO, 1969]). The increasing poverty of the majority can, of course, go hand in hand with the enrichment of a few, who turn this poverty to their advantage.

90 e.g. H.A. Alavi in R.D. Stevens, H.A. Alavi and P. Bertocci (eds), *Rural Develop-ment in Pakistan* (Ann Arbor, 1972); T.J. Byres, 'The Dialectic of India's Green Revol-ution', *South Asian Review*, 2 (1972); I. Palmer, *Science of Agricultural Production* (Geneva, 1972).

integrate into industrial society, local homogeneity by region ('regional peasantries') and marginal exchange give way to local heterogeneity, national division of labour and extensive exchange of goods and money traffic on nation-wide markets.[91] It is worth noticing here not only the phenomenon itself, however, but also the slowness with which these developments advanced. On the other hand, in societies of 'agricultural involution' market exchange remains limited or a reverse process may even take place, with the peasantry retreating into a semi-autarky determined by poverty, if not hunger.

The major developments in the character of exchange in the peasant societies linked into rapid industrialization are of two categories. Firstly, fully formed market relations take precedence over the direct market exchange between producers, with professionalization of trade and increasingly universalized prices, levels of occupational performance, levels of profit, and so on. General price system and exchange-values thus established take the place of use-values in the determination of the production choices. As market places decline in importance, market principles become the general rule of economic planning. Moreover, while markets of direct producers' exchange may have strengthened the internal cohesion of peasant communities,[92] generalized market relations lead to the disintegration of traditional social networks, which reflects in turn on further economic action. Secondly, the disappearance of restrictions on the sale of factors of production, especially land and labour, extends the scope of market relations, promotes capital formation and facilitates budgeting and profitability checks in abstract economic terms. Money and market relations advance side by side, as money becomes the major medium of evaluation and exchange. Credit facilities become increasingly professionalized, formalized and controlled by banks. A reminder of the specific character of agriculture is the exceptional importance of short-term and medium-term credit within farming.

The diversity of the peasantries in terms of political economy has been expressed through relations with political rulers and by the character of the internal peasant hierarchies. It has run therefore from serfdom to civic freedom and has seen various degrees and forms of socioeconomic differentiation and local oligarchy within the peasant communities.[93]

In its impact on social transformation of societies *in toto*, peasantry played a major role at the early stages of industrialization, contributing

---

91 E. Wolf in Dalton, *Tribal and Peasant Economics*.
92 Ortiz in Firth, *Themes in Economic Anthropology*, p. 206.
93 e.g. Stavenhagen, 'Social Aspects of Agrarian Structure in Mexico'.

to capital accumulation and labour supply.[94] Beyond this stage the impact of agriculture has dropped in its importance as a source of national income and of profits for those in power. While the peasant economy is transformed into capital-intensive farming, integrated into capitalist national economy, the major source of income drawn from agriculture by non-producers shifts from land rent to the control of supply, transport, credit and other necessary services. The importance of bureaucratic 'plenipotentaries' grows also. On the other hand, this is also the stage at which attempts are made to organize politically through peasant parties and farmers' pressure groups, to turn parliamentary structures to the advantage of the peasant-becoming-farmer. The rural–urban contradiction 'competes' here with inter-peasant class division in influencing the peasants' political stand.

In the societies of delayed industrialization the ruling group remains closely linked with landlordism. Even though its income increasingly comes from the town, from abroad or from the use of the machinery of state, land remains a major source of political power, especially in Latin America.[95] When land is short, the rocketing rents and prices for it hinder the intensification of landowners' estates, while land is often sold or rented to peasants. Large units disappear, outcompeted, as it were, by the starving peasant sharecroppers.[96] The town/village division deepens into a split structural in form and exploitive in its determination. 'Peasantization' and 'agriculturization' appear here as indicators of the crisis of rural economy which turns it into the major bottleneck of the national economies in the numerous 'developing societies' of today.

Inside the peasant communities, 'individualization' and increase in the social division of labour, coupled with commercialization and the emergence of new sources of income, often lead to socio-economic polarization. Part of the incomes from usury, controlling rural services and mediation in trades fall into the hands of the top peasant farms. Socio-economic polarization in rural localities is often related to the local division of political power, while some peasants play leading roles in both.[97] The development of capitalist economic relations in its full sense is slow, however, even at the richest and poorest poles of the peasant society, which are more exposed to it; the diversity is rather that of rich versus poor within a variety of traditional dependencies. The speed and character of such a development has been very much subject to the major economic trends of the broader 'encircling' society.

94 E. Preobrazhensky, *The New Economics* (Oxford, 1965).
95 Feder, *The Rape of Peasantry*.
96 e.g. Chayanov, *Theory of Peasant Economy*; Geertz, *Agricultural Involution*.
97 Wolf, 'Aspects of Group Relations in a Complex Society'; W.F. Wertheim, 'From Aliran towards Class Struggle in the Countryside of Java', *Pacific Viewpoint*, 10 (1969).

Finally, the policies of modern states and the impact of major political movements turn the modern state into a major determinant of the present and the future of peasant agriculture. We shall turn to it in Section 4.

3.2 Stability and Intervention

There seem to be two points of agreement within a wide range of analysts of economic change in peasant societies. The first is that structural changes have been largely generated, or at least triggered off, by forces outside peasant society, and the second that both changes in economic organization and the production increase in peasant agriculture have been much slower than planners and scholars predicted. Such conclusions should direct attention to the reasons for the remarkable stability of this social entity which, with remarkably little change, lasted for millennia.[98] It has outlived most of the non-peasant societal forms and still manages to constitute a major headache for the politicians of today. Clarification of the mechanisms reinforcing social stability must form a major component of any substantive consideration of social change.

Cultural 'inertia' rooted in the way of life of peasant communities and in the characteristics of peasant agriculture (e.g. the three-field system) has often been considered as a reason for the high structural stability of the peasant economies, and indeed contributed to it. The interest and will of the large landlords, backed by political power to keep things as they are, may act similarly. However, such determinations have operated on a par with conserving socio-economic processes, without which the results would have been very different indeed.

Pre-industrial society presents us with a variety of structural arrangements and of patterned processes which reinforce stability and cohesion by dampening the socio-economic polarization of the rural communities. Those arrangements also limit what has come to be called 'economic growth', i.e. both the rise in per capita production and the changes in the organization of the economy which facilitate such a rise. The 'pre-peasant' *potlach* of the hunting Indian and the Eskimo tribes may here provide an example: at some stage each family which has accumulated a surplus of goods uses them up by giving them away at a major gathering. This adds to the family's prestige and the community's pleasure and cohesion. It also brings the family 'back to square one', i.e. to the accepted level of normal poverty.[99]

---

98 See Redfield, *Peasant Society and Culture*, and especially his comparison of Hesiod's book from the third century BC with the evidence concerning contemporary peasantries.
99 e.g. P. Drucker, *Cultures of the North Pacific Coast* (San Francisco, 1965).

Peasant economies incorporate a variety of levelling mechanisms specific to them. For example, levelling by 'scrambling wealth to inhibit re-investment in technical advance and thus prevent crystallization of class lines on an economic base' is reported for the Indian communities of Latin America.[100] It operates through the fragmentation of property by inheritance and through obligatory ceremonial offices which are imposed on the richer members of the community and either severely limit incomes or make extensive spending necessary. Such social arrangements operate, or even become reinforced, with peasantry crossing the threshold of 'modernity', as it comes under the impact of the commercial and industrial town or foreign powers. In many peasant societies powerful, cyclical mobility operates then, with peasant family-farms continually changing their economic position as a result of the simultaneous opposing processes of cumulation of economic advantages versus the levelling trends (reflecting the rate of partitioning of wealthier households, the impact of nature, selective extinction, and so on).[101] The selective character of rural emigration usually abstracts from the peasant community its richest and poorest members, i.e. leads to equalization of those who stay, at the same time ridding it of its most aggressive and change-prone members. And so on. All these processes produce a powerful levelling impact and reinforce communal homogeneity and stability. They usually interlink with egalitarian norms of the 'golden mean', collectivity and sociability, accepted as self-evident by most of the peasant community. Together with the operating system of political economy, the heavy toll taken from agriculture by the urban controllers of power and the relative backwardness of rural resources generally observed,[102] this limits the polarization processes in peasant communities and puts a brake on structural changes. On the other hand, the existence of social forces impeding polarization of peasant societies does not necessarily mean that it does not take place.

Many of the specific characteristics of modern societies reflect directly the ways in which their peasantries entered the modern world.[103] The main triggers of structural change seem, however, to be placed outside peasant society. To be sure, in this period peasant revolt and revolution shake societies and make some regimes and social classes fall.[104] Yet,

100 M. Nash in Dalton, *Tribal and Peasant Economics*.

101 P. Stirling, *A Turkish Village* (London, 1956); Shanin, *The Awkward Class*; I. Ajami, 'Social Classes, Family Demographic Characteristics and Mobility in Three Iranian Villages', *Sociologia Ruralis*, IX (1969); M.C. Yang, *A Chinese Village* (New York, 1945); Nash, *Primitive and Peasant Economic Systems*.

102 e.g. A.N. Agarwala and S.P. Singh (eds), *The Economics of Under-development* (Oxford, 1970), pp. 381–3.

103 Moore, *Social Origins of Dictatorship and Democracy*.

104 Wolf, *Peasant Wars of the Twentieth Century*.

when the dust has settled (and possibly after some 'repeasantization' of society through egalitarian land reform), non-peasant elites and forces reassume their advance against the typically peasant way of life. The political will of the ruling classes and elites when ruralites are concerned has been increasingly expressed in conscious agrarian policies, stated and unstated. It is by the interplay of spontaneous and directed change as well as 'external' impacts and 'internal' reactions that peasant society and economy are altered. The changes may result from direct pressure but, at times, even more from the undermining or destruction of the specific 'stabilizers' which have formed part of the peasant social structure. Rapid population growth and ecological crises, mass communications and crises of traditional authority, new personal opportunities for some to accumulate political and economic power by linking into the new national network and policies of economic growth exercise increasing influence, which is destructive of the typically peasant social and economic organization. So does penetration of the market economy, public transport, mass media and so on. Moreover, the very advance of peasant agriculture may provide the base of industrialization and urbanization, contributing to the destruction of the peasantry as a specific social entity and a particular type of economy.

The stage at which the peasant economy is transformed as a social system, as a typical economic strategy or as a habit of mind of the individuals concerned,[105] presents a major analytical problem. The proclivity for both stability and change of the peasant economy must be tested for different historical eras and different societies, as well as against different variables like the availability of land, alternative employments, etc. Such comparative analysis is still in its infancy.[106] The disintegration of peasant social structure is, also, not unidirectional. The processes and policies facilitating the peasant socio-economic structure may take the upper hand, with societies 'repeasantizing' as a result, especially when a revolutionary agrarian reform is taking place.[107] Yet the general direction towards destruction of the typically peasant social and economic structures seems unavoidable.

The contemporary initiative to reshape peasant societies has been very much in the hands of non-peasant organizations and organizers. Their ability to achieve their aims has depended, however, on a number of major factors. It has been subject to their own class interests and ideological visions of society *vis-à-vis* those of the peasants. It has been

105 Nash, *Primitive and Peasant Economic Systems*,
106 e.g. Galeski, *Basic Concepts of Rural Sociology*; Mendras, 'Un Schème d'Analyse de la Paysannerie Occidentale'.
107 Chayanov, *Theory of Peasant Economy*, p. 28; Galeski, 'Social Organization and Rural Social Change'.

influenced by the extent of their understanding of peasant economy and society. It has also been subject to their ability to enlist peasant support or at least to have the peasants effectively neutralized or suppressed. In this sense the economic change of peasant communities increasingly finds its explanation in the totality of the policies and the political sociology of the societies within which peasants live.

4 Peasant Economy – Policy and Intervention

Contemporary peasant economies are located mostly within the so-called 'developing societies'. A high ratio of ruralites, mostly peasants, in the total population seems indeed to provide a reasonably close quantitative index for the delineation of the 'developing societies' today.[108] Powerful reminders of the specific character of the peasantry are still in evidence also in a variety of societies which are not the 'developing' ones by the UN designation.

Policies toward the peasantry formed a major component of political strategies, legislative action and the ideologies of nationalism, economic growth, democratization, social justice etc. The results of these policies, those which were successful and those which failed, past and present, have been crucial to the character of the world we know. Barrington Moore has offered a challenging historiography which defined the contemporary political divisions of the world at large by the alternative ways the relations between the peasantries and those who dominated them were being resolved.[109] As to the strategies and processes of today and their explicit mainsprings, the bulk of the societies with a large peasant population share governments and policies largely concerned with 'modernization' and 'growth', visualized as 'catching up' with the industrial societies in terms of national income, capital formation, education, and so on. By all these indices the peasantry represents the backward part of society and a major obstacle to its general advance. Low levels of income and of production per capita, under-employment, high mortality rates and so on, bad as they are in these countries, are particularly prominent in the countryside. While some of the 'developing societies' can show an impressive advance in new urban industries (but often manned by few and benefiting few), agriculture has often remained static or has even declined in per capita terms. 'Vicious circles' of 'cumulation' of backwardness, said to operate to the disadvantage of the 'developing countries' in the world economy,[110] operate also inside

108 e.g. FAO, *Progress in Land Reform*, Fifth Report (Rome, 1970), pp. 332–4.
109 Moore, *Social Origins of Dictatorship and Democracy*.
110 Myrdal, *Economic Theory and Underdeveloped Regions* (London, 1957).

each of those societies, with the peasantry very often playing the role of the weaker brethren increasingly falling behind.

The projection of all that in the planners' minds has been much accentuated by the depths of the cultural split between the peasants and 'the educated'. To most of the young, smart and impatient BA-holders in national administrations, as well as to many of their short-stay-in-the-tropics advisers, the peasant mass appears as the major obstacle to progress, its backwardness matched only by the conservative bloody-mindedness with which it resents new policies. Particularities of local agriculture (especially its relatively slow rhythms) and peasant knowledge of matters on which their livelihood depends (especially local ecology) are usually dismissed out of hand. At the same time what happens to the rural sections of the population cannot be simply ignored. Annoyance with peasant backwardness and a peculiar compassion without empathy mingle in a variety of ideologies and policies, most of which aim at hammering peasants into 'what is good for them'.

4.1 Aims and Policies

Economic advance and egalitarian justice, the two formal aims of the contemporary reforms directed towards the peasantry, have meant widely different things in different settings. A policy of increasing productivity (or marketability) may aim at the needs of the countryside, i.e. at the increased consumption or capital formation there, but alternatively it may be directed towards goals outside the rural sphere, i.e. at capital formation, market development and export, cheap wage labour, etc., especially when industrialization strategies are afoot. The official goals of social justice have to be taken with a grain of salt; at times they have 'beautified' policies clearly aimed at the enrichment of the few. In other cases, especially when agrarian policies resulted from a recent revolutionary surge of the ruralites, a genuine egalitarian tendency has made its impact felt.

Two more points should be stressed at the outset. First, the aims of economic advance and egalitarian justice may (and indeed, often do) clash, and the accepted resolution of that contradiction would define the specific character of the policy adopted. (For example, egalitarian land division has led in some cases to a drop in the production or marketability of basic foodstuffs.)[111] Second, the real content of whichever policies are adopted can be understood only in relation to the nature and actual interest of the dominant groups as well as of the adminis-

111 D. Warriner, *Land Reform in Principle and Practice* (London, 1969).

tration charged with the execution of the reforms and of their inter-relations with the peasant communities.

For varied reasons and under different circumstances, the official aims of most of the governments of chiefly peasant societies agree in their wish to dismantle the traditional peasant socio-economic structures in an attempt to 'modernize', to obtain rapid economic growth, and at times also to secure democratization of the society *in toto*. Their problem is how to advance such a development without leading peasant societies into pauperization and 'agricultural involution'. To governments committed to egalitarianism it means, additionally, finding ways to check the growth of new agrarian capitalism without, however, limiting the increase of agricultural capital formation and production. It means also overcoming the opposition of the powerful, privileged groups whose advantages depend on the peasants staying as they are.[112]

The contemporary policies aimed at the transformation of peasant economies can be divided into two basic categories which may appear simultaneously but often act as the stages of a long-term policy. The first centres on *land reform* and tends to reinforce specific peasant economies (although it may form but a step towards its radical transformation and disappearance). The second aims at the establishment of a *new and different agrarian economy*, more closely 'embedded' in and conducive to the growth of the national one. Depending on the ruling ideology this may take one of three forms: that of promotion of large-scale capitalist enterprises, or of modern and efficient family-farms, or else of collective units of production (and collective ownership, full or partial).

4.1.1 Land Reform Land reform has been authoritatively defined as 'redistribution of property or rights in land for the benefits of the small farmer and agricultural labourer'.[113] In this sense it, indeed, 'belongs therefore to the same family of economic tools as fiscal and monetary policy, subsidies, rationing, tariffs, nationalization, etc.'.[114] It is also a political measure, possibly involving expropriation, introducing compulsion, and encountering various degrees of opposition from the traditional large land-holders of the countryside.[115] It has resulted, therefore, in open and frequently brutal rural class warfare and also, often, in severe conflicts between the traditional and the modernizing

---

112 S. Andreski, *Parasitism and Subversion* (London, 1966); R. Dumont, *Lands Alive* (New York, 1965); W.F. Wertheim, *Resistance to Change – From Whom?* (Singapore, 1971).

113 Warriner, *Land Reform in Principle and Practice*, p. xiv.

114 E. Flores, 'Definition and Typology of Land Reform', *Journal of Administration Overseas*, VII (1968), no. 3.

115 e.g. Feder, *The Rape of Peasantry*; A. Blok, 'Mafia and Peasant Rebellion as Contrasting Factors in Sicilian Latifundism', *European Journal of Sociology*, X (1969).

urban classes and elites. The political and economic changes are as a rule formalized in extensive legislation: new rules about property, association, rent and lease, etc. The place of land tenure in peasant life being what it is, such reforms bear crucial significance. The power and the ability to resist by those who oppose those charges mean that for such reforms to work as a levelling measure they must be rapid and backed by extensive political mobilization of the peasantry and/or the machinery of the state.

The issues and the actual scope of land reform are, however, much broader and more complex than that of egalitarian land redistribution. To begin with, the redistributive aspect of land reform is on the whole supplemented by other 'corrective' steps concerning the land-holdings. The aim of such corrective measures is often to improve the efficiency of land allocation, productivity and use of labour, and to optimize the size of the land-holding by consolidating some and limiting the fragmentation of others. It may also aim at shortening the distances between the peasant's house and his land, at the improvement of communal services (education, health, transport) through consolidation of households into villages (e.g. the 'villagization' in Tanzania), and so on.

Expropriation and redivision of land in use has been often complemented by the settlement and colonization of virgin lands. The 'new' land may come from the unused parts of private property, customarily held tribal lands or state-owned lands, often 'virgin' and opened up by new holders. At times new settlement has followed successful land reclamation or new irrigation schemes (for example, the Nile-based schemes of Egypt and Sudan).

The creation of new patterns of land tenure have seldom come as a single measure. The capacity of the peasant to cultivate new land successfully and not to let it slip rapidly into other hands is conditioned by a variety of additional measures: provision of credit and/or equipment, new market outlets, reorganization of local authority, regional services, changes in the structure of production. Often enough the stratum exploiting peasant majorities through rents, etc., has been simultaneously operating as a barrier/mediator between the villagers and the national economy. Breaking or limiting this hold necessitates the organization of new types of economic interaction between the village and the 'outside'. Land reform has come increasingly to be viewed, therefore, as a general agrarian reform, a set of interlinked measures which, while changing land tenure, provides also for new social and economic arrangements of much wider scope, or else must grind to a halt.

The character of the land and agricultural reforms has been related to the broader economic, political and social setting and must be understood in such a context. To exemplify, the extensive studies by FAO have stressed the differences between the three continents of the so-called Third World.[116] In Latin America it is mainly the breaking up of large feudal estates which is crucial; in South Asia it is the problems of share-cropping (and of related patterns of usury) in an extremely densely populated area; in 'Black Africa' it is the problem of customary land holdings, colonial plantations, and a marketing monopoly which have been the focus of attention. In each of the major regions land tenure corresponds to a broader structure of social relations and any reform must necessarily mean the reform of both.[117]

The 'land to the toiler' type of land reform facilitated specific peasant socio-economic structures based on the family-farm, operating within the framework of traditional village communities. Its adoption has been influenced by peasant consciousness which, highly diffused as it had been, clearly pointed towards such steps. That has, indeed, been the direction of changes spontaneously adopted when armed peasantry was able to dictate its wishes.[118] In addition, land reforms were often introduced out of the belief of the non-peasant political elites that such is the peasants' wish and, consequently, that their implementation would secure peasant support (or else undercut peasant support for some rebels). On the other hand, it was usually the assumption of the non-peasant legislators that such a reform would produce a 'new' free peasantry; free, that is, from the conservative and crippling impacts of a traditional and/or feudal society and free to integrate in terms of market and labour into the national economy and to contribute to its rapid advance. Ideally, it was also to inject additional vitality into the general system of political economy promoted by the reformers. The process of transition following the land reform, but often overlapping with it and at times independent of it, provides the second major category of political intervention.

4.1.2 Shaping a New Agrarian Economy The general wish of the governments concerned to see the transformation of peasant economy into a modern and effective agricultural sector of an industrial society does not result in single and self-evident political prescription. The issues are political rather than technical, and 'to govern' is indeed 'to choose' between a variety of alternatives and underlying assumptions and criteria. The main alternatives which face policy makers are three: (1) 'betting on the strong', as against 'betting' on the mass, i.e. the attempt to reform or advance the small-holders' agriculture by concen-

116 FAO, 'Land Reform as an Instrument of Progress', *Land Reform*, I (1970).
117 FAO, *Progress in Land Reform*.
118 e.g. J. Womack, *Zapata and the Mexican Revolution* (New York: 1968); Shanin, *The Awkward Class*.

trating on a chosen few, supposedly the ablest or wealthiest, as against an attempt at a slower advance of the bulk of the farming population;[119] (2) large-scale farming based on extensive use of wage labour as against family farming; (3) building up an interactive as against a directive economic system, i.e. a system based on volunteer and partial association from below by family farmers as against tight state control of the agriculture. The farming units actually adopted to be aimed at in the process of reform were those of a capitalist enterprise, a collective or state-owned large enterprise and a technologically advanced family-farm within a cooperative network. These have been loosely related to the major frameworks of ideology and political practice, of 'Western-like' capitalism, Soviet- or China-like socialism and the 'populism' of, say, contemporary Tanzania respectively.

One should not overstate this association. Family-farms and state enterprises appear as the pre-eminent form of organization of agriculture in each of the political systems named; for example, both Denmark and Poland today centre on family-farms, while the Shah's Iran experimented, like the USSR of the 1920s, with state promotion of collective farms (of the 'Kolkhoz' type). Also, the actual reforms of the rural economy and society did not ever follow absolutely the conceptual models (1), (2) and (3) in a way which was total and exclusive of any other form. The family plot of the Kolkhoz member in the USSR provides an example of such solutions, which have been 'impure' in logic but to be preferred politically, and clearly helpful in letting the ends meet when farming populations are concerned.

For each of the major categories of the reforms discussed one should consider its goals side by side with the assumptions (or legitimations) of the reformers as well as the misgivings of the critiques, all to be tested in the light of the actual results.

As to the actual strategies of reform adopted, those aimed at the *promotion of capitalist farming* laid stress on the so-called farming elites, synonymous on the whole with the wealthier peasants and with those larger land-owners who directly engage in intensive farming. A farmer-entrepreneur of this elite is assumed to possess initial capital, knowledge of agrarian techniques and general manipulative capacities in excess of those of his rural neighbours. The larger size of farm, better equipment, use of wage labour and entrepreneurial skills secure the more effective use of the factors of production. The consequent rise in productivity and marketability leads to a deepening involvement in the national economy, higher rates of investment and further accumulation of socio-

119 For a most interesting exposition of this debate's second solution by the so-called Stolypin Reforms in Russia, 1906–10, see Robinson, *Russia under the Old Regime*.

economic advantages by such farms in the rural community, which
result in their expansion. Agriculture becomes business consisting of
large- or medium-scale enterprises run on capitalist lines. The economic
growth thereby secured does not require large-scale reorganization,
nationalization or complex administration, and the process may be
treated as a natural further development of rural socio-economic
polarization, with the ablest and best at profit-making increasing their
share of rural production. The less successful gradually lose land and
turn to wage labour ('more suitable for them') on the capitalist farms
and in towns.

The 'betting on the strong' state policies of promoting capitalist
farming include the promotion of a free and flexible market for the
means of production (especially land), land consolidation measures,
credit easily accessible to the wealthy (i.e. proportional to property
owned), maintenance of low enough agricultural wages, subsidies which
benefit mostly larger agricultural producers, and so on. Placing (or
leaving) the local political authority in the hands of the local rich greatly
facilitates such developments. The systematic discussion of the pros and
cons of this strategy and a tentative selective evaluation of them in
historical terms, i.e. in relation to the stage of socio-economic development of the society analysed, has been on the increase during the last
decade.[120] The Green Revolution in South Asia has been providing of
late an increasingly important testing ground for this debate.

Criticism of this economic strategy related firstly to the fact that
agricultural advance, rise in market supply and demand, etc., for a small
minority may mean little in national terms or may even coincide with
actual economic backsliding. Also, wealth and power do not necessarily
signify readiness and capacity to advance; conservatism and conspicuous
consumption often characterize the social milieu of the rural rich. The
use of economic resources by the wealthiest farms may be less effective
than their use by their poorer neighbours.[121] Even when the advance of
capitalist farming leads to general increases in food production, the fact
that peasant smallholders and share-croppers often lose their land
without being absorbed into permanent wage labour can lead to severe
social and economic problems. Mechanization of large-scale agriculture
may aggravate this situation. In broader social terms, issues of social
equality and conflict are at stake. Social tension created by polarization
in rural communities may explode into a political revolt of the poor
leading to the dislocation of economy, to direct challenge to its rulers

---

120 R.O. Dore, 'Land Reform and Japan's Economic Development', *Development
Economics*, III (1965), no. 4.

121 S.G. Madiman, 'Small Holder Agriculture versus Large Scale Production in Asia',
Land Reform, II (1970), pp. 65–6.

and promoters or even to the abolition of the socio-economic system which generated it all.

Collectivization has been directed towards the mass of peasant households, has assumed the superiority of the large enterprise and has a strong directive tendency. Large-scale integration of production resources in agriculture is assumed to secure their more efficient use, increasing productivity and rapid capital formation and expanding the technological base of farming as well as its contributions to the industrial town. It should also secure increased supply of food as well as of labour, both freed from their rural setting to be invested in industrialization. (In this sense the aim is indeed 'just to do what free trade did in Western Europe'.)[122] At the same time the egalitarian cooperation in production should put an end to the polarization processes in the countryside and secure social equality and a decent livelihood for all. The democratic organization of the collectives should place control of production in the hands of the farmers, while support of the peasant majority overcomes the expected obstruction to the egalitarian measures by a small exploitive minority.

A few years before the first massive collectivization in the Soviet Union, a systematic criticism of its possible shortcomings as a reform strategy was developed by some of the Russian scholars; especially by A. Chayanov. In that view the enlargement of an agricultural enterprise does not secure increasing productivity since the maximum size is not necessarily an optimum one (the optimum differs for each particular branch of agriculture). It claimed also that large-scale 'horizontal' integration would leave the peasants without local leaders able to handle the large-scale enterprises, and would cause the actual government of the collective farms to slip into the hands of bureaucratic outsiders. Finally, it anticipated the powerful and destructive opposition of the peasantry as a whole to measures which run counter to its experience of farming and tradition of organization, and which may land peasants in conditions which couple the alienation of the industrial worker with the insecurity of the smallholder. An alternative plan of 'vertical co-operation' was suggested.[123]

The increasing volume of research concerning the collectivization in the Soviet Union, now in its fifth decade, provided new materials for evaluation of this debate.[124] It is significant that agriculture still seems to

122 Warriner, *Land Reform in Principle and Practice*, p. 194.

123 A.V. Chayanov, *Oeuvres Choisies de Chayanov*, vol. V (The Hague, 1967). For a short discussion in English, see T. Shanin in P. Worsley (ed.), *Two Blades of Grass* (Manchester, 1971).

124 e.g. Warriner, *Economics of Peasant Farming*; N. Jasny, *The Socialised Agriculture of USSR* (Stanford, 1949); M. Lewin, *Russian Peasants and Soviet Power* (London, 1968);

constitute a major bottleneck in the Soviet economy. The growth of state farms may indicate here the direction of future advance but its results still need thorough investigation.[125] The heterogeneous experience of Eastern Europe, Asia and China, including the decollectivization in Jugoslavia, Poland and, temporarily at least, parts of North Vietnam adds an important dimension. China's collectives and communes offer an interesting field for further investigation, for which the existing data is very limited, especially so since the Cultural Revolution.[126] The heterogeneity of China and the prominence of local leadership of peasant stock, as well as experiments with new types of social structure and human motivation, may make the Chinese experience particularly important.

An intensive and efficient *family-farm linked into cooperative organizations of supply and marketing* provided the third alternative model of agricultural reform aimed at by the contemporary reformers. It means 'betting' on the mass, giving preference to small enterprises essentially based on family labour and to an interactive (at least formally so) organization of agriculture. Such a choice has usually been based on an egalitarian ideology, but also on assumptions of the economic preferences of family farming, at least at the given stage of economic and technological advance.[127] This view has put particular stress on the specific nature of agricultural production and the scope it still leaves to individual action, on processes which cannot be easily mechanized, etc. Fuller employment and better use of scarce resources in family farming, together with the broadening of the mass market for the basic products of national industry, are also cited in support of this view. The family-farm solution is considered less destructive of the initial peasant social structure, and therefore more capable of mobilizing the genuine good-will of the peasant majority towards the utilization and adoption of new technology and forms of organization.

The potential disadvantages of policies attempting to transform peasant economies into modern capital-intensive family-farms are numerous. Small farms often find it difficult to adopt new techniques and to generate additional capital for the investment needed to secure 'self-sustained growth'. Family-directed fragmentation of holdings through inheritance interferes with their economic advance. Limited state credit,

K.E. Wadekin, 'Soviet Rural Society', *Sociologia Ruralis*, XXVI (1971). See also a large number of articles in Soviet Studies.

125 e.g. Galeski, *Basic Concepts of Rural Sociology*.

126 We have some monographs on specific communities; e.g. W. Hinton, *Fanshen* (New York, 1966); G. Myrdal, *Report from a Chinese Village* (London, 1965).

127 e.g. Warriner, *Economics of Peasant Farming*, pp. 140–64; Madiman, 'Small Holder Agriculture versus Large Scale Production in Asia'.

if thinly spread on an egalitarian basis, may do little good. Under the pressures of market relations rural communities tend to stagnate or to polarize, spontaneously producing marginal capitalist farming and under-employed labour. The injection of state aid under such a system frequently turns into a directive and highly bureaucratic running of agriculture 'from without'. When the free market economy prevails the agrobusiness centring on banks and mortgage institutions, foodstore chains, monopolies of supply, etc. uses family farming to the best advantage of its own profit making.

Attempts to proceed with modern family farming while overcoming tendencies destructive of it have recently taken the form of 'communal development' schemes and of rural cooperation. The 'communal development' programmes aimed at inducing individual family units to join in voluntary collective projects: building local schools or roads, improving farming, reclaiming land, etc., while at the same time overcoming localist xenophobia. Some of these attempts were doubtless beneficial,[128] while others degenerated into a 'moronic stereotype in which so-called experts use high pressure salesmanship techniques on villagers to induce them to build village halls and other local projects'.[129]

Rural cooperation, while somewhat similar to communal development schemes, is on the whole older in experience and more fundamental in its purpose. An egalitarian ideology is usually accentuated in it. In socio-economic terms 'the real strength of the cooperation . . . lies in services',[130] i.e. an increasing range of processing, exchange and provision of credit, tools, storage facilities, etc. 'Vertical integration' of family-farms may result, enabling them to benefit from large-scale organization when it pays, while not committing them to it when it does not.[131] The success of cooperatives was, on the whole, subject to a fairly high degree of sophistication of farming and of the farmers. The experience of the last generation has been rather disappointing to the egalitarian ideologists of cooperation, as cooperatives often disintegrated or else slid towards capitalist farming and/or increasing bureaucratic control 'from above'. Sons of cooperative farmers were often not ready to proceed within the same social framework, and a 'second generation crisis' put in question the whole of the system. At the same time the capacity of cooperative family-farms to modernize and hold their own

128 G. Huizer, 'Community Development, Land Reform and Political Participants', *American Journal of Economics and Sociology*, XXVIII (1969), no. 2.

129 Warriner, *Land Reform in Principle and Practice*, p. 63.

130 FAO, *Progress in Land Reform*, p. 350.

131 Chayanov, *Oeuvres Choisies de Chayanov*, vol. V; P. Sinkvitz, 'Structural Change in Agriculture', *Sociologia Ruralis*, X (1970), no. 4.

within an industrial society at least for a while has been amply demonstrated by, for example, the Danish farmers.[132]

It may be useful to recollect at this stage that the aims, forms, successes and failures of contemporary agrarian reform must be considered within the framework of broader (i.e. national and international) economic, political and social schemes.[133] (The cited success of the Danish farmers in transforming peasant economy into efficient modern family farming was very much the result of their political successes, which gained them the support of the state, and of the fact that a rapid and selective urbanization purged the villages of both the very rich and the very poor, strengthening the egalitarian base of the farming communites. It also depended on the state of the world markets of food.) Moreover, once again, the mores and policies of the dominant urban society play an increasingly prominent role in the shaping of agricultural communities. Finally, such processes are two-directional. Non-peasants are crucial to the way in which the peasantry disappears while the patterns of depeasantization shape the future of a post-peasant society.

5 Afterword

'It may be politic to report that the FAO world plan to modernize and improve agriculture could be implemented without painful reform, but it would not be true.'[134] That statement holds true for the whole complex of the issues of transformation of the peasant economies and societies in a rapidly changing world. To put it in the right perspective, all this determines the livelihood of one-half of humanity while deeply influencing the future of the whole of it. Even the most revolutionary changes and speediest industrialization will still leave much of the world's population rural, and peasant, for at least a generation. Moreover 'the tragic fact of the matter, deeply relevant here, [is] that in most of the past experience the poor bear the heaviest cost of modernization under both socialist and capitalist auspices.'[135]

The character of the changes and reforms discussed was being determined by the prevailing political and economic group interests and power relations, as well as by direct political struggle. But this has been only part of the truth. It was also powerfully influenced by the accepted meanings, views and categories, by the entrenched information and

132 Warriner, *Land Reform in Principle and Practice*.
133 Flores, 'Definition and Typology of Land Reform'.
134 FAO, 'Land Reform as an Instrument of Progress'.
135 Barrington Moore, *Social Origins of Dictatorship and Democracy* (Harmondsworth, 1967).

misinformation, in short by all that we call knowledge. When agrarian policies lead to unexpected results and to shattering failures it was often 'because it has not always been realised that . . . villagers are peasants'.[136] Knowledge, especially the knowledge of a field the social significance of which is matched only by its complexity and elusiveness, has the power to influence, to mobilize human beings for action, to make changes and to halt them. All this may make the life of the students of peasant societies, who know their job and speak their minds, worthwhile and exciting, or, to put it boldly, path-breaking and revolutionary.

136 Mann, *The Social Framework of Agriculture*, p. 304.

8

The Peasants Are Coming
Peasants Who Travel, Migrants Who Labour and Marxists Who Write *(1977)*

This text was written as an intervention in the topical debate concerning inter-state migration of labour which was then changing the ethnic map of Europe. It was first published in Race and Class, *20 (1978). The comprehension of a new underclass of menials – Turks in Germany, North Africans and Spaniards in France, Italians in Switzerland, and so on – became a focus of debate. What follows was written as a polemic against the characteristic blind spot where peasantry is concerned in what passed as the orthodox Marxist political economy of migration. It exemplified how much the removal of this particular blinker matters for better comprehension of actual social issues, offering a more comprehensive historical, social and global perspective to social analysis of contemporary societies.*

Since the late 1950s the so-called labour migration of 15 million has literally changed the face of Western Europe. It has come unexpectedly, leaving the social scientists once more behind – a new theoretical problem *ex post factum*. The dispute which followed has led during the last half of the decade to the remarkably general acceptance of an essentially Marxist analysis of labour migration as the dominant mode of explanation of that phenomenon. While the list of publications resorting to it grows, the spokesmen for other views have recently kept remarkably silent. By now the essential tenets of this explanation have penetrated even into the objectivized language of UN and EEC bodies, boards and reports, becoming increasingly repetitive – a sure sign of maturity or senility within social sciences. One can treat in the same vein the recent call for the formalization of it all within a specific 'theory of its own, which would then have to be integrated into a general theory of the capitalist system of production'.

It is probably time to try to take stock of the new conceptual arrivals before new common sense and/or new orthodoxies rigidify and settle.

What is the place of this new wave within social theorizing? How satisfactory is the new approach in explaining 'stubborn data' which refused to fit other theories and concepts? How consistent is it within the Marxist theoretical heritage it claims? Most importantly, where do we go from there? (Or alternatively, is it all closed and shut with the major components of the formula established?)

To make it less abstract let us refer to a specific text. Nikolinakos's article in *Race and Class* has presented the paradigm in an orderly enough fashion to bring out its points of strength and weakness.[1] It also called for a debate, a call not yet heeded. The notes which follow are not directed at the author but simply put to use a crisp presentation of what it is all about – 'it' being the current stage reached in the mainstream of theorizing about labour migration, declaring allegiance to Marxist political economy.[2] Also, the form used there will be followed, i.e. notes concerning essentials without much attempt at final cosmetics or full display of evidence.

Nikolinakos's thesis begins by a self-definition, placing those views in contradiction to classical and neo-classical economics. These, we are told, assumed a harmonious society and explained migration of labour as mobility of factors of production, determined by laws of supply and demand. Such an approach is castigated as ahistorical, abstract and one-sided because it leaves out the political, structural and demographic factors which matter. Instead accumulation of capital is placed in the centre of the explanation offered, clarifying the native workers' shift into better-paid jobs, while emigrants take on the role of the labour 'reserve army', thereby securing 'the growth and the standard of living of the West European countries', providing a structural substitute to external colonies by internal ones. The demographic processes involved (e.g. 'population pressure' in the countries of emigration) are not autonomous but also a function of capital accumulation, perpetuating dependency between the capitalist centre and its peripheries. Countries of emigration are those which have been dependent on the colonial powers and assigned to produce food and raw materials. Through

---

1 M. Nikolinakos, 'Notes Toward a General Theory of Migration in Late Capitalism', *Race and Class*, XVII (1975), no. 1, from which the quotation above was taken.

2 The most significant work published in the UK was probably S. Castles and G. Kosack, *Immigrant Workers and Class Structure in Western Europe* (London, 1973). For a few more examples differing in particulars but close in general conclusions, see P.M. Worsley, 'Proletarians, Sub-proletarians, Lumpenproletarians, Marqinalidados, Migrants, Urban Peasants and Urban Poor', *Sociology*, 10; A. Ward, 'European Capitalism's Reserve Army', *Monthly Review*, 27 (1975), no. 6; A. Sivanandad, 'Race, Class and the State', *Race and Class*, XVII (1976), no. 4; J. Power, *Western European Migrant Workers* (London, 1976).

migration, capitalism stabilizes this state of affairs as potential social disturbances and de-revolutionizing workers are exported, while the metropolis benefits from being able to send them home in the periods of recession. Migrant sub-proletarians are exploited simultaneously as individuals, as a class and as natives of a dependent country. All the same to them it means material improvement. The class analysis offered places to labour migrants as sub-proletarians, unmasking the structural character of exploitation, and is expressed in the political call to migrants and native workers to unite, because 'in the final analysis there is objectively no interest specific to migratory workers.'

Without doubt the global process of accumulation of capital is central for the understanding of the stream of labour into Western Europe during the last two decades. Focusing on it made for the considerable achievements of Marxist analysis in the field and explains its persuasive power even with its ideological foes and with the 'non-committed'. To say this is to say much. To stop at this is to fail to see what still needs doing. It is my contention that the earlier paragraph faithfully codifies, beside considerable achievements, a related list of widespread and often repeated conceptual weaknesses and blind spots which weaken its illuminations. It is so in terms of the general characterization of the phenomenon and the data selected. It is also so on its own theoretical terms, i.e. those of Marxist thought. What follows therefore is not a dismissal, or substitution for, this analysis, but rather a claim of the necessity of its supplementation and critical review before self-congratulatory trivialization takes its toll.

1 Old Fogies and Fair Enemies

One of the favourite sports of academics on the Left is to caricature those they criticize, i.e. to present them as silly old fogies, and then to amuse the admiring public of believers by knocking them down. It is indeed abstract, not to say untrue, to refer to alternative/past migration theorists as claiming simply a harmonious world reflected in economic laws. To begin with, the very model of harmony assumes a problematic of disharmony and adjustment (e.g. 'moving equilibrium', etc.) and not only harmony *per se*. More importantly, the issue was never treated in a one-disciplinary format, i.e. as that of economics, for sophisticated non-Marxists know also that it will not do. That is where sociology comes in ('bourgeois' can be prefixed by those who like such labels). Within the relevant conceptual framework (mostly that of functionalism) the problematic and harsh realities of migration were since the days of Park both acknowledged and extensively studied in ways far from simplistic.[3] These theorists' conceptual framework (i.e. 'economizing'), the attempts to treat it all as problems of 'culture', 'assimilation' and 'acculturation', the tendency to treat migrants as individuals only (within a 'melting pot'), the vagueness about class hierarchies within the 'host countries', were all analytically limiting and inherently ideological in nature. The model of harmony was duly attacked and is by now very much 'in the dog-house' even with many of its past adherents. Which is all very far from treating it as non-existent or devoid of any illumination.

It will be only fair to say here that, while my criticism is true of Nikolinakos, other writers closely similar in outlook do not leave functional sociology out of consideration. Yet practically all of them assume at least a fake dualization of the conceptual field into 'them' (i.e. believers in social harmony) as against 'us' (i.e. Marxists, of course). That will not do, even if caricatures are otherwise avoided. Historically 'in between' and as an important stage before the Marxist impact came to be felt, a third conceptual position became a rallying point of many of the radicals. I am referring to the 'race relations theories', which for a spell took the lead in criticizing functionalism, offering an alternative designation of the issue as a group problem with a distinctive type of theorizing (usually close to symbolic interactionism) and terminology (e.g. 'visibility', 'dualistic folk-taxonomy', etc.).[4] Once again, these were rightly attacked for being theoretically insufficient and partial, politically open to xenophobic excesses and in considerable troubles with evidence once they depart from their Anglo-Saxon lands of origin (for how does one account this way for the treatment of Italian migrants within Switzerland or the preference of the very black people of Martinique over the Algerians in France?).[5] Its retreat, often blending into some sort of Marxism, does not mean its non-existence or the possibility of dropping it from conceptual debate.

All that is important not only because of the virtues of exactitude within a scholarly discourse. Far from belonging to the history of misconceptions (by now 'overcome') or else to the ideological armoury of the enemies (to be sunk), the views, achievements and limitations of those schools are immanent in the Marxist analyses of today. Which is not to call for a purge but to recall Marx's belief that only by integrating the best of his opponents' knowledge and achievements can his own type of social science flourish. Moreover, it is to assume with fair

---

3 R.E. Park, 'Human Communities', *Race and Culture* (New York, 1952). For a contemporary study of relevance see S. Patterson, *Dark Strangers* (London, 1976).

4 Most of the 'Black Power' publications took up that position. For an academic presentation see M. Banton, *Racial Minorities* (London, 1972).

5 Castles and Kosack, *Immigrant Workers*, p. 444; M. Bennoune, 'Meghribin Migrant Workers in France', *Race and Class*, XVII (1975), no. 1.

certainty future conceptual reappearance of the earlier paradigms with their sophistication enhanced by Marxist critique.

2 Class 'Here' and 'There'

Much more central and specific to the issues in hand is the peculiar, not to say amazing, class analysis offered within the theses referred to. We see a global society consisting of metropolis and periphery, the first exploiting the second. There is a class structure at the metropolis side of the picture: the bourgeoisie (late-capitalist) which controls the means of production, workers who do not, a foreign sub-proletariat at the very bottom. So far so good. But something dramatic happens to this class analysis once it turns to 'countries of emigration'. For there seem to be no classes there, at least none mentioned. The every-so-often repeated global model of migration is that of ethnic groups, i.e. Turks, Algerians, Spaniards, etc., which, by the fact of crossing frontiers, perform the no mean trick of becoming a class, i.e. proletarians, to which a prefix 'sub' can be added on demand. A non-class society of emigration (or is it one-class society of potential migrants?) is postulated by omission – a conceptual twin brother to the non-class 'host societies' of the models employed by the functionalist theorists of migration not so long ago.

Who are 'the migrants' at the other side of the divide which seemed to stop the penetrating gaze of the 'Western' class analysts? With few manifest exceptions (e.g. the West Indians in the UK), those are mostly peasants in the sense in which this class has been specifically defined.[6] Furthermore, for classes do not exist in a vacuum, the peasants referred to belong to the stage in history which was usually defined in Europe as the 'early stages of industrialization'. Many of them come directly from the villages of Turkey, India, Algeria, Morocco, Portugal, Sicily, etc. Some of the others puzzle statisticians by going first into the slums of the native towns to proceed within a few years to the foreign metropolis and be registered as 'from Istanbul', etc. (This is not the place to offer the proof of all that but enough of the proof exists by now.)[7] In some of the expositions the fact of 'rural origin' of the migrants (whatever that

6 Be it by Marxist originals or contemporary analysts; i.e. K. Marx, *Precapitalist Economic Formations* (London, 1964); or B. Galeski, *Basic Concepts of Rural Sociology* (Manchester, 1972); T. Shanin, *Peasants and Peasant Societies* (Harmondsworth, 1971); E.R. Wolf, *Peasants* (Englewood Cliffs, NJ, 1966).

7 e.g. for North Africa, see Bennoune, 'Meghribin Migrant Workers in France'; for Turkey see A. Kudat, *Stability and Change in the Turkish Family at Home and Abroad* (International Institute of Comparative Social Studies publication: Berlin, 1975), or N. Abadan-Unat, *Migration and Development* (Ankara, 1976); etc.

means: gentlemen farmers? rural priests? wage labourers? paupers?) is indeed mentioned in a passing fashion. The reference is usually as dismissive as silence in so far as its class significance is concerned.

But what does it matter? Granted the good joke, and the sociology-of-knowledge-insights, of the analytical short-sightedness in presenting such a lopsided omission as a paper 'relating every aspect of the phenomenon of migration to its class characteristics' (Nikolinakos, 'Notes Towards a General Theory of Migration in Late Capitalism', p. 14), is it all truly relevant to the understanding of labour migrants? After all, they are now mostly urban and (sub-) proletarian. What does it matter what they *were*?

It does matter most decisively because a Marxist, or any other, class analysis can dismiss history only at its analytical peril. Migration is a sequence even to those least inclined to see the present as history. Peasants in towns differ from old proletarians. Labour migrants cannot be fully understood as a group without bringing into the picture their origins, dynamics and global context. Without such any class analysis will be indeed ahistorical and one-sided.

To specify the significance of that one must look more closely at peasants who travel, migrants who labour and Marxists who write.

3 Peasants Who Travel

The process of industrialization has been also a process of depeasantiz-ation. To remember (or to remind oneself of) this context is to be able to call for our purposes on comparable data, comparative experience and analytical expertise already available. It is also to delineate relevant comparisons elsewhere, e.g. Mexicans in the US, Finns in Sweden, or 'blacks' in South Africa, as well as to categorize diversity between the labour migrants from essentially peasant societies and those (in the minority) who are not, e.g. the Punjabis versus the West Indians in the UK. Sivanandan's discussion of the differences between the West Indians and Asians in England can be indeed considered in those terms.[8] To proceed farther afield and deeper, one is guided towards the relevant writings of Znaniecki and Marx, surprisingly 'fresh' in clarifying the two poles of depeasantization via migration into foreign metropoles (on one hand when villages stay, on the other hand when villages collapse).[9] It is also to have a further insight reinforced: peasant fodder has been

8 See Sivananadad, 'Race, Class and the State', pp. 359–62.

9 See W.I. Thomas and F. Znaniecki, *The Polish Peasant in Europe and America* (New York, 1958); K. Marx, *Capital*, vol. I (Harmondsworth, 1976).

necessary to have the industrialization wave going at its most effective. The explanation of that is, once more, very much an analytical achievement of the past presented in the studies of 'primitive accumulation' from Marx through Preobrazhenskii and as far as Baran.[10] The availability of peasants, to be 'structurally disintegrated' and squeezed, has been central to industrialization/capital accumulation in that it offered cheap, hardened manual labour eminently exploitable and with the expenses of its reproduction charged elsewhere (i.e. carried by their own villages). 'Enclosing' peasant lands, the expansion of markets through destruction of crafts, and the squeeze of cheap raw materials out of the colonial peasantry were also highly relevant here. But it was the peasant labour input which seems decisive, for it could rarely be substituted. To get it 'all' moving, one has to make peasants move.

That was made easier by the fact that the often-accepted image of static, land-bound peasants is but a prejudice of the jet-traveller's point of view. The world we live in is still very much defined by peasants and peasant sons who travelled and pushed forward frontiers in their inevitable and powerful search for land, be it in Russia, China, Vietnam, Sudan, America, etc. To make their 'programme' complete, a dream of somewhat unspecified liberty was often added and a stubborn will to repeasantize as soon as possible. Such moves were specifically patterned and well institutionalized within the life of the peasant communities: the peasant son going away to settle anew, or to come back after having provided for (impending) marriage or to pay off taxes, etc. There was also a clear and consistent selection of the more educated and adventurous, the often poor yet not the poorest. There were other consistent and institutionalized correlations there, e.g. the relation between family position, the land available and the tendency to return.

During the last two centuries a new stage in peasant migration has begun with the gradual closing of 'open frontiers' and at the same time industrialization, and so peasants have been increasingly redirected into towns, often foreign. Yet within this new stage peasant migrants have usually carried many of the old characteristics: the specific self-selection of those who migrate, the group character of migrants in the new place, the dream of return. Peasants were never the only newcomers into the industrial milieu of the West, but they were the most numerous.

One immediate conclusion is that any analysis of labour migration must consider not only the characteristics of metropolitan capitalism but also the processes of disintegration and change in the rural economies and societies. Both are doubtlessly related, yet at the same time rela-

10 Marx, *Capital*, vol. 1; E. Preobrazhensky, *The New Economics* (Oxford, 1965); P. Baran, *The Political Economy of Growth* (New York, 1962).

tively autonomous in characteristics. This is why no simplistic 'background' which 'disintegrates' under the impact of 'capitalism' (all non-specified) will do; there must be a more substantial analysis of actual happenings.[11]

Secondly, one cannot quite proceed to study labour migration without incorporating in it a considerable amount of study of urban processes within the so-called developing societies and 'peripheries', especially of their slums.[12] The discussion of the dual economy by Santos is relevant here, while McGee's very title speaks for itself: 'Peasants in the cities: a paradox, a paradox, a most ingenious paradox'.[13]

Some of the conclusions up to date should be critically examined, opening vistas for further thought. The model of capitalism implicit in the approach discussed above suffers from over-rationalization or 'hyper-intentionality'. To put it otherwise, it is based on the assumption that a class of capitalists knows best what is best for the development of capitalism and runs national and international affairs accordingly. Yet a possibility and indeed necessity of what the late Ossowskii once called the problem of 'unexpected results of socialist planning' must be at least as significant within the capitalist realm. The belief in the unlimited capacity of capitalism to expand under its own steam has been a favourite self-mystification of capitalists and economists alike. One of the expressions of it was the politically promoted state policy of de-peasantization in Western Europe, which considerably strengthened the spontaneous processes already operational in that direction. It meant over-depeasantization, which turned into a major bottleneck in the 1950s. Within a short time the still remaining local peasants (of, say, South Italy) and other sources of available labour force (e.g. East Germans leaving for West Germany or the French Algerians 'coming back home') were 'utilized'. The answer to the still ongoing shortages was found in labour migration, i.e. a 'repeasantization' of Western Europe from foreign sources. Which should help to place and 'date' it all historically and globally.

More importantly, it should put at doubt and open for new debate the analysis of the mechanism of self-perpetuation of industrial capitalism. The assumption has been that once the input of peasant sweat, local and colonial, got the accumulation of capital going, capitalist expansion

---

11 e.g. E. Wolf, *Peasant Wars of the Twentieth Century* (London, 1969), for discussion of a relevant crisis of peasantry.

12 For an example of such work see M.B. Kiray, *Squatter Housing: Fast Depeasantation and Slow Workisation in Underdeveloped Countries*, (Proceedings of the World Congress of Sociology: Varna, 1970).

13 T.G. McGee, 'Peasants in the Cities: A Paradox, A Paradox, A Most Ingenious Paradox', *Human Organization*, 32 (1973), no. 2.

would be self-perpetuating and extend itself at a brisk and incessant pace, some jerks and jolts admitted. Is it so? Should it be the case that European capitalism is unable to perform 'booms' without 'primitive accumulation', i.e. by swallowing peasants (and not only oil or 'environment'), what does it mean in terms of prediction and prejudices concerning its growth and future global development?

4 Migrants Who Labour

All those considerations apart, how does the upgrading of peasants from the footnote to the page help us to understand the characteristics of the present labour migrant/sub-proletarian communities? The answer to that must be related to a three-fold consideration.

Firstly and generally, class analysis which disregards the historical past is an abstraction at its worst, i.e. a reification. Consciousness and action are doubtlessly shaped by the objective context of economic conflict, the 'place in relations of production', as well as by social structure in the broadest sense. Within these structures of determination 'men make their own history', even though 'they do not make it just as they please: they do not make it under circumstances chosen by themselves, but under circumstances directly encountered, given and transmitted from the past.' That is why, and as a part of that past, 'the tradition of all the dead generations weigh like a nightmare on the brain of the living.'[14] To see only the immediate determinations is the type of theoretical history which is no good for man or beast, except in the clearance of PhDs or in impressing male and female 'blue stockings'. Anything more practical and relevant, from political mobilization through policy intervention and as far as the prediction of the actual reality, necessitates analysis in which past and present, structure and process lock.

Next, a central component of our whole attitude to the issue in hand must be the measure of contact with and the tendency to return back into the villages by the ex-peasants/labour migrants/ sub-proletarians. In the terms of political economy, this is a major way in which they differ qualitatively from the native working class (with colour, nationality and culture dropped from consideration by the terms of analysis). This is also the way to pin down retained 'peasanthood' in aspects open to inspection. Once again one runs into two economists' prejudices: (1) the belief that the 'reserve army' will be sent back when the capitalist 'boom' ends; and (2) the assumption that labour migrants will not go

14 K. Marx and F. Engels, *Selected Works* (Moscow, 1969), p. 398.

back spontaneously (for who in his right mind would go back into poverty and lower income-per-capita rates?). That is wrong on both counts.

The replacement of the 'boom' by an economic crisis after about 1972 did not reduce the numbers of labour migrants in Western Europe. Nor are their rates of unemployment higher than those of the natives. A new situation developed in which the labour migrants are able to take over the lowest paid, 'dirtiest' and most unpleasant jobs in society from the native workers, the latter group preferring to fall back on unemployment 'dole' rather than to accept such jobs any more. The influx of new labour migrants is limited by legislation, but no legal steps have actually dislodged migrant communities or made much impact on the massive 'illegal' migration which is taking place. The explicit interest of the local employers in having them, and the strategems of survival of the migrants, secure it well enough.

The dream of return, rich and successful, into one's own village has been the grand utopia, round which strategies, norms and claims were structured by the migrants. Nor were those only dreams, for one can barely find a South Italian or Irish village without some 'Americans', i.e. returnees. Indeed, to sustain a dream one usually needs some consistent proofs of its realism, even if only limited in scope. We are still short of serious and long-term studies of the matter, but some earlier comparative figures may prove indicative here. The figure for Poles, mostly peasants, who returned at the turn of the century from the rich, prosperous and free US into the poverty-stricken oppression and landlessness of Poland was 30 per cent, while the whole rate for migrants to and emigrants from the US to Europe during 1897–1918 was estimated to be 47 per cent.[15] Furthermore most of all those seemed to return to villages.

In so far as Western Europe today is concerned, many of the migrants stay on – as expected. More than expected seem to return of their own volition despite fear of not being able to come back again to the larger incomes etc. of the West.

Collective dreams interwoven with some measures of reality are a serious business when characterization of social groups is concerned, and especially so when political consciousness is analysed. Consider economics: these sub-proletarians show the highest percentage of savings ever seen within the societies they live in – quite exceptional for proletarians (especially 'sub-proletarians') of any type. Consider the invested savings: massive components of it go into land and houses back

---

15 Thomas and Znaniecki, *The Polish Peasant in Europe and America*, p. 1511; C.P. Kindelberger, *European Post-War Growth – The Role of Labour Supply* (Harvard, 1967).

home or else are saved in local banks.[16] Consider the structure of
political organization: the labour migrants are said to organize within
associations which play a multi-faceted role as a union, a party, a club, a
cooperative; very different from what is happening around them, yet
directly related to the peasant way of doing things, as reported by every
student of political sociology of peasantry.[17] (Also, labour migrants,
supposedly backward in the experience of class struggle, consistently
and loyally support native strike actions, while the natives do not
support theirs.)[18] Consider mental illnesses: Nikolinakis and many
others are quite behind the times in assuming higher rates among
migrants, for the opposite is true – a peculiarity which puts them apart
when compared to the native proletarians.[19] One can proceed, but by
now conclusions can possibly be drawn.

To recount, labour migrants cannot be realistically treated either as
'objectively' similar to local proles or simply a downtrodden group of
people who fell from the moon. One must see them in a context which is
both global and dynamic, assuming movement of people, resources and
communication in both directions as well as history in its broadest sense.
The labour migrant community is a residuum resulting from selective
return, i.e. very much an on-going process. In their social and political
characteristics, besides the effects of a late capitalist society, labour
migrants carry aspects of peasanthood not only through the traces of the
past in the present, but also in terms of contacts, both real and imaginary (but remember the importance of dreams, especially in the political
context).

5 Marxists Who Write

Analysis is ever a two-sided process. Learning Marxism comes best
through working with it. While the Marxist analysis clarified much of the
labour-migrant problematic, it is as true that these studies advanced
Marxist analysis *in toto*, by bringing closer the desks of those who write
to human experience and to struggles which matter. In that dual sense,
even with all of the points already made we are not yet at the end of

16 e.g. for Turks in West Berlin: land purchase 30.6%; home purchase 20.7%; bank
deposits 40.9%; luxury investment 6.5%; technical equipment 1.3%. Total 100.0%
Kudat, *Stability and Change*, p. 77.

17 Worsley, 'Proletarians, Sub-Proletarians', as compared to Galeski, *Basic Concepts*.

18 Power, *Western European Migrant Workers*.

19 S. Ramon, T. Shanin and J. Strimpel, 'The Peasant Connection: Social Background
and Mental Health of Migrant Workers in Western Europe', *Mental Health in Society*, 4
(1977).

even the most cursory list of questions concerning labour migration which need investigation.

Firstly, there is the question not yet even posed, let alone tackled, of why social analysts, Marxist and non-Marxist, failed to predict one of the most significant changes in the social face of Western Europe. If the most current theorizing is right and Marxism carries straightforward answers to all, why did it come *ex post factum*? Were there no Marxists around before? Or is something the matter with Marxist analysis (like, for example, an in-built West-centred bias)?

Secondly, the concept of 'false consciousness' for the explanation of the anti-labour-migrant 'prejudices' within the native working class will need much more analytical muscle and sophistication before its value becomes clear. How far does interest in 'final results' go in defining actual class consciousness and political struggle? Where does it all place labour migration as against the European socialist movement? What policy of migration is to be fought for other than the self-evident and rather toothless declaration of 'equal treatment' and control of local police harrassment running wild? Moreover, how about the case made by Emanuel that the consciousness of the native and migrant workers reflects correctly a basic structural difference of interests between both?[20] To recall, his analysis reproduces in a new form what used to be referred to as the 'labour aristocracies' thesis. The conclusion may be programmatically unpleasant, but that is, if anything, an additional reason to look at the issue with particular care.

Thirdly, consideration of the future must be related to reconsideration of past and present. The issue of the 'second generation' of labouring migrants within the cities of Western Europe looks different once related to the disappearance of what was referred to as peasant background (to show once more the value of comparison and the general character of the issue, see for example Vol. 2 of the study by Thomas and Znaniecki referred to above).

Finally, the theoretical issues of the links of class and history, of global dynamics and national structures, etc., are of course far from being simple issues of labour migration. The problems involved will need more than discussion of a specific issue of migration can offer. It is resolvable within a broader framework of analysis or not at all.

20 A. Emanuel, *Unequal Exchange* (New York, 1972), especially pp. 178–82.

9

Social Characteristics of Peasant Political Action (1965)

What follows is part D of the article initially entitled 'Peasants as a Political Factor' (The Sociological Review, 14 [1966]), *the earlier part of which appears as item 2. It is linked also to the short aside about peasantry as a class (item 10).*

The extensive work concerning peasant political action published since these notes went into print (e.g. Womack, Wolf, Scott, Esteva, Zamosc, to name but a few,[1] as well as my own work devoted to Russian peasants in 1905–7,[2] supported, on the whole, these tentative generalizations. Their main weakness lay in their rather sketchy nature and scanty consideration of the impact on the peasants of non-peasant political forces which the peasants faced. Such a broadening of focus in my work came later, especially in the 1980s.

The political impact of the peasantry has been marked on the whole by its socio-political weaknesses. The segmentation of peasants into families, local communities and clans and the differentiation of interest within the communities had made for difficulties in the crystallizing of nationwide aims and symbols and the developing of national leadership and organizations (this made in turn for what I have called 'low class-nesses'). Technological backwardness, especially in the field of communications, weaponry and tactical expertise, has brought to naught many attempts at political action. Peasantry has had its socio-political points of strength, however, especially its being the main food producer, being dispersed in rural areas and being numerically preponderant. Monopoly of food production often proved of crucial importance in times of crisis and provided for an extra measure of ability to survive in

1 For particulars see T. Shanin (ed.), *Peasants and Peasant Societies* (Oxford, 1987), second edition.
2 T. Shanin, *Russia 1905–7: Revolution as a Moment of Truth* (New Haven, 1985).

confrontations. The vastness of the countryside could serve as a stronghold. Numerical strength could tip the balance. Yet in the long run it was rather the basic weaknesses of the peasantry which tended to stand out. The peasantry usually proved no match for smaller, closely knit, better organized and technically superior groups, and has, time and time again, been double-crossed or suppressed politically or by force of arms. Yet peasantry cannot in consequence be ignored and its actions dismissed. It is not only victors and rulers who determine political reality.

In the last one hundred and fifty years the spread of industrialization and mass culture has given peasantry some new possibilities for communication and for cultural and political cohesion. Yet, at the same time, it has lowered the importance of the countryside in terms of national production, curbed the impact of its 'food monopoly' by developing international trade, stimulated village-level polarization and increased the government forces' relative advantage in terms of organization, mobility, weaponry and other forms of repressive power. The course of historical development has seemed therefore to weaken farther the peasant's political power and potential. Yet it has been the twentieth century when the political role of the peasantry has proved particularly significant and begun to draw growing attention.

This is influenced by the broader societal context. The peasants' chances of influencing the political sphere increase sharply in times of national crises. When non-peasant social forces clash, when rulers are divided or foreign powers attack, the peasantry's attitude and action may well prove decisive. Whether this potential is realized is mainly dependent on the peasants' ability to act then in unison, with or without formal organization. This, in turn, has been dependent on the cohesion of the peasantry, i.e. its economic, social and cultural homogeneity and the reflection of these in the ideological and political spheres.

The particular patterns of peasant political action are determined by the peasantry's character as a social entity. In the contemporary world we may discern three main types of it:

(1) *Autonomous class action*, in the sense suggested by the class theory defined in Marx's own lifetime. In this type of action, a social class crystallizes in the course of conflict, creates its own nationwide organization, works out its ideology, aims, and symbols, and produces leaders, mostly from within its own ranks. For today's peasantries, this pattern of political action is the least frequent. Some of the 'Green International' parties in the Eastern Europe of the 1920s, the peasant unions in Russia in 1905 and China in 1926, the Zapata movement in Mexico and their counterparts in the rest of the world need to be studied comparatively to understand the mechanics of this type of peasant

action as well as its relatively limited occurrence and scanty final success.

(2) *Guided political action*, in which the social group concerned is moved by an external power-elite which unites it. This pattern of action is especially important where peasantry is concerned. The cyclical stability of the farm and the village and the political implications of this are generally overcome only by a severe crisis, matched by an exogenous factor of sweeping political and emotional power. Such an external organizer of the peasantry may be found in millennial movements, secret societies, the Russian cossacks, French Bonapartism or Mao's people's army, which were alike in providing the peasantry with the missing element of unity on an inter-village and inter-regional scale. The common element found in these very different movements is the existence of a closely-knit group of activists, with its own impetus, specific organizational structure, aims and leadership – a group for which the peasantry is an object of leadership or manipulation. The peasantry, in this case, may be 'used' (i.e. deliberately tricked into some action alien to its own interest) or 'led to achieve its own aims': but the very definition of 'aims' is in the hands of the qualitively distinct leaders. The peasants' interests and attitudes are only one of the factors taken by them into account. Marx expressed such a situation when referring to the French peasantry in the mid-nineteenth century: 'they are . . . incapable of enforcing their class interest in their own name, whether through a parliament or through a convention. They cannot represent themselves, they must be represented. Their representative must at the same time appear as their master'.[3] The only thing to be objected to in this statement is its absoluteness, which was refuted by later events.

The low 'classness' of the peasantry makes the study of peasant movements especially illuminating for the sociological analysis of the external elites which lead them. The peasantry's limited counter-influence on such leaders makes the elite group's dynamics appear in 'purer' form. Moreover, it also helps us look at the problem of social groups (such as Russian soldiers in 1917–18) which are acting temporarily as class-like entities but do not bear all the features of a social class, and at their place in political processes.

(3) *Amorphous political action.* This pattern seems to be highly typical of peasants' impact on politics, and may take two forms:

3 K. Marx, 'The Eighteenth Brumaire of Louis Bonaparte', in K. Marx and F. Engels, *Selected Works* (London, 1950), vol. 1, p. 302.

(a) Local riots which 'suddenly' emerge as short outbursts of accumulated frustration and rebellious feeling. On the whole easily repressed by the central authorities, these riots may act as a check on the state policy and stimulate its change. When related to crises in other spheres, riots may develop into nationwide movements capable of a determining effect on major political processes.

(b) Peasant passivity. The conceptual grasp of passivity as a factor of dynamics poses some complex questions. Yet the spontaneous restriction of production by the Russian peasantry in 1920 proved strong enough to frustrate the will of a government victorious in a war against numerous and powerful enemies.

Government decrees and orders the world over have been voided of effect by their spontaneous, stubborn and silent non-fulfilment by peasantry. As suggested in a recent lecture by R.E.F. Smith, passive resistance is actually a specific peasant contribution to politics, elaborated, sophisticated and articulated as it became by Tolstoy and Gandhi. The relationship between basic social features of peasant society as discussed above and passive resistance seems evident. On the other hand, the influence of conservative peasant 'apathy' has often proved decisive for the victory of the 'establishment' over revolutionaries. Once again, such events must be understood in relation to the peasant social structure, consciousness and experience.

Finally, turning to other forms of political activity, *armed action* has had a special place of importance in the internal life of societies which include numerous peasants. Clausewitz's remark that war is an extension of politics by other means holds true not only for the relations between states. As to this extension of peasant political action, its particularities were expressed mostly through three areas: army service, guerilla activity and the military culture of the armed forces, often labelled their 'morale'.

(1) The modern conscript army is one of the few nationwide organizations in which the peasantry actively participates. The segmentation of the peasantry is thereby broken. The cultural intercourse involved, even when there is no nationalist indoctrination, teaches the peasant soldier to think in national and not only village-limited terms. He is also taught organization, complex cooperative action, coordination, modern techniques and military skills. The army provides him with a hierarchical institution in which he may rise as a leader and receive the training necessary for it. This increase in the peasant's ability to act politically would, while in the army, be largely curbed by rigid disciplines and by

the controls exercised by the non-peasant officer corps. Yet, in a time of crisis, the self-evident nature of authority declines and the preferences and attitudes reflected in the action (or in the refusal to act) of a largely peasant army may well become decisive.

Moreover, the experience gained in army service acts as an important influence in the villages. The ex-serviceman may become a leader and a channel through which outside influences reach other villagers. In attempting to organize politically, peasants frequently refer back to their army experience. The Russian *Tamanskaya armiya* and 'Green Army of the Black Sea', the FLN of Algeria, the Chinese 'People's Militia', and the Zapata and Villa armies in Mexico served not only as military organizations but also as the main political organizations – as political parties in arms. An army may bear, therefore, the marks of both the first and second type of political action described – i.e. of peasantry as 'a class for itself' and as a 'guided' socio-political entity.

(2) During the last decade, the success of guerilla warfare has moved it into the centre of public attention. American strategists tend to approach guerilla warfare as a military technique or tactic, to be taught by smart sergeants along with drill and target practice. Their failure in both guerilla and anti-guerilla warfare in Vietnam is the best comment on this view.

The social essence of guerilla warfare is that it offers the most suitable form for armed peasant action. The record of it seems to be as old as peasantry itself. Innumerable rebels, brigands and outlaws appear in the myth, the folk memory of every people, as well as in its real history. The ability of the guerilla 'army' to dissolve in times of need into the sympathetic peasant mass, to vanish into the expanses of the countryside, its ability to utilize various degrees of peasant militancy and friendly passivity, its capacity to survive without outside supplies and the adequacy for this type of warfare of relatively primitive weapons may make a guerilla force unbeatable by modern military methods.

Yet the essentially peasant character of guerilla warfare explains not only its strengths but also its weaknesses – the segmentation, the lack of crystallized ideology and aims, and the lack of stable membership. These essential weaknesses may be overcome by the injection of a hard core of professional rebels, turning the revolt into 'guided political action'. The professional rebels' nationwide ideological and organizational cohesion, their stability and zeal and their ability to work out a long-term strategy may turn a peasant revolt into a successful revolution. But the key to the understanding of successful guerilla warfare must be sought not in the marvels of the rebels' organization, but in their relationship with the peasantry; not in the military techniques of the few, but in the sociology of the mass.

(3) Last, there are the cultural and subjective determinants of military action generally labelled 'morale', whose resistance to quantification does not negate their importance. Peasant revolts all over the world display some common cultural features which seem to have been better caught by the arts than when dissected by the analytical tools of the social sciences. The picturesque image of the young peasant rebel challenges the mundane nature of everyday peasant life. The childish display of exhibitionism, described by Znaniecki[4] as typical of the peasant's attempt to establish his own personality when breaking out of rigid family ties, explains much of the spirit of the peasant fighters. The leader-hero, the legends which surround him, his 'personal charisma', to a large extent may take the place of ideology and organization as unifying factors. All these features influence the general character of peasant units as a fighting force, especially so in conditions of civil war.

4 W.I. Thomas and F. Znaniecki, *The Polish Peasant in Europe and America* (New York, 1958).

10

Peasant Politics: On the Empirical Peasantry and the Hypothetical Proletariat

An Extract (1971/1982)

The segment to follow formed a part of an article and debate about peasantry's political propensities and socialist revolution which linked to Vietnam's independence struggle. It was published first in Journal of Contemporary Asia, 1 (1972), no. 2, *created by Malcolm Caldwell to challenge the solid wall of specialized academic journals hostile to the cause of the Vietcong. To me it came as a polemical extension of my initial analytical work concerning peasant political action (items 2 and 9). To sweep away ideological chaff was then as important for the comprehension of the issue discussed as any statement of fact. In many ways this still holds true.*

The reconsideration of established concepts in the light of new, often non-European, developments lies at the core of the post-1968 debate. The discussion of the early 1970s about revolutionary classes and perspectives was both an example of it and an important case in itself. The argument unfolded within the basic framework of the Marxist tradition. This implied a common commitment to change aimed at abolishing the social base of exploitation and domination of human by human. It accepted a sociological perspective whose major components are the determining impact of political economy and of class conflict within social structure. It accepted revolutionary violence as the probable and indeed usual – though not obligatory – way of bringing about the necessary social changes. At this point, however, paths began to diverge.

One group of analysts looked to the Third World as the area where revolutionary conditions are ripe and where revolutions, which might develop into socialist ones, are on the cards. The industrial working class of the advanced capitalist societies, on the other hand, was increasingly diversified in numbers and sunk in complacency, derived in part from the benefits of the imperial spoils. The main weight of global capitalist exploitation fell most heavily upon the 'developing societies', in particular on the peasants and the urban poor of peasant background, who together form the major oppressed class(es) there. The established industrial working class in these countries has been privileged in relation to the peasant majority, the poorest urbanites, and the unemployed. It is also relatively small in numbers and will remain so until the imperialist controls that result in 'underdevelopment' are broken. Therefore, 'the masses in the exploited dependencies', i.e., the underprivileged classes – the peasants, the urban poor, *and* the workers, plus, perhaps, the 'intelligentsia' – 'constitute a force in the global capitalist system which is revolutionary in the sense Marx considered the proletariat of the early period of modern industrialization to be revolutionary.'[1]

Against this, others stuck to the more orthodox Marxist guns. The most advanced technology, the centres of power and knowledge, lie in the industrial societies, and it is therefore from there that socialism has to be established around the globe. It is the social character of the industrial working class – its unity on the shop floor, its skills acquired in dealing with advanced technology, its size, its propertylessness, and its explicit relations of conflict with the capitalists – which make it into the most – indeed the only – revolutionary and socialist class of our times.[2]

A closer look indicates that some of the very premises of that comparison were spurious. The peasants of the 'Proletarianists'' argument often seem realistic enough, their images backed by political experience and study. It is the image of the proletariat that has remarkably little to do with the actual life of the contemporary working class in industrialized capitalist societies. Indeed, the more one tries to match the real working class with its hypothetical model, the more the model looks either prehistoric, i.e. irrelevant to our times, or ahistoric, i.e. utopian. It is this hypothetical proletariat that outstrips real peasants in its revolutionary and socialist potential.

Let us try to turn this comparison of incomparables into comparative analysis of real social classes in a real world. An article by N. Harris published as part of the Third-Worldist/proletarianist debate provides a list of characteristics of the peasantry, or rather, of its political short-comings – as compared to the proletariat of an industrial metropolis.[3]

---

1 Paul M. Sweezy, 'The Proletariat in Today's World', *Tricontinental*, 9 (1968), p. 33.
2 For example, Ernest Mandel, 'The Laws of Uneven Development', *New Left Review* 59 (1970).
3 N. Harris, 'The Revolutionary Role of the Peasants', *International Socialism* (December/January 1969). See also a reply by Malcolm Caldwell, 'The Revolutionary Role of the Peasants', in the same issue.

Let us go through that list, comparing the political characteristics of empirical peasants with those of empirical industrial workers, rather than attempting to deduce them from a 'historico-philosophical theory whose supreme virtue', in Marx's words, 'consists of being supra-historical'.[4]

Peasants in their political struggles tend to fight for land rather than for broader political aims, to be preoccupied with local day-to-day concerns rather than with general long-term aims and complex ideologies. That, no doubt, is true. But so do industrial workers: wages, pensions, and holidays simply take the place of land, rent, and taxes (the name for this limitation of horizons in the revolutionary lexicon is 'bread and butter issues', 'unionism', or 'economism'). Only at long intervals and under conditions of extraordinary crisis have the workers directly attacked the system of property relations by seizing the means of production, what-ever the explanation and immediate impulse – in Russia in 1917–18, in northern Italy in 1919, in Shanghai in 1927. So did Mexican peasants under Zapata, Russian peasants in 1905–6, and again in 1917–19, and Chinese peasants in 1926. Both peasants and proletarians in these confrontations dominated the political scene for a short while, were eventually 'calmed down' by reforms and/or brutal suppression, and finally lost impetus and impact while different social forces took over.

The workers develop nationwide class consciousness and class organ-ization, becoming consequently 'a class for themselves', while the peasants remain disunited and politically naive. (Harris uses the example of the Russian peasants who, while fighting landlords, worshipped the tsar.) The claim that there are important differences between workers and peasants holds true for the reasons indicated, i.e. that working in large industrial structures facilitates organization and self-organization. Not surprisingly, therefore, workers have often shown superiority over peasants in organizing nationwide associations and adopting nationwide symbols. But the relationship is anything but one-to-none. The political and revolutionary potential of the workers is by no means constant. We will return to this point shortly. On the other hand, the 'green move-ments' of the peasantry in Eastern Europe between World Wars I and II provide ample proof that peasants have the capacity to consolidate as a class and to create their own organizations through which to fight for political power. Poland, to give a specific instance, has seen powerful peasant parties (the SL, Piast, etc.), a real peasant prime minister (Witos, who to the horror of his staff was said 'not to use handker-chiefs'), and even, in the 1930s, a nationwide and reasonably successful peasant 'general strike'. The differences are therefore mainly ones of

4 For the full text, see the beginning of the second section of this essay.

degree and context. Incidentally, the bulk of Russian workers worshipped the tsar in 1904 as much as did peasants, as 'Bloody Sunday' in
January 1905 clearly proved. Only by 1917 had the bulk of the Russian
working class finally shed this faith – but by that time so had a crucial
part of the peasants.

*The peasants do not control their leaders; they are the object and tool,
rather than the subject, of political action.* That has been true, once
again, for peasants and workers alike. The article pointed to the fact
that the Communist Party of China was not an agent of the Chinese
peasant class, and that its leadership was drawn mainly from the urban
intelligentsia; one could add that it was mainly of rural origin and that it
directed and utilized the rank and file, at times against the immediate
interest of peasants. No doubt this was substantially so. The same seems
to apply to the relations between the Bolsheviks and the Russian
workers. Lenin's writings (from *What Is To Be Done?* onward), and in
particular the type of organization he built, made this clear and legitimized it within the socialist movement as one of the necessities of
revolutionary action.

Time has not made that debate obsolete. The essentials of the
'proletarianist' view have been repeated with few modifications. Some
of the recent writings deconceptualized peasants altogether labelling
them the 'rural detachment of the petit bourgeoisie'.[5] What is at issue is
not simply the social and political characteristics of peasants within
different areas and conditions. (Indeed, a similar conceptual denigration
could be documented for other social classes and groups in contemporary societies.) The image of the peasant is clearly used as an 'anti-model'
– an abstraction and a punching bag – in order to elevate the hypothetical proletariat and to justify its monopoly over the revolutionary imagination.

There are reasons why this type of reification – which depends on
false comparisons – has persisted within Marxist orthodoxy. Wishful
thinking is, as always, one reason – a wish to see change in the world we
ourselves live in, since it is industrial workers who form the massive
'lower class' in the societies to which Western intellectuals belong.
Taken to extremes this turns into the fallacy of dismissing deductively

5 For example, an article by James Petras, 'Revolutions and the Working Class', *New
Left Review*, 111 (1978), in which the specificity of the 'developing societies' was essen-
tially disregarded, the revolutionary capacity of the proletariat assumed to be innate, and
any public way to prove or disprove it dismissed as self-evidently unnecessary, indeed
slanderous of the subject matter. The quotation is taken from J. Ennew, P. Hirst, and K.
Tribe, 'Peasants as an Economic Category', *Journal of Peasant Studies*, 4 (1977), no. 4.
For a different view, see Teodor Shanin, 'Defining Peasants: Conceptualizations and
Deconceptualizations', *Peasant Studies*, 14 (1980), no. 4 [reprinted here as item 4].

and automatically as 'unscientific' any evidence or analysis not reducible to the simple 'proletarians are revolutionary' proposition. Secondly, some of these images of peasants result from faithfully following Marx's views of over a century ago. Marx lived in a world in which peasants had formed the majority for millennia, while the industrial working class was still in nappies, something new, promising, and exciting. During the following century, there was a particularly rapid transformation of urban-industrial society in the centres of world capitalism. Hence, whereas the majority of students of 'developing societies' can still recognize contemporary peasants from the picture drawn by Marx in the *Eighteenth Brumaire*, and his comments there seem still remarkably 'fresh' and useful,[6] a contemporary industrial worker in Detroit or Coventry is nearly unrecognizable in terms of nineteenth-century descriptions of workers, whether they be by Marx, Booth, Zola, or Dickens. Marx was, after all, a better scholar than a prophet – an epitaph which would no doubt please him greatly. Finally, peasants (and intellectuals) do not fit well into global theoretical structures of elegant simplicity. Those who prefer pure deduction to social investigation do not like them.

The manifest disparity between 'proletarianist' images and actual reality does not mean that 'peasantism' is the 'correct' alternative. Quite the contrary. Recent history has brought into question any belief in a single, natural, and sole revolutionary class. Revolutions have happened. They will no doubt happen again, and provide abundant evidence of class-determined political action. But the same evidence also demonstrates that different classes can be revolutionary, and that the revolutionary potential of the 'same' class may vary greatly in different social and historical contexts. That is why one cannot simply deduce revolutionary potential from a general definition. The central question is what the general conditions are under which successful revolutions 'from below' occur.[7] In other words, what must we concentrate on in making such an analysis, what are the component elements, and what are the relationships and contradictions between these components in a general 'model' of revolution, in which class analysis in a narrow sense constitutes a major and necessary input, but is insufficient on its own?

During the 1968 wave of revolutionary optimism, the discussion of revolution tended naturally to focus on the revolutionary camp, i.e. on those who are, or may become, revolutionaries. It usually underestimated the intrinsic power of the systems of social domination to mobil-

6 Karl Marx and Frederick Engels, *Selected Works*, vol. 1 (Moscow, 1973), especially pp. 478–83.

7 'Revolution from below' in the sense attached to the phrase in Isaac Duetscher, *The Great Contest* (London, 1960), i.e. when popular mass intervention plays a major role.

ize resources, to manipulate, and to readjust. Those capacities are not only immense, but still growing, and a more realistic way of putting the questions is, 'How do revolutions take place and succeed at all?' rather than, 'Why do revolutions not take place more frequently?'

11

Peasant Politics: Outsiders and Plenipotentiaries

An Extract (1970)

This item is taken from The Awkward Class *(Oxford, 1972), which followed my PhD study of Russian peasantry, 1910–25. The core of the book was devoted to reconsideration of the links between peasantry's social economy, mobility and political action in the Russian revolutionary era. (See item 14.)*

The text looks at the state-representing 'plenipotentiaries' – one of the major social categories in which peasant majorities meet directly the worlds outside the communities they live in. Up to a point it overlaps with the concept of 'a brocker' (as used by students of Latin America's rural environments), but it represents particularities of fact and of analysis.

Different scholars have stressed a peculiar characteristic of the inner diversity of peasant society. Marx's striking 'sack of potatoes', Durkheim's 'segments' in a society of 'mechanical solidarity', the 'vertical integration' of contemporary scholars have dealt with the same phenomenon of what may be termed the vertical segmentation of the peasant community.

. . . The Russian villages of the early New Economic Policy (*NEP*) era, 1921–7, showed a distinct pattern of vertical diversity and segmentation. A household, an informal group of friends, neighbours, a commune, and, at times, even a district (*volost'*) could validly be analysed this way. If attention is focused on the commune, as the peasants' most meaningful framework of political consciousness, the internal cohesion of its members was matched by the strain of their external relations with a variety of outsiders. The rural outsiders to a Russian peasant commune could be classified by a threefold typology: neighbours, strangers, and plenipotentiaries. (1) *Neighbour outsiders* may be defined as members of other peasant communes, essentially similar and sharing territorial boundaries which made both contact and conflict over land-holding unavoidable in the conditions of traditional farming. (2)

Stranger outsiders would be those who brought into the countryside social and cultural components alien to the peasant commune, disturbing to the basic consensus and violating the homogeneity of units. (3) *Plenipotentiary outsiders* would be agents of external centres of power acting as their rural transmission belts.

The revolution resulted in significant changes in the make-up of what were the rural outsiders to the peasant commune. The Russian landed nobility was eliminated at a single blow in 1917–18. The agrarian revolution led also to the destruction of the majority of enclosed farms; those remaining were an insignificant factor except in the west and north-west of Russia.

The unification of the bulk of the peasants in the communes and the increase in homogeneity of peasant households did not preclude neighbour outsiders' conflicts within the peasantry. Rural Russia witnessed unending hostility, quarrels, and blood-feuds between communes over land, meadows, forests, or over past grievances whose actual content had long been forgotten. Homogeneity did not equal unity, and segmentation (and consequent socio-political weakness) of the peasants on a national scale found ample local expression in the relations between neighbouring villages within the Russian peasantry of the post-revolutionary period. However, it was the interaction with qualitatively different groups and social structures which proved crucial for the Russian peasant communities . . .

1 The Plenipotentiary Outsiders

Examination of those in the villages who were 'outsiders' as far as the peasant commune was concerned reveals a complexity of groups and interrelations. Classification could be attempted by arranging these groups in order of their relative dissimilarity to or separateness from the majority of peasants. Such a scale would range from, at the bottom end, those peasants who were well integrated into the community but displayed some cultural characteristics brought from outside (e.g. re-immigrants from towns and ex-servicemen) to, at the top, some of the state-employed professionals sent down into an alien countryside and having barely any contact with peasants at all. Another classification could rank groups of outsiders according to their *type* of dissimilarity from the peasantry: the scale would range between two conceptual ideal types – stranger outsiders and plenipotentiary outsiders (the rural intelligentsia and the local administrators respectively, say). However, the major issue in the countryside was the problem of authority and power. Identification of the centres and of the structure of power-relationships provides yet another highly relevant classification of rural groups. Furthermore, this issue is related to the question of the execution of Soviet state policy in a situation in which there actually obtained a supremacy of communes over Rural Soviets. Analysis of the power structure may also clarify what were the dominant conflict-relationships in the countryside and what their impact was on the various possible future lines of social development.

The next layer 'up' from rural communes in terms of territorial organization was the *volost'*. A major centre of local power in the Soviet countryside of the 1920s was what might be called the '*volost'* caucus'. It drew its strength from representing and reflecting the two major national bureaucratic organizations; the state and the Bolshevik Party. Its hard core consisted of two substantially overlapping groups – the heads of the major branches of *volost'* administration (its *volost'* executive committee – the VIK – the militia, the judiciary) and the members of the party branch in the village which was the *volost'* centre. This hard core was surrounded by a small circle of close associates; the other members of the party in the *volost'*, Komsomol activists, and party sympathizers among the higher grade officials. The rank and file of the Komsomol, the majority of the chairmen of Rural Soviets, some ex-servicemen of the Red Army, and a few party sympathizers formed its periphery.

With Congresses of Soviets meeting rarely, the Executive Committees became the agencies of Soviet power. The VIKs developed into major centres of the Soviet administration of the peasant countryside. The membership of a VIK overlapped with that of the local party branch and of the other agencies located in the *volost'* centre. Somewhere in this complex – at a meeting of the VIK, at a meeting of the party branch, or just at an informal gathering – decisions on local administrative affairs got negotiated among the members of this small, closely-knit group of activists. The decisions were then fed into the administrative channels available.

The *volost'* leadership had great power over the inhabitants of its *volost'*. The authority of the *volost'* leadership was wide and ill-defined – and therefore arbitrary – including, for example, the power to arrest suspects and 'enemies' practically at will. However, wide powers in relation to the peasants *did not* mean autonomy for the *volost'* leaders in relation to the higher authorities. Their position was seen as mainly executive, and its maintenance was conditional on their success in executing the orders of the higher ranks. It was a highly centralized organization, to which party members belonged, which used its right to assign them to work in a particular field, to a specific responsible post and place of residence; the Party presupposed absolute discipline in carrying out orders from above. In actual fact, the VIKs consisted of appointees of the leaderships of higher level. The Success and advancement for members of the '*volost*' caucus' was measured in terms of competent execution of commands from above (chiefly relating to collection of taxes, smooth procurement of grain for the towns, carrying out the numerous campaigns, and ensuring the absence of major disturbances in the area). A study of local government (*nizovoi apparat*) carried out in 1925 by the People's Commissariat of Workers' and Peasants' Inspection (NKRKI) reported: 'VIKs have proved good executors of tax-collection work for the higher authorities, but independent work done by VIKs in serving the basic needs of the village is negligible.' This seems equally applicable to all the rural organizations of the plenipotentiary outsiders.

The discrepancy between the aims and requests of higher authority and the resources of the *volost*' leadership was stupendous. The Soviet local executive lived under perpetual pressure from an everlasting string of orders, requests, instructions, and threats coming from the various branches of the state and party machinery. He was kept in an atmosphere of perpetual involvement in several simultaneously running campaigns, generally without the allocation of any additional resources. The Weberian model of ideal-type bureaucracy acting in an apolitical, rational, and objective manner would, no doubt, have seemed ridiculous to this group. Not objectivity, but zealous devotion was required by the higher authorities; personal failure had the smell of treason and counter-revolution. Silent peasant defiance of orders added to the general atmosphere reminiscent of a harassed and besieged garrison.

An additional element of tension was that this heavily overworked group was extremely badly paid. Salaries varied in different areas and periods, but in 1924 members of VIKs received an average monthly salary of less than 20 roubles; it amounted to as little as 12 roubles in many cases. Chairmen of Rural Soviets were reported as receiving less than 10 roubles a month. The average salary of an urban state employee during the same period was 36 roubles per month whilst for those in Moscow the sum was 42 roubles per month.

The discrepancy between aims and resources, between personal power and limited income, between the authority granted and the insecurity felt in the position led to two opposite reactions. On the one hand, recourse to harsh administrative methods, arrests,[1] and beatings

---

1 For example, during 1922 (the first year of the NEP), according to the records of the People's Commissariat of Finance (*Narkomfin*), the peasants in Smolensk province lost 2,007,000 days as defendants in court or in gaol, not counting the time spent in court as witnesses. The court proceedings and arrests were mainly due to tax offences and were the equivalent of 1,672,000 work days – or 299 work days per 1,000 *puds* (1 *pud* = 16

of the peasants by particularly zealous devotees of the Party were widely reported. This reflected the difficulties experienced in trying to carry out the orders of the higher authorities, the common lack of administrative experience, and the tension generated by the feeling that peasant households 'had it too good'. On the other hand, cynicism and corruption spread; this is evidenced by the frequently reported embezzlement of public funds, bribes, and cases of gross drunkenness indulged in in company with the richer peasants.[2]

The heavy external pressures, the similarity of their problems, and a way of life far removed from the great majority of the rural population all tended to produce small and exclusive groups of 'outsiders', sharing a particular subculture, in the *volost'* centres. Their members lived in their own world of problems, images, values, friendships, and sociability which centred around the VIK and the local party branch, and was vastly remote from the world of the surrounding peasant communes. Many of the plenipotentiaries were, in fact, newcomers to the *volost'* centre; they had no local contacts whatsoever, except those with the local executive group which they had been sent to join. Similarity in educational background[3] added to the group's cohesion. The eagerly read publications of the central party press helped to maintain the political unity and the feeling of belonging to a big and powerful force. Unity of basic aims and shared conflicts made for basic group solidarity; this did not exclude, of course, personal clashes over power and influence. Small closed communities of outsiders, both plenipotentiary and stranger, had come to be built up in the peasant countryside of Russia.

This was the social situation in which the peasants' image of the party members as those who 'collect taxes and order people around' came close to the party members' self-image; as reflected in a proposition, voiced in some rural party branches, to pay party salaries to all party members, because 'there are only about half a million of us, and it's we, after all, who hammer the taxes out of them' (*ved' nalogi my vykolachivaem*).

In these conditions, communication between the local administration and the peasant population became a major problem. The Soviet authorities were caught in a major dilemma. On the one hand, both the implementation of short-term policy and the attainment of the long-

---

kilograms) of grain collected. (A. Vainshtein, *Oblozheniya i platezhi krest'yanstva v dovoennoe i revolyutsionnoe vremya* (Moscow, 1924), p. 162.)

2 Drunkenness, in particular from *samogon* – the illegal home-brewed vodka of the Russian peasants – became a major problem in the Russian countryside. The anti-*samogon* policy of the Soviet state and the Bolshevik Party was another lost battle.

3 Generally primary education, Red Army service, some party experience, and a fairly limited administrative know-how.

term aim of socialism could be effected only through close contact with the peasantry. On the other hand, close contact with the peasantry could (and at times did) develop into corruption – i.e. the development of personal loyalties taking precedence over loyalties to the state and the Bolshevik Party. This dilemma was clearly felt in the party slogans of the NEP period, which called for a closing of the ranks between party members and peasants (*smychka*) but, at the same time, heavily castigated what was seen as effectively absorption into the peasantry (*vrastanie*). However, in these conditions, these were unavoidably linked. It seems that the main socio-political boundary ran through the group of chairmen of the Rural Soviets. Above this line, the Soviet electees overlapped with the party members and Soviet white-collar workers, and constituted the small local élite, traditionally referred to by the peasantry as 'the authorities' (*vlasti, nachal'stvo*) – or simply as 'them'. A peasant who happened to join the 'caucus' was rapidly faced with an unavoidable conflict of loyalties.

In these circumstances, the periphery of the *volost'* power caucus was of particular importance, both as the main non-administrative bridge to the peasant population and as the potential ally in the villages. Yet the polarizing of loyalties between the members of the *volost'* caucus and the peasant commune made the position of the bridging groups both unstable and precarious. The chairmen of Rural Soviets, as we have seen, were a good example of this. Both the members of the Komsomol and the Red Army ex-servicemen constituted a group of potential party sympathizers but, under the pressure of this deep political and cultural polarization of rural society, they tended either to join the administration or to dissolve into the peasant mass. The members of the Komsomol were prevented, what is more, by the older generation, from making any real impression on the *Volost'* Executive. Party reports of this period complain endlessly about the lack of non-party peasant sympathizers in rural areas, ready to shoulder the burden of political work. The Bolshevik Party did not fare much better with the rural intelligentsia, which remained isolated.

The power structure of Russian rural society, was, therefore, characterized by a profound dualism. Real power was held, on the one hand, by the peasant commune gatherings and, on the other hand, by the plenipotentiaries of the state administration, embodied in the VIKs and the party branches; the Rural Soviets played a mainly subsidiary role. The members of the *volost'* power caucus did not operate as 'power-brokers', to use J. Steward's and E. Wolf's term (i.e. as a buffer group typical of many rural societies, mediating between the state power and the peasants, having resources of its own and a reasonable field of manœuvre), but were totally dependent on the national leadership.

Polarization was in fact reinforced by the weakness and lack of stability of what buffer groups there were and by the cultural diversity of the members of the major groups. The image of a dual society resembling the one depicted by Boeke as typical of rural areas in the contemporary 'developing societies' was further complicated in our case, however. The essential dualism of the power structure was associated with an essentially threefold division in the cultural sphere: the Russian rural intelligentsia constituted a third closed group – that of 'stranger outsiders', who lived alongside the peasant communes and the other distinct group of 'plenipotentiary outsiders'. Moreover, once again the overlap between the three groups was very limited and the groups which could possibly bridge the gulf were notably weak . . .

On the local level, the revolution led to considerable changes in the patchwork of the socio-political groups in the Russian countryside. Some of these groups had disappeared completely (e.g. the landed nobility), the importance of others had increased (e.g. the ex-servicemen and the women), and significant new groups had come into being (e.g. the Party members). The source-group and the personality-type of those recruited to man the local administration had also changed, reflecting the needs and views of a new and radical national leadership. At the same time the socio-economic differentiation of the peasantry diminished, mobility went up, enclosed farms disappeared, and the engagement in crafts and trades lessened, increasing the homogeneity of the peasant communes and limiting chances of a 'Western' path of modernization by the growth of the market economy. These changes made the political divisions of the Russian rural society all the more significant for future developments.

The political dynamics of Russian rural society in this period were related to a variety of conflict-relations at work, one of which seems clearly to have overshadowed the others and to have become predominant in the political life of the countryside. This conflict-relationship developed between peasant communes and the plenipotentiary outsiders, reflecting on the local level the relationship between the peasantry and the Soviet state.

The position and actions of the plenipotentiaries were to a decisive extent determined by the national organizations and leadership. The implementation of state rural policies was strongly influenced by the depth of the gulf existing between the members of the peasant communes and the plenipotentiaries in the Russian countryside. The possibility of the latter's influencing the Russian peasant communities by political mobilization of various groups of the peasantry was limited to an extreme; various exercises in pressure and coercion were the main, if not the only, contact and in these the power of the state found its match in the silent stubbornness of the peasant communities.

On the other hand the political stand and the social impact of the peasant communes was a result of the peculiarities of the peasant social structure. Defensive conservatism faced state pressures. The vertical segmentation embodied both the strengths and the weaknesses of the peasant groups: the intense solidarity of each village meant disunity between the villages; the division into cohesive households and communes gave rise to the socio-political weakness shown by the peasantry as a whole. Without outside organizers, peasant action and pressure remained, as a rule, localized; the peasants lacked national organization, symbols, and leaders and stood little chance in an open clash with the bureaucratic organization which the state and the ruling party constituted. Yet the ability of the state machine to break peasant resistance by a full display of force did not mean that it had the ability to shape the future in accordance with its untrammelled will. The choices open were determined by the existing social structure, by the resources available, and by the apprehension of reality by the major political 'actors'.

During the NEP period, the tremendous passive power of the Russian peasant communities proved incapable of generating a political alternative and uniting for political action. The Soviet state machinery and the Bolshevik Party did have the power, but lacked a perception of the real social processes going on in the Russian countryside. Worse still, the remoteness of the local representatives of the Bolshevik Party and the state from the peasantry blocked the very channels by which an adjustment of concepts and policies to reality could have taken place. With the political leadership committed to a misleading conception of rural society, with its local representatives out of touch with the peasantry in nearly all contexts other than coercive administrative force, with the power of the communes decisive in local affairs, yet unable to dictate national policy and bound to be defeated in a full-scale confrontation with a modern state, the stage was set already in the mid 1920s for the drama of collectivization.

12

The Peasant Dream: Russia
1905–7 (1981)

This paper formed part of an extensive study of the peasantries of Russia in the 1905–7 revolution, undertaken in 1978–83. It was written up for discussion and published first in a volume of Historical Workshops entitled Marx and the Russian Commune, *No. 21. The paper eventually became a section of the book* Russia 1905–7: Revolution as a Moment of Truth, *but it forms a separate entity devoted to peasants' political perception within a large, complex and multi-ethnic society involved in revolutionary confrontation within itself. What gives it its broader significance is the extraordinary wealth of direct evidence concerning peasant political choices and demands which was then articulated and accumulated in Russia. Peasants are often mute when* literati *are concerned. In Russia in 1905–7 they spoke their mind.*

Dreams matter. Collective dreams matter politically. That is a major reason why no direct or simple link relates political economy to political action. In between stand meanings, concepts and dreams with internal consistencies and a momentum of their own. To be sure, their structure bears testimony to the relations of power and production they are embedded in and shaped by. However, such interdependencies are never one-sided. Patterns of thought, once established, acquire a causal power of their own to shape, often decisively, economy and politics: that is true particularly of the political impact of ideology, understood here as the dream of an ideal society in relation to which goals are set and the existing reality judged.

Doubts have often been expressed about the very possibility of studying peasant ideology or thought. Such an analysis can never be undertaken, so the argument runs, for lack of convincing evidence. Peasants differ between regions and between villages as well as within every village: the rich and the poor, the farmer and the part-craftsman, the man and the woman, the old and the young – how can one generalize about 'the peasant mind'? To make things worse, most of the peasant lore is oral, while most of those who write of the peasantry are outsiders to it – how can one trust such testimony? Anyway, collective thought is notoriously difficult to express, to record and to divine. Nor does it quantify easily and relevantly – a major sin to those to whom mathematics is synonymous with true scholarship.

Yet, on the other hand, a prudent refusal to generalize about peasant thought would also mean giving up the full analysis of peasant political action, for there can be none without considering peasant goals. Nor would the problem be resolved by narrowing the analysis to a specific peasant stratum or to a single village. The same argument applies to each such subdivision, until one is left with many single, different and unrelated personas – a caricature of social reality if ever there was one. That is why the alternative often adopted was simply to deduce patterns of consciousness from the interest of classes, groups or societies. Such a short-cut, a substitution for actual consciousness of its presumed causes, is tautological and resolves little. The causes and context of consciousness must be explored, not postulated.

Can one provide any meaningful and significant generalization about the collective thought of the Russian peasants? If so, is there sufficient evidence to study the peasant political ideology?

A major case in point may help us answer the first of those questions. The rules of inheritance within the Russian peasantry from 1861 to 1911 were never legislated by the state but explicitly left, at Emancipation, to the 'local custom' as understood by the peasant magistrates of every community. Our knowledge of the procedures which actually resulted is fairly good. Several intensive studies of the decisions made by peasant magistrates were undertaken by the Russian court of appeal. These studies concerned the decisions of peasant courts in many thousands of villages, differing as regards their history, climate, riches and type of agriculture as well as their interaction with the nobility, the towns and the broader economy. Besides the diversities, the studies reveal a repetition of the basic principles of inheritance and property relations throughout the Russian peasantry. This evidence is all the more striking in that these principles differed consistently from the corresponding relations operating within the other social classes of Russia as well as from the 'national', i.e. non-peasant, official legislation.[1] We are talking here of family property (as against both private and collective ownership), the non-admissibility of the will, the equal division of land between all resident sons and sons-in-law, the specific female property,

1 See the codification of peasant common law by V. Mykhin, *Obychnyi poryadok nasledovaniya u krest'yan* (St Petersburg, 1888).

and so on. It goes without saying that these generic characteristics of the norms, views and actual procedures concerning property were closely linked with the nature of the peasant economy and the structure of the peasant households and villages. However, this was a link of mutual interdependence and not a simple reflection of the one in the other (whichever the 'one' and whichever the 'other'). The Russian peasant common law is central to any consideration of the peasant economy and its dynamics. To conclude, generalizations about the Russian peasant mind find justification in a major piece of evidence. This massive and strategic example should suffice to show that such generalizations are possible and, when justified, provide considerable illumination.

Despite the fact that a major part of the Russian peasants were illiterate, extensive evidence relevant to the study of peasant collective thought in Russia is available, representing in particular the political views of the peasantry during the period 1905–7, when thousands of petitions, resolutions of communal assemblies (*prigovory*) and instructions to delegates (*nakazy*) were recorded. They were addressed to the tsar, to the government (especially after the Decree of 17 February 1905, which actually called for their submission), to the deputies of the Duma and to the All-Russian Peasant Union. The Peasant Union congresses also passed a number of major resolutions. Later, the peasant deputies addressed the Duma, putting the case of their electorate. A number of relevant reports by observers as well as by police and army chiefs and by state administrators about the peasant's views and moods are also available,[2] and so are some memoirs of officials, nobles and 'intelligentsia'. The evidence is rich, if uneven, and within the heterogeneity of expressions shows considerable consistency of content.

One may begin the review of the peasants' views about the type of society they wished to see, from the debates and the decisions of the two 1905 congresses of the All-Russian Peasant Union of which the protocols were published.[3] A broad consensus was clearly established at both. While well aware of the limitations of their capacity to impose their wish fully on the tsarist state, the peasant delegates showed considerable unanimity in their preferences. The ideal Russia of their choice was one in which all the land was to belong to the peasants, to be held according to a roughly egalitarian division and worked by family labour only, without the use of wage-workers. A pool of all Russian farming lands

2 e.g. the reports of the governors of the provinces, of the officers in charge of pacification and of the punishment expeditions, collected in *Revolyutsiya 1905 goda i samoderzhavie* (Moscow, 1928).

3 *Uchreditel'nyi s'ezd vserossiiskogo krest'yanskogo soyuza*, (Protokol) (Moscow, 1906); *Protokoly delegatskogo soveshchania vserossiiskogo krest'yanskogo soyuza* (Moscow, 1909).

was to be established and the land-holdings equalized in accordance with the size of the family and/or a 'labour norm', i.e. the amount of labour of which the family was capable. Trading in land was to be abolished and the actual control of land placed in local hands. The local authorities, elected to represent equally the entire population, were to be invested with considerable powers, to oversee land-holding and redivide the land in case of need, as well as to run the public services, among which free education for all was particularly emphasized. At the state level, a parliamentary monarchy was somewhat more vaguely envisaged, with civic equality, freedom of speech and assembly, and 'compassion' as a major principle to guide state policies – a semi-religious formulation of an idea not unlike that of a 'welfare state'. The officials were to be elected. Women were to be granted an equal vote ('which may help to fight against drunkenness'). Solidarity was strongly expressed with all those engaged in the confrontation with the government: the workers, the soldiers, the 'intelligentsia' and the 'ethnic peripheries'.

There was also a fair consensus at the congresses of the All-Russian Peasant Union as to the delineation of the evil forces which had stopped peasant dreams from coming true. Those were first and foremost the state officials (*chinovniki*), described succinctly as 'malevolent to the people' (*narodu vredny*). The squires, the Kulaks and the local Black Hundreds[4] were also named as enemies (in that order) but ran a clear second to the 'apparatus of the state'. In the major transformation aimed at, the squires were to lose their land, the Kulaks their ability to exploit the neighbours and threaten village unity, the Black Hundreds their capacity to perpetuate terror in conjunction with the local police. Some of the decisions voiced a moral-political consensus, relevant once more to the peasant ideal of society: rejection of the death penalty, a demand for general political amnesty, a denunciation of drunkenness and condemnation of the anti-Jewish *pogroms* as 'shameful and sinful'. Much of the debate was couched in moral, often biblical terms of the fundamental rights and wrongs, assumed to be as evident to all good men as the difference between day and night. An endlessly repeated statement 'Land is God's' is an example and a central case in point – a *Weltanschauung*, a moral judgement, a political stand, and a strategic demand, all in one.

The many disagreements within the All-Russian Peasant Union congresses mainly concerned the road towards realization of these goals and not their nature. They were related principally to the issues of land

4 A xenophobic monarchist organization known for its physical attacks and intimi-dation aimed at the radicals, the non-Russians (especially Jews) and others suspected of liberalism.

redemption and the form that the struggle should take, i.e. how far it would be accomplished by revolutionary violence. To begin with the first issue, everybody agreed that the land of the state should enter the redistributional pool free of charge. A majority preferred the peasant control of Russia's land to include also the 'buying-off' of private owners, financed by the state, while a substantial minority objected to any such payments, for 'land was created by the holy spirit' and not being man-made should not carry a price-tag. An image of a peaceful and orderly transformation of land and power with a new consensus safeguarding the stability of that change was often referred to and was clearly at the root of the tactical preferences of the majority of the delegates. The issue of tactics was central to the Peasant Union's debate. The awareness of confrontation with the combined weight of the state machinery and the landed nobility, a confrontation which would grow harsher, was strong in the minds of the peasant delegates. The methods of struggle agreed on were the boycott of state officials and their appointees, the removal of 'loyalist' elders by holding new elections, the setting up of Peasant Unions' committees called upon to take over local affairs and the passing of resolutions formulating demands (*prigovory*) by the assemblies of peasant communes and districts. The very spread of the Peasant Union branches, district organizations and conferences, both legal and illegal, was also a direct challenge to and pressure upon the authorities. The November 1905 Congress extended the above measures by banning the sale or rent of lands, and by declaring that any increase in police pressure on the union activists would be countered by refusal to pay taxes and draft recruits. In line with the position taken by all the revolutionary parties and the Petersburg Soviet of Workers' Deputies, the November Congress decided to boycott the Duma – the parliament granted – until a fully democratic electoral law was accepted by the government. At the same time, the All-Russian Peasant Union dissociated itself from the 'taking apart' of the manors (which was declared counterproductive but explicable in terms of the peasant grievances, bitterness and disorganization).[5] Further progress in peasant organization and an amnesty were to take care of that. The next step in the escalation of the struggle was to be a 'general peasant strike' (doubtless with the example of the success of the urban strike in October 1905 in mind). The general peasant strike would mean the withdrawal of peasant labour from the manors and the refusal to pay rent and taxes. Many of the speakers called for resistance by

---

5 'When strong we got our way by peaceful means, when split we turned to arson and similar means. As long as we are not organized, arson and bloody means will continue.' Report of a delegate from Minsk *guberniya*, *Protokoly*, p. 61.

force (*dat' otpor*) as a way of keeping the 'forces of order' under some constraint. The possibility of a massive invasion and *de facto* takeover of the manorial and state lands 'in the spring' was seriously discussed. A call for an armed uprising was considered but refused.

The attitudes to the tsar were one of the major issues over which the particular mixture of peasant radicalism and peasant conservatism (or caution) found its expression. The state and its officialdom were rebuked and abused constantly, yet the tsar was usually 'left out of it'. To some of the delegates, doubtless representative of a sizeable part of the peasantry, it was still the belief that the tsar must be misled by some wicked ministers not to understand what was so self-evident to them. An increasing number of the peasant activists clearly knew better but voiced suggestions (especially at the November Congress) to continue 'not to touch him', as their villagers might not be ready for such a challenge and a split over monarchist loyalties might be disastrous. To nearly all the delegates, while struggle for the peasant control of all lands and a change in the local power were central, the attitude to the state, the capitals, and the national centres was more distant. A peasant delegate expressed this in a half-jocular, half-serious report to the November Congress. He proudly recounted his *volost'* assembly's reply to an official who, after listening to their debates about the future, demanded to know 'where did you place the tsar in all that?' The peasants' answer was 'of him we did not speak at all.'[6] Schweikian wit and tactics of avoidance were still the old and tested peasant weapons, a fine way to face a puffed-up outsider and to draw a quiet grin of appreciation from one's neighbours.

The intellectuals watching peasant congresses often expressed surprise or dismay at the discrepancy between the powerful rhetorics and the actual decisions. Members of the revolutionary parties craved revolutionary action. Peasant violence was reported all through Russia. At their congresses of 1905 peasant delegates spoke sharply of grievances and demands but did not endorse violent action (without actually ever refusing it either.)

Yet that contradiction lay mostly in the eyes of intellectuals; every peasant assembly-man knew the difference between a true wish (carefully hidden from the 'outside', yet forcefully expressed to unite the assembly round him) and the recognition of the realities one had to live with. Every peasant also understood the simple tactics of any peasant market: to bluster, then try to settle by a compromise which secures the concession and is 'right' within the peasant code of propriety (*po chesnomu*). There was in such attempts neither surrender nor despair.

6 ibid., p. 8.

The delegates of the mostly unarmed and land-bound villages called for an attack but were not ready (yet?) to adopt the tactics of armed struggle.

Peasants also knew the limitations of their own political organization. To unite localized peasant power nationally and to do it effectively, one needed either a base outside, i.e. a revolutionary army or an established guerrilla force ready to march against the peasant enemies, or else some measure of legality, which makes communication and unification possible. With the first not in evidence, peasant activists tried to make use of the second, while building up their power. They brushed aside advice to the contrary offered by the revolutionary parties, both the Social Democrat (SD) representative's proposal of a republic and the Socialist Revolutionary (SR) delegate's call for an armed uprising. The majority of the peasants, in the eyes of whom power (and particularly local power) was central, clearly strove to minimize violence, that is, to use it limitedly, selectively and on the whole defensively. These were not, however, the decisions of some distant, opportunist leadership playing parliamentary games of respectability. The local reports showed the consistency of the opposition to the destruction of manors by the 'conscious' peasants on the spot, even though they did not usually break ranks when their villages went on the attack. Nor was there lack of courage in it all, for the extent of calm bravery shown by many of the peasant activists in the face of the pacification squads, prisons and trials was impressive, and these were the very villages from which the Russian infantrymen who fought in the wars and the civil wars were to come. The sober realism of recognizing the superiority of strength of the regular army in any face-to-face engagement was proven well enough by the entire experience of 1905–7. That is also why, all in all, the delegates of the peasant union seem to have represented the 'conscious' peasants' grasp of their own interests well. It was characteristic that the great realist, Lenin, admitted to just that.[7]

The representative nature of the Union's view of the Russian peasantry at large was challenged at once by its contemporary critics. The popular press supporting the government and usually financed from its 'secret funds' ('loyalist' in government designation, 'reptile' to its enemies), promptly denounced the All-Russian Peasant Union as an organization of arsonists and its congresses as a conclave of the intelligentsia dressed up as peasants. At the other end of the political scale, an SR delegate to the November Congress (Studentsov) claimed that the congress was

7 'It was truly popular mass organization, which has shared, of course, many of the peasant prejudices . . . but definitely "of the soil" real organization of masses, definitely revolutionary in its essence . . . extending the framework of the peasant political creativity.' V.I. Lenin, *Sobrannye sochineniya* (Moscow, 1968), vol. 10, pp. 232–3.

dominated by its presidium, representing intelligentsia and/or rich peasant delegates. That was how he explained the November Congress's refusal of the SR delegate's call for an armed uprising.[8] Shestakov, an SD Bolshevik representative at the July session, felt similar dismay at the peasant congress's moderation,[9] and subsequently explained, in a fairly similar way to the SR delegate, the refusal of the first congress to declare for a republic, its decision to give partial compensation to private landowners, and the November Congress's refusal to give the SD workers' delegates the privilege of addressing it and so of allowing the peasants to learn from the workers' superior revolutionary experience. Maslov, the major Menshevik theorist of rural society, eventually accepted, like Lenin, the assumption that the peasant congresses of 1905 did represent peasant political thought, but claimed that they were socially an exclusive expression of the remainders of the peasant repartitional commune and geographically restricted to the areas where those existed.[10]

It so happened that these doubts and comments of contemporaries concerning the impact of the liberal or populist 'intelligentsia' on the Peasant Union came speedily to an acid and spectacular test. As already mentioned, the Peasant Union's decision to boycott elections and the mass arrests meant a veritable purge of Peasant Union activists from the first Duma. With the call for a boycott universally rejected by rural Russia, the peasant deputies were also mostly unattached to any political party. During the election campaign, the arrests and deportations of the rural radicals produced as pure a case as can ever be of peasants' choice uninterfered with by the political organizers of the day – in the language of a 1906 report about the pre-election atmosphere, 'all of the political life in the villages seemed dormant.'[11] The impact of the authorities was mainly exercised through pressures against candidates deemed unreliable rather than through organizing a faction of their own. The liberals of the KD, the only party which proceeded with a systematic electoral campaign, did little in the countryside and gained the support of less than one-sixth of the peasant-elected deputies.

The resulting first Duma, with its massive 'non-party' peasant representation, produced a sigh of relief in the Establishment: the Duma's conservatism seemed assured. The parties of the left agreed with this

8 A. Studentsov, *Saratovskoe krest'yanskoe vosstanie 1905 goda* (Penza, 1926), pp. 42, 46.

9 A.V. Shestakov, *Krest'yanskaya revolyutsiya 1905–1907gg v Rossii* (Moscow, 1926); V. Groman, *Materialy po krest'yanskomu voprosu* (Rostov, 1905).

10. T. Maslov, *Agrarnyi vopros v Rossii* (St Petersburg, 1908), pp. 277–81.

11. B. Veselovskii, *Krest'yanskii vopros i krest'yanskoe dvizhenie v Rossii* (St Petersburg, 1907), p. 138.

expectation, and so did the liberals. What actually followed sent a shock of surprise through the Russian political scene for a moment, drawing attention from the triumphant reaction following the defeat of the revolutionaries in November/December 1905. The largest group of the 'non-party' peasant deputies promptly banded together into a Labour Faction (*Trudoviki*), incorporating representatives from all over Russia, inclusive of a number of delegates from the Western provinces where the repartitional commune did not exist. Within a month the Labourites produced demands, both 'agrarian' and more general, which were practically indistinguishable from those of the All-Russian Peasant Union.[12] Any idea that some hidden agents of the left or of the All-Russian Peasant Union had hijacked the peasant vote was dispelled by the political position of the peasant deputies who stayed outside the Labour Faction. To the further shock of the authorities, the KD majority of the Duma and their Marxist critics alike, the peasant deputies spoke what was described by a Soviet scholar of our own generation as 'the language of Socialist Revolutionaries'[13] – one must add, in all but the desire for a revolution. Even the self-declared peasant conservatives and monarchists among the peasant deputies supported the agrarian programme tabled by the Labour Faction. Some of the peasant deputies from the ethnically non-Russian areas joined national factions ('the autonomists') which stressed the demand for self-rule along ethnic lines. They consequently objected to the national 'pool of land' demanded by the Labour Faction, but once again agreed with the rest of its programme. The peasant deputies who joined the KD faction supported, unlike the Labourites, redemption payments for *all* private lands but wanted them requisitioned in full and turned over to the landless and small-holding peasants. Cross-cutting boundaries of party allegiances, regions and ethnicity, the peasant land demands were well put in the words of the somewhat later instructions (*nakaz*) given by the otherwise highly conservative and monarchist Krasnichinsk Orthodox Parish of Lublin *guberniya* to its deputy to the second Duma: 'You can compromise on all other issues but in the question of land you should join the extreme tendency, that is, without fail demand the transfer to peasants [*nadelenie*] of lands and forests.'[14] Not land alone was at issue. To a major part of the peasantry, the resolution (*prigovor*) of the

12 The 'Project of the 104', for the text of which see *Agrarnyi vopros v pervoi gosudarstvennoi dume* (Kiev, 1906), pp. 5–9.

13 M. Gefter in *Istoricheskaya nauka i nekotorye voprosy sovremennosti* (Moscow, 1969), pp. 22–3.

14 The archives of the second Duma quoted after E. Vasilevskii, *Sotsial'no-ekonomicheskoe soderzhanie krest'yanskikh prigovorov i nakazov* (Vestnik MGU, 1956), no. 179, p. 132.

assembly of the village Shnyak in Kazan *guberniya* was clearly as relevant: 'Worse than poverty, more bitter than hunger is the suppression of the people by absolute arbitrariness/powerlessness [*bezprav'e*]. Without a permit, you cannot take a step, say a word or else it is a fine, prison or exile to Siberia. . . . Instead of the courts it is the local police which passes all sentences.'[15]

The homogeneity of the positions taken by the peasant communities and the peasant deputies in fact increased even further after the government's 'declaration of intent' in the first Duma, by which any takeover of privately owned land was flatly rejected. As the work of the Duma proceeded, the opposition of the peasant deputies to the government solidified, while outside its walls the peasants' direct attack against the landowners reached a new peak in the summer of 1906.

The next stage, and one more test of peasant consistency of beliefs and demands, came when the government banned the majority of the deputies to the first Duma from re-election. The second Duma, which met in 1907, therefore carried a new slate of deputies. Despite the heavy government pressures on the electorate, the second Duma proved more radical in membership than its predecessor. A quarter of the deputies of the new Duma were by now self-described revolutionary socialists of the SD and SR, another quarter belonged to the Labour Faction which increased considerably, and a quarter went to the KD – a formidable opposition line-up against the government. The Labour Faction, nearly totally new in its membership and without any proper extra-parliamentary organization to secure its consistency, promptly repeated all its initial 'Labourist' demands (i.e. the 'Project of the 104'). Meeting directly after the enactment of the so-called Stolypin Reform, a government decree promoting the privatization of communal land, it also showed unqualified hostility to this. An equal hostility was expressed in the instructions to the Duma deputies voted by villages all through Russia.

In the second Duma, a number of other substantially peasant factions (e.g. that of the Cossacks) once again came out in full support of the land demands of the Labour Faction. Significantly, even the deputies of Volyn' – the one place where the Black Hundreds swept the peasant vote – presented agrarian demands not unlike those of the peasant radicals elsewhere. In the ethnic context of Volyn' such demands were directed against the Polish nobles and Jewish merchants, which secured a victory for the Black Hundreds' xenophobic appeal.

Even the elections to the third Duma in 1907 still produced a massive peasant vote for the opposition. The new electoral laws had now

15 ibid., p. 130.

stopped most of the Labourists from reaching the Duma, but those few who succeeded came to state once more similar demands and preferences. A major proof of both the substance of the peasant demands and the surprise and fury they caused was offered by a sequence of vitriolic attacks by government supporters and the right-wing parties on the Labour Faction. To give an example, one such publication described the Labour Faction collectively as a group consisting of people with

(1) half-way arrested natural abilities resulting from incapacity as much as from lack of a consistency which can be acquired only by good education, (2) incredible self-esteem resulting from supremacy over one's own ant-hill, i.e. an environment which is lacking in any culture, (3) untrammeled utopianism determined by a mixture of half-education and insolence, (4) a hate of everything which is cleaner, whiter, more sophisticated – a type of hate without which the impudence and the utopianism would lose any meaning or justification.[16]

The author clearly knew all one could know about class hate and about the depths of the deepest class gulf in Russia. His own emotions centred, typically, on the plebeian elite representing the mainstream of the Russian peasant movement, supported by considerable groups of workers, intelligentsia and some of the ethnic minorities.

While the deputies and delegates to the peasant congresses and to the Dumas argued out the demands and dreams of the Russian peasantry *in toto*, every village proceeded with its own never-ceasing debate throughout 1905–7. Scraps of news were endlessly retold, discussed and embellished, printed sheets were read and read out, the thirst for knowledge seemed infinite. A rumour that a meeting was to be held or that a 'knowledgeable man' was visiting a village brought neighbours on foot, in carts, and on horseback from many miles away. The villagers also sent out delegates 'to find things out' and to invite 'an orator' from the local towns or neighbourhoods. A village in the south specified such a request, ordering its messengers 'to bring over a student or a Jew to tell of the news' while another village voted to offer payment of an 'orator's' wages from the communal purse. At the centre of this immense process of communication was not outside propaganda, but rather a grandiose and spontaneous effort at political self-understanding by millions of illiterate and half-literate villagers. In an endless, slow, often clumsy and ill-informed and ever heated debate, masses of peasants looked at their life and environment anew and critically. They conceived and expressed what was often unthinkable until then: an image of a new world, a dream of justice, a demand for land and liberty. For, once again, it was not only land which was in question.

16 Quoted from N. Vasil'ev, *Chto takoe trudoviki* (St Petersburg, 1971), p. 4.

It is usually the local evidence which is the most difficult to come by where peasant movements are concerned. However, for once, in Russia 1905–7, much of the peasant thought was expressed publicly, formulated and written up. An Anglo-Saxon parliament, in which its members are free to act as they deem fit, would have struck the Russian peasants as distinctly odd. The experience of communal self-management taught them otherwise. A deputy was to be told specifically what he was sent to say – hence the *nakaz*, somewhat along the lines of the *Cahiers de doléances* of the French Estates General in 1789, but more direct as regards the legislation demanded. The authorities and especially the Duma were to be told of the peasants' hardships and needs – hence the communal decision (*prigovor*) and the petitions. Major waves of these documents corresponded to (1) the government's official call for legislative suggestions in early 1905, (2) the peak of the All-Russian Union activities in November 1905, and (3) the first and (4) the second Duma in summer 1906 and spring 1907 respectively. The revolutionary parties, especially the Social Democrats, opposed the petitions to the government and Duma as Utopian and reformist, but failed to make any headway with that position.[17] The communal and *volost'* assembly offered a ready-made machinery for such actions, while, for once, the newspapers and the analysts publicized them broadly.

The direct and representative nature of the peasant petitions and instructions was manifest. The documents themselves declared time and time again 'we wrote it ourselves' (*sami sochinili*), to which the language used readily testified. So did the signatures, which usually began with that of the village elder (the document 'certified true' by his stamp) and continued with those of all the village literates. Then followed a long line of crosses made by the illiterates, declaring not only the support of a view formulated by somebody else, but direct participation in the wording of the letter or the decisions. The sophistication of some of these tracts, especially in areas from which every active member of the intelligentsia had by then been removed by arrest or exile, showed to what extent knowledge of politics is not chiefly a matter of books or of universities.

A collection of documents addressed to the first Duma from the villages of Sumara *guberniya* offers a fair example of the species.[18] Of

---

17 Maslov, *Agrarnyi vopros v Rossii*, p. 214; Shestakov, *Krest'yanskaya revolyutsiya 1905–1907gg v Rossii*, p. 59; Lenin, *Sobrannye sochineniya*, vol. 13, p. 121. To quote chapter and verse, the whole petitions movement was described as 'the fruit of the governmental demagoguery and of the political underdevelopment of the peasants' by the future president of the USSR, Kalinin, in the 9 August 1905 issue of the main Bolshevik newspaper, *Proletarii*.

18 *Krest'yanskie nakazy samarskoi gubernii* (Samara, 1906), pp. 6–80. See p. 40 for a

the seventy-eight items, thirty-eight were addressed to individual deputies, thirty-one to the Duma *in toto*, and nine to its Labour Faction collectively. They asked for land, for lower rents, for agricultural credits and for progressive taxation of incomes. They asked also for 'liberty', amnesty of political prisoners, free election of officials, free education for all, state salaries for the clergy (which would free the peasants from the necessity to pay their keep), and for courts whose proceedings would be 'equal, prompt, just and merciful'. The leading complaint in its frequency, next to that of shortage of land, was that concerning *proizvol*, i.e. official lawlessness and the arbitrary nature of the local authorities' rule – the peasant's main antonym to liberty, self-management, and good order. One village told the Duma deputies that it did not take over the land of the local manors by force 'which could easily be accomplished' because 'a law is needed.' Many others called on the deputies to stand fast and not to yield over the basic demands. The villagers clearly appreciated, more realistically than the Russian liberals, what might happen to the peasant delegates who did just that: the deputies were told 'to bear their cross for they are the last hope' and 'God and their people will stand by them.' Last, a village assembly announced to the deputies its decision to close the local church, 'for if there were a God, he would not permit such injustices to continue.'

A single letter to the Duma may be of particular interest here, representing as it did a deep stirring of the most neglected half of the peasant population. It came from the peasant women of three villages in the Tver' *guberniya* who met in secret. Once again, no 'rural intelligentsia' was involved – the text was written down by a young pupil of the local primary school. The letter addressed to the members of the Duma protested against the fact that while 'our men are quite ready to entertain themselves with us [*gulat' s nami rady*] they refuse to talk to us about the land and the new laws. . . . Before now, they admittedly beat us at times, but serious matters were decided together. Now they say that we are not partners any more, for only they elect the Duma.' The women asked for an equal vote, which was necessary 'to handle matters in a godly manner'. The Duma 'must offer expression to all: the rich as well as poor, the women as well as men, for otherwise there will be no truth on earth and no peace in the families either'.[19]

Soviet historians have attempted to analyse quantitatively the large numbers of peasant petitions and instructions available in the archives. Such a content analysis was performed on the above documents from

petition which carries forty signatures and 280 crosses to represent all of its households – a literacy index of 12.5 per cent for the heads of households.

19 Quoted after Maslov, *Agrarnyi vopros v Rossii*, p. 308.

Samara *guberniya*, on the 146 instructions from branches of the Peasant Union, on 458 instructions to the first Duma, on some 600 village petitions to the second Duma, and so on.[20] Once again, the fundamental homogeneity of the results, concerning documents originating from different peasant communes and groups, over a huge country, is most striking. A comparison of the petitions and instructions of villages in the poorer (northern) part of Samara *guberniya* as against those of its richer region in the south showed a more intensive participation of the relatively richer areas in the 'petitions campaign', these areas also laying more stress on the political demands. In general, in terms of the socio-economic indices, the participants in the 'petition movement' were said to be mostly 'middle peasants', i.e. both the poor (but neither landless nor the destitute *golytba*) and the better-off (but not the richest) within the rural population. The inhabitants of the larger villages were shown to be more active than those of the smaller ones. Overwhelmingly, any comparison of local evidence leaves the impression of mainstream similarities – a unified ideology, a dream remarkable in its consistency, overriding the socio-economic, regional and local differences.

The terminology of peasant political thought is itself of interest. Some of it has been referred to already. Words to express the new experiences and demands were sought and found in tradition or in legend as much as in the new vocabulary of the newspapers and towns. Some of it was produced by the intelligentsia, other terms came from the peasants themselves and entered the language of the educated. The 'golden manifesto' and the 'second freedom' expressed the hope in a decision by the tsar to follow up the emancipation of serfs in 1861 by dividing the rest of the nobles' land between the peasants. The concepts of 'equalization' (*uravnitel 'nost'*) and of the 'labour principle' (*trudovoe nachalo*) – i.e. the adjustment of the land grant to the extent of the family labour of each unit – were used by peasants and the intelligentsia alike. The Black Repartition (*Chernyi peredel*) and the global all-embracing commune (*Vselenskii mir*) embodied the most radical designation of change – a world of peasant righteousness, of total and equal redivision of all land and of Russia as a commune of communes, with very little social

20 See O. Bukovec, 'K metodike izucheniya "prigovotnogo dvizheniya"', *Istoriya SSSR* (1979), part 3. Also for the first Duma sources see V. Mikhailova, 'Sovetskaya istoricheskaya literatura of krest'yanskikh nakazakh i prigovorakh', *Nekotorie problemy otechestvennoi istoriografii i istochnikovedeniya* (Dnepropetrovsk, 1972). The second Duma found a much better coverage, especially in the works of Maslov, *Agrarnyii vopros v Rossii*, pp. 282–8; E. Vasilevskii, *Sotsial'no-ekonomicheskoe soderzhanie krest'yanskikh prigorov i nakazov*, and A. Nilve, *Razvitie V.I. Leninym agrarnogo voprosa v teorii nauchnogo komunizma 1893–1916*, (Moscow, 1974).

space left to the non-peasants. There were some words whose declined in usage signalled the new times. The word 'humbleness' (*smirenie*), so often used in the descriptions and self-definitions of the Russian peasants of old, was fading away. The term 'strike' came to symbolize a class attack and a challenge – 'we have struck [*zabastovali*] the grazing lands', the peasants said of the land seizures in the south of Russia. The word 'student' became synonymous with 'revolutionary', and so on. The government press referred to all this as the infestation of the peasant mind by the 'rural intelligentsia' or else a proof of illiteracy or miscomprehension on the part of the peasant mass. Yet these were the new dreams which found expression in new words. One could not make them up synthetically any more than one could produce by stealth the political dreams which came to move masses of Russian peasants in those days.

The nature of the peasant dream of a good society which surfaced in 1905–7 was interlinked with and generated by the way of life we refer to as peasanthood: the specific economy, policy and communal life as well as the cognitions involved. This was what had underlain the stubborn consistency and generality of peasant 'dreaming'. Both comparison with other peasant societies of the day and consideration of Russia's past made it clear. The slogan 'land and liberty' expressed those dreams remarkably well as slogans do, i.e. it pinpointed the essentials without quite exhausting their full content. Production on the land, usually operating within a three-field system, with family labour as its main output, related directly to the demand: the land to those who till it and to them only. The idiom of survival was characteristic of and necessary to a way of living in which survival had been the essential goal for millennia. It meant also the deep suspicion of all other land-holders in the area and both considerable tensions and overwhelming unity when facing outsiders within every rural commune. Liberty was envisaged mainly as the freedom from external restraints. It was to a decisive degree the image of self-management known to all of the peasant communities, writ large and idealized. Education was mainly the access to literacy and to the skill of a village scribe – a badge of equality with the non-peasants as much as a way to new non-farming jobs for the 'surplus' son or daughter, who could be 'educated out' in that way. It was therefore definitely a 'good thing' and to be open to all of the peasant youth. The demands for charitable government, 'fair and merciful courts', the election of the officials and popular control came as much from legends as from the rural life experience, mostly negative. Past traditions mixed with new characteristics of the peasantry in crisis – the type of crisis referred to today as that of the so-called 'developing societies'.[21] The forms in which it was expressed have shown it clearly: cognition and terminology of conservatism, conventionality, patriarchalism, and semi-magical beliefs injected with new words, views and experiences, and put to use to grasp and shape a rapidly transforming society and to understand a revolution in which the peasantry was massively involved.

The Russian peasant rebellion also prefigured some features of contemporary peasant unrest and revolt: (1) the 'crisis of authority' linked to the ecological and demographic crises as much as to the impact of markets and 'monetization' associated with socio-economic polarization and pauperization; (2) the 'opportunities' granted by extra-rural confrontations which weakened, split and immobilized the powers-that-be; (3) the socio-political points of strength and weakness of the major peasant populations – their size, spread and monopoly of food production as well as segmentation, backwardness and low 'classness'.[22] Also the peasant demands were often legitimized by reference to the good old times, i.e. the past rights lost unjustly – '*das alte Recht*' for which the German peasants fought in the Peasant Wars of the 1520s, before and after. The non-economic aspects of peasant struggle must be seen also to understand its characteristics, stages and connotations. The Russian peasant struggle of 1905–7 has shown what was called in a different time and place the peasant 'moral economy' – a peasant ideology of righteousness – at the root of their revolt. That is where the patterns of cognition and dreams link directly into political confrontation and peasant war.[23] That is also why the ideas, words and symbols of the Russian peasants during the revolutionary epoch would have been more easily understood by peasants from far off than by most of the well-educated Russians of their own generation. A few Russian poets like Klyuev offered an exception but paid the price of being treated rather as a curiosity only, tolerated for a while. The basic disunity between the *literati* and the ethnically 'their own' peasants often

21 For particularly important work on the Russian peasant ideology and its early semantic expressions see H. Wada, 'The Inner World of Russian Peasants', *Annals of the Institution of Social Science*, no. 20 (Tokyo, 1979). His article has drawn in part on the recent works published in the USSR by A. Klibanov, V. Kristov and N. Gromyko.

22 For discussion see E.R. Wolf, *Peasants* (Englewood Cliffs, NJ, 1966), part 4; T. Shanin, *Peasants and Peasant Societies* (Harmondsworth, 1971), part 4; G.M. Foster, 'The Peasants and the Image of Limited Good', *American Anthropologist*, 62 (1965), no. 2; J. Berger, *Pig Earth* (London, 1979), etc.

23 For the major attempt to consider these matters see E. Wolf, *Peasant Wars of the Twentieth Century* (New York, 1969); also J.C. Scott, *Moral Economy of the Peasant* (London, 1976); T. Shanin, *Peasants and Peasant Societies*, part 4; E.J. Hobsbawm, *Primitive Rebels* (London, 1963).

hid, at least for a time, the consistency and the rationale of peasant demands and dreams from the Russian officialdom and intelligentsia. In that, once more, the Russian peasantry was not exceptional.

Issues of consciousness and struggle cannot be disconnected from the Russian peasantry's past. In the most direct sense, its older generation still remembered the emancipation from serfdom in 1861, both the dramatic change and the many disappointments. However, one can and should go further back historically. There is enough evidence to show that, well hidden from 'official Russia', the memory of great peasant rebellions of the sixteenth and seventeenth centuries was never quite extinguished in some areas of Russia, especially in the mid-Volga (to recall an area particularly active in the 1905–7 peasant rebellions, e.g. Saratov *guberniya*.) For centuries the state meted out punishment even for mentioning Ryazin or Pugachev, and the church anathemized them, yet legends were told, ballads sung and millennial dreams woven – well described as a veritable 'samizdat of those illiterate'. Those songs and legends carried the message of peasant defiance, but also some basic ideas round which new ideology could take shape. The idea of turning all the peasants of Russia into Cossacks – i.e. independent, free, armed and self-ruling peasant communities – was remembered: the model used by Ryazin and Pugachev alike was that of the Cossack *Krug*.[24] The call for land for all and war on the landowners, on officials and on corrupt clergy, and even the tale of the 'just tsar' whose 'golden manifesto' was hidden by evil advisers, were all still in use in 1905–7. Some of it was carried through centuries by the Old Believers' sects who added to it a specially xenophobic dimension – to them Tsar Peter was the symbol and root of oppression as well as of devilry; an anti-Christ invented by the Germans.

This historical consistency of the political ideas of the Russian peasants was expressed in relation not only to the past but also to the future. The end of the revolution and 1907 left the Russian peasant with more tangible results than any other social group which rebelled. Those who fought for a republic seemed utterly defeated, the main organizations of the intelligentsia and workers suppressed, the liberals' parliamentary dream caricatured and rendered powerless in the third Duma. Russian peasants did not receive all the Russian land they fought for and the 'liberty' they demanded. However, a considerable amount of land was now rapidly being transferred into peasant hands, admittedly benefiting more the better-off, but not exclusively. The sales of the lands of the nobility to peasantry and the Peasant Bank activities peaked dramati-

24 See P. Longworth, *The Cossacks* (London, 1969).

cally from 1906 onwards. Also, most of the peasant debt was cancelled
by the state. More generally, the authorities were taught a major lesson
with regard to the peasants' anger, that of their potential strength and
something of the limitations of their patience, a lesson which nobody
was likely to forget for a while. Yet the majority of the Russian peasants
were neither mollified nor ready to retreat from their basic demands.[25]
The *prigovory*, *nakazy*, the reports and the election results and the
reports of the police show that while the mass of the peasants was
silenced by 1907, they remained dissatisfied, they knew it clearly and
more than ever before were conscious of the class divisions, the political
camps and the possible alternatives they faced. Not only land and abject
poverty remained at issue, but also the societal division, fundamental
and sharp, into the peasant 'us' and the variety of 'them': the state, the
nobility and the 'clean quarters' of the city, the uniforms, the fur coats
and the golden spectacles, or even the elegantly rolling phrase. Within a
decade this peasant awareness and self-awareness, as well as the political dreams deeply rooted within peasant practice and crystallized by the
1905–7 experience, came to play a decisive role in a new revolution and
a revolutionary war, which ended differently from 1905–7 and made
Russia, for a while, more peasant than ever before or even after.

25 For evidence, see the investigation by I. Chernyshev, *Obshchina posle 9 noyabrya
1906 g.* (Petrograd, 1917); also N. Perris, 'The Russian Peasantry in 1917', *Historical
Workshop* (1977), no. 4.

13

Four Models: Soviet Agriculture under Perestroika
The Most Urgent Task and the Furthest Shore *(1987–8)*

It was Gorbachev who declared at the party conference of 1988 that the economic transformation of perestroika *must begin with the transforming of Soviet agriculture. The old Muscovite joke still holds – the one about a child being left on its own because dad is away, having flown to the moon, while mum is in the queue for sugar. But the joke has by now grown into a public scandal, the result of which may stop short Gorbachev's renaissance. Once again, as so often in the past, the context of agriculture and rural policies defines a much broader set of issues in the political life of the country, and in the careers of its leaders – Vitte and Stolypin, Stalin and Khrushchev, and now Gorbachev. Also, in agriculture one can see the microcosm of the national economy, its stagnation and potentials for change. The debate about agriculture defines, therefore, not only pere-stroika's problems but also its programme's diverse interpretations and the political forces coming to bear.*

This text is an extensively amended and updated version of a paper published first in French translation under the title 'Soviet Agriculture under Perestroika' in 1988 in Les Temps Modernes.

During the second half of the 1980s the Soviet Union was going through a fundamental reconsideration of its alternative futures. At such a time the human-made nature of social structures becomes suddenly apparent and for a while the sky is the limit – everything seems changeable, possible and debatable. This is also a time when a gap opens between plans and the social realities inherited from the past, and much depends on the way it is to be closed. Be this as it may, these are times never to be forgotten by those who live through them. As with 1968 for Western Europe, a political generation will feed on images and ideas established at this time. And there is also a fighting chance of victory for radical reformers striving towards fundamental restructuring of Soviet society. Accepting that plans and results would always differ, even a partial

victory for the reformers could make *perestroika* into the most significant social transformation the world has seen in the late twentieth
century.

When the waves and froth subside, a number of arguments about
Soviet agriculture will stand out as central for the revolution in perceptions and ideas which has been taking place. Some were obvious,
presented in places where public attention was purposely focused, such
as the plenary sessions of the Central Committee. Yet the two most
significant signposts-cum-documents were both published in March 1987
in places which were somewhat unexpected or not easily accessible to
Western specialists. The third major event of the 1987 revolution in
perceptions was the rehabilitation of Chayanov and other senior scholars
condemned in 1931 for sabotaging Soviet agriculture. It was followed in
1988 by the rehabilitation of Bukharin. An October 1988 meeting about
agriculture, presided over by Gorbachev, made it clear how central
these signposts and events are now to the political strategy of rural
reform.

1 Poltava 1986: Past and Present

'*Three Days in Poltava*, or a monologue about agricultural labour and
the farmers' *weltanschauung*' was first published in March 1987 in
Znamya.[1] All this needs some explanation for the Western reader.
Three Days in Poltava is anything but a monologue. It is a record of a
conference which took place in late 1986. The gathering was composed
of farmers, administrators and social scientists but also teachers, professional philosophers and writers. It was called by Fedor Morgun, then
the provincial party secretary of Poltava, that is the senior figure in its
administration, known for his radicalism and thorough knowledge of
agriculture. Poltava is a provincial town in the Ukraine, in the heart of
the Soviet Union's best farmland. *Znamya* is a journal of the writers'
union, recently transformed by a newly elected executive. The place of
publication reflects the way writers moved to the forefront of debate
about social issues, often overtaking social scientists. The publication
itself was typical of radical supporters of Gorbachev and of the new era,
in dealing as much with farming as with social structure and applied
ethics.

The debate in Poltava had on its agenda the state of farming, of rural
communities and of agricultural policies in the province, but it also

1 'Tri dnya v poltave' (Three Days In Poltava), *Znamya* (1987), no. 3. For a fuller
version see *Cheloveki Zemlya* (Humans and Land) (Agropromizdat, 1988).

considered the state of affairs in other grain-producing areas of the country. It therefore summarized half a century of history for the bulk of the Soviet countryside, following Stalin's collectivization.

Three terms were suggested in Poltava to describe the mood and practice of agricultural policies of the recent past: profitless zeal, self-cannibalism and gigantomania. The Soviet Union now produces twice as much chemical fertilization as the US, has four times the number of dairy cows and uses five times the tractor power, yet endless shortages of agricultural goods have been matched by endless demands for more, and more, and still more farming inputs. Demands for more chemicals, more energy, more iron and steel were linked to growing claims about shortages of land, labour and resources and stagnation of per capita production. In the Ukraine grain production showed no improvement over fifteen years. Increase in size of enterprises rather than improved efficiency of farming was underwritten by the centralized system of management and incentives. The 'zealous effort' of this administration was said to have created rather than resolved shortages. The repetitive noisy campaigns to improve farming, the endless rush of orders, threats and busybodies, produced no result in terms of goods in the market place, while food imports continued to increase.

The longer-term cost of 'endless zeal' was ecological disaster and the alienation of those directly involved in production. As to ecology, some of the signs are globally familiar: destruction of forests and soil erosion, the disappearance of smaller rivers and the pollution of larger ones, acid rain which the winds blow for a thousand miles, the worsening of the macro- and micro-climates. The ecological impact on agriculture and the quality of life of rural communities in the Ukraine has been particularly severe, with much of the arable land destroyed or its productive capacity lost. What made Poltava soil, the *chernozem*, among the most fertile in the world was the *ten per cent* humus content created by millennia of natural grass growth. This percentage is now down to *five* through over-ploughing, while gullies spread rapidly. The exceedingly high percentage of produce wasted by being left to rot in the fields, inadequately stored or badly transported could be considered as yet another aspect of ecological-cum-social mismanagement. The human-made disasters were produced by what was described as 'self-cannibalism', that is exploiting agricultural resources for the sake of short-term gains, regardless of longer-term consequences (and so having to run faster and faster just to stand still). This produced in Soviet agriculture a profiteer mentality not unlike that of the nineteenth-century 'robber barons' of the US frontier. But rather than having the land despoiled by individual greed and a profit-making 'free for all', in the USSR this mentality had at its roots a system of management and a social structure set up under Stalin and fully elaborated under Brezhnev.

Gigantomania was said to have offered an important complement to 'futile zeal' and ecological degeneration. Much of it reflected the transfer of insufficiently digested experience of heavy industry to an environment where such innovations were counterproductive. Larger equals more efficient, more mechanized equals more effective, more chemical input equals more output – none of these statements is unproblematic, to say the least. Yet all were adopted as articles of faith and a badge of Progress. The ideology of gigantism has often combined with simple opportunism: heavier equipment produces larger premiums for producers of rural technology, larger-scale enterprises secure faster promotion for provincial bureaucrats. The country which has the world's largest mine, largest steel oven and largest excavator also has the largest agricultural tractors on earth (so heavy that they systematically destroy the structure of the soil they roll over) and the largest gangs of permanent workers (in which effective administration becomes a major issue). This countryside has also been desperately short of the small and sophisticated implements on which modern farming depends, as well as the servicing necessary to keep existing equipment in working order. Summed up by a labour economist taking part in the Poltava conference, policies failed to take into account the fact that in agriculture 'there is no direct relation between labour input and its results' and the kind of division of labour used in heavy industry is 'unjustified both socially and economically'.[2]

The actual results of gigantomania were once again detectable as 'more' rather than 'better' in the way plans were set and achievements tested. An example presented was the comparison between trends in milk production in the USSR and the USA. Over the last twenty-five years the number of dairy cows in the USSR doubled (with corresponding massive rises in fodder and construction costs), while the number of cows in the USA dropped by two-fifths. At the same time milk production per cow in Soviet agriculture, which was initially 72 per cent of that in the USA, is now down to only 38 per cent. Most of the speakers had no doubt, however, that production figures were not the worst feature of Poltava's agriculture. It was the rural social structure and the environment which suffered most.

Before turning to these issues, let us put on record some past policies concerning agriculture, representing an assumed hierarchy of preferences, which speakers attacked with particular fury. These belong to the Brezhnev era but were actually rooted in the Stalinist and still earlier conceptions of Agrarian Progress. All have been condemned by Gorba-

2 'Tri dnya v poltave', p. 206.

chev's leadership as gross mistakes, but the animus with which they were attacked made it clear that the issue is not one of past history only. Nor were the speakers simply 'joining a bandwagon'. To make these points at a time when such expressions were unpopular, come what may, has an honourable pedigree in the USSR.

Three major policies-cum-perceptions came under attack. The first was the view that family plots of members of collective or state farms were a particular form of capitalist agriculture, small and subsidiary as they are. Growing restrictions placed upon them with a view to eventual elimination must form, therefore, a natural and necessary part of the advance of socialism. Second, in the same hierarchy the state farm stood higher than the collective farm, state ownership being equated with socialism. Third, larger units being considered naturally better than smaller ones, a systematic effort was made to enlarge both collective and state farms. As part of the same sequence 40 per cent of existing villages (more than half in many areas of the country) were declared 'localities of no prospect'. This was promptly followed in the 1970s by the running down of all services there and evacuation of inhabitants to larger villages, or else their departure from the area altogether. Villages' being 'decommissioned' is now being seen as a major factor which promoted the depopulation of the countryside, detrimental to its social content and ecologically dangerous.

The human picture of the countryside painted in Poltava was indeed worse than the dismal review of productive capacity. Massive immigration depopulated the European Russia's midlands (outside the *Chernozem* areas) where nearly half the rural population used to live. Hundreds of villages there stand empty. The speed and the selective character of the rural immigration (as the young, the healthy and the better-educated move first) gutted local communities and turned many of those which remained into rural slums of human failures. Vodka and crime have overwhelmed many rural areas. Services are poor, supplies of goods inadequate, cultural life sluggish. Birth-rates in the countryside are often lower than in the crowded towns. The will to work, the traditional love of the land and preference for farming as an occupation were described as casualties of this rural environment. Losing farmers, the speakers at Poltava concluded, is worse than losing production and much more difficult to rectify. Bad as the problems of agrarian production are, it is the social reproduction of the farmers and the countryside which is far more troublesome.

Finally, the general system of state management of agriculture came under critical scrutiny which carried important social and ethical connotations. The system was described as over-centralized, over-interventionist and standing in the way of effective farming practice. Yet it is rational within its own terms; that is, it is said to represent the individual and corporate interests of those of whom it is made up. To them good work and good citizenship are comprised of total loyalty and prompt execution of orders from above (or at least, a prompt report that the orders were executed). The other side of the coin is public apathy, a lack of initiative which is regarded as civic virtue. Slavish scientists of nature and society who obediently and cheerfully tell administrators what they want to hear form part of this management system. Dual morality and double vision developed into 'the way things are done'. The burning of flax which was left uncollected in the field year after year was taken as a symbol of this mismanagement from above and apathy from below. To overcome bureaucratic management one must overcome apathy, but to root out apathy one must fight the institutionalized social injustice in the Soviet countryside, the unearned privileges and the powerlessness of farmers, the 'yes-men' and the accepted lies. Typical of the tenor of the debate, this view, coupled with the name of Tatiana Zaslavskaya and her new essays, was quoted nearly as often as Marx or Lenin.[3]

One important piece of evidence capped this argument. The main device used by the new Gorbachevian regime to stimulate agriculture has been the contractual team (*podryad*), which enables single rural families or cooperative groups to rent land and implements from the collective farm for a given period and, using them with their own labour and management skill, to maximize production and incomes. The Soviet press of 1988 pointed to successes along these lines. The message of Poltava was that in that province most of the contractual teams existed 'on paper only'. Why was this? Because the powerful bureaucratic system proceeded to dictate to the producers. And 'regardless of our attempts to try to restrict our agricultural administration it proceeds as a super-structure, as an office. And every office needs to keep itself busy, every office needs reporting . . . while a contractual team cannot be made to work when the team itself has no power to decide anything at all.'[4]

2 Four Models of Rural Change: Past and Future

How far did *Three Days in Poltava* offer a realistic general picture of Soviet rural life? Before extrapolating one must remove from the picture much of the non-Slavic ethnic peripheries of the Soviet Union,

3 T. Zaslavskaya 'Chelovecheskii faktor razvitiya ekonomiki i sotsialnaya spravedlivost' (Human Factors in Economic Development and Social Justice), *Komunist* (1986), no. 13.
4 'Tri dnya v poltave', p. 212.

where climatic and social conditions differ, often very profoundly. In many ways parts of the Estonian and Lithuanian countryside look more like Hungary than Perm or Poltava. But as for Russia, the Ukraine or Belorussia, the three Slav republics which contain more than three-quarters of the USSR's population, the evidence from different sources build up a picture which fits the Poltava discussion. During the 1980s it was supported by increasing statistical evidence (gathered especially by the Novosibirsk team of rural 'economic sociologists').[5] Corroboration can also be found in a variety of Western sources as well as 'dissident' writings of the recent past.[6]

The evidence and the argument would leave us puzzled without some focusing of the numerous views and new evidence. Let me suggest four models of agriculture and rural society around which the Soviet policies and disagreements have developed. First, it must be kept in mind that an analytical model is a purposeful simplification of a complex social reality, aiming to throw into sharp relief its principal characteristics and dynamics. At best it clarifies through overstatement; that is to say, operates the way a well-drawn caricature would. In the present case each model carries the powerful combined charge of taken-for-granted perceptions and appropriate political alternatives, but also of an indication of embodiment in the social structure and an intellectual history linked to an applied political ethic.

For a century or more, agriculture and the rural inhabitants who made it work were seen by the country's rulers as an object – a problem to be solved and a population to be transformed. Russia's peasants were consistently treated as the bottleneck in the country's development and the main reason for its backwardness – a barbarian hinterland of the destitute and under-civilized. This hinterland had to give way while a new and better world was being established.[7] As from 1917, for those who ruled, the future world was to be socialist.

During the period of interest here – the half century from the end of the 1920s – four fundamental sets of images lay at the heart of the debate policies. The first of these models dominated Stalin's Collectivization. While legislation and tactics turned and twisted, the principle

5 T. Zaslavskaya and Z. Kupryanova, *Sotsialno-ekonomicheskoe razvitie sirbirskogo sela* (The Socio-economic Development of the Siberian Village) (Nauka, 1987).

6 See in particular the *Newsletter for RSEEA* published in Portland, USA. For an example of 'dissident' writings see L. Timofeev, *Soviet Peasants (or The Peasant Art of Starving)* (New York, 1985). For a recent overview see Z. Medvedev, *Soviet Agriculture* (London, 1987).

7 For discussion see T. Shanin, *Russia as a Developing Society* (Yale UP, 1985), especially chapters 4 and 5; T. Shanin, *Russia 1905–7: Revolution as a Moment of Truth* (New Haven, 1985), chapters 1, 3 and 5.

behind them did not change for two generations. The core of this *Model 1* can be defined simply: 'the larger and more mechanical the better'. Poverty in the Russian countryside, low production within agriculture and the underdevelopment of the country at large were thus seen as rooted in the small and nature-dependent character of the peasant family-farm. What was therefore urgently needed to break free from it all was the transformation of peasant farming along the lines tried out successfully by the manufacturing industries of Manchester, Sheffield, Saar and Detroit. As for the rural population, it was to be civilized and brought into a new world through colonization by the industrial culture – a new, socialist Fordism brought forth by the proletarian party cadres. The losses the peasants might suffer and their possible opposition were treated as short-term problems. Later benefits were to be broadcast accordingly. Fiscal manipulation was to help it along (in the planes proposed by theorists like Preobrazhenskii), or else Stalin's dictum, 'when the forest gets cut, splinters fly', would be used *vis-à-vis* peasants in the imposing of what was good for them. Once put in motion, the new system of increasingly mechanized large-scale units would, in this view, bring about the long-term resolution of its own problems. The resulting increase in production would overcome rural poverty and constitute the final argument for socialism and for collectivization.

The party purges of 1929–32 and 1934–8 were a sign that even within the party cadres of the 1930s, good Stalinists all, some felt uneasy with the rural solutions adopted. But it took Stalin's death for a systematic criticism of Model 1 to surface and for a new model to be brought forward and adopted. It was clear by then that Model 1 did not work. The countryside of the larger units was still desperately poor and its agricultural production stagnating. The destruction of the 1941–5 war had, of course, had a major influence but it was becoming evident that this was not all that was wrong with Soviet farming. Even 'squeezing agriculture for the sake of industrial growth' did not work, for agriculture was manifestly failing to produce enough to be of use elsewhere.

Model 2 reiterated the preference for the large scale and the extrapolation from the industrial experience of the nineteenth century. Indeed, unit size was being increased still further. However, for production efficiency in industry, as in agriculture, size was assumed to be beneficial only in conjunction with a steep increase in inputs. What followed in the Khrushchev period and, more so, in the Brezhnev period was a sharp increase of investments in the manufacture of agriculture inputs such as tractors and fertilizers. More resources were also put into rural infrastructure and training. Extra land was also being utilized in considerable quantities, in Khrushchev's 'Virgin Lands Programme'.

To close the urban–rural gap, a *de facto* bondage (refusing rural inhabitants internal passports; that is, the right to migrate) was ended in this period. Food procurement prices were increased. Minimal rural wages were set and pensions granted to members of collective farms. The taxation of family plots was relaxed. But all these were treated as preliminary adjustments or the removal of extraordinary measures imposed by war. Long-term plans and policies concerning the future of agriculture were based on the described general view of its dynamics.

This strategy for agriculture saw a surge in rural production and productivity in the early periods of Khrushchev and again of Brezhnev. The Model 2 approach of 'the larger the input the greater the result' seemed to work. But within a few years the improvement began to level out and, with both population and consumer demand growing, Khrushchev found himself importing grain in 1963/4. Brezhnev came to import still more year after year, exhausting in the process the riches extracted from Siberia. Subsidies to keep food prices to consumers low, while offering inducements to farmers, reached staggering proportions. Most important, while becoming a major drain on the national economy, the policies of ever-increasing investment and input did not lead to a steady increase in food production. Huge investments were producing little return and, after 1982, none at all. At the same time the countryside was manifestly declining socially and ecologically. *Three Days in Poltava* is in fact the moment of recognition that the second model has been running out of steam.

The *Model 3* under debate in the USSR is easily recognizable to agricultural economists of the West. Size of farm is left open (even though the majority of Western economists would rather have it large). Increasing inputs are also taken for granted. The additional component is personal motivation for farmers to work hard and to economize to fight waste and strive for the most effective methods. This motive is associated with profit-seeking, competition and the fear of bankruptcy – the full paraphernalia of *homo economicus*. To activate pressure one needs a free market for agricultural products and inputs. A large body of Soviet public opinion and many economists accept this view as a satisfactory new description-cum-strategy for agriculture, with some important 'non-Western' amendments to be added, however. These include the view that the sale of land and private use of wage-labour should continue to be prohibited, as a hedge against capitalism. Also, in keeping with this scenario, the government should retain broad powers to secure national interests (a view with which, in their own countries, most Western economists would heartily agree).

Yet contrary to the view proferred by the Western media, the Soviet alternatives are not simply the conservatives' preference for centralization versus the reformers' wish to follow 'Western' ways (with the main argument reduced to how much the capitalist economy is to be allowed to penetrate Soviet agriculture). Such a solution fails to take into account the scope of actual experience or the projections of the future preferred or assumed by Soviet scholars and planners.

Concerning experience, it would be reasonable to keep in mind the USA, where a market-centred agriculture flourishes. While many participants in the Soviet debate look to it as a solution to all ills, the US social scientists are becoming increasingly alarmed at their own version of the agrarian and ecological crisis. Farm bankruptcies have reached massive proportions. Subsidies are large and rural communities disintegrate despite all efforts, often becoming the refuge of the backward and the poor. While US grain farmers struggle to make ends meet and are frequently defeated, staggering profits are made by increasingly bureaucratized agribusiness, often out of state subsidies. In the US a free market for farm products is becoming a myth.[8]

More importantly, major elements of the Poltava debate are not addressed at all in Model 3, such as the view that the most significant long-term problem that Soviet agriculture and the countryside face is not production but social reproduction and quality of rural life. A socialist vision of the future must give this particular priority.

This is where *Model 4* comes into play. It represents the views recently put forward by the Soviet radical rural sociologists-cum-economists ('economic sociologists' in their own parlance). To them the long-term development of agriculture depends on the social structure of rural life. Either the general quality of life meets the needs of the rural population or the best and brightest leave the land. Simply increasing income will not stop this process (as it failed to do under Brezhnev). Only living and flourishing communities can secure sufficient and balanced rural populations and lay the foundation for sound ecological policies, avoidance of waste and effective local management of resources. This must mean more material comfort in the countryside but also relative autonomy, richer cultural life and more opportunity for vocational choice (and thereby a more balanced rural economy, with small-scale manufacturing, services and creative arts, etc., as part of it).

Growing awareness of ecological danger and the waste of inputs and production in the Soviet countryside in the last few years has led to the continuous outcry, 'the land needs a master.' 'Masterlessness' is used as a synonym for 'nobody being responsible', and its solution is seen as an

---

8 For discussion see F. Buttel and H. Newby, *The Rural Sociology of the Advanced Societies* (London, 1980); E. Havens et al., *Studies in Transformation of US Agriculture* (New York, 1986); H. Friedmann, 'Family Farm and International Food Regimes', in T. Shanin (ed.), *Peasants and Peasant Societies* (Oxford, 1987).

essential plank of development policy. It needs the farmer's confidence that he and his family will be able to farm the same land in the future, and to continue living in the same place, to underpin his efforts. Simple privatization and marketization would not do; on the contrary, they could lead to further ecological decline of natural resources and the environment. The only effective solution seems to be a long-term transfer of 'mastery' and responsibility for the countryside to communities and to producers, who are made strong enough to withstand external bureaucratic pressures and egoistical insiders acting with an eye to only short-term gains.

What has been indicated as Model 4 is not to supplement or confront 'narrow economic interests' with other factors defined as social, cultural or communal. The use of private profit to enhance production is on the whole accepted. But to improve production means making farmers act responsibly as masters of their own production units, communities and environments. To achieve that one must not only secure private profit but also change power relations in rural areas – by debureaucratizing them. One cannot remove modern bureaucracies by frowning on them nor abolish them outright, but one can change their impact, size and status by establishing alternative centres of power, authority and responsibility.

Like Model 3, the fourth model can be challenged on grounds of experience and logical inadequacies. Rural communities which have disintegrated can seldom be brought back to life. Rebuilding the power of rural communities in the face of a bureaucratic state may sound Utopian, especially as the social agency of it is not clearly defined. Local autonomy would carry some parochial tendencies and dangers. The actual experience from which lessons can be drawn, be it the Russian *artel'* or commune under the NEP of 1921–8, or else parallel institutions in certain non-European regions today, is ambivalent. It is indeed a question of choices having to be made between long-term alternatives, none of which is easy or should be idealized. New is the understanding that the current state of the countryside cannot proceed for long even at its current inadequate level. It must be restructured or it will proceed to decline.

The very nature of analytical models means that none of them can be adopted directly as a programme of reform. Models are heuristic devices which help to explain the internal logic of an argument. The way these are combined and the emphasis they are given defines actual political programmes. Put another way, a political programme is always a combination of traits reflecting different interests, needs and perceptions. In the USSR of today the choices and emphases lie mostly between the accentuations of what have been described as Models 2, 3 and 4. These three models are associated with different general approaches and political forces within *perestroika* – reactionaries who look to the past for inspiration, conservatives who support only economic modernization and wish to blunt its anti-bureaucratic edge, and radicals who see it as a revolution due to transform social relations and bring about socialism (in the other versions socialism has already been achieved). The radicals of *perestroika* do not object to new technologies and would dearly like to link productivity more closely to personal gain. Yet there is an unmistakably 'non-economistic' emphasis to their message.

3 Zaslavskaya, Danilov, Chayanov: Future and Past in the 1987 Debate

The next significant development in the 1987 debate about Soviet agriculture and rural society was an internal document produced in Novosibirsk and signed by T. Zaslavskaya, V. Smirnov and A. Shaposhnikov.[9] In September 1987 it was debated by senior economists, sociologists and political scientists in Moscow. It offered further systematic evidence, expanding on the criticism voiced in Poltava. Over the last twenty years, it said, the average annual productivity increase in agriculture in each five-year period dropped from 4.2 per cent to 1.2 per cent. Worse still, despite state targets for agricultural improvement being reduced, the rate of achievement actually dropped from 84 per cent to 46 per cent. Still more dramatic, the productivity of agricultural labour in the USSR had not increased in the last twenty years. All this occurred while massive investment was being poured into agriculture and the income of farmers was growing. The document listed deepening ecological problems: forests, soil and water. As to rural services, the health of rural people was shown to be far worse than urban, while medical institutions saw no improvement. The quality of housing in the countryside was particularly bad, yet state investment was very limited indeed. The same held for education.

Opinion surveys in the Novosibirsk document did show a strong preference on the part of rural managers for larger units, because these were easier to manage. Managers also preferred to advance regional autarchy. Massive state subventions to cover losses were taken for granted. Personnel were appointed 'from above' while 'rivers of un-

9 T. Zaslavskaya, V. Smirnov and A. Shaposhnikov, *Metodologiya i obshchie kontury kontseptsii perestroiki upravleniya agrarnym sektorom sovetskogo obshchestva* (The Methodology and General Outline of the Idea of Perestroika of the Management of Soviet Society's Agricultural Sector), Academy of Sciences Siberian Branch discussion paper (preprint), (Novosibirsk, 1987).

necessary paper' flowed endlessly. Most important, only 22 per cent of those involved in agriculture considered themselves to be working at full stretch, even fewer when the managerial middle stratum was concerned. Opinion studies for the last decade reported also a striking increase in the expectations and demands of the majority of the rural population for better income, better conditions and a better quality of life. The rural population was increasingly objecting to 'living in the old way'. Yet the only clear improvements the document could report were some decrease in manual labour and some increases in educational standards in the villages.

On this evidence the Novosibirsk paper pointedly rejected the 'larger-the-better' vision, suggesting in its stead the need to combine large and small units, a view whose origins in the USSR can be traced back to Alexander Chayanov's theory of cooperation (see item 19). They also rejected Model 2, coming down on the side of Abel Aganbegyan's argument for the whole of Soviet economy, of the need to move from the 'extensive' mode of development to an 'intensive' one, that is from a simple increase in inputs to a focus on improving quality and utilization.[10] The view offered was a combined Model 3 and Model 4, but leaned far towards the latter. It set out schematically the mutual dependence of the 'economic' and the 'social' in village life. (For example, the 'social' sphere defines migration patterns, influencing in turn rural production, while the 'economic' defines job opportunities, reflected in the social sphere. Growing rural demands over the quality of life result in migration while shortage of labour puts increasing restrictions on agricultural production.) A list of particularities of rural labour was drawn up: the human qualities demanded for working with living organisms, the devastating impact of high labour mobility in farming, the psychological significance of division of labour and the need for highly flexible management to secure effective production.

The strategy offered was to construct a rural social system which would activate 'the human factor', relating personal effort to collective interest, increasing social justice and debureaucratizing management. Families and cooperatives must be freed from paternalistic and bureaucratic restriction to become the mainstay of a large-combined-with-small system of agricultural production. To improve ecological conditions, unified management of farming and territory must be introduced. To provide for this one must democratize local power, which calls for

10 A. Aganbegyan *The Challenge: Economics of Perestroika* (London, 1988), chapters 1, 3 and 11. See in particular Victor Danilov's article 'Kolektivizatsiya' (Collectivization) in the Soviet Historical Encyclopedia. For basic Western studies see M. Lewin, *Russian Peasants and Soviet Power* (London, 1968) and R.W. Davies, *The Socialist Offensive* (Cambridge, 1980).

division between party authorities and local authorities and organizations. Every enterprise or farm should be put on an equal footing
where execution of mutual obligations and contracts is concerned. Also,
and highly controversial, to promote self-regulating economic arrangements and self-accounting, food prices must increase. Finally, the future
planning of agriculture must be based on a variety of alternative projects
being considered before any decision is taken.

To sum up, a credo of combined regeneration of communal power
and enlightened long-term self-interest was put forward as the way to
improve farming, and also to rid the countryside of petty corruption,
drunken stupor, feelings of alienation and long-term degeneration. The
goal was to make the rural world efficient, comfortable in daily life and
of higher quality in an ecological and ethical sense – a place people
would like to stay in and come back to. The immense difficulty of
pursuing such a goal is clear to the authors but the long-term social cost
of not following it provided, in their view, a decisive incentive.

These interventions by social analysts of the present were matched by
extensive arguments between Soviet historians. An immense appetite
for historical writings was stimulated by Gorbachev's reforms. As to
agriculture, explanations of its sorry state and the problems of food
supplies could not but relate to the origins of Stalin's collectivization.
The work of Victor Danilov's department (suppressed in the 1970s) in
the Institute of the History of the USSR in Moscow offered important
insights and further data.[11] But the argument has by now moved on. The
repressive and destructive nature of the Collectivization of 1929–40, its
human price (including the death of millions in the human-made famine
of 1932) and its effect on current farming are common knowledge. But
explanations differ sharply and have become part and parcel of a debate
in which the problems of the future are often approached by arguing
about the past.[12]

Of an avalanche of views expressed, some do not seem to merit
serious scholarly discourse, offering a peculiar concoction of half-truths,
Stalinist apologia and Russian chauvinism. For example, Mozhaev's
recent novel put forward the view that the 1930s collectivization was
designed by the arch-devil Trotsky, executed by Kaganovich and actually restrained by Stalin.[13] To decode this message, collectivization was

11 e.g. the team work published as *Kollektivizetsiya sel'skogo khozyaistva v SSSR*
(Moscow, 1982).
12 e.g. Danilov's interview in *Pravda*, 4 June 1988, and the responses to it as well as
contributions by Yu. Afanasev, V. Tikhonov, etc. See also 'Issues in the History of
Cooperation and Collectivisation of Soviet Agriculture', *Journal of Historical Sociology* 2
(1989), no. 1, and the Afanasev interview in *History Today*.
13 In an influential *perestroika*-type of novel by B. Mozhaev, 'Muzhiki i a baby'
(Peasants and Peasant Women), *Don* (1987), nos 1–3.

what Jews did to good Russian folk, with Stalin in the role of the charitable tsar advised by bad ministers. Simple recitation of facts and names (Trostky was then in exile as an 'enemy of the people', Kaganovich was but one of the pack of executives to which Molotov, Ezhev or Voroshilov, all ethnically Russian, also belonged) demolishes the credibility of this version of events. It lingers in some darker corners but is not really about agriculture.

As to the historian's history of Soviet agriculture, past versus present, there have been three basic views on offer. Firstly, some of those engaged in the debate (often pensioners who began their careers as young collectivization firebrands) defend their own and their government's past as justifiable harshness in the face of world dangers and enemy opposition. The mounting evidence of cruelty and destruction are therefore treated as propaganda of less-than-patriotic whiners (*nytiki*) who give comfort to the country's foreign foes. In this view, it was discipline which secured the major achievements of the past and can be used again to cure the current ills. But more influential and more central to our issue are two further views in the current debate about alternative interpretations of history. On the one hand are those who now accept that Russia's collectivization was a terrifying event made considerably worse by Stalin's cruelty. This needs to be acknowledged. But there was no other option in the 1920s.[14] Against this is the view that there were a number of alternatives for socialist development of agriculture in the 1930s and, in particular, the early version of the Five Year Plan (of Groman and others), the suggestion made by the Academy of Agricultural Sciences (by Chayanov and others), the Bukharin 'line' in party leadership. Stalin rode roughshod over these projects and once his version of collectivization was enforced the rest followed: the peasants' confrontation with state plenipotentiaries, the hunger of 1932, the purge of 1937, agricultural stagnation and runaway migration. As Danilov put it in a 1987 lecture, there were alternative strategies for agriculture and rural society's further development: 'the terrible thing is that we had chosen the worst of them.'[15] The 'need to rectify a wrong turn' view of Soviet rural history forms a major element of the approach of the radicals of *perestroika*.

Still in 1987, Chayanov and his friends were fully rehabilitated in August. This tale needs to be told separately[16] but, to indicate the

14 e.g. I. Klyamkin, 'Kakaya ulitsa vedet k khramu', *Novyi mir* (1987), no. 11. For review and response see *Detente* (1988), no. 11.

15 The quotation comes from a lecture delivered in Moscow at a forum in its Institute of Archival Studies.

16 In a text still to be finalized by me, under the title of 'Chayanov's Treble Death and Single Resurrection'.

significance of this event, it offered a powerful link between the sociologists' and economists' argument about present/future and the historians' considerations of present/past. In September 1987 A. Nikonov, President of the Academy of Agricultural Sciences, made this clear.[17] He spoke of the direct and immediate significance of Chayanov's theory of cooperative collectivization as a way to reconstruct agriculture under *perestroika*. Chayanov's books were to be reproduced as a matter of urgency. Chayanov's fundamental ideas of cooperation were accepted: the 'vertical' division of labour, the 'differential optimums' combination of small and large units and the use of different cooperative schemes for different branches of rural production, a rural environment which is a cooperative of cooperatives.[18] Past, present and future met as honour was restored to Russia's great social scientist of rural affairs, who was 'purged' with the onset of Stalin's collectivization, to be summarily executed in 1937.

4 Gorbachev 1988–9

Without political resources and will, the 1987 feast of intellectual regeneration and debate over Soviet agriculture could still have remained empty of real political content. The occasion when the fully-fledged views of Gorbachev could be ascertained came in autumn 1988, when in snap meetings of the Central Committee and the Supreme Soviet he took practically unlimited authority. This meant less need for muted definition of goals. The sluggish development of the contractual team, indicated in Poltava, was now generally recognized. Agriculture and food supplies have increasingly become, to mass public opinion in the USSR, the measuring rod for *perestroika* and a source of growing doubts about its chances of success.

Gorbachev's major public engagement with agriculture came within days of his assuming the presidency, at a meeting of agrarian specialists and farmers in early October 1988.[19] Much of his introductory speech was taken up with the usual recitation of rural ills and the praise of exemplary districts, enterprises and farmers who had been successful in

17 At an Academy of Agricultural Sciences meeting devoted to Chayanov and addressed by the author in September 1987.

18 A. Chayanov, *Osnovnye idei i formy organizatsii sel'-khoz kooperatsii*, (Basic Ideas and Organizational Forms concerning Agricultural Cooperation) (Moscow, 1927). See also pp. 262–7 of his *Theory of Peasant Economy* (Manchester, 1986).

19 Published as 'Razvivat' arendu, perestreivat' ekonomicheskie otnonheniya na sele' (To develop renting-out, to transform economic relations in the village), *Izvestiya*, 14 October 1988.

finding new ways of organizing farming. But Gorbachev also laid down the basic elements of his vision of social transformation of the country-side and used for that purpose ideas and language drawn directly from the 1987 debate regarding goals, concerns and solutions.

Measured by the four models suggested, his message was explicit. Massive capital inputs did not produce satisfactory results – Model 2 was quickly dismissed as a solution to the agrarian crisis. Model 1 was not even accorded a hearing. It was a combination of Models 3 and 4 which was to be applied with all vigour. The immediate goal was the improve-ment of a productivity in terms of goods in the shops. Only through a major transformation of the agricultural economy could this be achieved. At the heart of the solutions offered was, in Gorbachev's own words, the 'centrality of humans' in determining necessary rural regen-eration. Far from operating as a propaganda slogan, this view acted as a linchpin of the whole programme Gorbachev was arguing for, relating the economic and the social, the collective and the individual. It linked the projects of reconstruction of the social environment, improvement in profitability, farmers' rights to long-term leasing of land and equip-ment, moral regeneration and rekindling the will to work at full stretch. Following closely on the Poltava debate and the Novosibirsk document of 1987, Gorbachev summed up the aims of rural reforms as creation of conditions, economic as well as social, which would make the country-side a place worth living in and facilitate the return of some of those who have left the villages.

Gorbachev expressed his ideal of the future economy of the country-side as one of a cooperative of cooperatives. This should be based on a multiplicity of forms of organization and rural production, Chayanov's 'differential optimums' clearly being expected to come into play. 'Peasant psychology' was quoted as a virtue – a synonym for 'feeling of mastery' (*Chustvo khozyaina*) and responsible behaviour towards work, output and the environment. The political message of Gorbachev's inter-vention was a call for an alliance of the 'top' and the 'bottom', the national leadership and the direct producers, in newly formed coop-eratives, grass-roots teams and family-farms, to put pressure on the 'middle' of bureaucratic managers, who hold on to resources, controls and the ceremonial briefcase. To be specific, these are mostly the officials of Agroprom and the rural party functionaries, with their appointees in the local authorities and collective or state farms. With increasing clarity a fundamental causal chain was being defined: to put an end to inadequate food supplies, a new rural economic system must come, rooted in cooperatives and family-farms, this being secured by transformation of rural social structures, which necessitates clipping bureaucratic wings, which can only come following the shift of power towards local authorities, communities, grass-roots organizations and families of producers.

What follows is a matter of political struggle between *perestroika*'s radicals, the conservatives who would like to change the way the economy works but without an anti-bureaucratic edge to it, and the reactionaries who oppose it, hankering after Stalin's 'iron discipline' or the Brezhnevian *dolce vita* for the elite. It is mostly a confrontation between an enlightened minority attempting to energize and mobilize others, and bureaucratic conservatives, as well as social inertia. To succeed in the long term the former will have to mobilize on its side those 'from below' to whom the chance for improvement must be demonstrated before they will act. It is in this context that Soviet agriculture is being closely watched as the make-or-break point for Soviet socio-economic reform. Once again in the history of this country, agriculture is central to the most immediate plans as well as to designs for long-term reconstruction aiming to transform society right down to its roots. Crucial to this effort must be the ability of Soviet social scientists to assess their country's alternative futures, to offer convincing solutions and to win the battle of ideas central to the country's existence and to its effort at a revolutionary change.

Part III

Measuring Peasants: Communities and Cyphers

14

Socio-Economic Mobility and the Rural History of Russia 1905–30 (1970/78)

This paper carries the shortest possible version of an alternative expla-nation to the puzzle of Russian peasantry's place in the 1917–30 revol-utionary period and its aftermath, presented in full in part II of my The Awkward Class *(Oxford, 1972). It used the work of Russia's rural statisticians to reconsider the impact of socio-economic differentiation on peasant political perceptions and action. The significance of this issue to the understanding of Russian history is matched by its relevance for the realistic class analysis of contemporary societies. To that purpose the study designed or adopted a number of new concepts and methodological tools relevant to rural society in transition, e.g. that of 'cyclical mobility' or 'plenipotentiaries' (see also item 11). It challenged the self-defeating tendency to use substantively static methodology for the study of pro-cesses. All this can show, hopefully, how much measuring peasants can help us grasp many things besides cyphers themselves.*

The paper was published first in Soviet Studies, *23 (1971), no. 2, and re-edited for publication in* Cambridge Anthropology, *4 (1978), no. 1.*

As recorded by the 1897 census, there were in Russia 2½ million industrial workers, 1¼ million soldiers, 1 million officials, 300,000 con-victs, 17,000 students and 100 million peasants – not less than 85 per cent of the population of the realm. In purely numerical terms, peasants were Russia. Not so in the terms of political economy, for both power and wealth were developed and accumulated elsewhere. Yet few of the Russian scholars and politicians doubted the fact that it was the future of the massive peasant majority, its stability or disintegration, its political passivity or revolutionary upswing, its possible alliances, struggles or ineffectuality which would define the future of Russia. Nor were they in much doubt about the fact that the crunch was coming, a decisive period when history might take an irreversible turn. (Lenin's comment about the 1905/6 revolution providing 'a rehearsal' is typical of the mood.)

With a language of class analysis very much accepted by both 'the establishment' and those who challenged it, the political camps were remarkably specific and 'sociological' in their predictions and aims. The most efficient of the tsarist prime ministers – Stolypin – was to 'place the wager not on the needy and drunken but on the sturdy and strong' – on the emerging capitalist farmers – 'called upon to play a part in the reconstruction of our Tsardom on strong monarchical foundations'.[1] The Liberals took capitalist development, urbanization and the rise in strength of the urban middle classes for granted – a path to a necessary constitutional evolution. To the Marxists, the inevitable Western-like rise of capitalism was to lead, through the social polarization and proletarization of the peasantry, to the once more inevitable proletarian revolution and a better civilization. To all those three schools of thought, the differentiation of the peasantry and indeed depeasantiz-ation of Russia were vital for their most sacred plans. The process of differentiation was to produce and/or enhance the class which would be called upon to dominate and ensure a better future, be it the protective wall of monarchist farmers, the camp of middle-class respectability, or the proletarian revolutionary army. On the other hand, the populist faith in peasant revolution presupposed the ability of the peasant class cohesiveness to withstand the pressures of capitalist differentiation. Scholarly analysis and political strategy and tactics intertwined at the dawn of the new century in Russia.

Not surprisingly, at the beginning of the century Russia led the world in studies of peasantry. The unusually high quality and the extensive nature of the Russian rural data gathered in the last decades of the nineteenth and first quarter of the twentieth centuries was a result of the historically extraordinary encounter between the massive traditional peasantry and a highly sophisticated and committed intelligentsia facing a problematic of exceptional and explicit significance. Since the 1880s many of the elected local authorities (*zemstvos*) had developed into strongholds of the liberally minded nobility and middle classes who considered studies of peasant life and improvement of peasant con-ditions their major task. Dozens of radicals, often in their employ, engaged in studies and analysis. The constant harassment by the tsar's government (all studies of peasantry were forbidden for long periods in a number of regions) failed to stop these enquiries. Indeed, some of the research workers embarked on their studies as a direct result of being banned, because of revolutionary activities, from living in big cities and

---

1 Quoted from Stolypin's speech in the Russian Duma in 1907 (A. Bol'shakov, *Istoriya khozyaistva Rossii*, vol. III [Moscow, 1926], pp. 26–7). For the best analysis of the period available in English see G.T. Robinson, *Rural Russia under the Old Regime* (New York, 1949).

holding university positions. Many others volunteered for this work out of commitment to the populist or the socialist cause.

The data collected by the *zemstvo*s approached 3,000 volumes by 1917. The experience amassed and the conceptualizations attempted show a variety of extraordinary insights. Studies were somewhat hampered by the lack of a national centre. The needs of World War I and later the commitment of the Soviet regime to national planning led to a unified national system of data gathering. After then, and up to 1928, Russian rural data was gathered within highly sophisticated annual representative samples of up to 600,000 households – in many ways superior to the more recent studies of peasant societies and, indeed, still unique.

Considering the extensive knowledge amassed, the history of the implementation of Russian Soviet rural policies 1906–30 was plagued to a surprising degree by failures and unexpected effects. A policy adopted – unexpected results – crisis and attempts to solve it by new political measures – once more an unexpected crisis, followed each other in monotonous sequences. Even today, many of the theoretical constructs accepted as self-evident for the analysis of rural Russia 1900–30 clash with available evidence. The fact that issues of Russian history and historiography seem to meet here a number of comparable problems in the contemporary sociology of some of the so-called 'developing societies' makes all that particularly significant.

To review it, the concept of the basic dynamics of peasant society accepted by Russian policy makers and, indeed, by the majority of educated Russians at the beginning of the century can be outlined in a few sentences. It was based on a closely studied social history of Western Europe and supported by Russian data. It assumed that economic development is accompanied in all societies by increasing social division of labour, the establishment of market relations, the accumulation of capital, and social diversification. It was believed that these processes are centred in towns but inevitably spread into the countryside. Rich peasant farms, which are large and well equipped and enjoy a higher capital/worker ratio, are able to deploy and accumulate capital better than poor peasant farms. Continuing cumulation of economic advantages on the one side and of disadvantages on the other leads to the polarization of peasant society. The rich farmers develop into capitalist entrepreneurs; the poor farmers lose their farms and become landless wage-labourers in the employ of rich farmers, estate-owners or urban entrepreneurs. Some of the characteristics of a traditional peasant family-farm may still be seen in the middle strata of the peasantry, but these disintegrate or change in the inevitable process of economic advance. With them disappear the survivals of traditional peasant society, and a new social structure based on capitalist farming is finally established in the countryside.

The tradition of thought rooted in Russian populism challenged the above analysis, insisting on the basic cohesion of the Russian peasantry as a class and on the stability – at least relatively – of peasant social structure. However, this approach never came to guide policies of state and, often, suffered badly from idolization of the peasantry.[2] To those who ruled, the general picture of the dynamics of peasant society, described above, was firmly established as a piece of self-evident knowledge, i.e. it had become part of the prevailing ideology not only in the normative but also in the cognitive sense. It was thus taken as given, and incorporated into the rural policies of the Russian state during the politically crucial quarter of a century which followed the 1905–6 revolution. The political perspective was that the peasantry would break down into new rural classes typical of capitalist society, i.e. capitalist farmers, wage-workers, etc., which would demonstrate increasing self-awareness, cohesion and a tendency towards political action in support of their own interests. This expected development was, in fact, a precondition for the success of the policies pursued by all Russian governments from 1905 to 1929, in spite of their conflicting purposes and convictions.

The crucial fact of Russian rural history in this period is that the predicted major development both of the class structure and of the political response of the peasants did not happen. The richer farmers and the rural wage-earners (or poor peasants) on the whole failed to act as independent factions. One can scarcely doubt the fact of socio-economic differentiation in Russian peasant society in the period; the evidence is ample. Yet, in spite of the socio-economic differentiation revealed by those studies, Russian villages went on showing remarkable political cohesiveness and unity of response. This is particularly striking in the 1905–6 and 1917–19 revolutions and during collectivization, but seems to hold true for the whole of the period 1905–30.

Soviet historians have repeatedly spoken of the 1905–6 agrarian revolution as a dual civil war of (1) the peasant poor against the peasant rich, and (2) the peasantry as a whole against the landed nobility. However, a glance at their work casts doubt on such an explanation. The most important part of the evidence is based on police reports of 'agrarian disturbances'. In these reports for 1905–7, 62 per cent of the cases are quoted as peasant action aimed against nobility estates, 13.4 per cent as rural strikes (once more aimed mainly at the big land-

---

2 Even during the short domination of the Russian government by the SRs in 1917 the ruling group did not in fact put 'populist' policies into operation.

owners), and 14.5 per cent as action against the police and army (which, on the whole, rushed into the countryside to defend the estates).[3] Only 1.4 per cent of the cases relate to inter-peasant warfare, i.e. were aimed against the wealthy or 'enclosed' peasants. What is more, the percentage of 'revolutionary acts' of peasants against other peasants in fact diminished during the revolutionary period.

The following period saw the bold attempt of Stolypin 'to place the wager not on the needy or drunken but on the sturdy and strong' – to promote a new stratum of independent and wealthy peasant yeomen settled on enclosed farms and, in his words, 'called upon to play a part in the reconstruction of our Tsardom on strong monarchical foundations'. If one is to believe reports, a decade of active and essentially successful implementation of these policies followed.[4] Yet it turned out to be surprisingly easy to reverse all these far-reaching changes in the following period.

The most widely accepted description of the 1917–19 agrarian revolution has its roots in Lenin's predictive analysis, by which an anti-feudal revolution of peasants as a whole would be closely followed by an anti-capitalist revolution of the rural poor against the rural capitalists.[5] Accordingly, the first stage of an agrarian revolution in which the lands of Russian landlords were taken over by the peasants is said to have been followed in 1918–19 by the takeover of the lands of the rich 'kulaks' in an egalitarian revolution of the rural poor. The relative success of the Stolypin reforms in establishing and reinforcing a stratum of rich farmers would lead one to expect this inter-peasant war to be particularly intense.

However, there definitely seem to be flaws in this scheme. The Russian peasants had almost uniformly opposed the 'Whites' in 1918–19, and by the end of 1920 were in active and passive revolt, this time against Bolshevik policies, again acting with remarkable unity. How does one explain such political unity of village neighbours within a year of an alleged 1917/18 fratricide and mutual land expropriation? Moreover. the kulaks, according to Soviet historians, comprised 20 per cent of the peasant population, up to 20 million 'souls' organized in the

3 The evidence in this paragraph comes from *Osobennosti agrarnogo stroya Rossii v period imperializma* (Moscow, 1962), pp. 36, 80. The trick of fitting such data into the general picture of a dual civil war was performed at times by adding the figures of rural strikes to those of attacks on rich peasants under the common heading of 'anti-capitalist revolution'.

4 See Robinson, *Rural Russia under the Old Regime*, chapters VI, VII; see also S. Dubrovsky, *Stolypinskaya zemel'naya reforma* (Moscow, 1963).

5 V.I. Lenin, *The Two Tactics of Social Democracy in the First Russian Revolution* (1907).

best-managed households of rural Russia.[6] With their relatives, depend-
ants and mature sons freshly back from the army and on the whole
armed, the kulaks would represent a formidable force. These 'sturdy
and strong' of the Russian countryside are said to have been stripped
within a year or two of up to 50 million hectares (about 125 million
acres) of their land and enclosures by the rural poor. One would expect
a gigantic inter-peasant civil war, and yet any substantial evidence of
this is lacking. To be sure, five decades of studies have shown some riots
in the countryside in 1917–19. But these were remarkably insignificant
in size when compared with the peasant uprisings of 1906 and 1920.
More important, a closer study even of these reveals as a rule a picture
of anti-taxation riots in which no class conflict can be traced and in
which peasant communities showed, if anything, remarkable unity
against outsiders.[7] We are left with a question: what was it that made the
powerful kulaks accept meekly what would have amounted to robbery
in their eyes? Alternatively, what is wrong with the two-stage theory of
the agrarian revolution?

Finally, the October revolution marked an attempt by the new government to 'put the wager' on the rural proletariat, to activate and unify the
rural poor as the natural allies of the urban proletarian revolution.
Rural Committees of the Poor (*Kombedy*) were set up to secure food
requisitions for the needs of the towns, but also to socialize the countryside by mobilization of the rural poor for a second revolution against the
wealthy peasants. Yet within less than a year this policy had to be
abandoned and the Committees of the Poor which had been set up
disbanded. This step is described by a leading historian of the period as
'timely recognition of failure – a retreat from untenable positions'.[8]
Similar results occurred with the so-called policy of 'directed agriculture' in 1920.[9] The attempts of the Soviet government to split the
peasantry and establish a Bolshevik foothold among the rural poor
failed.

The New Economic Policy (NEP) at the end of 1920 amounted to a
government surrender to the pressure of peasant will, and an explicit
recognition of the Russian peasantry as a cohesive, specific and powerful social class. Sporadic attempts to organize the rural poor on class
lines were, it is true, made during the NEP period, but were

6 *Bol'shaya Sovetskaya Entsiklopediya*, second edition, vol. 23, p. 327, estimates the
kulak households as 15 per cent of the total, whilst their membership size far exceeded the
average one. See also the more recent M. Rubach, *Ocherki po istorii revolyutsionnykh
preobrazovanii na Ukraine* (Moscow, 1956), pp. 20–3.

7 For example, see the introduction to V. Aver'ev, *Komitety bednoty* (Moscow, 1933).

8 E.H. Carr, *A History of Soviet Russia*, vol. II (London, 1963), p. 159.

9 See, for example, I. Teodorovich, *O gosudarstvennom requirovanii sel'skogo khozyaistva* (Moscow, 1920).

unsuccessful.[10] When major efforts to socialize the countryside were revived in the form of imposed collectivization, the anticipated socialist revolution of the rural poor (supported by urban allies) against their exploiters, again turned into 'a battle . . . more perilous and formidable . . . than the battle of Stalingrad',[11] between the forces of the Soviet state and the Russian peasantry acting once more mostly as a united whole.[12]

Basic discrepancies between the expectations and the results of rural policies in so far as the cohesion and militancy of peasant communities is concerned thus constitute the crux of the political history of rural Russia from 1904 to 1930.

The apparent failure of accepted theories to accord with the evidence of Russian rural history can be approached in several ways. One can simply deny the existence of the problem, i.e. of the inexplicably high political cohesion of Russian peasants in the period in question. Many of the Soviet historians (especially after collectivization) and some scholars in the West, for example, have persistently retained the image of a dual peasant revolution both in 1905–6 and in 1917–18. Alternatively, one can abandon the premise of class analysis by denying correlation between socio-economic positions and political attitudes and actions. Neither the Russian evidence available nor the contemporary political sociology support such solutions.

Another approach is to retain the initial theory while claiming that the predicted changes did not have time to mature. Interest and further research promoted by this approach concentrates, therefore, on factors of 'social inertia' which may have acted as a brake on the predicted changes, i.e. on static factors which reinforce stability. Research on these lines has produced interesting results in the form of studies of peasant culture, and of the structure of peasant communes.[13] Discussion of the influence of a low starting point (i.e. the general poverty and low surpluses in rural areas) on slowness of capital formation has been

10 See, for example, L. Kritsman, P. Popov and Ya. Yakovlev, *Sel'skoe khozyaistvo Na Putyakh vostanovleniya* (Moscow, 1925), p. 318.

11 Stalin's description of collectivization as reported by Churchill in F. Maclean, *Eastern Approaches* (London, 1951), p. 360.

12 E.H. Carr, 'The Russian Revolution and the Peasant', *Proceedings of the British Academy*, XLIX (1963); see also M. Lewin, *Russian Peasants and Soviet Power* (London, 1968).

13 See, for example, D.J. Male, 'The Village Community in the USSR: 1925–1930', *Soviet Studies*, XIV (January 1963), no. 3; Y. Taniuchi, *The Village Gathering in Russia in the Mid-1920s* (Birmingham, 1968).

another facet of this approach. Such factors retarding social change will no doubt have played a role; yet an explanation based solely on them seems doubtful in view of the extreme persistence of peasant political cohesion shown through one of Russia's stormiest periods of history, in time of revolution and of economic boom and disaster alike.

One can finally examine the possibility that some aspect of the basic processes has been ignored, and specifically examine and check against the evidence the assumptions made by both common sense and theory about basic socio-economic developments in the Russian countryside. Let us examine such a possibility.

Turning back to the evidence, the most important data both establishing and explaining the socio-economic polarization of rural society were those provided by the so-called Budget Studies, first presented in advanced form by Shcherbina in 1900, and later based on regional and national annual samples covering 30,000 households. These studies provided a systematic input/output analysis (including labour, production, consumption, sales, tax and accumulation) of each peasant farm of a selected sample and a census of its major factors of production, i.e. land, workers, equipment, etc. These data were then categorized by socio-economic strata. Both pre-revolutionary and post-revolutionary studies showed a correlation between size and wealth of peasant households and also a clear and constant tendency for cumulation of advantages and disadvantages. Productivity in particular (both total and per capita) was higher in the wealthier and larger peasant households and lower in the poorer and smaller ones. All that evidence provided clear proof of socio-economic differentiation, and suggested, at least at first sight, an ongoing socio-economic polarization of Russian rural society. (A single exception in the direction of the process was noted during the 1917–19 agrarian revolution and land redistribution, when levelling was reported.)

Furthermore, a number of Rural Censuses were conducted in Russia during the period discussed, including comprehensive national censuses in 1916, 1917, 1919, 1920 and 1926. The evidence of these censuses has again shown differentiation of the peasantry into richer and poorer strata. What is more, comparison of successive censuses seemed to support the view that with the exception of the 1917–19 period a reasonably constant, though admittedly slow, process of polarization was taking place.

Yet in spite of the seemingly self-evident truth of the suppositions discussed above, and the important empirical support provided for it by the evidence of the Budget Studies and Rural Censuses, the story of polarization as the main socio-economic process among the Russian peasantry is not true, or, more precisely, is not the whole truth. More sophisticated methods of study suggest that the main form of socio-economic mobility in Russian peasant households at this time was *multi-directional*. The polarizing trends were powerfully challenged by simultaneous mobility of the opposite type, in which large numbers of wealthy households deteriorated while the position of a considerable number of the poorer ones improved, at least in relative terms. The comparison of successive censuses of peasant households has displayed but the 'tip of an iceberg' of actual socio-economic mobility, i.e. the access of dissent over assent or vice versa. Moreover, a substantial number of peasant households seemed *successively* to ascend and descend with cyclical regularity. A definitely possible (if not finally proven) interpretation of the dynamic is to see it as *cyclical*, i.e. the higher the relative socio-economic position of a household the *greater* on the whole the chance that it would begin to deteriorate (and, conversely, the lower the position the *better* the chance of improvement). On the face of it, all this sounds quite incredible, especially to an observer trained in neoclassical or Marxist traditions of economic thought. It was duly greeted, even at the time, with expressions of disbelief and a tendency to dismiss such evidence as spurious, accidental or temporary.[14] Yet, as a Russian saying has it, 'facts are stubborn', and despite the denials the proofs of these processes failed to disappear. Indeed, some recent studies of peasants in China, Iran and Turkey point to the possibility that similar processes seem to exist in a number of peasant societies in other parts of the world.[15]

The evidence which suggests multi-directional and possibly cyclical processes of socio-economic mobility in the Russian peasantry is supplied by the so-called Dynamic Studies (*Dinamicheskie issledovaniya*). The method used resembles what modern psychologists and demographers call the study of cohorts. A comparative study of the same sample is repeated at various intervals of time so that we are able to locate not only social and economic changes in peasant society as a whole but also those of individual peasant households. The life histories of these families, statistically analysed and related to socio-economic strata, are then presented and analysed. Table 14.1 presents the results of a pre-revolutionary Dynamic Study by Rumyantsev, and can be used as an example of the method.

A straight comparison between the socio-economic differentiation of the households studied in 1884 and that in 1900 showed practically no

14 See, for example, Kondratiev's view in *Puti sel'skogo khozyaistva* (1927), no. 5.
15 Yang Chang Kun, *A Chinese Village in Early Communist Transition* (New York, 1959); I. Ajami, 'Social Classes, Family Demographic Characteristics and Mobility in Three Iranian Villages', *Sociologia Ruralis*, IX (1969), no. 1, pp. 62–72; P. Stirling, *Turkish Village* (London, 1965).

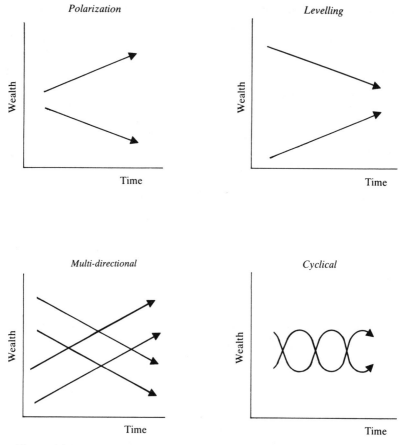

Figure 14.1 Patterns of socio-economic mobility of peasant households

further polarization and a slight improvement in the economic position of the community as a whole. Altogether, 9.7 per cent of the households seem to have changed their position in terms of the arbitrarily defined socio-economic strata. However, the Dynamic Study of the same sample and period proves that in fact nearly half of the households accounted for in 1900 found themselves in different strata, and that the changes were particularly predominant amongst the poorer and the wealthier (of the last category four-fifths lost their position within the period).

The Dynamic Studies were initiated by N. Chernenkov in 1897, and four more of them were published before the revolution.[16] In the

16 First published in N. Chernenkov, *K kharakteristike krest'yanskogo khozyaistva* (Saratov, 1905).

Table 14.1 The mobility of peasant households in Vyaz'ma uezd, 1884–1900

A. Changes in socio-economic differentiation

Year	Households sowing (% of total)				
	Nil	Less than 3 desyatinas	3–9 desyatinas	More than 9 desyatinas	Total
1884	14.3	24.2	56.9	4.5	100
1900	9.5	24.6	59.2	6.7	100
Households changing stratum 1884–1900	–4.8	+0.4	+2.3	+2.2	9.7

B. Dynamic study

Of which households sowing in 1900 (%):

Households sowing land totalling:	Number of Households in 1884	Nil	Less than 3 desyatinas	3–9 desyatinas	More than 9 desyatinas	Total	Households changing stratum 1884-1900 (% in stratum)
Nil	1,329	49.0	26.3	23.6	1.1	100	51.0
Less than 3 desyatinas	2,249	10.7	39.7	48.3	1.3	100	60.3
3–9 desyatinas	5,238	4.1	19.6	68.7	7.6	100	31.3
More than 9 desyatinas	413	3.2	10.6	65.3	20.9	100	79.1
All strata	9,294	–	–	–	–	–	44.5

Source: This Dynamic Study was carried out by the statistical department of the *zemstvo* in Smolensk *guberniya* and published in P. Rumyantsev, 'K voprosu ob evolyutsii russkogo krest'yanstva', *Ocherki realisticheskogo mirovozzreniya* (St Petersburg, 1906). One Russian *desyatina* = 1.09 hectares = 2.7 acres.

post-revolutionary period TsSU established a special section for this work (headed by A. Khryashcheva), which produced increasingly sophisticated annual studies of representative samples, and also provided reliable sampling and regional breakdowns. The size of the samples had grown by 1926 (the last study to be published) to about 600,000 peasant households each year.[17] The evidence gathered during four decades of Dynamic Studies of Russian peasantry reveals a clear and persistent uniformity in the pattern of mobility of peasant households on lines described above and exemplified in the study by Rumyantsev. This process proved, without exception, qualitatively similar in Dynamic Studies of samples representing different periods, drawn from different areas and using different categories of peasant wealth (e.g. land held, land sown, number of horses and even 'the extent of exploitation' in terms of wage-labour). The recorded differences between the results of the various Dynamic Studies were as a rule only quantitative in nature: an increase in the extent of mobility in the post-revolutionary period and somewhat higher rates of mobility in the agricultural south and south-east of Russia than in the north and west.

Before attempting to show how an unexpected pattern of socio-economic mobility may help to explain the unexpected socio-political behaviour of the Russian peasantry, let us outline in short a possible explanation of such mobility patterns.[18] The picture of the socio-economic mobility of the Russian peasant households which emerges from these studies is more complex than the monistic model of polarization described earlier; it suggests the existence of three types of process, operating simultaneously, and partly autonomously – polarizing, levelling and multi-directional.

(1) A cumulation of advantages and disadvantages favouring polarization, as documented by the Budget Studies and predicted by classical and neoclassical economics.

(2) A number of processes of a levelling nature, related to the selective character of peasant mobility correlated to the stratum involved:

(a) Among Russian peasants there was a strong positive correlation between wealth of household and size of household; the richer the household the bigger its membership, and consequently the more numerous the units resulting from division of the household be-

17 Last published in 1928: see *Itogi desyatiletiya Sovetskoi vlasti v tsifrakh* (Moscow, 1928), pp. 124–36.

18 For a more comprehensive treatment, see T. Shanin, *The Awkward Class* (Oxford, 1972).

tween the sons according to egalitarian partitioning customs. (The word inheritance would be misleading: the majority of peasant sons received their share before their parents died.)

(b) A substantial number of mergers between peasant households (mainly by marriage) was reported, on the whole negatively correlated with household size, i.e. the smaller and poorer households had the best chance of an increase in size, and hence in prosperity. The poorest and smallest households often lacked one of the production factors essential to a peasant economy, such as male labour, or horses; a merger (e.g. a marriage of a boy with land and a girl with a horse) would restore such a household to 'normality'.

(c) A high rate of extinction and emigration of peasant families was reported in negative correlation with size and wealth, i.e. the poorer and smaller the household the greater the chance of its disappearing. The selective extinction and emigration of households constantly 'purged' villages of their poorest and deteriorating members.

The differential character of all the processes of substantive change (*organicheskie izmeneniya*, in the accepted Russian terminology) in peasant households, i.e. of partitioning, merger, extinction and emigration, provided for a considerable egalitarian trend. It was reinforced by egalitarian communal land redistribution in those places in which this still operated. The simultaneous operation of polarizing and levelling trends found expression in multi-directional and possibly cyclical mobility.

(3) Some ongoing processes were multi-directional or cyclical by their very nature, e.g. the chance factors in peasant life, in particular the powerful, arbitrary and uncontrollable impacts of nature, market and state policies on the peasant economy of limited resources.

This preliminary analysis of 'causes' of unexpected patterns of mobility was hotly debated in the early 1970s. In addition to the usual and useless crop of friendly and unfriendly labels (e.g. the author is or is not a bloody or else nice Marxist, anti-Marxist, Populist, neo-crypto-semi-reactionary radical) a number of interesting comments were offered, and in particular some alternative or supplementary explanation of mobility was discussed. The most important of those included E. Vinogradoff (University of Pittsburg) pointing to the three-field agricultural system's impact on mobility and cohesion between Russian peasant villages, M. Harrison's (University of Warwick) suggestion that it is only multi-dimensional mobility we see and that can be explained by the economic instability typical of 'developing societies', and J. Peel's (University of Liverpool) stress on the possible illumination which can be shed by comparison with son/father coalitions within an African rural context.[19] Whatever the outcome of this debate (the advance of which is subject to further analysis of Russian materials and comparative analysis elsewhere), the essential data concerning mobility within the Russian peasantry stood up to scrutiny.

The handbooks of TsSU and the works of its leading members published in the 1920s provide here particularly extensive evidence and can be referred to with relative ease. The Dynamic Studies presented in tables 14.2 and 14.3 bring two more examples of it. The first (see table 14.2) was carried out by TsSU on a representative sample of villages of European Russia (exclusive of the areas hit by the 1920–1 famine). Horses per household were used as the accepted index of peasant wealth. The second (see table 14.3) uses sown area per household as the index of prosperity (as in figure 14.1 above), and is based on a representative sample of 265,436 households in sixteen *guberniyas* of European Russia. Both of them (and many others) repeat the essential characteristics represented in table 14.1.

The acceptance of a strong and consistent multi-directional and possible cyclical tendency in peasant socio-economic mobility must, in turn, lead to a reconsideration of the nature of the socio-political effects of polarization on peasant communities. In the first place, the effects on the polarization process will be weakened and may be cancelled or even reversed by a stronger opposing trend resulting in levelling. Indeed, recognition of this may help to clarify the puzzle of the 1918–19 'second agrarian revolution' referred to above.

Ideology aside, the main evidence supporting the claim of a second revolution lies in the comparison of the 1917 and 1919 (or 1920) rural censuses. These showed extensive levelling of the Russian peasantry, in terms of land owned and horses owned per household, while the number of households rapidly increased.[20] There can be little doubt of the genuine economic ascent of the landless and the poorest, who shared in the distribution of the lands of the nobility in 1917–18. However, to attribute the levelling of the wealthier peasant households to expropriation of the richer peasants by the poor means to disregard the simple fact that after a four-year period in which partitioning had virtually been suspended, millions of peasant sons suddenly came back from the army. They were mature, aggressive, marriageable, and keen to claim their share in a society in which wealth coincided with numerous sons, and equal sharing-out of the farm holding to all mature sons

19 Based on correspondence and personal discussions with those mentioned, and published since.

20 *Ekonomicheskoe rassloenie krest'yanstva v 1917 i 1919 gg.* (Moscow, 1922). See also A. Khryashcheva, *Gruppy i klassy v derevne* (Moscow, 1926).

Table 14.2 The mobility of peasant households in regions of the RSFSR, 1920–4

A. Changes in socio-economic differentiation

Year	No. of Households Owning (% of total):				
	No horse	1 horse	2 horses	More than 2 horses	Total
1920	30.0	63.9	5.8	0.3	100
1924	33.3	61.1	5.4	0.2	100

B. Dynamic study

Households in 1920 owning:	Number of households in sample	Households undergoing 'substantive changes' in 1920–4 (%)				Households not undergoing 'substantive changes in 1920–4 (%)				All households (%)
		Partitioned	Merged	Emigrated or extinct	Total	Unchanged	Ascended	Descended	Total	(%)
No horses	22,364	3.6	3.8	13.2	20.6	56.4	23.0	–	79.4	100
1 horse	47,534	10.7	1.8	2.1	14.6	68.5	5.0	11.9	85.4	100
2 horses	4,344	28.2	1.4	1.6	31.2	29.8	2.0	37.0	68.8	100
More than 2 horses	211	43.6	2.8	0.9	47.3	9.5	–	43.2	52.7	100
All strata	74,453	9.7	2.4	5.4	17.5	62.3	10.3	9.9	82.5	100

Source: A. Khryashcheva, 'Usloviya evolyutsii krest'yanskogo khozyaistva', Sotsialisticheskoe Khozyaistvo, (1925), no. 5, p. 59.

Table 14.3 Peasant mobility in sixteen *Guberniyas* of European Russia, 1924–5

Stratum	Households in 1924 with area of sown land totalling:	Households undergoing 'substantive' changes in 1924–5 (%)				Households not undergoing 'substantive' changes in 1924–5 (%)											All households (1–3+A–H)
		Partitioned	Merged	Emigrated or extinct	Total (1–3)	Of which, by 1925, showing membership of stratum:								Total (A–H)	Showing stratum change(%)	
		1	2	3		A	B	C	D	E	F	G	H			
A	0.1 *desyatinas*	0.3	1.2	15.7	17.4	58.1	20.3	3.1	0.8	0.2	0.1	0.0	0.0	82.6	24.5	100
B	0.1–2 *desyatinas*	1.3	0.7	3.5	5.6	1.1	74.8	17.7	0.7	0.1	0.0	0.0	0.0	94.4	19.6	100
C	2.1–4 *desyatinas*	2.7	0.3	1.9	5.0	0.1	9.1	71.1	13.4	1.3	0.0	0.0	0.0	95.0	23.9	100
D	4.1–6 *desyatinas*	4.0	0.3	1.5	5.9	0.1	0.8	17.3	60.0	15.5	0.4	0.0	0.0	94.1	34.1	100
E	6.1–10 *desyatinas*	7.5	0.2	1.2	9.1	0.1	0.2	3.0	17.6	63.2	6.6	0.2	0.0	90.9	27.7	100
F	10.1–16 *desyatinas*	12.0	0.4	0.8	13.5	0.0	0.1	1.4	5.7	29.2	44.6	5.4	0.1	86.5	41.9	100
G	16.1–25 *desyatinas*	12.2	0.6	1.2	14.4	0.0	0.2	0.6	0.8	6.1	32.7	39.9	5.3	85.6	45.5	100
H	>25 *desyatinas*	17.4	0.6	–	17.4	0.0	0.0	0.8	0.0	1.7	5.8	28.9	45.4	82.6	37.2	100
All strata		2.7	0.5	2.8	6.0	2.1	33.4	34.6	14.9	7.5	1.2	0.2	0.0	93.9	34.2	100

Source: A. Kyryashcheva, *Gruppy i klassy v krest'yanstve* (Moscow, 1926), pp. 15, 146–7 and 139–40.

was customary. The return of ex-servicemen must have led to rapid partitioning of the richer households. And what could be more sensible in anticipation of the progressive taxation and possible egalitarian policies of the socialist government? The few relevant studies of this period indeed show that more than half the wealthier households were partitioned between 1917 and 1919–20, and estimates were made of a rate of partitioning ten times higher for this period than for the period 1914–17.[21] The data also show an extraordinary decrease in the size of membership of the wealthiest households in this period. The puzzling notion of a 1918–19 inter-peasant revolution (for which there is very little evidence), followed within a year by a powerful peasant rising all round Russia, in which the same peasant communities acted as remarkably united wholes (evidence for which is rich to overflowing), may after all be laid to rest. The inter-peasant war and the kulak counter-revolution of 1918 failed to materialize because the anti-kulak peasant revolution had never taken place. The socio-economic dynamics of the peasantry in 1917–19 are reflected in the peasant unity of 1919–20 and after.

The consideration of levelling trends by no means exhausts the consequences of an analysis of socio-economic mobility. The massive mobility revealed would limit the chances of class crystallization of rich and poor strata within the peasant communities, an effect well known to social scientists.[22] Indeed, as early as 1907 Sombart noted high vertical mobility as a major determinant of low degree of 'class-consciousness' and of limited political 'class antagonism'. If, indeed, 'each class resembles a hotel or an omnibus, always full, but always of different people',[23] the rate of turnover will be particularly relevant to the tendency of a socio-economic stratum to develop from a 'class in itself' to a 'class for itself', from a socio-economic category into a politically self-conscious conflict-group. Such high mobility will also necessarily influence the character of local leadership of the peasant communities.

Before proceeding with the discussion of the political relevance of such analysis, it may prove useful to say what it *does not* attempt to do. The concepts of multi-directional and cyclical mobility are not intended to provide a general master key to the understanding of peasant societies *in toto*, unrelated to time and space. Also, while analytically distinguishable, they are in reality always enmeshed within a variety of other factors. The impact of socio-economic differentiation on the

---

21 See A. Khryashcheva in *Sotsialisticheskoe khozyaistvo* (1924), no. 2, p. 57. For the estimates see A. Bol'shakov, *Sovremennaya derevnya v tsifrakh* (Moscow, 1925), p. 32.

22 See, for example, *Transactions of the Third World Congress of Sociology*, vol. 3 (1966), etc.

23 J.A. Schumpeter, *Imperialism and Social Classes* (New York, 1951), p. 165.

political consciousness of the Russian peasantry and the possible division of the peasantry into conflicting classes must be understood in the terms of the specifically peasant social structure, its basic units, i.e. the family-farm and the village, its dynamics and its placement within the broader society ruled by others. Also, the patterns of mobility have to be related to the extent to which the dominant conflict-relations in rural society develop along the lines of socio-economic differentiation.

The political life of the peasantry is ridden with a variety of latent and manifest conflicts and tensions between socio-economic strata, sex and age groups, 'vertical segments' of households, factions and networks of patronage. The crucial issue of the political sociology of Russian peasantry lies in establishing what was for each period the *dominant* conflict which overshadowed, structured and utilized other conflict situations and determined the main boundaries and major camps of political struggles. During the 1919–29 decade the social controls of the peasant communities and the patterns of mobility discussed combined to weaken considerably the expression of inter-communal strife and in particular the tensions between socio-economic strata or rural communities. The dominant conflict of rural Russia was set at its most explicit between peasantry and the Soviet state and was locally expressed in the conflict between peasant communes and the *volost'* (sub-district) caucus of Soviet local authority. The semi-formal peasant communes of this period showed remarkable independence. They were faced by small, hard-core groups of outsiders, in which a dozen or so local party members closely overlapped with the local officialdom. These small groups of state plenipotentiaries lived and operated very much like a fortified camp in hostile territory, to which they transferred demand after demand of the central authority. The structural conflict between this group and the peasant communes provided an important unifying link to peasant localities, overshadowing time and time again other potential boundaries of tension. The patterns of mobility discussed contributed to such tendencies and were increased by them.[24]

To recall, during this period the multi-directional and/or the cyclical patterns of mobility at work checked the crystallization of peasant socio-economic strata into classes and made possible the relatively high political cohesiveness which the peasant communities in fact showed. The peasant community and its immediate neighbourhood provided the peasants with their most meaningful framework of political consciousness and political involvement. In the conditions then obtaining, the external pressures and conflicts tended to limit and to overshadow the

---

24 A systematic discussion of the political sociology of Russian villages during 1917–25 is presented in part III of Shanin, *The Awkward Class*. See also item 11 above.

tensions created by socio-economic diversity within peasant communities. Furthermore, in the struggle with outsiders and nature, a successful farmer, head of a big and relatively wealthy household which had arisen in many cases within living memory, was usually accepted as a natural leader rather than a 'class enemy'. No propaganda effort could make the peasants accept a townsman's picture of class relations and class warfare which contradicted their everyday experience. They knew better.

To put it all from 'the other side', that of the *post factum* analyst, the character of the rural involvement in civil war, 1917–21, and the civil-war-like character of 1929–33 collectivization were defined by social processes within which social mobility is crucial. The widely accepted variant of Russian rural history and of the historiography of its peasant society needs serious modifications. The consideration of the role of socio-economic mobility in the rural history of Russia helps to explain the failure of analyses and policies which implicitly presumed relative stability of the socio-economic strata among the peasantry, and/or a deductively ascertained rapid polarization. The evidence of the political history of rural Russia does not after all invalidate the essentials of classical political economy and political sociology but only demolishes its crude and static forms. It calls for more complex, more sophisticated and more dynamic expressions of class analysis.

15

Measuring Peasant Capitalism
(1977)

Written nearly a decade after the work carried out on Russian statistical analysis of peasantry's socio-economic differentiation (item 14), this text returned to it in a broader context of comparison. The direct topic was the measuring of exploitation as a dimension of social change within peasant societies transforming under the impact of market economy. The paper formed part of a general discussion, polemical in this case, about studying rural India, and was used to introduce English-speaking audiences there to the methodological achievements of the Russian tradition of rural studies. I treated it as a stepping stone towards a planned larger study of Russian intellectual tradition – a memorial to an outstanding project carried out by a generation of scholars whose analytical capacities were matched by their commitment to the betterment of the livelihood of their people. By now, with Gorbachevian Russia opening new doors daily, this general task can be left to the Soviet scholars looking critically at their countryside's past and present.

The paper was first published in Economic and Political Weekly (Bombay), XI (1977), no. 47.

1 A Problem and a History

The operationalization of concepts finds its significance and its limitations in the problematic posed. By those standards, our topic – measuring peasant capitalism – lies at the heart of the major concerns of contemporary social science. It has to do with capitalism as a process; it relates the understanding of the origins of our time to the characterization of the essential tenets of the global system we live in.[1] It is both

---

1 For elaboration, see 'The Third Stage: Marxist Historiography and the Origins of Our Time', *Journal of Contemporary Asia*, VI, (1976) no. 3.

central and controversial, for, while different schools multiply argument and terminology, none has managed to avoid the issue of peasant differentiation and structural change. The basic concepts of classical and Marxist political economy as well as those of the mostly neoclassical economics – the contemporary academic discipline – have been created to explore and to explain capitalism. All of them took shape outside peasant economies and societies. All the schools accepted, at least originally, Plekhanov's crisp contention that, 'historically speaking', the peasantry does not exist, implying the rapid global spread of capitalism in its 'classical' sense and the assumption that capitalism equals de-peasantization. Consequently much of economic theory disregards peasants entirely. Otherwise these analytical paradigms focused on the dual process of the peasantry's disappearance and capital formation.

Within the perspective of political economy, and especially in the various Marxisms of our time, three related issues are central. First is the process of differentiation of peasantry, confidently expected to produce or reinforce the basic social classes of capitalism – the capitalists and proletariat. Secondly there is the problematic of 'primitive accumulation', i.e. the exploitation and destruction of the mostly peasant modes of production and livelihood, which makes for the necessary pre-conditions for capital formation and capitalist industrialization – accumulated surplus, 'free' labour and an expanding market.[2] Finally, and on the whole, rooted in the last generation's experience and analysis, there is the question of the ways by which the world capitalist system can actually stabilize, reproduce and even extend peasant economies and societies via their exploitive integration or marginalization.[3]

Of these three only the first will be discussed here, as I consider the literature on Russia's 1920s, for possible insights into the so-called 'developing societies' of today. This date (the 1920s) and place (Russia) limit the discussion to the problematic of socialists arguing over the realization of their ideals. Within those circles the conceptual characteristics of the issue of peasant differentiation make it of high ideological relevance. Indeed many radical movements have divided and split, predicted and planned, were consolidated and purged in accordance with the way questions concerning the peasantry's differentiation were answered. Basic political strategies and class alliances have been treated and anticipated accordingly.

Indeed, no less than the very creation and existence of the proletariat as the major political actor are at stake – hence the extent of the debate

---

2 E. Preobrazhensky, *The New Economics* (Oxford, 1965).
3 J.R.B. Lopez, *'Capitalist Development and Agrarian Structure in Brazil'* (Sao Paulo, 1976).

and the powerful emotional undercurrents. When such confrontations increase, dictated by the turns of political and economic history, leaders and militants turn into (or turn to) social scientists. Some of them stay at the level of deductive elaboration of categories and programmes, but others proceed to look at relevant data, leading to greater awareness of the complexity and ambivalence of 'simple facts' as well as to greater analytical sophistication. It is usually a sign of maturity when the bridge between theory and *empeiria* comes into focus. The differentiation debate becomes, in part, an operationalization debate.

The translation of the 'algebra' of theory into the 'arithmetic' of field notes or the statistics of censuses and vice versa is, at the best of times, the major difficulty of the social sciences – the more so within a problematic loaded with conceptual ambivalence and a politically tense situation. The numerous ways of avoidance testify to these difficulties, e.g. the ever-increasing tendency to pepper 'pure' concepts with a few 'empirical' examples. The central problems here are those of a meaningful quantification and comparison of diversity within the peasantry, as expressed in peasant wealth, mobility, patterns of exploitation, capital formation and structural transformation.

It was in Germany that, for the first time, leaders of a socialist mass movement had to confront the fact of the peasantry as a major component of their society, and of central importance in any political strategy they were to design. It was therefore, not surprisingly, the place where the differentiation debate took shape.[4] Russia was a natural next in line, the attitude to peasant differentiation forming dividing lines between the main revolutionary movements as well as between the main factions of every one of them.[5] Russia was also the place where those involved most deeply were given the opportunity not only to use statistical data collected by officials and official academics, but also to undertake field studies on their own.[6]

Those opportunities blossomed fully in the 1920s when the new revolutionary regime stimulated massive and representative studies of peasant differentiation while opening the field wide enough to adherents of different approaches to facilitate debate. Consequently, while in Germany the interest in problems of operationalization was limited, it became central in Russia. To proceed, the next socialist mass movement

4 The debate between Kautsky and David, etc., in the German Social Democratic Party.

5 For discussion see T. Shanin, *The Awkward Class, Political Sociology of Peasantry in a Developing Society: Russia 1910–25* (Oxford, 1972), chapter 3.

6 For example, Khryashcheva, a Bolshevik, Groman, a Menshevik, and Kushchenko, close to the populists in his outlook, directed, before the revolution, *zemstvo* rural censuses in Tula, Mokshan'sk and Surazh respectively.

and major country in which original analyses of differentiation within peasantry developed were China's CP and the writings of Mao. His conceptualization has found a rather under-developed operational appendix in the works of Chen Po-ta – the head-to-be of the Academy of Sciences of post-revolutionary China.[7]

Most recently, India's radical academics took their turn at the differentiation debate. It goes without saying that no 'discovery of an issue' is claimed; Marxists of various hues and other students of the peasantry have discussed it before often enough – the overspill of debate within the Third International would be enough to provide for that. All the same a 'break in continuity' since 1970 was evident in the intensification of the debate, in the new suggestions offered and, to an extent, also in the new terminology applied. The issue has been posed in terms of the characterizing modes of production within India's agriculture.[8] A number of 'specifically Indian' problems like that of the colonial mode of production have formed part of the discussion. All the same, while no debate repeats itself in its entirety, the essential structure and problematic of the peasant differentiation debate of the past is being reproduced. With the debate growing sharper the consideration and reconsideration of data is increasingly coming into focus. The differentiation debate is turning into an operationalization debate.

Such a stage of development offers an opportunity to improve our knowledge of the issue in hand, but there is also the danger of going into a blind alley of a few academics duelling over words and struggling over prestige. One of the ways to 'up the odds' is to broaden the debate by indicating a comparison, the fruitfulness of which has been proven often enough.[9] I am referring to the achievements of the Russian scholarly community by the late 1920s and how their analyses relate to the India of the mid-1970s.

2 India's 1970s

Comparisons are always tricky and to make this one less abstract let me refer to a specific text. Utsa Patnaik's 'Class Differentiation within the Peasantry'[10] is relevant here as a major effort at operationalizing the

7 Chen Po-ta, *A Study of Land Rent in Pre-Revolution China* (Peking, 1966).

8 D. McEachern, 'The Mode of Production in India', *Journal of Contemporary Asia*, VI, (1976) no. 4.

9 The impact of a single translation of Chayanov into English has been indicative enough since Daniel Thorner initiated it. See A.V. Chayanov, *The Theory of Peasant Economy*, (Homewood, IU., 1966).

10 U. Patnaik, 'Class Differentiation within the Peasantry', *Economic and Political Weekly* (September 1976).

growth of capitalism and of the class divisions specific to it within the Indian peasantry. There are things besides that in the article, but I shall focus only on the issue chosen.

To recapitulate the relevant part, the paper suggests a labour exploitation ratio E as the empirical approximation and methodological tool to pose and quantify class analysis of the peasantry. In the author's words 'use of outside labour in relation to the use of family labour' is 'the most reliable single index of categorizing peasants' (p. A-84). There are said to be two main ways to exploit labour in the Indian peasant context (similar to the China of 1930 but different from, say, the Russia of 1910). These are the direct hiring of labourers and the indirect exploitation through leasing out land (p. A-87). This labour/land equation of exploitation 'does not give an exhaustive coverage of all agrarian relations, but only those arising directly in the production process' on the rationale that 'other relations such as those between the trader and money-lender on the one hand and different classes within the peasantry, are themselves conditional upon the existence of class differentiation arising in the production process' (p. A-90). The non-incorporation does not, however, stop there. There is no way to calculate leasing out in labour-days equivalence, and therefore the actual E is limited to the balance of labour hired in as against labour hired out (pp. A-92, A-84). In other words, while the leasing out of land is identified as a major component of class characterization and typified in Patnaik's tables 3, 3A and 4, it is not incorporated on the scale of quantification, even though the possible contradictory cross-cutting of the two types of category is mentioned. A single scale of mutually exclusive groups based on the labour balance within every specific household unit then follows (Patnaik's tables 2, 6), putting households into classes on the assumption that 'from a statistical point of view the E criterion simply represents the translation of economic class in agriculture into an empirically applicable form' (p. A-91).

As it stands Patnaik's discussion is important, significant but, at the same time, insufficient or not quite sufficient. Its importance lies in the very issue discussed. It is enhanced by a sophisticated discussion of relations between theory and operational categories. It is significant because the labour exploitation index is doubtless central to any attempt to understand the structure and the dynamics of capitalism within peasant agriculture. In this sense it will doubtless 'work', i.e. offer a way to identify peasant strata in a way relevant to the major issue raised. At the same time it is insufficient or not quite sufficient for the following reasons:

1 It lacks a workable common denominator to quantify ratios of exploitation, even in so far as its two declared major components are

concerned. Labour time cannot operate as such a common denominator, despite a variety of attempts to use it so in the past. Nor is an alternative way offered to integrate major empirical aspects of rural exploitation in an unequivocal way. The E ratio translates 'class in agriculture' but does not do it 'simply'. Indeed, the resulting reduction to a single index necessarily means a considerable inbuilt mistake. To avoid this one must have a multiplicity of indices, or else a composite index of several components. When these indices or components clash, arbitrary solutions necessarily follow.

2 It leaves out major causalities of the processes of rural exploitation, capital accumulation and the peasantry's disintegration (called rather vaguely 'agricultural relations'). As it stands, such a strategy would seem particularly unsatisfactory at delimiting the entrepreneurial/rich end of the scale of E proposed. To study a peasant community without a money-lender and a trader and their impact is to disregard what every peasant knows to be central, and also to omit some of the very springs of change one tries to understand (and can be left out only *after* establishing their secondary or dependent character). Not to do so within Marxist analysis because of its being Marxist is to me a caricature of Marxism as a major tool of thought and action. Those who doubt the Marxist propriety of such an eclectic realism should go back to the first pages of *The Class Struggle in France* (and many other pages besides). The primary nature of relations of production as against those of circulation, declared by Marx, does not translate into disregard of the latter when class relations are considered. An operationalization within which the richest trader-usurer of a village (and a capitalist farmer in a year?) can be delineated as 'middle peasant' is 'insufficient or not quite sufficient'.

3 It accepts by default the core of the existing methodology concerning data collection and analysis, although introduced and crystallized at a considerable conceptual distance from any concern with peasant differentiation and exploitation. It is barely possible that the problematic of peasant differentiation and exploitation can be fully discussed without relating it to alternative methods of empirical study. At the very least such a position cannot be left implicit.

The fact that the labour theory of value forms the core of Marxist economic theory does not necessarily make labour time sufficient to index classes and exploitation within a specific context. Nor is it sufficient to study accumulation of capital, despite its doubtless relevance to it. And so on. Clearly much additional work on operationalization is still pending, even in so far as the specific issue of indices of exploitation is concerned.

Instead of asking if there is anything useful one could learn from the Russian analyses of similar problems half a century ago representing five decades of accumulation of data and expertise, let us instead go to those whom the Russians themselves would accept as experts at the time when the relevant analysis reached its peak, i.e. the late 1920s.

3 Russia's 1920s

The 'peasant differentiation debate' within Russia had commenced by the middle of the nineteenth century and was to reach a new stage in the populist/Marxist debate at the century's end. It proceeded unabated, rapidly increasing in sophistication, to reach a new and final height in the official 1926 debate conducted by the Soviet Agricultural Academy. It was the last time that important exponents of major theoretical schools within the USSR crossed swords in an attempt to understand the differentiation processes within the Soviet countryside – neoclassical economists, populists, Marxists of different shades. Nor was the discussion limited to that debate, for relevant books and articles published in the late 1920s ran into many dozens.[11]

The operationalization debate within Russia came at the end of the nineteenth century. It took place mostly among the so-called rural statisticians (who were in fact also economists and sociologists by our own disciplinary standards), largely employed by the *zemstvos*, the Russian regional authorities established in 1861. The outspoken commitment and the ideological heterogeneity of this group facilitated lively debate. Much of it took place within the national congresses of rural statisticians, spilling over often enough into the public press and party argument, especially on the left. A number of methodological queries found their final resolution via consensus within this manifold group. For example, the peasant household was accepted as the main unit of analysis, a resolution less self-evident than it seems today. More 'technical' issues (e.g. the 'optical statistical mistake' in which some usage of samples results in a mistaken appreciation of differentiation) would also belong there.[12]

At the very centre of this debate lay the issue which bridged the pre-revolutionary and the post-revolutionary concerns and related them both to our times. It is the issue of empirical representation or at least approximation of peasant socio-economic differentiation, i.e. the issue of capital and capitalist class formation within Russian peasant society.[13]

11 A word-by-word report of the debate was published in *Puti Sel'skogo Khozyaistva* (1927) nos. 4–9. A great number of relevant articles was also published in *Na agrarnom fronte* of the relevant period.

12 See note 21.

13 See E. Volkov, *Agrarno-ekonomicheskaya statistika Rossii* (Moscow, 1923).

To put it differently, these are the problems of the relevance and validity of the operational definitions and categories used to express, to analyse and to refute conceptual claims and theoretical constructs within the peasant differentiation debate.

At the core of this issue are two related questions. Firstly, what is the way to establish an empirically meaningful scale of categories and/or classes into which peasant households can be divided? Secondly, there was a quest for a workable methodology to monitor and explain relevant socio-economic processes, e.g. polarization, in a more satisfactory way than the ordinary census could do. While the first of those methodological problems seemed about to be solved by the late 1920s, the second had been resolved to a considerable degree during the earlier three decades by the so-called Dynamic Studies and Budget Studies. Let us review those questions in turn.

Attempts to apply to Russian peasant communities a purely Marxist typology of classes under capitalism (as defined by the ownership and the use of the means of production) had failed empirically often enough to be abandoned by its early Russian proponents with few exceptions, e.g. Sukhanov. The heuristic value of an operationalization in which nearly every unit finds itself in the middle category of 'petty bourgeoisie' was next to none. While consequent recategorization was taking place (e.g. 'poor peasants' increasingly replacing 'rural proletarians' in most Marxist writings), those 'in the field' adopted land sown and horses owned as the major indices of differentiation by wealth of the peasant household. Marxist analysts, Lenin included, have usually accepted those empirical categories (at times 'under protest', pointing out their limitations). The rationale of these indices was that agriculture was highly grain-centred with no mechanization to speak about, and also that accountancy was easier within these categories. The limitations were very considerable, however. Major aspects of production and exploitation were left outside the main typological scale of empirical studies. An attempt to tackle those aspects and to double-check results was made through multiplication of indices incorporating more than 'land sown and horses'. Both quantitative and qualitative indices were experimented with accordingly, reaching a new stage of sophistication at about 1910. For example, Khryashcheva's 1911 study in Tula used simultaneously five indices in which the 'two greats' were supplemented by those of family labour, cows owned and land owned.[14] Baskin's 1913 study in Samara introduced qualitative categories of wage-labour usage, non-agricultural income and enterprise-ownership together with land

---

14 A. Khryashcheva, *Krest'vanskoe khozvaistvo po perepisyam 1899–1922* (Tula, 1916).

sown to establish a scale of mutually exclusive categories of peasant households: (1) entrepreneurial: (2) part-exploitive; (3) family farming; (4) trading and craft-producing; (5) poor and proletarian.[15]

The 1917–21 Revolution and Civil War led to a considerable levelling within the Russian peasant villages. It also aggravated the operationalization problems of the Russian statisticians. Private land ownership was abolished, land holdings were massively redivided, 'surplus horses' were requisitioned by the army, and so on. The new egalitarian policies of the state and its tax collectors made old indexes, as recorded, less reliable. Under the circumstances the 'land sown' and 'horses owned' categories used by the state planning and statistical authorities were highly suspect, as hiding rather than revealing the actual extent of differentiation. Worse still, even the extent of wage-labour did not any longer express the class diversity clearly, because in the context a rich peasant was increasingly hired together with his equipment and horses by his poor neighbour.

The possible elusiveness of peasant differentiation to the scrutiny of the operational tools used was debated mostly by the Marxists. The somewhat acrimonious debate between the two Bolsheviks, Khryashcheva and Kritsman, could provide here an example. The issues could not be settled by the usual reference to Lenin's own writings, which offered little guidance in matters of operationalization. While the ignorance of the Russian language in the Anglo-Saxon realm and its dependencies overseas turned volume III of Lenin's *Collected Writings* into a never-ending source of quotations concerning peasant differentiation in Russia, the sources used there, e.g. Postnikov, are methodologically prehistorical. By the time the Russian operationalization debate reached its final peak, Lenin was gone from the realm of the living.

During the 1920s Kritsman of the Agrarian Section of the Communist Academy was a persistently severe critic of the operational methods used by the Central Statistical Board. In 1928 a team headed by him published a massive re-study of peasant households in accordance with three indices simultaneously and comparatively used – (1) land sown, (2) the 'strength' of the household, defined by the extent of cattle owned and the type of equipment used, and (3) the use of wage labour. The aim of this analysis was explicitly set out as identification of the classes among the 'pseudo-neutral' majority of peasant households 'defined negatively', i.e. as neither wage employers nor wage employed, and usually referred to as 'middle peasants'.[16] By 1928 a number of Krits-

---

15 V.S. Nemchinov, *Izbranne proizvedeniya*, vol. I (Moscow, 1967), pp. 71–2.

16 L. Kritsman et al., *Materialy po istorii agrarnoi revolyutsii v Rossii*, vol. I (Moscow, 1928).

man's associates, like Gaister, had begun to produce field studies in which peasant households were classified by capital and income in monetary terms.[17] Their opponents did not fail to open fire, pointing out the considerable difficulties of estimating such categories in a partly monetized economy, and expressed doubts about a classification which disregarded land held (following both the nationalization law and the strictly Marxist interpretation of capital). Alternatives and alternative indices were suggested. The air was thick with methodological suggestions and experiments – the last blossoming of a social world and a scholarly community destined for instant oblivion.

At this stage there came the intervention of a bright young man from the provinces. His name was V.S. Nemchinov, born in 1894, graduated in 1917, and by 1926 head of a regional statistical department in the Urals (and due in 1928 for the chair of statistics in the Agricultural Academy – one of the highest tokens of academic appreciation then available). In his general outlook Nemchinov was a Marxist who, while finding much in common with Kritsman's criticism, offered somewhat different solutions to the problems under debate. In particular he accepted a number of the contentions of those Kritsman argued against. Nemchinov set out to establish a satisfactory index of exploitation by which Russian peasant households could be empirically classified to make possible study of capitalist accumulation and class creation, exactly the problems discussed in India fifty years later. In a number of ways a new peak in the relevant Russian methodology is reflected in Nemchinov's work and suggestions.

In 1926 Nemchinov published locally a paper which commences with a comparison of eleven variants of methodology used or suggested in so far as the empirical studies of differentiation of Russian peasantry were concerned.[18] These included methodological suggestions by Baskin (one), Khryashcheva (three), Kritsman (one), Gaister (one), Groman (three) and himself (two). Nemchinov proceeded to synthesize all of the qualitatively specific categories and relations, referred to as 'topological groups'. This synthesis is presented in table 15.1.

Nemchinov suggested the definition of every peasant household in accordance with the basic topological categories expressing its input in monetary terms divided into the entrepreneurial component $(a+d+j+k)$, the dependency component $(b+c+i+l)$ and the independent operation component $(e+f+g+h)$. (It goes without saying that this division is specific to its historical context, for renting in land was 'entrepreneurial' there, but can be, and is, a representation of 'depen-

17 A Gaister, *Ressloenie sovetskoi derevni* (Moscow, 1928).
18 Nemchinov, *Izbrannye proizvedeniya*, pp. 44–62.

Table 15.1 Conditions and means of production within a peasant household

	In own household		In other households
Means of production	Owned by others	Self-owned	Self-owned
A Land	a En	e In	i De
B Fixed capital	b De	f In	j En
C Circulating capital	c De	g In	k En
D Labour	d En	h In	l De

Note: (En) Entrepreneurial, (De) Dependent, (In) Independent.
Source: Based on Nemchinov, *Izbrannye proizvedeniya*, vol. I, p. 48.

dency' elsewhere.) In cases in which both the entrepreneurial and the dependent component existed, a balance of both was to be used. Estimates and averages were to be used to establish annual input. Relevant 'price tables' were worked out empirically by Nemchinov's statistical outfit for their own district. The category 'land' (A) was represented by the actual rents of land in the area. Fixed capital input (B) was represented by estimates of amortization. Actual average prices as established were used for circulating capital (C) and labour (D). Every peasant household of the sample was then to be characterized in percentages which can be represented by a formula

$$\frac{\text{En} - \text{De}}{\text{Total input}} \times 100$$

Table 15.2 explains this with an actual example.

In this case the entrepreneurial component would be 413.75 roubles and the dependent component 31.35 roubles. The total input being 1381.25 roubles, the results in terms of the formula used would be

$$\frac{413.75 - 31.35}{1381.25} = 27.7\%$$

i.e. the household shows an entrepreneurial component of 27.7 per cent. In cases of trading and similar activities outside agriculture Nemchinov suggested adding their input to the entrepreneurial component of the present household (*Izbrannye proizvedeniya*, p. 50).

To try it out, Nemchinov proceeded to re-study one of the sample areas of the national annual census within his region. It consisted of 835 peasant households which did not undergo 'substantive changes' within the 1924–5 period (i.e. did not partition, merge, emigrate or liquidate).

Table 15.2 An example of a peasant household estimate (in roubles of input)

Means of production	In own household		In other households	Total
	Owned by others	Self-owned	Self-owned	
A Land and meadows	*a* 127.25	*e* 176.85	*i* 21.10	325.20
B Equipment and livestock	*b* 10.25	*f* 104.60	*j* 35.50	150.35
C Seeds and fodder	*c* –	*g* 289.70	*k* –	289.70
D Labour	*d* 251.00	*h* 365.00	*l* –	616.00
Total	388.50	936.15	56.60	1381.25

Source: Nemchinov, *Izbrannye proizvedeniya*, pp. 49–56. Figures realistic for
the period and the area (a rich household).

For every peasant household a balance of basic components of input was
prepared in accordance with the programme presented above. All of the
peasant households were then divided into six strata/categories. Table
15.3 gives the results.

This stratification was subsequently compared to, and cross-tabulated
with, the groupings of the same households by the 'natural' indices of
land sown, horses owned, etc. The same households were also re-
grouped once more in accordance with the estimates of value of constant capital in each of them. A number of analytical conclusions was
then drawn, reflecting both the content of table 15.3 and the others. For
example, Nemchinov concluded that any attempt to delineate 'kulaks' –
a major concern of those times – must take into consideration both the
'social characteristics' as defined on the scale in table 15.3 *and* the fixed
capital as estimated. (In his studies he divided households into three
basic categories of rich, middle and poor.) The consequent analytical
operation showed as 'kulak' eight households in his sample (0.96 per
cent), taking only those units which appear in the top category of both
scales under consideration. Further, he was able to demonstrate that
within the independent producers category about one-third of the
households was poor by the standards of value of capital, while about
one-tenth was rich. The typical 'middle peasant' in terms of both the
scale of 'social characteristics' and that of wealth would consist thereby
of only 43 per cent of the households studied.

At the beginning of 1927 Nemchinov presented his methodological
suggestions in two 'theses' presented to the All-Union Convention of
Statisticians. Much of Nemchinov's contribution simply restated system-

Table 15.3 The differentiation of 835 peasant households in Troitskii area, 1925 characterized by input

Category	Percentage
Dependency above 50%	9.70
Dependency above 15 and under 50%	13.05
Dependency above 2.5 and under 15%	9.70
Up to $2\frac{1}{2}$% of either entrepreneurial or dependency	52.93
Entrepreneurial $2\frac{1}{2}$% to 15%	12.10
Entrepreneurial above 15%	2.52
Total	100.00

Source: Nemchinov, *Izbrannye proizvedeniya*, p. 58.

atically the essentials of his methodological attempt in the Urals. A class delineation of peasant households was stated to be its aim, expressed in its classical terms as the process of alienation of means of production from the direct producers and the expropriation of surplus value via control of means of production. The issue of modes of production was mentioned but deliberately put aside in view of the 'total lack of suitable statistical characteristics dividing the pre-capitalist mode and the other ones' (p. 63). Nemchinov suggested that his new categories were to be used simultaneously with those of land sown within a section of the national sample selected for more intensive study. The earlier attempt at categorization was extended by incorporating a broader review of pre-revolutionary works of rural statisticians, adding Rumyantsev and Shlipovich to those already named. From what we know, the 1927–8 dynamic census was to incorporate Nemchinov's methodological suggestion. It was caught up in the collectivization upheaval and never published.

That is not all, for Nemchinov's work in the Urals was directly related to specific methodologies designed to study peasant differentiation as a process. While his work on the expression of exploitation was no doubt original, by the time he entered the scene the other methodologies referred to had already been established as a solid achievement of Russian scholarship. Consequently, they had been incorporated into, and were at the very centre of, the work of the state statistical board and planning outfits in the 1920s. As the head of a regional statistical board, Nemchinov participated in all that work; his insights and his very professional knowledge formed in close relation to them. Those studies, specifically designed to approach peasant differentiation and the opera- tion of peasant households as a process, fell into two major types referred to as Dynamic Studies and Budget Studies respectively. By the end of the 1920s both were carried out annually on samples representative of all of the regions of the USSR. (The size of the annual sample was by 1926 about 500,000 peasant households for the Dynamic Studies and up to 30,000 households for the Budget Studies.)

Dynamic Studies were introduced first at the turn of the century out of dissatisfaction with conclusions drawn about a process of socio-economic mobility from a census – in everybody's view a spurious procedure, yet often used for lack of any better data. Much of what was and still is presented as empirical analysis of a process is actually very much akin to guessing from a snapshot how a ballerina dances – an attempt to look at processes through an inherently static reflection. The author of the Dynamic Studies, Chernenkov, claimed that even a study of two consecutive censuses of samples drawn from a similar area must hide much of the socio-economic change and mobility involved, by showing only the residuum of upward and downward mobility and disregarding non-quantitative changes which occurred. What was needed was a re-study which went back specifically to every peasant household in the sample initially studied to represent the totality of changes statistically. Such an analysis enables one to single out substantive changes, i.e. the rate at which peasant households of every peasant stratum transform or disappear via partition, merger, emigration and disintegration; and to grasp the full scope and direction of socio-economic mobility within every chosen stratum and category of peasant households. His results were revealing enough for the methodology to be adopted by five more major studies before the Revolution and to be incorporated into the core of the basic data and annual report by the Central Statistical Board as from 1920.

To exemplify the potential insights of the Dynamic Study, Nemchinov's work on the period of 1924–5 revealed, in addition to a 'class map', the fact that the peasant households with a high rate of dependency were highly unstable, 16 per cent of them disappearing within one single year, mostly through self-liquidation and merger (p. 56). Other dynamic studies monitored the extent of upward and downward mobility within different peasant strata and specific groupings, e.g. those deeply engaged in craft and trade, etc. And so on. Instead of 'statistical snapshots' or a sum total residuum, Soviet scholars established a system of analysis and a body of data annually reviewed, reflecting the sum total of mobility and structural transformation within the countryside.

Russian Budget Studies developed on a tradition essentially borrowed from the West, mostly via the works of F. le Play.[19] Its use for the study

19 See, for example, A. Chayanov, *Byudzhetnye issledovaniya* (Moscow, 1929).

of peasant households and its 'modern' form were established by Shcherbina in the *zemstvo* of Vorenezh during 1887–91. By moving its focus from families as consumption units to the peasant household, as a production–consumption unit, the whole character of this methodology was transformed. It came to consist of systematic input–output analysis of representative samples of peasant households for the whole of an agricultural year. This information plus the amount of labour, land and equipment available for every peasant household were then presented and analysed statistically in strata defined in terms of wealth. Such a study enabled the explication of specific characteristics of different strata and categories of peasant households in terms of typical production techniques, productivity, consumption patterns, income, accumulation and so on. Despite considerable technical and methodological difficulties, the Russian scholars persistently developed Budget Studies, turning them into a basic tool to monitor and reveal actual processes rather than to assume them on the basis of the empirical studies of their results only.[20]

The considerable conceptual achievement of these Russian scholars cannot be understood at all without an awareness of their major methodological achievements, which put them ahead of anybody else in so far as empirical data available and its analysis were concerned. In the words of one of them, 'the *zemstvo* statisticians constructed a tool, unique of its kind, for studying the life of the peasantry, such as no other country has at its disposal.' He has also pointed out that it 'substantially diverged in almost every respect from West European models'.[21] For once we are not dealing here with a typical display of Russian boastfulness. The claim was true and became even more so while methodological thinking in the 1920s gathered momentum. It still remains true in 1977.[22]

4 Heritage and Usage

What are the possible uses of the Russian methodological heritage for the resolution of contemporary problems? Specifically, what can one

---

20 Volkov, *Agrarno-ekonomicheskaya statistika Rossii*.

21 Quoted from the item '*Zemstvo* Statistics' in the Russian encyclopaedia, *Novyi entsiklopedicheskii slovar*, vol. XVIII (Petersburg, 1913).

22 For elaboration and examples in English see Shanin *The Awkward Class*, which also carries references to the main Russian sources. For alternative review of material available in English see Chayanov, *Theory of Peasant Economy*, and, much more limited, in P.A. Sorokin, F.F. Zimmerman and C.J. Golpin, *Systematic Source Book in Rural Sociology* (New York, 1965).

learn from it to facilitate the gathering of an analysis of empirical evidence concerning exploitation and class formation within the Indian peasantry?

Following the chosen path of methodological comparison, I shall not refer here at all to the relevant aspects of the issue of modes of production, to be taken up elsewhere. At 'the other end' of the conceptual spectrum numerous technical and methodological 'tips' of immediate interest can be culled from Russian experience and put to work anew. Yet it is the way comparison helps to formulate the problematic which is to my view the most important. In so far as the issue of indexing exploitation and stratifying peasant households accordingly is concerned there seem to be three stages of necessary procedure. Each of them represents an answer (or a cluster of answers) to a question crucial for the setting out of those issues in a language directed to field work. These are the questions of types, of the common denominator and of categorization or scales. The whole range of specific projects in Russia, India and elsewhere is definable in terms of the resolution of these questions. Moreover, the way each question is resolved narrows down the possible choices further within the sequence.

(1) Contemporary peasant societies present a complex network of relations and determinations relevant to the issue, i.e. patterns of exploitation and class formation. To typologize them is to establish a qualitative list of different categories ('topological' in the Russian professional jargon). Within such a taxonomy every peasant household can be defined by a set of binary yes/no answers or else by being placed on a scale of more/less. For example, a peasant household in a sample can be categorized by answering the questions: (a) does it employ wage labour on the farm (yes/no)?, (b) what equipment does it use (simplest/also a drill/also tractors)?, (c) does it also own non-farming enterprises, i.e. a shop, a truck, or a workshop (yes/no)?

A household X employing wage-labour on the farm, owning a drill but not a tractor, as well as a truck, may be then defined accordingly (into, say, the group of the well-to-do and to be watched for possible transformation into a capitalist farm). Such an example brings out clearly enough the gratifying, if relative, simplicity of usage as well as the limitations of such an attempt using qualitative characterization only. To begin with, there is no direct way to compare relatively the significance of each of these categories. An attempt at further specification rapidly increases the number of the theoretically available slots, making the whole system unwieldy. (There are twelve such possibilites in the example offered above, while a list of this kind actually discussed at the Statistical Convention of 1926 in the USSR included forty-five such groups.)

While some of the analysts stop at that stage, the validation of many of the major conceptual questions necessitates a further step – the meaningful integration of these categories. To be truly effective, such a 'step forward' must begin with a satisfactory clarification of the full 'list' of the relevant qualitative categories of rural exploitation and a reasoned decision in so far as consequent selection for usage is concerned. This decision will necessarily dictate subsequent procedure.

(2) An attempt to integrate and represent the nominal 'topological' categories established can be expressed as the problem of a common denominator. To begin with, for such a need to arise the number of relevant categories must be large. The least unequivocal solution would then be to use simultaneously a number of scales and to trust to either some arbitrary rules of procedure or else the analyst's intuition (when results on different scales contradict each other). A half-way solution, developing further the idea of 'rules of procedure', is to establish multi-variable indices, as for example in defining as middle peasant households all those which have *either* ten acres of operational landholding and two bullocks, *or else* seven acres of operational landholding and four bullocks, etc. An optimal solution would consist of a formula and a 'common currency', making possible integration via meaningful quantification of all of the qualitative aspects of the issue in hand. One index and one quantitative scale only would result.

(3) The definition of peasant households in terms of quantified expression of exploitation, empirically recognizable, is not the end of the matter. At the centre of studies of peasant differentiation stands the problem of comparison between specific peasant households and their grouping into conceptual categories rooted in theoretical analysis. In operational language it must involve expressing the empirical results on a scale of peasant groups/categories. Proceeding once more from the least satisfactory, such a scale can consist of categories which are arbitrary (e.g. placing a household of ten acres and two bullocks above a household of seven acres and three bullocks). More satisfactory would be a *quantitatively integrated* scale with arbitrary cutting-off points (e.g. from 5.1 per cent to 10 per cent, from 10.1 per cent to 15 per cent, etc.). The ideal would be a scale translatable directly into the language of social classes, dividing most of the population exclusively into owners of means of production as against proletarians, with very little else. Peasants are not civilized enough to offer such solutions to the purist, but a delineation of optimal solutions is useful for illuminating directions of advance and realistic possibilities at hand. More importantly, any

solution to such queries must be closely related to the dynamics, which cannot be 'thrown in' here without a more specific methodological conclusion. I shall turn to it shortly.

A lengthy epistemological discussion of the relations between aims and tools of empirical study could begin here, easily stretching into several volumes. Instead, I shall simply say that I accept most of what was said by those referred to above about the complexities of the matter and the fact that operational solutions can only approximate concepts, not match them. Also, any questions and/or answers would be subject to their context, both social and conceptual as well as related to what can be defined as subject/object relations involved. In this sense different indices can and should be used to illuminate different aspects of a problem and to throw additional light on each other's results. It goes without saying that making use of different indices does not mean their equality in some eclectic sense, but must be seen in hierarchies of significance defined by the conceptual structure of the question posed. All that accepted, it is still the attempt to push closer the conceptual to the empirical which is the focus of operational debate, past and present.[23] Let us return to that.

The strategies suggested for the class analysis of peasantry can be placed in relation to the sequence of questions/stages suggested. Patnaik's position is to fasten on wage labour and land rent as the main categories. She then declares the impossibility of a common denominator between these categories and subsequently settles for a quantitative scale of one of them, to which a qualitative lessor/lessee category of exploitive relations is added, the operational relation between which is not (not yet?) fully worked out. Its limitations and strengths as well as my reasons for believing in its qualified usefulness were set out above. As it stands, it should probably be referred to as *LER* (labour–exploitation ratio), rather than an *E* one. The different Russian approaches can also be defined via diverse combinations of characteristics, different ways to solve the problems of integration and differences of scale.

Nemchinov's approach reviewed above seems to offer the advantage of high flexibility at stage (2) in its openness to extension and change in the list of qualitative categories without a collapse of integration in the scale used. With a few adjustments (e.g. fertilizers instead of fodder, etc.), it can probably be put to an immediate use in most of the contemporary 'developing societies', India included. The value of extending the list of exploitive relations relevant to peasant societies must

23 Those who would like to challenge my views on that matter should first read Shanin, *The Awkward Class*, chapters 3–7, or Shanin, *The Rules of the Game: Cross-Disciplinary Essays on Models of Scholarly Thought* (London, 1972), etc.

be set against 'the other side of the coin', i.e. the more eclectic nature of the categorization. But it is worth the trouble for it keeps 'in the picture' channels of rural accumulation, exploitation and control. However, such problems cannot be usually solved by pure deduction. An experiment will doubtless be beneficial.

It is important not to treat Nemchinov as a new and final master key. His main importance is in providing a lesson in thinking for oneself, for every social scientist must be also his own methodologist. Both general approach and actual usage must be adjusted to local circumstances. Let us offer an example of how to build on Nemchinov's scheme by developing new indices. A concept of Net Conventional Income (*NCI*), as developed and defined within Russian studies of peasantry as the sum total of a peasant household's income less all of its input with the single exception of family labour, could be used in monetary terms, as a common denominator. The study would commence with a consideration of the basic dimensions of exploitation and capital formation within the relevant peasant society. These could then be categorized to establish two lists of types of income typical of the entrepreneurial/capitalist households (*EI*) on the one hand and the proletarian/poor ones (*PI*) on the other. For example, the *EI* group would include renting out bullocks, renting out land, money-lending business income, income resulting from use of wage-labour at the farm*, etc., while the *PI* group would include wage labour, income from land rented*, etc.

In both groups the last item, marked (*), presents a problem which can be resolved by further analytical work, as long as one remembers that approximation rather than absolute exactitude is sought. Entrepreneurial income resulting from use of wage labour at the farm (*EI**) can be, for example, estimated as the percentage of wage-labour within total labour multiplied by the Net Conventional Income from farming. The income from land rented by a poor household (*PI**) can be estimated likewise as the Net Conventional Income with the price of rent incorporated in input. A formula can then be used to define every peasant household, so permitting classification of the sample in terms of the extent of the entrepreneurial self-producing or proletarian tendency within each household, according to the formula

$$\frac{EI - PI}{NCI} \times 100$$

The longer the list of components, the more difficult the task of empirical estimates and their integration. A balance will have to be struck in such cases. Nor must the choice be arbitrary or purely deductive. Budget Studies can be used as guidance to locate within praxis the most decisive dimension and directions of development of exploitation. In all probability work of lesser depth on large samples and more intensive study of smaller samples will proceed simultaneously.

The paragraph above does not carry a 'better' suggestion, but exemplifies possible ways to extend procedures. The actual job must be left to the practitioners of the work itself. Field work is not conducted by telegrams from abroad. Nor for that matter can it be structured in advance by brilliant deductions from a study room within the 'native' campus, often as far removed from villages as the foreign campus.

Finally, a short comment about the second cluster of issues referred to in section 3 – the methodology of studying differentiation *as a process*. Once again it is the formulation of the problem which is decisive, and here we can directly benefit from comparison with the work of the Russian scholars. The principles established by them by the late 1920s were straightforward enough. To study a *process* one must establish methodology directly relevant to change, i.e. to overcome both the inherent static bias of the ordinary census and the inbuilt descriptive narrowness of monographic studies. All those cannot be resolved simply by high abstraction. The Dynamic Study and Budget Study offered a methodological tool to do it at a level which could be, and was, operational and indeed put to use in work on massive empirical data. There is no way to present it here over and above the one-sentence definitions of section 3. The only way is to refer those interested to the basic sources and either make them overcome linguistic idleness or else, 'to take a leaf' out of Thorner's book, get further translations going. Russian Dynamic Studies and Budget Studies are not the last possible word and further methodological development will still be necessary. Before that begins, one should first try to climb up on 'the shoulders of giants' for a look ahead.

Which is the moment to bring it all to a close and also back to its beginning. The operationalization of concepts finds its significance and its limitations in the problematic posed.

Part IV

Theorizing Peasants: The Classical Roots of Debate

16

Peasants and Capitalism: Karl Kautsky on 'The Agrarian Question'

(written together with Hamza Alavi, 1986)

One of the paradoxes of publishing is the fact that Karl Kautsky's highly acclaimed The Agrarian Question *(1899) has seen the light of day in English with a delay of nearly ninety years. This paradox carries some illumination. Promptly translated into dozens of languages, this text 'got stuck' where peasants were mostly non-existent and the evolutionist idiom well established by the industrial revolution. At the same time the peasants of the Anglo-Saxon empires, far away but also as close to the UK as Ireland, were made invisible by prejudice, and by the refusal to give space to what were considered vestiges of barbarism and pre-civilization.*

Within a couple of decades Kautsky became a non-person of the pro-Bolshevik left, while at the other end of the scale virulent anti-Marxism extended to include him to the full in its attack.

Kautsky's The Agrarian Question *was a particularly insightful contribution that is also relevant today. Much of what was written since develops themes and insights Kautsky introduced, often quite unconscious of their true author. This is why Hamza Alavi and myself accepted with considerable interest the task of introducing the first English edition of the book which, after some further delays, came out recently (ZWAN, 1988). It was a particular pleasure to work on it through discussion with a friend I respect, combining in our effort experiences of different environments and different biographies-cum-histories.*

Item 1 of this book should help to place Kautsky's broad approach in the context of theoretical traditions concerning peasant economy. On re-reading the item that follows here, I would now have examined more closely the concept of subordination (or subsumption) as a not-one-to-zero game to stress the 'weapons of the weak' and the measure of autonomy of the expolary economies (see item 6). But then, one would rewrite most of one's articles endlessly as life and one's work unfold.

'Kautsky's' book is the most important event in present day economic literature since the third volume of *Capital*. Until now Marxism has lacked a systematic study of capitalism and agriculture, Kautsky has filled this gap.'[1] Lenin could not have praised Kautsky's *The Agrarian Question* more highly, ranking it after the great work of the founder of Marxism himself. Kautsky's study appeared in 1899. At the time Lenin had himself just completed a study of the impact of capitalism on Russian agriculture which formed the first part of his book on *The Development of Capitalism in Russia*. In a postcript to it Lenin expressed regrets that he got Kautsky's book too late to make use of it to illuminate his own work. The dissimilarities as well as similarities of context and argument between these two major contributors to Marxist analyses, at the turn of the century, of the impact of capital on agriculture and rural societies, offer valuable insights into their respective analytical and political positions and their bearing on similar issues of today, notably with respect to the 'developing' societies.

In view of the acclaim with which Kautsky's work on *The Agrarian Question* was greeted by his contemporaries, as well as the vigourous controversies that it sparked off, it is quite extraordinary to see how much the work has been neglected by twentieth-century theorists not only in the context of European rural history but also, and especially, in that of changes in the contemporary peasant societies of the Third World. Part of the reason for that neglect might lie simply in the fact that knowledge of the German language, which for much of the nineteenth century was an indispensable mark of scholarship in Europe, was soon displaced by English; and it is only now, after a staggering delay of ninety years, that this first English translation is at last being offered. Nor was *The Agrarian Question* available in other West European languages until quite recently, for the first Italian translation appeared only in 1959, a Spanish one in 1970, while the French edition of 1900 was quickly out of print, to be renewed only in 1970. The main explanation for the neglect must lie, however, not in the linguistic barriers but in the general disenchantment with the Marxism of the Second International, a positivistic, deterministic and evolutionist Marxism which was epitomized in the work of Karl Kautsky. Much of this was reincarnated in the ideological forms of Stalin's Marxism.[2] Thereby it survived for much longer than might be inferred from the infrequency of references to Kautsky. It has survived also as a stereotype of Marxism in the works of its opponents. But the actual writings of those progenitors of 'orthodox Marxism' were mostly relegated to oblivion by official spokesmen of the

The authors are grateful for comment and advice offered by Geof Eley and John Kautsky. The usual disclaimer about responsibility for the arguments expounded here applies.
 1 V.I. Lenin, *Collected Works* (Moscow, 1977), vol. 4, p. 94.
 2 e.g. 'On Dialectical and Historical Materialism'.

renewed Marxist orthodoxy of the Third International. As a US communist of long standing said to one of the writers of this introduction: 'It took me 40 years to discover that Karl and not Renegade was Kautsky's given first name.' In Germany, Kautsky's opposition to the Bolshevik revolution set the seal on his post-1914 status as an ideological pariah in the eyes of revolutionary Marxists. He was equally unacceptable to the Social Democratic Workers Party of Germany (SPD) majority because of his refusal to go along with the policy of the leadership to give total support to the war and to exchange Marxism as he understood it for their own brand of post-war 'pragmatism'. His decision to leave Germany in 1924 was an admission of his growing isolation.

With an upsurge of Marxist scholarship in the 1960s–70s and the recent reconstruction of the history of German socialism, increasing attention is now being given to the work, and the role, of Karl Kautsky. A great deal has been written about the Marxism of the Second International and what Lichtheim has called the conceptual 'drift towards positivism and scientism which accelerated after Marx's death and [was] formalised by Kautsky . . . [as] a cast-iron system of 'laws'.[3] The authors of this introduction would accept such a critique of Kautsky's Marxism. But they do not conclude therefore that all of Kautsky's work is barren and should be discarded or assigned to the past; nor can they accept, contrariwise, the somewhat naive attempts to re-legitimize the pre-1914 Kautsky by making a Leninist out of him. Kautsky's work on *The Agrarian Question*, particularly, does not fit such dismissive or subsuming categorizations. Much of Kautsky's analytical achievement is particular to him. Much of it is also relevant to contemporary analyses and puzzles. Between the most interesting and theoretically fruitful aspects of his work are those that have to do with structural aspects of the transformation of peasant economies by capital, illuminating complex and contradictory directions of that process, although linear and scientistic models do lurk under the surface of his explanations. In order to see this work in perspective it may be helpful if we begin by identifying five principal points of analysis which characterize his study.

1 Peasants: Processes, Perspectives and Prescriptions

The first of these issues is that of processes of class differentiation of the rural society as a consequence of the impact of capital. Kautsky's arguments in this connection are often misread, especially by eyes

---

3 G. Lichtheim, *Marxism: A Historical and Critical Study* (London, 1961), p. 238.

trained to equate them with the analysis offered by Lenin. Moreover, to add to the problem, having started with certain preconceptions Kautsky modifies his views quite radically in the course of his work itself, in the light of his findings as his analysis progresses.

Kautsky's initial presumption was that just as the tendency towards concentration and centralization of production, set in motion by the dynamics of capital accumulation, eliminated petty commodity production in manufacturing, likewise in the field of agriculture it would result in the dissolution of the peasantry and a polarization of rural society into two classes, the rural proletariat and capitalist farmers. In so far as the rural censuses of Germany did not actually show progressive concentration of land in fewer hands, increasing levels of intensification of capital investment could still provide the road to the emergence of capitalist enterprises in agriculture leading towards the demise of the peasantry (potentially so, at least, for Kautsky did not find sufficient evidence that this was happening either). Theoretically, the actually existing peasantry would then be subsumed under the residual category of petty commodity producers, destined to disappear under capitalism. As Kautsky proceeds with his analysis, however, he defines with increasing clarity significant structural differences between conditions of peasant production and petty commodity production in manufacturing, so that the peasantry cannot be assimilated into the category of petty commodity producers unproblematically.

This recognition becomes quite clear by chapter 7 of the work where Kautsky's analysis turns nearly a full circle. Having started with a presumption of a general tendency of capitalist development to dissolve and eliminate the peasantry, he finds himself explaining the opposite, namely why such a tendency does not actually prevail; why the peasantry may persist within the general framework of capitalism. At first he merely qualifies the operation of the presumed law of evolution. Later he points out, (in section [a] of chapter 7) that in Europe 'the small farm has not lost ground to the large since the 1850s. In fact, in terms of overall acreage, small farms seem to be growing in some areas.' He then considers, in section (c) of that chapter, factors that retard processes of centralization and concentration in agriculture where, he argues, they operate *more slowly* than in industry – the differences in the process of the dissolution of petty commodity production and of the peasantry by capitalism being posited merely as a matter of differences in relative speed of the process. By the time Kautsky gets to section (f) of that chapter, however, we find him pointing out the functional role of small farms as 'production sites' for labour power needed by the capitalist large farms and industry. Increase in the number of large farms relative to small curtails the rural source of supply of labour power while, at the same time, increasing the demand for it. That contradiction limits the general scope for wholesale displacement of the small farms by the large. He therefore concludes that 'This in itself is sufficient to ensure that despite its technical superiority, the large farm can never completely prevail in any given country . . . As long as the capitalist mode of production continues there is no more reason to expect the end of the large scale agricultural enterprise than that of the small.' More than direct production for profit is at stake, for the peasant family-farms are also ideal 'production sites' for army recruits – plentiful and conservative in their outlook (chapter 8, section [a]). Kautsky argues that there are built-in economic tendencies as well as sources of effective political pressures for state intervention, with the blessings of large landowners, which ensure the continued existence of the small family-farms. To see what that means one may best compare this to the unconditional statement from Lenin of 1899 that 'The old pesantry is not only differentiating, *it is being completely dissolved, it is ceasing to exist* it is being ousted by absolutely new types of rural inhabitants . . . These types are the rural bourgeoisie (chiefly petty bourgeoisie) and the rural proletariat – a class of commodity producers and a class of agricultural wage workers.'[4]

The thesis that the peasantry was inexorably being eliminated in the course of capitalist development was argued most strongly by the young Lenin in his *Development of Capitalism in Russia*. Lenin not only predicted that there was a necessary process of 'depeasantization', but also defined the rural Russia of the day (in 1899, or even by the late 1880s) as already having undergone this process of becoming capitalist. He was later to modify that evaluation in the light of the experience of the revolution of 1905, when he was led to make fresh assessments of the political role of the peasantry. To wit, 'the contemporary manorial economy of Russia is based on an enserfing rather than capitalist economy. Those who deny it cannot explain the current breadth and depth of revolutionary peasant movement in Russia'.[5] It is the early unrevised Lenin's 'model' of the 1890s which is often maintained as representing his definitive view. But even his revised view of rural Russia in 1905–6 was still premised on the 'classical' notion of its eventual transformation through polarization, which was bound to operate in rural Russia with the necessity and totality of a force of nature, tempered only by Russia's economic backwardness. Kautsky's 1899 perception of the processes of change in rural society as a consequence of the impact of capital and of progress is significantly different.

4 Lenin, *Collected Works*, vol. 3, p. 174.
5 Lenin, *Collected Works*, vol. 10, p. 177 (translation of the first sentence amended on the basis of the Russian original).

The next question posed by Kautsky's analysis, and a most relevant contribution to the understanding of the world we live in, concerns his conceptualizing of peasant production as an integral component of a capitalist economy and society, rather than holding the view that they were mutually incompatible. At the outset, he begins with the recognition that peasant production, understood as one essentially based on the family-farm and family labour, is not as such specific to any particular historically given mode of production. Peasants were the basis of 'archaic' societies organized communally, where each family-farm was a primary unit of the organization of economic activities, although some of these activities were organized on the basis of wider social units. Again, peasants, free or unfree, were components of feudal societies where a tribute in labour, in kind or in cash, was extracted from them by the dominant class. With the development of capitalism, the peasantry is incorporated into the capitalist mode of production and its structure and its dynamics cannot be understood except in those terms. Kautsky's analysis of the interaction of the peasantry with industrial and urban-centred capitalist economy can be extended to illuminate a variety of contemporary conditions which did not exist when his book came to be written.

We must begin here by recognizing the complexity of a subject matter involving the coexistence of partly opposing tendencies. We need to take account simultaneously of the specificity of peasant production, based on the family-farm, as a particular form of organization of productive activities and of the broader context of the capitalist economic system in which it is integrated. Kautsky emphasizes two aspects of the peculiarities of peasant family-farms as against the framework of capitalism. One concerns the character of land as a non-reproducible means of production. He points out the peculiar difficulties and contradictions associated with its concentration in the process of capitalist development as against the capacity of peasants to hold on to it. The other aspect is that a significant part of peasant production that provides for subsistence is not valorized through the market; nor are many of its inputs. These features distinguish peasant production from petty commodity production in manufacturing, an added reason why peasant production may persist within the capitalist mode of production in a form that integrates it into the capitalist economy without its dissolution. A foundation is laid for an explanation of family-farms as a particular yet integral category of a capitalist mode of production.

The third principal feature of Kautsky's analysis is the explanation of peasant farming in terms of over-exploitation of peasant labour power; that is, the characteristically lower than average price of labour power that is realized in agriculture, which reinforces its functional significance for capitalism. For Kautsky economies of scale and the potential of employing more advanced technology made large-scale agriculture necessarily more effective than peasant farming. But peasants survived all the same and even outbid capitalists for purchase of land, while tenants often produced more profit for the landlord than direct capitalist farming. In Kautsky's view this happens because peasants are ready to accept 'underconsumption' and 'excessive labour', underselling permanent wage-workers, caught in what Lenin was later to refer to as the 'plunder of labour' of the peasants and which formed a part of Chayanov's concept of 'self-exploitation.'[6] What it means for the 'national' political economy is a flow of extra surplus value extracted from the impoverished peasant unable to offer effective resistance to forces that dominate him. The peasant sector of the capitalist political economy is the source of continuous 'primitive accumulation' rather than being doomed to rapid dissolution.

Kautsky's reply to those who celebrate the seemingly eternal nature of the peasantry and use this against Marxist analytical predictions was to insist on the historical nature of the peasantry. He refuted the argument of E. David who put forward the view that larger units could not win against the small when more intensive agriculture is concerned.[7] The mistaken view that small farms were necessarily more effective than large agricultural enterprises was answered by Kautsky, however, by an equally debatable assertion that to enlarge is to improve. Consistently with it, the possibility of exploited yet highly productive and relatively prosperous family farmers in a capitalist world of mechanized enterprises was dismissed too lightly by Kautsky, for in his conception progress was unchallengeably related to size.[8] Kautsky also followed the same assumption as he took issue with those who proclaimed peasant survivability as a virtue. Family farming under capitalism was necessarily a poverty trap, its survival explainable by its tribute of labour

---

6 Lenin, *Collected Works*, vol. 16, p. 455 (the expression 'squandering of labour' is used in this translation). Chayanov's concept of 'self-exploitation' was broader in context, assuming the possibility of some advantages of family economy over capitalist production. For discussion see A. Chayanov, *The Theory of Peasant Economy* (Madison, 1986), chapter, 2 and item 19.

7 E. David, *Sozialismus und Landwirtschaft* (Berlin, 1902) and the shorter version of his argument in *Sotsializm i sel'skoe khozyaistvo* (St Petersburg, 1906) especially chapter 5.

8 For a pertinent discussion see J. Harriss (ed.), *Rural Development* (London, 1982), especially the contribution by G. Djurfield and M. Taussig; H. Friedmann, 'World Market, State and Family Farm', *Comparative Studies in Society and History*, 20 (1978), N. Swain, *Collective Farms which Work*, (Cambridge, 1985) for a relevant discussion of the 'large versus small' concerning units of production in agriculture, with reference to a case of the collectivized agriculture of Hungary.

power to large-scale farming and capitalist industry, by the brutalizing 'pre-capitalist impoverishment, child labour, premature ageing and other disabilities from which the majority of non-waged 'middle peasants' suffered worse than other exploited sections of the population. There could be little else to explain peasants' continuity as long as the economies of scale were held absolute.

The fourth aspect of Kautsky's work is his prognostication concerning the impact of capitalism on peasant agriculture during the period which he considered to be one of the 'run up' toward the socialist revolution. By then the proletariat would be massive, superbly organized and fully conscious of its role, dominating the political scene in the revolutionary task of dismantling the whole system of class society. Industrial capitalism and large-scale agriculture would represent the prevalent forms of production. Peasants might have disappeared by that time but that did not have to happen in advance of the socialist revolution. The definite end of the peasantry would result from technological progress rather than from the impact of capitalism as such, or indeed of socialism. As to the intermediate period, Kautsky's fundamental anticipation was of a political economy in which agriculture and peasant agriculture in particular would be increasingly outpaced and taken in tow by the technologically advanced capitalist, or later socialist, industry. That is why the peasantry could be discounted economically as well as politically when the grand historiographic scenario of the future was being unfolded. The stagnant sidestreams of the economy and in particular the peasantry must eventually be swept away by the mighty torrent of progress. To conclude as to the general outlook consequent on such a prognosis, the prospect of the peasants' actual non-disappearance is admitted, analytically explained and then politically and economically disregarded in so far as the dynamics of change is concerned. This brings us to the issue of the SPD's agrarian programme.

The fifth and last major characteristic of Kautsky's work represents his political conclusions – a party strategy concerning peasants that he outlines in the second part of his work. In a sense, these conclusions contradict the sophisticated analysis of part 1 of *The Agrarian Question*. They seem to follow, rather, from an over-generalized conception of the historical process in which 'progress' is inevitably defined by the 'forces of production' and by a mechanistic interpretation of laws of capitalist development, by virtue of which industrial capital has innate supremacy and only the industrial proletariat was to play the revolutionary role dictated to it by the forces of history. This order and hierarchy are central to a decisive statement of Kautsky's position when he declared that 'social development stands higher than the interest of the proletariat and of Social Democracy.' Progress before the proletariat and/or the party, let alone any of the other participants in the struggle for the realization of socialism!

Although by the time Kautsky began to deal with the agrarian policy of the SPD in part II of his book he had already reached the conclusion that the peasantry as a class may not disappear even at the most advanced stages of capitalism, he was nevertheless convinced that their significance for the socialist movement is either negligible or negative, for the peasantry (and even agriculture as such) is a conservative and not a progressive force. He sets out to lay the basis of a scientifically valid political strategy with these words: 'If there is any clear conclusion to be drawn from the developments in Part I, it is that industry will become the determining force in society as a whole, that agriculture will lose its significance relative to industry.' He qualifies this statement at once by saying that the SPD could not ignore agrarian issues. But he does not fail to add, in genuine bewilderment, 'It is a curious phenomenon that agriculture's *political significance* is in inverse proportion to its *economic significance*.' By virtue of the fundamental process of social transformation the peasantry would not be eliminated. But it was being marginalized. The main forces of the future were to be found in the burgeoning capitalist industry as against which peasants were an irrelevance, an anachronism. As to the coming class confrontation of capitalists with the proletariat, the peasants might prove to be a liability or even a source of potential danger, for peasants in uniform may be used against revolutionaries, as had happened in 1848. There were fortunately 'two souls in the breast of the peasant' and he was not necessarily a class enemy of the proletariat. He would show petty bourgeois ambivalence in the face of the confrontation of the main classes of capitalism. Peasants were not wholly and necessarily hostile to socialists and a few of them might even join the SPD in anticipation of their own future proletarianization. The political conclusion for socialists was to neutralize the peasantry rather than to mobilize it. No active role could be assigned to it in the forthcoming socialist revolution.

Once again, a comparison with Lenin makes Kautsky stand out in marked contrast. While there are some parallels between their analyses of the impact of capitalist development on peasantry, their respective conceptions of its revolutionary potential differed radically. Following the 1902 peasant rebellion in the Ukraine and especially the 1905–7 revolution, both Kautsky and Lenin accepted the revolutionary *élan* of the *Russian* peasants, rejected before by the 'orthodox' Marxists. Both explained it by the backward state of the Russian economy – a precapitalist class was engaging in a pre-socialist revolution. This similarity of assumptions and consequent strategy disappeared fully in the face of the Russian civil war which was to Lenin, at least as from 1919, a socialist revolution supported by and dependent on the peasant majority, while to Kautsky it was an aberration explained in part by the peasantry's conservative nature. Even before that, the similarities noted did not preclude differences, signalled by the different accentuation of revolutionary strategy and political will. The lessons of the 1905–7 revolution made the political mobilization of peasants, on the side of the socialists, Lenin's main concern.[9]

Let us recapitulate. The particular position offered by Kautsky in his fundamental study at the turn of the century was accepted by the orthodox Marxists of the Second International as the most authoritative extension of *Das Kapital* itself to the analysis of the peasantry – the majority of mankind and even of the Europeans of the day. Kautsky's work was, nevertheless, forgotten within barely a decade. Its existence has mostly been acknowledged at second hand and often not very reliably by those who have not read the original.[10] Kautsky's analysis is premised on the decisive nature but also the contradictory impact and effects of capitalist penetration into peasant agriculture. Other major elements of his analysis involve the conditionality of rural class differentiation (with a variety of possible outcomes); a structural explanation of the particularity of the peasant economy under capitalism which stresses over-exploitation and the functionality of the peasant economy for capital; a prognosis of the eventual depeasantization, resulting, however, from technological progress rather than from a transformation of social relations of production; and, finally, a political strategy of neutralization of the peasantry rather than their mobilization by socialists in the battle for power. Before proceeding to relate Kautsky's contribution to the understanding of and the efforts to transform the world that he lived in and the world we ourselves confront, let us look at the man and his immediate and most significant political environment – the Social Democratic Workers Party of Germany.

2 A Man and a Party: Theory versus Politics

Karl Kautsky was born in 1854 in Prague in a comfortable, professional, middle-class family which soon moved to Vienna. In Vienna University Karl studied history, economics and philosophy. He was the son of a Czech father and a German mother and for a while he moved in Czech nationalist circles. In 1875 he joined the Austrian Social Democratic

---

9 For further discussion see T. Shanin, *Revolution as a Moment of Truth* (New Haven 1985).

10 Most of those who have referred to Kautsky's *Agrarian Question* since the late 1970s

Party which had been founded the year before. His biographer, Steenson, comments that 'Kautsky's role in the Austrian Party was a model for all his later participation in the German and international socialist movements. He took no part in administration or organization, either of the Party of the trade unions; he neither held nor ran for public or party offices; he was exclusively a propagandist, teacher, and very occasional speaker. Though he frequently attended meetings of the Party leadership . . . he very rarely contributed.'[11]

The ideas of the young Kautsky were influenced first by the romantic radicalism then prevailing among Czech nationalists. The heroic but tragic fate of the Paris Commune helped him to develop an interest in socialism and in the aspirations of the working class. That interest was fed firstly by the ideas of Ferdinand Lassalle and French socialists, notably Louis Blanc. His encounter with Marxism was so far perfunctory. Kautsky was soon to come under the spell of positivist thought with its overwhelming acceptance of the models and methods of natural sciences – a dominating force in the intellectual climate of the late nineteenth century. Along with positivism another major influence was that of Darwin. As noted by Colletti 'only a slight knowledge of his [Kautsky's] work is sufficient to see that Marxism always appears in it as an extension of Darwinism; both are then seen as two particular moments of the genus "evolution".'[12] Kautsky himself did not deny the evolutionist cast of his thought or his fascination with Darwin. During the first years of *Neue Zeit*, the authoritative theoretical journal of the German Social Democrats edited by Kautsky, much space was devoted to Darwin's relevance to social evolution. 'Marx and Darwin were to be the twin pillars on which the *Neue Zeit* rested, and Kautsky obviously saw the two as a natural pair.'[13]

In 1880, at the age of 26, Kautsky moved to Zurich. He was to work closely there with Eduard Bernstein. It was also the time when he embarked on a systematic study of Marxism. In 1881 he briefly visited London, hoping to stay there to study under the direct guidance of Marx and Engels. He saw little of Marx, who clearly did not take to what he described as the young man's 'pedantry'.[14] Kautsky returned to London in 1885, by which time Marx was dead, and established with Engels a lasting intellectual and personal relationship. Kautsky was soon to

have actually used only its summation by J. Banaji in *Economy and Society*, 5 (1976), no. 1, which is problematic.

11 Gary P. Steenson, *Karl Kautsky, 1854–1938: Marxism in the Classical Years* (Pittsburg, 1978), p. 38.
12 Lucio Colletti, *From Rousseau to Lenin* (London, 1972), p. 25.
13 Steenson, *Karl Kautsky*, p. 52
14 Marx's letter to his daughter Jenny Longuet on 11 April 1881.

acquire a reputation as a major Marxist theoretician in his own right. After Engels's death in 1895 Kautsky took over the task of editing Marx's literary estate, a high point in his literary career. In fact he had already done some work on it, for in 1889 Engels had entrusted him with the work of editing Marx's *Theories of Surplus Value*, the projected fourth volume of *Capital*. Kautsky's authorship of the theoretical section of the new programme of the SPD, the 1891 Erfurt Programme (its tactics and programmatic section were written by Bebel and Bernstein), set the seal on his status as the principal theoretician of the Party.

It was as the editor of the influential *Neue Zeit* that Kautsky established himself as the arbiter of Marxist orthodoxy. He edited it from the inception of the journal in 1883 until 1917, when he was removed from this position. The journal dominated Marxist theoretical debate of the period throughout Europe. Besides the editorial privilege which gave him the power to pick and choose among contributors, Kautsky was himself a prolific and erudite writer and his works covered a wide range of themes.

Before the First World War Kautsky was not only the main theoretician of his party (and of the Second International, set up in 1879) but represented a specific tendency there. Since its inception there was growing evidence of a rift between the radical wing of the SPD, led by the towering, charismatic figure of Bebel, and an opposing faction whom Kautsky was to characterize as upholders of 'petit bourgeois socialism'. He spearheaded the theoretical attack against them. Kautsky's proclivity for theorizing was a particular asset to the SPD leader Bebel, legitimizing the latter's political and tactical stances. At the same time Kautsky, having little knowledge of organizational questions, depended heavily on Bebel for his bearings on practical political matters and was happy to be guided by him. Kautsky's biographer concluded that 'the two men co-operated out of shared interests and conviction, but they worked on different levels . . . What influence Kautsky did have usually came from his usefulness to SPD policy makers, especially August Bebel . . . [who] frequently used Kautsky's writings to bludgeon party opponents . . . But the relationship between Kautsky's theory and Bebel's practice was neither crude nor exploitative; Kautsky was rarely if ever manipulated by Bebel.'[15] It would be difficult to understand fully the role and importance of Kautsky, or his disorientation after the death of Bebel in 1913, without understanding this mutual relationship.

August Bebel, the practical politician and the SPD's undisputed leader, came from a background very different from that of Kautsky.[16]

15 Steenson, *Karl Kautsky*, pp. 248,159.
16 W.H. Maehl, *August Bebel – Shadow Emperor of the German Workers* (Philadelphia, 1980).

He was born poor and was orphaned at the age of four. His early life was a constant struggle for survival, his education was perfunctory. He found employment as a turner. He experienced directly his own exploitation and persecution and that of his fellow journeymen as he moved from city to city. He finally came to Leipzig where his genius was to have full play. Within five years he became the main figure in the Saxon workers' movement. Together with Wilhelm Liebknecht he led the Eisenacher Social Democrats, who united in 1875 with the ADAV initiated by Lassalle to establish the SPD. With Lassalle dead the Eisenacharian tendency, which considered itself to be the Marxist and the more radical wing of the SPD, came to dominate the party high command. Bebel's leadership of the SPD was linked to his leadership of the Eisenacharians and later of the 'orthodox' majority faction, which supported to the full an undiluted version of the Marxist party programme – the Erfurt Programme accepted in 1891. But Bebel was not a theoretician. Installing Kautsky as editor of *Neue Zeit* suited him admirably.

The SPD's internal ideological battles focused, then, on the issue of 'revolution or reform'. Until 1914 the political position taken by the majority of the party members and functionaries was one of participation in parliamentary life but non-collaboration with the government, and refusal to enter any political coalitions, in anticipation of the impending proletarian revolution that would be secured by the inevitable growth of the working class and its socialist consciousness. That position was rooted in an apocalyptic vision of the working of the inexorable laws of evolution of society, presumed to have been defined with finality by Karl Marx. The party minority which challenged this 'general line' was a diverse group representing a variety of political stances, assumptions and goals: trade union functionaries keen on 'pragmatism', party officials who saw themselves as 'practical' men, Southern German SPD parliamentarians concerned above all with winning elections, some theorists who wanted to use 'new economic findings' to revise their party's programmatic assumptions. Contemporary historians have argued extensively about the reasons for the SPD majority's Marxist revolutionary self-image and the abandonment of it in 1914–19.[17] In particular, they point to the impact of the heroic and exclusivist subculture established by the clandestine party organization during the period of Anti-Socialist Law, 1878–90, as well as the political context of the authoritarian and repressive state and what they describe as the consequent 'absence of opportunity for reformism'.[18] These are

17 For sources and excellent review see G. Eley, 'Combining Two Histories: The SPD and the German Working Class before 1914', *Radical History Review* (1984), nos. 28–30
18 ibid., p. 25.

explanations available *ex post factum*. In the period discussed the debate about reformism was a matter of deadly seriousness for the participants because for them it concerned issues that would decide the prospects of the realization of socialism expected in their own lifetime. This gave a keen edge to inner party debates about reformist or revolutionary paths to socialism, although as yet the Party was kept united by the common goal.

These ideological tensions came to a head when the reformist factions of the SPD found an articulate theoretical expression in the works of Eduard Bernstein – one of the leading SPD figures who had been befriended by Engels, Bebel and Kautsky. His call for 'Evolutionary Socialism' provided rationalization and legitimation for the political positions of the reformist wing. His views came to define the core of Revisionism – a call for the revision of some of Marx's basic assumptions and of the 'orthodox' Erfurt Programme of the SPD.

Bernstein repudiated historical materialism as a mechanistic philosophy, a criticism which, given the form in which it was presented by Kautsky, was not far off the mark. But unlike the theoretical critiques and political practice of later critics of Kautsky's version of Marxism on the left of the SPD, such as Rosa Luxemburg, Parvus or Karl Liebknecht, Bernstein did not move towards a philosophy of purposive, organized action by the working class and its revolutionary intervention to transform society. He argued rather that capitalism had changed by virtue of diffusion of share ownership of corporate capital – in this he prefigured later arguments about separation of ownership and control and the emergence of a post-capitalist society. The working class itself, Bernstein argued, was getting stratified and there was no more polarization of society into two antagonistic classes. Capitalist development did not entail its collapse. Parliamentary democracy, on the other hand, could go a long way towards amelioration of the conditions of workers within the framework of capitalism, through trade union struggle. 'The trade unions are the democratic element in industry. Their tendency is to destroy the absolutism of capital, and to procure for the worker a direct influence in the management of an industry . . . Democracy is in principle the supercession of class government, though it is not yet the actual supercession of classes.'[19] While socialism still remained the declared goal, gradualism was Bernstein's slogan: as he proclaimed, 'the movement is all, the final goal nothing.' In retrospect it is clear that Bernstein had made explicit what was already the dominant practice of the SPD, notwithstanding the verbal rhetoric about commitment to proletarian revolution. In the eyes of some SPD leaders Bernstein's sin

19 Edward Bernstein, *Evolutionary Socialism* (New York, 1961), pp. 42ff.

lay, indeed, in making explicit what they would much rather have left unsaid. A letter of the SPD party secretary, Ignaz Auer, to Bernstein made just that point: 'My dear Eddy, that is something which one does, but does not say.'

Kautsky seemed reluctant to take up the cudgels against Bernstein (Bebel wrote to him angrily 'What sort of devil is riding you that you make so many concessions to Ede [Bernstein]? . . . You really spit in my soup'). With Bebel at his back Kautsky eventually published a more biting critique entitled 'Bernstein and the Social Democratic Pro-gramme: An Anti-Critic'. Kautsky argued that the course of capitalist development had not superceded in any substantive ways the predic-tions of Marxist analysis. The growth of joint stock capital was not its diffusion but, rather, its in-gathering under more concentrated control. Some immediate gains by the proletariat were due to its growing organized power. That did not make the ultimate goal of socialism any less relevant. Bernstein's proposals would undermine the political struggle of the proletariat by its transformation from a party of revol-ution into a reformist party, which would put into jeopardy even those gains that the proletariat had achieved. Kautsky then proceeded to explain the rise of Revisionism itself as an example of a 'renaissance of bourgeois radicalism'. Given Kautsky's cast of mind, we are not sur-prised that he considered Bernstein's position to be a 'historically necessary manifestation' for German capitalist society at that particular stage of its development.

As to political strategy, to many in the SPD the state was a 'national' agency capable of rising above conflicts of classes and class interests. Vollmar, who led the powerful Bavarian section of the SPD, was particularly attracted by the paternalism of Bismarck's slogan of 'state socialism', a view which mirrored that of Lassalle. His 1891 'Eldorado speeches' were a clear affirmation of reformism, rightly described later as an 'apologia for a predominantly legalist, collaborationist, political tactic'.[20] The majority in the SPD, however, rejected conceptions of a paternalist state and were opposed to class collaboration and the con-cepts of 'national unity'. As to the road to socialism, Kautsky, speaking for them, characterized their party as 'revolutionary but not revolution making', emphasizing objective conditions of the inexorable march of history that would transform society and the state, and casting suspicion on conscious and forceful intervention in the revolutionary process by an organized proletariat as a 'putschist' thought.

The Russian Revolution of 1905–7 had a considerable radicalizing impact in Germany and elsewhere. Kautsky supported it and took a

20 Maehl, *August Bebel*, p. 179.

position closer to Lenin's than those of his less radical comrades inside Russian Social Democracy. In Germany and the rest of Europe a wave of strikes broke out. That gave rise to a debate about the general strike as a political weapon of the working class. This debate gave focus to a new inner-party challenge to the official positions of the SPD leadership, a challenge from the Left. This issue was to outweigh earlier debates about Revisionism in its practical political significance and long-term implications for the SPD and the European socialist movement. It entailed new alignments, a cleavage between those who were exclusively parliamentarian and the radicals, like Rosa Luxemburg and Karl Liebknecht, who acclaimed the role of direct action and of the mass strike, anticipating the struggle between the Second and the Third International in the post-1917 era. In that division the trade union hierarchy was firmly on the side of exclusively parliamentary struggle and against political strikes; they even sought to ban discussion of the issue. Kautsky was ambivalent, the beginning of what was later described as his 'centrism'. On the one hand he criticized 'parliamentary cretinism' and acknowledged, in principle, the weapon of mass strike. But he hedged it in with conditions that virtually ruled it out. About Kautsky's *Road to Power*, written in 1909, Lenin was to comment that Kautsky's pamphlet devoted to an analysis of political revolution, good as it was in sharp rejection of gradualism, evaded the question of state power. This was so and this remained a major weakness in Kautsky's political analysis. Kautsky was ambivalent on the colonial question, likewise, for he declared that the rising colonial struggles, while weakening capitalism, were themselves necessarily bourgeois, attempting only to substitute external capitalism by an internal (i.e. national) one and therefore violently hostile to workers and socialists. He called therefore for an unreservedly critical attitude to the 'non-European enemies of European capitalism'.[21]

World War I marked a watershed in Kautsky's career and brought to an end his influential role as the grand theoretician of European Marxism. There was a rapid polarization of forces in the political arena in which Kautsky's assumption of a 'centrist' position marginalized him. His friend and guide, Bebel, had died in 1913. (On Bebel's death Kautsky wrote to Adler 'The feeling depresses me not a little that I must now engage in practical politics without being able to follow a leader.') After taking a middle-of-the-road position over the SPD Reichstag vote for military budgets in 1914, in 1915 Kautsky approved of the 'majority resolution' at the internationalist conference of anti-war socialists in

---

21 K. Kautsky, *The Road to Power* (Chicago, 1909), p. 115 (This is the original German edition.)

Zimmerwald, Switzerland, which called for a peace without annexations. (It was opposed there by Lenin and his allies who called for the turning of the World War into a revolutionary civil war.) As time progressed the political inadequacies of Kautsky came to play an increasing role. His biographer summed it up thus: 'Without Bebel, Kautsky felt uncertain and he regretted his own confusion at the outbreak of the war . . . In retrospect Kautsky lost the basis for his historical importance on 4th August 1914 . . . The war and the rise of the Bolsheviks changed the main thrust of Marxism in such a way that Kautsky became a peripheral figure, at first viciously attacked and subjected to ridicule and scorn, but finally merely rejected.'[22]

Central to Kautsky's reaction to the October Revolution in Russia was his outrage with the un-scientificity of Bolshevism. The Russian stage of economic development did not permit direct transition to socialism as yet, but in April of 1917 the Bolsheviks had proclaimed just that to be their aim. The savagery of the Russian civil war of 1918–21 and the repressions by the Soviet authorities of many of Kautsky's political friends infuriated him as much. So did Lenin's personal attack on Kautsky, which did everything possible to demolish the prestige of the erstwhile 'pope' of pre-war Marxism, who now opposed the European revolution which was thought to be indispensable for the survival and success of the Bolshevik Revolution. For Kautsky, the socialist revolution was premature, a putschist act by a revolutionary sect which imposed itself on the masses, inclusive of the proletariat – a revolution out of turn. For him it was a new version of Asiatic despotism against European socialists and Marxists, who represented civilization at its most advanced stage.[23] Bolshevik rule, he was convinced, must collapse and lead to a Bonapartist military dictatorship of the right. Faced with this, the European working class must recover from the nationalist fever and regain its centrality in the struggle for progress and a socialist future. In his twilight years, in the 1920s and 1930s, he stayed consistent to this outlook while political events increasingly passed him by.

3 The Agrarian Question

Kautsky's dependence on Bebel for guidance through the minefield of German politics from the 1890s to 1913 did not mean that he followed Bebel's dictates slavishly, and it was on the 'agrarian problem' that they

22 Steenson, *Karl Kautsky*, pp. 159, 181.
23 In particular Kautsky's *Terrorism or Communism* (London, 1920), and his discussion of the Georgian Mensheviks' rule as an alternative to Bolshevism in *Georgia* (London 1921).

had their most celebrated clash. In 1894 the SPD congress decided to consider its position *vis-à-vis* the peasantry. Suggestions of its committees for an agrarian programme came up before the party's Congress at Breslau in 1895. There Kautsky led the forces which attacked the Committee's recommendations. He mobilized for this the support of Engels, who threw his authority on Kautsky's side by contributing an article in which he argued that the SPD should not engage in promises to the small-holder, who 'like every other survival of a past mode of production is hopelessly doomed'.[24] Alignments in that confrontation did not go along the usual factional divisions in the party. Those who supported Kautsky consisted of many on the party's left wing who combined, however, with followers of Lassalle and trade union bosses of the SPD's right wing in opposing any attempt 'to dilute' the party's proletarian character by 'pandering to peasants'. (It was Lassalle who first described all social classes other than the proletariat as 'one reactionary mass' and suggested that his party's membership must be restricted to wage-workers only.) On the other hand Bebel argued against Kautsky's stand on the issue and found himself and some of his closest allies, especially Wilhelm Liebknecht, aligned with many of the SPD reformists, led by Vollmar. The political goals of the supporters of an Agrarian Programme for the SPD differed. Vollmar's view was based on his wish to increase electoral support in regions like Bavaria, his own region, while his conception of the way in which the problems of the peasantry were to be tackled was limited to what a benevolent state might do for them. Bebel viewed the proposal to mobilize the peasantry as part of his 'orthodox and revolutionary' strategy.

As to the theoretical debate, a specific set of assumptions concerning the fundamental stability of small-holders' farming was injected into the Revisionist position by the agrarian analysis of E. David and a few others, and was used against the supporters of the Erfurt Programme to prove the incompleteness of Marx's analysis. At the centre of David's argument was a systematic exposition of what he considered to be the particularities of agricultural production which were imposed by nature and therefore absolute, in contrast to the conditions of manufacturing. Factors such as the necessary seasonality, organic relation and non-stereotyped character of labour, lack of static work-place impeding mechanization, and distance from the working site meant to him that intensive family-farms must eventually win in competition against large agricultural enterprises. The evidence of the 1895 rural census indicating the stability and even advance of the small-holders was presented as an economic law rooted in natural regularities.[25]

24 F. Engels, 'Peasant Question in France and Germany' (written November 1884), in K. Marx and F. Engels, *Selected Works* (Moscow, 1973), vol. 3, pp. 469, 460.

At the SPD Congress of 1895 at Breslau the view championed by Kautsky prevailed. The agrarian programme was rejected by a two-thirds majority. This was one of the rare cases when Bebel found himself outvoted on the party platform. (In a letter to Adler written in October 1895 he was to comment that his opponents had 'thrown out what should never have been thrown out . . . sealed the pass for years . . . [it] will make the worst possible impression in the country-side.' He added 'The worst thing, however, was the motivation . . . which . . . amounted to a dismissal of all demands which would benefit peasants, even those which would not cost us anything.') The Congress decided to request from party analysts a full study of this question before any steps were considered. Kautsky took this call seriously enough to undertake the systematic study which appeared in 1899 in the form of the work discussed. But, as Bebel understood only too well, for the majority of party leaders the call 'to study' was simply a device to bury the issue.

Kautsky's initial view of the 'agrarian question' was a simple deduction from the basic position that was already taken in his exposition of the SPD Programme, his best known and most translated work: *The Class Struggle: The Erfurt Programme*. That pamphlet was intended to provide a systematic presentation of Marxist revolutionary theory, as Kautsky understood it, and as the SPD majority accepted it, i.e. what was defined as 'orthodox Marxism'. Kautsky expounded there a model of capitalist development beginning with the dissolution of petty commodity production, polarization of society into two main classes, the proletariat and the capitalists, and sharpening of the class struggle. The proletariat was to liberate not only itself but all of humanity. Reference to the peasant question was remarkably absent, although it was already a contentious issue in the SPD. That was dealt with only tangentially and dismissed there in the few paragraphs that deal with petty commodity producers in general, as destined (with the peasants included among them) for extinction in the wake of capitalist development.[26] Kautsky did not then recognize any structural differences between peasant production and other kinds of petty commodity production, as he was to do later.

Kautsky's views on the subject were soon to alter considerably and in a later statement he was explicit about reasons for this change: 'On one major point we must change our outlook. The peasant does not

25 David *Sozialismus*; see also F. Hertz, *Die Agrarischen Fragen in Verhaltnis zum Socialismus* (Wien, 1899), etc. For a pertinent discussion of the argument and its context see A. Gerschenkron, *Bread and Democracy in Germany*, (Berkeley, Cal., 1943).

26 Karl Kautsky, *The Class Struggle: The Erfurt Programme* (Chicago, 1910), pp. 212–3.

disappear as rapidly as we expected. During the last decades he only very slowly lost his position, if at all.'[27] The evidence of the rural censuses was clearly taken on board. Consequently at the 1895 Congress Kautsky gave recognition to particularities of agricultural development under capitalism. This he was to explore at length in *The Agrarian Question*. Yet, while as his analysis advanced his view of the impact of capital on the peasantry was transformed, no new political conclusions were drawn. Kautsky insisted that as the party of the proletariat the SPD would not be true to itself if it offered a particular political programme for the peasants. He seemed to have moved further in this direction by declaring in 1909 that by then the (Lassallean) 'concept of a single "reactionary mass" had become a reality', and that the peasantry as well as the other petty bourgeois allies had 'turned into [the] most violent enemies' of the proletariat.[28] The proletariat and the SPD could rely only on themselves – a conception of proletarian exclusivity in revolutionary struggle.[29]

It is against this background, conceptual, historical and biographical, that we may attempt to evaluate Kautsky's contribution to the 'agrarian question' in the light of further experience and the knowledge gathered since, of arguments raised and the problems encountered or remaining unresolved in our own times. Within the confines of an introduction we shall limit our comments to a few main issues concerning German peasants at the turn of the century and Marxist analyses of small-holders' agriculture under contemporary capitalism.

4 German Peasants and the Socialist Movement

The stereotype of the German peasantry that was widely held at the time was that it was impervious to radical appeals, inherently passive and socially conservative, that it constituted a solid and unshakeable base for the traditional social order that was dominated in Prussia by the junkers. The junkers as a class, who as cereal producers were threatened economically by cheap grain imports, especially from the New World, responded to the loss of their economic power by organiz-

27 'Sozialismus und Landwirtschaft', *Die Neue Zeit*, 21 (1903) book 1, p. 685.

28 Kautsky, *Road to Power*, pp. 125, 108 (the English translation amended on the basis of the German original). See also pp. 123 and 103–5.

29 By 1919 Kautsky came to regard *The Agrarian Question* as outdated *because* of the changes in the conditions of the agriculture, especially the upturn in the prices of the foodstuffs. He insisted, however, rightly in our view, that his substantive viewpoint and analytical approach remained unchanged. See *Die Sozialisierung der Lendwirschaft* (Berlin, 1921), pp. 8–9.

ing politically to dominate the state. They used their command over state power to secure economic and fiscal concessions and privileges, among them higher grain tariffs on imports. To achieve that, it was believed, they harnessed the resentment of the peasantry against the liberals and the socialists who threatened their economic position by advocacy of free trade, large-scale production and statist solutions, compounded by the socialist threat of 'abolishment of all property'. A corresponding component of that consensual view was the deeply held belief in the SPD that the only issue for the peasantry was their attachment to property, and that this would turn out to be the principal obstacle to socialism if the peasantry acquired an influential position in the Party. It is a reflection on the SPD leadership and a mark of its isolation from the peasantry that they were unable to see what was actually going on at the time, for the decades of the 1880s and 1890s were actually a period of a great ferment which was releasing new forces in German rural society which that party failed to harness or even perceive.

In recent years important new work by historians of Germany has demolished old myths about a passive and immobile, junker-dominated and deferential German peasantry.[30] The new historians, their vision enriched by sociological insights, have shifted their focus from the grand council chambers of Berlin and the big cities to the actual ground on which the peasant stood. In doing so they have revealed and analysed a whole new world of peasant militancy in Germany in the closing decades of the nineteenth century. At the economic level they have pointed out that the issue of grain tariffs was by no means the only important one, for the area of large cereal producing estates was in the north-east. For small peasants who predominated in other parts of the country, especially in the south and the west, the main sources of discontent were different. This is too large a topic for us to attempt a summary here, except to point out that the landlord-centred reading of the situation that has generally prevailed is misleading for grasping the agrarian problem. What is central to our present purposes is the picture that we now have of the forceful expressions of grievances by the peasants that arose out of the transformation of the German peasant economy in the second half of the nineteenth century. Kautsky analysed these economic changes but failed to see their political consequences.

With the incorporation of the peasant economy within the capitalist

30 David Blackbourn and Geoff Eley, *The Peculiarities of German History* (Oxford, 1984); David Blackbourn, *Class Religion and Local Politics in Wilhemine Germany* (New Haven, 1980), Geoff Eley, *Reshaping the German Right: Radical Nationalism and Political Change After Bismark* (New Haven, 1980), to which an extensive list of German texts can be added.

system, it was firmly locked into a market economy, and the peasant found himself in the grip of new and unfamiliar forces over which he felt he had no direct control, which he often felt were even more relentless than capricious nature and oppressive landlords, with whom he had coped over the millennia. Depressed and unpredictable prices, rising costs, higher taxes and mounting burdens of debt were all new threats or, at any rate, threats that he had not encountered before on such a scale. That produced within the peasantry a new demonology and a rash of independent peasant movements, small and large. Failing to find a leadership that might have articulated such grievances from the platform of the socialist movement, the peasant unrest took on a variety of nationalist and reactionary forms, such as an anti-semitism that made the Jew a symbol of the anti-peasant establishment, alongside the official, the banker, the lawyer and even the traditional notables, together with the much-suspected urban political leadership and intellectuals. The Bavarian Peasant League, for example, fought the 1893 elections on the slogan of 'No aristocrats, no priests, no doctors, no professors – only peasants for the representation of peasant interests'. Their leaders resorted to vigorous anti-semitic rhetoric. It was bad that the political vigour of the peasantry was channelled in those directions. It was not inevitable that it should have been so.

Mobilization of the already militant peasantry by the socialist movement could have broken the mould of German politics of the day. But, as Blackbourn points out, 'The grievances and aspirations of rural communities were refracted through the prism of conservative politics. There is no doubt that in the process they were distorted and caricatured . . . Conservative and Centre Party demagogues encouraged the peasantry to attack symbolic but empty targets, like the Jew or the stock exchange, rather than the structural basis of their exploitation.'[31] The SPD leadership betrayed a singular inability to understand what really moved the peasantry at the grass roots and how their energies might contribute to a struggle for socialism. The ideological legacy of Lassalle and Duhring facilitated anti-peasantism. The reformist wing of the SPD was too dominated by statist and paternalistic ideas to capture the resonance of peasant radical aspirations either. An ideology of proletarian exclusivism in the socialist struggle dominated both the revolutionary wing of the SPD and its trade unions.[32]

The SPD leaders hostile to peasant mobilization unfailingly invoke the authority of Engels, who was persuaded to contribute his well-

31 Blackbourn, *Class Religion*, p. 66.
32 At a later date it was the most significant leader of the SPD's left wing, Rosa Luxemburg, who was to express extraordinary unease with the peasant component of the Russian Revolution. See her *The Russian Revolution* (London, 1959).

known article on 'The Peasant Question in France and Germany', published by Kautsky in *Neue Zeit*, in which he supported the Kautsky position. But if authorities are to be invoked, it must be recalled that Marx himself emphatically took an opposite view, notably in his critique of Lassallean ideas that had impregnated the 1881 Gotha Programme of the SPD. In his Critique of the Gotha Programme he challenged the Lassallean formula that 'The emancipation of labour must be the work of the working class, *relatively to which all other classes are one reactionary mass.*' Answering this Marx asked rhetorically, 'Has one proclaimed to the artisans, small manufacturers and *peasants* [emphasis in the original] during the last elections: Relatively to us you, together with the bourgeoisie and feudal lords, form one reactionary mass?' Elsewhere in the same document Marx reminded those to whom his critique was addressed: 'In the first place, the majority of the "toiling people" in Germany consists of peasants and not of proletarians.'[33] In his notes in 1881 he also expressed the view that the Russian peasants and their organizations might play a major autonomous role in the socialist transformation of their society.[34] Neither Kautsky, the 'orthodox Marxist', nor the Revisionist leaders of the SPD were to grasp this insight or to follow its broader implications. Kautsky's political programme and strategy concerning the place of peasants in struggles for socialism was, however, to be repudiated in practice by the subsequent history of revolutionary experience. But that orthodoxy was to survive to haunt numerous Marxist movements, as in the Li Li San strategy in China, the Bulgarian internal wars of the 1920s or the Russian collectivization.

5 Marxism and Agrarian Capitalism

Kautsky's enduring contribution to the 'agrarian question' lies not in his position on the political role of the peasantry in the socialist movement. Rather, his achievement lies in illuminating the different ways in which capital makes its impact on the peasantry. Contemporary debates have followed many of these analytical insights. By now the globality and historicity of the transformation of rural production, its economic logic, processes and social organization, as well as the multiplicity of forms

33 Marx and Engels, *Selected Works*, vol. 3, pp. 20–1, 24.

34 In a remarkably apt anticipation of the different results of the different ways toward collectivization adopted by twentieth-century socialists, Marx also defined the conditions under which peasant support can be secured (i.e. the revolutionary context) and systematic transfer of resources of society to the peasant communes (i.e. the reversal by socialists of 'primitive accumulation'). See T. Shanin, *Late Marx and the Russian Road*, (London, 1983). pp. 111–14, 116–17.

which capitalist extraction of surplus value takes – features that Kautsky highlighted and examined – are often taken for granted. The influence of international markets for foodstuffs, as shown by Kautsky, can be seen to reach into every village and farm, transforming their character-istics and redefining the way in which they function. Kautsky also traced the regularities and stages through which peasant family-farms were transformed under the impact of capital, the agriculturalization of the peasant (i.e. the increase of farming activity as against the self-supporting crafts), the commercialization and monetization of their economic activities, and the increasing engagement in extra-farm wage-labour, providing for the possible restabilization of the farm but linking it increasingly into the capitalist mode of production. Peasant farms have survived through the millennia by functioning within differ-ent types of socio-economic formations and they must be understood in each case in the context of the structures of the broader society and economy. Those elements of Kautsky's explanation are still with us, being built into the general analysis of contemporary rural societies, particularly in the 'developing societies'.

The most significant in terms of contemporary relevance was Kauts-ky's explanation of the incorporation of peasant family-farms within the capitalist mode of production, providing for their continuity under capital, which dominates them and exploits them without dissolving them absolutely. The classical conception of capitalist social relations of production is premised on the separation of the producer from the means of production, resulting in the division of society into a class of free but propertyless producers and a class of non-producers who own and control access to the means of production. Peasant production does not fit neatly into such a definition of capitalist production. The develop-ment of capitalism in agriculture has therefore been ordinarily deduced as a process of depeasantization, the family-farms being doomed, like all petty commodity production, to extinction. Kautsky learned from his analysis of European agriculture at the turn of the century (and others have learned since) that this is by no means the whole story. In so far as the actual facts did not fit the preconceived formula, he accepted the facts and advanced an explanation, even though he seemed to be troubled by the ambiguity of the phenomenon, namely that of a peasantry which was incorporated as a part of capitalism without being fully 'capitalist' as the term was understood. All the same, he rightly recog-nized the specific manner in which peasant production was transformed by capital and became an integral component of a capitalist economy, putting aside both of the opposing 'essentialist' notions, namely that of peasants who never change and that of capitalism which takes only one possible form.

In the last decades it has been increasingly accepted that we have two alternative forms of agricultural production under capitalism, namely farming based on wage-labour and, secondly, a form of organization of production based on the family-farm which is incorporated into the capitalist mode of production without losing some of its substantive particularities. Keeping Kautsky's frame of reference in mind we may recognize the condition of separation of the producers from the means of production as one type of agriculture in a capitalist mode of production, say type 1. But, given the dominance of the capitalist mode of production, we also have the further possibility of a type 2 form of subsumption of peasant production under capital without the separation of the producer from the means of production, which is therefore distinct in reality and particular in its analytical implications. The peasant economy is then structurally integrated within the capitalist mode of production. The peasant's labour is objectified in his product, for which he is paid less than full value by virtue of unequal exchange.[35] Surplus value thus extracted from the peasant, through the agency of commercial capital and credit institutions, is appropriated by capital as a whole and contributes to capital accumulation, but outside the peasant economy from which it is drawn. Peasants are integrated into the circuit of generalized commodity production of global capitalism. The growing impact and explicit intervention of capital via technological packages, credits and contracts as well as the controls of modern storage, transport and consumer outlets has been changing the nature of family farming, providing for its ever deeper insertion into capitalist political economy.[36] But failure to recognize the distinctiveness of the type 2 mode of subsumption of peasant production under capital, and the universalization of type 1 (namely production based on the capitalist farmer and wage-labourers) as the only way in which capital incorporates agricultural production, obscure a crucial dimension of the dynamics of contemporary agriculture, its relationship with capital and the wider economy.

Kautsky's analysis lays important foundations for the understanding of the impact of capital on agriculture and of family-farm production as a particular yet integral part of the capitalist mode of production, not its negation. This part of his work also offers analytical 'openings' to other contemporary problems which were not on Kautsky's agenda, namely

---

35 Argbiri, *Unequal Exchange: A Study of the Imperialism of Trade* (London, 1972).

36 For further discussion and contemporary evidence see footnote 6 above. Also see the contributions of J. Harris, H. Friedmann, A. de Janvry and E. Taylor in the revised edition of T. Shanin (ed.), *Peasants and Peasant Societies* (Oxford, 1986). Historically the issue first came to light in the European cooperative movements of family farmers at the turn of the century, especially the Danish one.

questions about the integration of the peasantry into the political economies of post-revolutionary societies with extensive and/or advancing state ownership or direct control of means of production and state monopoly of international trade. The significance of the family plot in a Soviet Kolkhoz, the surprises and successes of the combination of family-scale and collective-scale agriculture in Hungary and the recent developments in China can be better understood if we keep Kautsky's analysis in mind.[37] This also accentuates the moment when Kautsky's work becomes inadequate or, putting it differently, when the further experience of nearly a century has left Kautsky behind. This concerns particularly three issues, namely the assumptions about the inevitability of rural misery, the advantages of large-scale technology, and the possible Marxist designation of the difference between peasants as conventionally understood and the highly capital-intensive family farmers in North America, Western Europe and elsewhere.

In his early days Kautsky assumed a general law of increasing misery that was presumed to operate under capitalism as one of its necessary consequences. This element of what was once considered to be an axiom of 'orthodox' Marxism was eventually discarded in its more general form by Kautsky himself, but it lingered on in his view of family farmers as a pre-capitalist survival within the capitalist world. In this view peasants survive in the face of triumphant capitalist entrepreneurship and the dominant use of wage-labour only by virtue of the over-exploitation of their own family labour and by their 'artistic capacity for going hungry'. The evidence has since taught us a much more complex lesson. There is neither the inevitability of family farmers' exceptional misery under the capitalism of today nor a guarantee of their wellbeing. One can see evidence, not only from Holland and Austria but also from Turkey, Egypt, Venezuela or the Indian Punjab, of small-holders farming successfully and avidly absorbing new technology, adjusting to contemporary markets and securing a livelihood which is as good as or better than that of the local wage-labourers or of the clerical salariat. But such agriculture is also much exposed to the heavy weather of capitalist economic cycles, resulting in bankruptcies, and social attrition through selective village-to-town migration of the young, the bright and the best educated. On the other hand stand those family farmers of 'developing societies' whose farming has not moved into the new era, whose poverty makes them indeed the lowest of the low even in the impoverished societies they live in, and whose growing destitution and 'involution' would well qualify them as carriers of 'increasing misery' and marginalization, to appear in the focus of international attention

37 N. Swain, *Collective Farms which Work.*

only when yet one more famine relief operation fails to save another million of human beings. But this is by no means the universal picture of family-farmers under capitalism.

This brings us to the next and linked issue of the contemporary stage of technological revolution in the context of crop and animal farming. Kautsky's images of technological advance, derived mainly from the type of equipment manufactured in his day, was that of the application of large-scale machinery operated by large numbers of manual labourers.[38] Modern technologies of agriculture, mechanical, chemical and biological, are much more divisible. This has made possible further advances in farming, by way of a new division of labour, new types of service and new significance of skills. All this has altered the criteria of optimal size of the labour team, lowering it for some branches of contemporary agriculture. A family-farm is not necessarily privileged over a large enterprise, but it is not debarred from utilizing new technology. Subject to that and given the right combination of productive activities, flexible use of family labour and cooperation through the social networks of a rural neighbourhood, it is often more effective and stable than a parallel large enterprise based on wage-labour. Subsumed under capitalism as the dominant mode of production, it can secure higher or safer profits for agribusiness while at the same time providing an improved livelihood to its own members – an equation which means the continuity of family-farms as a social form, at least for a time.

Thirdly, moving further from Kautsky's initial preoccupation with peasant farming in the Germany of the 1890s, is the problem of a Marxist conceptualization of the transformation of the peasant into a 'farmer'. Kautsky visualized prospects of the pauperization of a peasant into a peasant-worker, increasingly involved through wage work in capitalist production of surplus value, with some peasants becoming rural capitalist entrepreneurs operating mainly with wage-labour. His family farming alternative was equated with survival in misery on the margins of capitalist advance, as islands of technological backwardness. This did not allow for the emergence of highly capital-intensive farming based on a family labour which has escaped theoretical specification, becoming a blind spot. A conceptual step forward within a Marxist frame of reference has been recently suggested in this connection by a Soviet scholar, V.P. Danilov.[39] In Danilov's view the distinction based

38 For a little-known yet excellent discussion of the differences between fundamental levels/forms of production, i.e. gathering, husbandry and manufacturing, see M. Malita 'Agriculture in the Year 2000', *Sociologia Ruralis*, XI (1971).

39 V.P. Danilov et al., 'Osnovnye etapy razvitiya krest'yanskogo khozyaistva', in *Agrarnye structury stran vostoka* (Moscow, 1977).

on the respective relations of production, which delimits family labour from wage-labour under capitalism, must be supplemented by a further distinction based on qualitative differences in the forces of production deployed. Peasant production is family agriculture where natural forces of production, land and labour predominate. Farmers, on the other hand, represent family-farms in which the human-made forces of production, mostly industrial in origin, come to play a decisive role. The particularity of family farming as a form of organization of production does not disappear thereby but the characteristics of the two different types can be distinguished more clearly. The issue is certainly alive and other approaches to this problem have recently been attempted also by some of the Western Marxists.

The state of theorizing about the place of the peasantry in contemporary societies, especially those of the Third World, and of its future, is in considerable disarray. Most non-Marxist approaches seem to be unable to go much beyond the market-model search for technological solutions and legitimate concerns about ecological issues in considering the implications of capitalist development for peasant societies. The mainstream of Marxist thought, on the other hand, has branched out in two rather different directions. One characterizes peasants as pre-capitalist and, given the manner in which peasant societies serve the purposes of the wider capitalist economy, the relationship between the two is represented as a non-contradictory articulation of two modes of production, one pre-capitalist and the other capitalist. The other approach follows an older orthodoxy, one which Kautsky himself started out with when he embarked on his major study, by virtue of which peasant production is no more (or less) than petty commodity production in general and, like the latter, doomed to extinction with the advance of capitalism. Both of these views are constrained by a common assumption that the concept of capitalism cannot accommodate any form of production other than that based on the separation of the producer from the means of production. Capitalism in agriculture, for both these alternative approaches, can mean only one thing, namely the emergence of a rural capitalist entrepreneur employing wage-labour. Peasant production is excluded from capitalism as a matter of definition. Kautsky's seminal analysis of this question invites us to reconsider these assumptions.

In the course of his analysis Kautsky proved able to move beyond his own initial presuppositions and to recognize ways in which peasant production, whilst retaining its particular character rooted in the family-farm, was, nevertheless, radically transformed by the impact of capital. Its new features could no longer be explained within the conceptual framework of a pre-capitalist economy; it was structurally integrated into the wider, indeed global, capitalist economy. Nor could the peasant economy be characterized as one more example of petty commodity production in general. Kautsky demonstrates a variety of ways in which the peasant economy differs from petty commodity production in manufacture. As a consequence the dynamics of the two, in the context of capitalist development, are different. What we have is the specific case of peasant economies transformed and subordinated under capital, with a dynamics and a future that must be considered both in terms of their specific structural conditions and those of the conditions and contradictions of capitalist development in general.

It remains true that Kautsky's conception of capitalist development, of historical materialism, was substantively reductionist, a deterministic and linear vision in which the economic logic of capital accumulation inexorably ground its way to the final goal of socialism. Human agency and questions about organized political intervention were devalued in that vision, for politics, ideology and culture were seen as essentially epiphenomenal superstructures of the economic base whose logic unfolds with inevitable necessity. Kautsky's politics too remained ambivalent and, after the death of Bebel, rudderless. His last years were to be those of bitter isolation, for he outraged revolutionary Marxists by his opposition to the Bolshevik revolution and was shunned by the right wing of the Social Democrats for 'still' being a Marxist. Today, however, Kautsky's politics of his day or his general theoretical stance are less of an issue. More relevant are questions concerning contemporary peasantry and rural societies – the agrarian question. In the continuing debates about this issue the appearance at long last of this translation of Kautsky's seminal work into English will make its mark.

17

Orthodox Marxism and Lenin's Four-and-a-Half Agrarian Programmes: Peasants, Marx's Interpreters, Russian Revolution (1989)

For reasons discussed in the book's item 1, Lenin's views and those of other interpreters of Marx concerning peasant economies are also significant as a category of approach, shared by people whose political outlook has been far removed from that of Lenin's own. The same holds for rural political strategies and their dramatic changes, associated with Lenin's leadership of his party in Russia's revolutionary era and the growing gap between his theory and his political intuitions or tactics. This paper is devoted to this issue of cognition. Exploring it can help us understand the way peasantry was considered by 'orthodox' Marxists and Marxist revolutionaries. It also bears significantly on the contemporary debate in the USSR concerning its countryside's past and future (see this book's item 13). On the other hand no substantive argument concerning the social reality v. Lenin's analysis of Russian rural political economy is undertaken, readers being referred to the sequence of my three books relevant to it.[1]

This paper was written for this book of essays to round out its part IV.

1 Making Sense: Theory v Revolution

Born in 1870 and dead by 1924, Lenin's maturity spanned two centuries and two fundamentally different types of political experience. The first was that of an all-encompassing Socialist International, 1889–1914, the

A number of basic publications quoted repeatedly are referred to in the text by the following codes:

PSS   V.I. Lenin, *Polnoe sobranie sochinenii* (Moscow, 1968–75), fourth edition.

BPSR N. Bukharin, *Puti sotsialisticheskoi revolyutsii* (New York, 1965).

GPS   G.V. Plekhanov, *Sochineniya* (Moscow, 1923–6).

MES K. Marx and F. Engels, *Selected Works* (Moscow, 1973).

1 *The Awkward Class* (Oxford, 1972), *Russia as a 'Developing Society'* (London, 1984) and *Russia 1905–7: Revolution as a Moment of Truth* (London, 1986).

second that of the 1905–20 period of wars and revolutions. The intellectual formation of the whole turn-of-the-century generation of European Marxists was shaped by this dual experience, the contradictions it uncovered and the ways each and every one of them made sense of it. That was also where the particularities of Lenin stood out in sharp relief to give real meaning to the concept of Leninism.

To the Marxists, i.e. the International's most influential and coherent intellectual elite, the project and promise of their credo was the global integration of the working-class parties and of an accomplished social science. This was due rapidly to transform the world, creating a universal socialist civilization of humans made equal, affluent, wise and free. Following directly on the ideal of the nineteenth-century sciences, their achievements and their scorn of any ambivalence, 'scientific socialism'-cum-'orthodox'-Marxism offered an absolute method of analysis and prediction. The fundamental optimism and outstanding self-assurance of this *Weltanschauung* was based on the assumption of full integration between logic, scientific methodology applied to society and a theory of necessary progress, with the most progressive class as its social agent. This class was directed by a party which mastered the new and progressive social science. The logical 'fit' between correct theory and correct policies being naturally perfect, it could be disturbed only by human error, archaic prejudice (not unlike astrology), or else the designs of the exploitive minorities defending their privileges. Such impediments (their true nature explicated, once again, by the scientific analysis offered) could be temporary only. So was the power of the privileged minorities facing inevitable doom. Social revolution by the working class was approaching rapidly with the certitude and intelligibility of Newtonian laws of mechanics.

The 'fit' of theory with historical evidence and political praxis encountered by the leaders of the Second International of 1889–1914 was in fact much more ambiguous. This found its early expression in a number of repetitive debates in Marxist ranks concerning the theory's correct interpretation and usually coded as 'questions': the national question, the agrarian question, the class alliances question, etc. Later came a debate as to the general theory: the question of revisionism. But only the wars and revolutions of the twentieth century exposed fully the problematic nature of many deductive chains on offer within the nineteenth-century social sciences, Marxist and non-Marxist. The weaker joints between the social theory and political strategies of 'scientific socialism' were being driven apart by dramatic political experience. Of these weak joints the most significant to the 'orthodox' Marxists proved the actual extent of workers' international solidarity vis-à-vis war as well as the ethnic processes and conflicts, the relations of revolutionary elites with movements of popular dissent (and consequently the issues of state and bureaucracy), the social placement of peasants vis-à-vis social 'progress' and the regional particularities vis-à-vis global history. The last two are the core of our issue, i.e. that of the way Lenin as a Marxist made sense of the peasants of Russia in the period from the 1890s to the 1920s.

2 'Orthodoxy': The First Post-Marx Generation

The Grand Deduction: Peasants and 'Orthodox' Marxists

Marx did not bequeath an integrated science of society and politics. To have it established, elements of Marx's views were culled by interpreters from articles, books (especially the single published volume of *Capital*) and Engels's works, especially from his *Anti-Duhring*, which Marx read, accepted and supplemented. The authority of Engels as Marx's interpreter was made unique by years of friendship and association but the publication of Marx's heritage was taking most of his energy in the last decade of his life, 1885–95. In the face of then rapidly growing workers' parties and factions ready to seek out Marx's theory of socialism as guidance to themselves, the elaboration of a 'Marxism' was undertaken by the next political generation of socialist theorists: Kautsky, Bernstein, Plekhanov, Loria, etc., as well as a number of leading socialist politicians ready to use their pens, e.g. August Bebel. An early construction of Marxism as a social theory explicitly linked to the political strategy of a major workers' party was the 1891 Erfurt Programme of the SDP in Germany.[2] It defined for a generation what was to be full-blooded Marxism as a global analytical system from which the policies of the day were to be deduced. Plekhanov christened it 'dialectical materialism'. As with the natural sciences of the day, further unfolding of the system was expected, but no challenge to its essential logic and methods was seen as permissible – hence the self-definition as 'orthodoxy'. The author of the Erfurt Programme's theoretical part was Karl Kautsky (increasingly referred to as the 'pope' of Marxism). The exclusive prestige of Kautsky's interpretation was sustained by his very effective books of popularization and application, a near consensus of major interpreters of Marx and, especially, Kautsky's support by Engels. It also drew strength from becoming the official creed of the most theoretically minded workers' party of Europe – the SPD.

The Erfurt Programme began with the assumption that the essence of contemporary history is the rise of bourgeois society and at its core are

2 For an English version see G.P. Steenson, *Not One Man, Not One Penny* (Pittsburgh, 1981), pp. 247–50.

the laws of capitalist accumulation and concentration. Immutable laws of political economy lead 'by natural necessity' to the separation of workers from their means of production and the 'downfall' of small enterprises. These processes are being caused by and, in turn, advance further the growth of forces of production as well as the unification and uniformization of society. On a par with the social unification come new powerful contradictions and a growing class division. The 'evermore bitter class struggle between the bourgeoisie and the proletariat' is the expression and logical extension of objective laws of capital accumulation – a 'distinctive feature common to all industrial societies'. Unable to absorb its own achievements and riches, the capitalist systems enters a crisis as existing property relations turn into a source of misery and the fetters of society's productive forces. As a result, the class offensive of the proletariat increases. The eventual victory of the proletariat is destined not simply to establish a new system of class privileges, however. The working class, which is unrestricted by property interests of its own, comes to act in the general interest of progress. While liberating itself the working class must liberate others, i.e. abolish the class system as such, establishing fundamental social justice and bringing the prehistory of human society to a close.

This is where and why the tracing of causal chains, the evidence drawn in its support and the political prescriptions offered, do not quite exhaust the actual message of Erfurt Marxism. Its emotional charge, political drive and power to convince were rooted as well in a basic ethical scheme and a general creed of Progress, i.e. of nineteenth-century evolutionism. Put in a nutshell it was expressed in the optimistic postulate that the inevitable, the rational, the good and the programmatic are the same.

No place has been assigned to peasants in the Erfurt charter of progression through capitalism towards the socialist revolution. It clearly assumed that countries the population of which consisted nearly without exception of peasants were bound to follow industrial societies. At the industrial core of capitalism the still existent peasants were part of the amorphous mass of 'decaying middle layers', whose 'insecurity of existence, poverty, oppression, servitude, humiliation and exploitation' were necessarily on the increase and whose rapid demise through proletarization was certain (and progressive). The objective reasons for the necessary disappearance of the 'middle layers' was assumed to lie in the necessarily higher productivity of the larger units of production, especially so when mechanization and high capital investment are involved. While the workers are being shaped by capitalism into an increasingly organized, class-conscious and uncompromising socialist force, the subordinated middle layers are being politically weakened and necessarily display reactionary cravings resulting from their social and historical placement. A declining class would hold on to past-directed Utopias, its political ambivalence would follow from neither-worker-nor-capitalist conditions. Peasants are a 'decaying middle layer' with a vengeance. They are exceptionally insecure, poor, oppressed, servile and humiliated. They are also mostly illiterate and particularly narrow-minded because of the experience of village life. Never a subject of history, they can be only its victim, a raw material from which general processes and other classes or leaders will shape humanity's future.

When the growing parliamentary effort of the German SDP made some of its leaders clamour for an agrarian programme to court the peasant vote, it was the formidable ideological alliance of the two most authoritative and 'orthodox' Marxists of the day, Engels and Kautsky, which came to defeat it on ideological grounds. They also formulated and put in full the 'orthodox' Marxist view of the place of peasantry in the revolutionary struggle to come. In Engels's words then:

The peasant has so far largely manifested himself as a factor of political power only by his apathy, which has its roots in the isolation of rustic life . . . [he is the] strongest pillar not only of the parliamentary corruption in Paris and Rome but also of Russian despotism . . . Small production is irretrievably going to rack and ruin . . . The small peasant, like every other survival of a past mode of production, is hopelessly doomed. He is the future proletarian.

The political conclusion was as clear:

We can do no greater disservice to the party as well as to the small peasants than to make promises that even merely create the impression that we intend to preserve small-holding permanently. . . . Let us say outright that in view of the prejudices arising out of their entire economic position, their upbringing and their isolated mode of life, prejudices nurtured by the bourgeoisie and the big landowners, we can win the mass of the small peasants forthwith only if we make them a promise which we ourselves know we shall not be able to keep . . . it is not in our interests to win the peasant overnight only to lose him again on the morrow if we cannot keep our promise. (MES, vol. 3, pp. 457, 460, 469)

Accordingly, Kautsky put to his party congress of 1895 the following resolution: 'The programme of the agrarian committee should be rejected for it offers the peasants hope to improve their conditions . . . etc.' The congress of the SDP affirmed this view by a two-thirds majority vote in which the party radicals joined hands with its right-wing union bosses in the defence of the proletarian exclusivity of their party's struggle for socialism.

Five years later, in a book Lenin was to describe as the most significant Marxist contribution to agrarian theory since Marx, Kautsky offered a different analysis of peasants versus capitalism, but his political prescription did not change. There was no place for an 'Agrarian', i.e. peasant-directed, programme of the SPD. A few selected peasants could be expected to commit class emulation by joining the proletarian stand of this party. To defend itself from peasant counter-revolutionary propensities and an army of peasant sons which could be marched against the socialist cities, the SPD should strive to neutralize the peasantry politically. That was the most socialists could expect from the peasant mass.

How far was the Erfurtian Marxism's attitude to peasants one of Marx's own? Without doubt, the fundamental components of the theory of progress suggested by Kautsky matched Marx's views: history as the passage through modes of production, capitalism's dynamic as defined by capital accumulation and the necessary eradication of smaller economic units, social polarization into capitalists and proletarians. Marx's list of negative characteristics concerning peasantry as a way of living and in political action was also impressively long: their cultural backwardness ('idiocy of rural life'), and their fragmentation ('a sack of potatoes'), their hopeless poverty, petty-mindedness and lack of social space for individual development. Prudhon's ideas of attempting to keep such entities alive were dismissed by Marx as sentimental utopianism. Marx would probably accept Engels's statement that one remedy to the limitations of small enterprises was a large enterprise. Moreover, in his 1850 view:

Peasant interests beget no community, no national bond and no political organization among them . . . [making them] consequently incapable of enforcing their class interest in their own name . . . They cannot represent themselves, they must be represented. Their representative must at the same time appear their master. (MES vol. 1, pp. 479, 482)

But this was not all of Marx. Some of his comments treated as condemnation were actually more complex than later readers would have them. (To exemplify, in the usage of a German scholar in the middle of the nineteenth century the word 'barbarian' spelt not only backwardness and crudity but also strength.) In parallel with disparaging remarks about peasants, one can find in Marx's writings of the 1850s and 1860s different motives, especially so when his attention moves from industrial England to other countries. The two most relevant elements of the 'kitchen' of Marx's thought, indicating his changing view of peasantry, came in what we call today the *Grundrisse* and, more manifestly, in the late Marx of 1875–82.[3] However, these texts remained

3 See in particular K. Marx, *Precapitalist Economic Formations*, ed. E. Hobsbawm (London, 1964); T. Shanin, *Late Marx and the Russian Road* (London, 1983).

mostly unknown to the generation which followed him directly. On the face of it, the Erfurt Programme and Engels and Kautsky's writing of 1895 spoke on behalf of the master.

Plekhanov: Peasants and the 'Father of Russian Marxism'

Of Europeans who formed the Second International the country which seemed to out-peasant all others was Russia – up to nine-tenths of its population was officially designated as such. The *Weltanschauung* of the small band of Russia's Marxists who came to join the Second International was dominated by Georgii Plekhanov. It was he who declared at the first congress of the International that 'the revolutionary movement in Russia can triumph only as a workers' revolutionary movement . . . [and it is] the proletariat, created as the result of the disintegration of the rural commune, which will deliver the mortal blow to the autocracy' (GPS, vol. iv, p. 54). The Marxism of the young Lenin and that of his generation in Russia began with Plekhanov as well as Kautsky, Engels and Marx's *Capital*.

Plekhanov was both an adherent of and an important contributor to 'orthodox' Marxism. He shared and elaborated the image of immutable laws of progress through the modes of production. He also shared and advanced the fundamental self-image of a new science as integrating the basic insights of Marx and Engels into a system of laws concerning all the world around us, but especially its human history, past, present and future. Accordingly, in Plekhanov's words, Marx was 'Copernicus' who moved men from the centre of the universe through establishing the objective, i.e. scientific laws of society. Those who offered alternative explanations of society or of socialism to those of Marx's were consequently 'alchemists', 'romantics', and 'Utopians' – a pre-scientific breed. Plekhanov shared in the select network of personal friendships and animosities at the very top of the Marxist camp – diffidently corresponding with Engels, mutually admiring of Kautsky, friendly with Bebel and Lafargue, he shared with them some pet enemies like Bakunin and, later, the once devotee and latter revisionistic Edward Bernstein.

The German SDP was Plekhanov's admired political model: its massive working-class membership, its scientific programme and leadership, its manifest goal of socialist revolution and its strategy of proletarian exclusivity in organization. Another element of SPD strategy with which Plekhanov identified was expressed succinctly in Bebel's 1895 statement that 'he always asks himself if a step suggested will disturb the development of capitalism. If so, he is against it'.[4] Here was the clearest link of

4 G.V. Plekhanov, *Izbrahnye filozofskie proizredeniya* (Moscow, 1956), vol. 1, p. 822.

social theory and political strategy. A progressive party of the most progressive class strictly adhering to the Theory of Progress – an ideal the Russians were to reproduce once their country entered the right stage for it.

As against the other leading lights of 'orthodox' Marxism, Plekhanov stood out mostly by his style and by the Russian 'brief' he held. His personal style was strongly coloured by philosophical inclination, exacting logic and abrasive militancy expressed in biting argument in defence of the creed. The term 'Monism' was used by him as a badge of full consistency necessary for every true science. The best theoretical thought was to him uncompromisingly materialist and any idealism was blind, but Plekhanov's particular wrath was reserved for any admixture, for eclectism and/or for agnosticism, all of them to his view intellectually second rate and rooted in petty-bourgeois philistinism. Also, in a social world ruled by objective laws, the role of any individual was one of carrier of historical necessity only or none whatever. Wisdom as well as ethics were equated with the service to Progress. Those who refused the light of truth were not only wrong but stupid and obnoxious, while the Revisionists were personally reprehensible.[5] Aloof and distant in life, Plekhanov the polemicist poured on his opponents endless scorn and abuse. These were not only, however, matters of the language he used. The 'orthodox' Marxists of Germany were surprised and dismayed by the factional animus of their Russian counterparts: Engels refused Plekhanov's demand to join an anti-populist crusade, Kautsky was stunned when Plekhanov suggested that Bernstein should be expelled for revisionism from the SPD. But there was also a measure of admiration of the uncompromising stand of Russian revolutionaries. Kautsky was to remark in 1902 that it 'may possibly become a powerful force to purge the spirit of soft philistinism and sober politicking which begins to spread in our ranks'.[6]

Plekhanov was expected by his allies as much as by himself to provide the dual service of introducing Marxist theory to Russia while simultaneously introducing Russia into the camp of true Marxist theory. Often designated the 'father of Russian Marxism', he was in the realm of theory its supreme authority for the two decades of 1885–1905.

In the 1880s Plekhanov concluded that 'in Russian history there are no essential differences from the history of Western Europe', and those who treated Russia as 'a China' were simply wrong (GPS, vol. 4, p. 53, etc.). He partly modified this view later as he came to accept Russia to

5 See Plekhanov's correspondence with Axelrod, reviewed in S.W. Baron, *Plekhanov* (Stamford, 1963), pp. 172–80. See also GPS, vol. 18, p. 219.
6 K. Kautsky, 'Slavs and the Revolution', published in Russian in 1902 and quoted after K. Kautsky, *Doroga k vlasti*, (Moscow, 1959), p. 139.

be a version of oriental despotism (as Engels did in his *Anti-Duhring*). Either way, the core of the matter had been Russia's backwardness as against the other parts of Europe, while its way out of it was the necessary growth of capitalism. Capitalism was synonymous with Europization and to be followed necessarily by a socialist revolution. The making of Russian capitalism was to Plekhanov's view well advanced already by 1885, while the Tsar Alexander II (1855–81) was the country's first 'bourgeois monarch'. Russia's particularity lay in the feebleness of its capitalists and that was why the revolutions due to occur would have to be carried out by its workers' revolutionary movement. Being privy to the science of society made Marxist intelligentsia into a necessary ingredient of this move. The first task was to provide for political liberty by destroying autocracy, i.e. to remove the pre-capitalist burden on Russian civil society (GPS, vols. 2–6).

Some decades earlier, Russia's major indigenous theorist of socialist revolution, Chernyshevskii, to whom Plekhanov often returned in a curious love-hate relation, suggested a triple class division of the Russian society. In his view it consisted of *Svet'*, that is the state's elite in bureaucracy and nobility (i.e. the tsar's direct social environment), *Obshchestvo*, i.e. the literate middle classes who acted as carriers of the country's public conscience, and *Narod*, i.e. the common people, mostly peasants, who were the still silent yet potentially all-powerful arbiter of Russia's future.[7] While Plekhanov's 'scientific socialism' set the bourgeoisie and industrial workers at the centre of his class analysis, Chernyshevskii's 'social arbiter' still loomed large on the actual social scene. It was its interpretation which was being changed. By the middle of the 1880s Plekhanov came to see Russian peasants as an inert mass immune to revolutionary appeal, their reactionary views rooted in objective backwardness and in the necessary decline of the type of economy they represented. Their political ineptitude was objectively necessary because of their fragmentation, low educational standards and the unresolvable ambivalence of the peasants' class standing – being both owners and employees within the advancing system of capitalist market relations. In all these he anticipated and doubtlessly influenced Engel's and Kautsky's general argument of 1895.

The issue of the land commune (the *mir*), Russia's significant particularity and the basic social organization of its peasant farms, was central to political debate between Russian socialists.[8] Egalitarian images of the communes and the repartitional arrangements in them were to Plekha-

---

7 N. Chernyshevskii, 'Letters Without an Address'. For discussion see F. Venturi, *Roots of Revolution* (London, 1971).

8 For particulars see T. Shanin, *Russia as a 'Developing Society'* (London, 1984).

nov nominal only, a mockery of social justice but a real enough restraint on economic progress. He concluded that the peasant commune's historical origins and function lie in the system of fiscal exploitation by the tsarist state. The commune facilitated the lingering apathy of the peasant mass, sustaining a pre-capitalist state which was defying Progress in Russia. A morbid remainder of pre-capitalist formations, it was, fortunately, in the process of rapid disintegration.

As against his past effort as a revolutionary populist to subvert peasants for socialism, Plekhanov believed now that there could be no place for this. A peasant socialism could be imagined only as an Inca-like paternalistic despotism, stagnant and destructive of individuality. Politically the Russian peasants were synonymous with Asia'ness (*Aziyatchina*) and China'ness (*Kitaishchina*) – both used as terms of extreme abuse. Populists who at the turn of the twentieth century still considered peasant revolution and its socialist potentials (to Plekhanov the 'so-called party of so-called Socialist Revolutionaries') were the Bakuninistic representatives of petty bourgeois, unscientific and Utopian misperceptions.

To Plekhanov, while Russia's archaic legislation and common destitution could give them a spurious air of similarity, the peasants and the workers were two fundamentally different social entities. The first represented Asia, the East and humanity's past, the second represented Europe, the West and humanity's future. Nor could one speak of them even as two parallel social classes. Capitalism transformed Russia and within this context peasants were not any longer a class but a legal notion imposed by the state (*soslovie*). Beneath this legal fiction lurked a highly differentiated social universe, deeply divided between rural capitalists who used the peasant commune to enhance their exploitive power and those whom social differentiation turned into paupers and eventually made into proletarians. To expect class action from such a social mishmash was ridiculous. To compare them with the industry-shaped workers was outrageous. Harsh as this all might seem, there was no place for sentimentality in the scientific pursuit of truth.

By the 1890s there were indeed clear signs of rapid capitalist development in Russia's industry, railways and mines. This and a number of major industrial strikes offered powerful support to the 'orthodox' Marxist view of Russia. But the core of the debate concerning the development of capitalism in Russia still lay with its agriculture and the more than four-fifths of total population in it. Plekhanov had no doubts. But for such certitude his evidential base was remarkably thin.

There was in fact a major divergence between Plekhanov's adopted self-image and his writing about rural matters. A devotee of 'scientific socialism', he did not really engage in the systematic evidence collection, verification procedures and discourse which twentieth-century social scientists would recognize as the particularity of their trade. For a man who furiously argued for the economic base of any social structure he made remarkably little use of Economics. He mostly philosophized about social structures and processes using examples drawn from the works of Russian economists and from historical comparisons. He was impressive in his confrontation with those who argued on similar grounds of social and political philosophy. He was often brilliant in his polemic. He made his particular mark when tearing at the weak joints of analysis offered by the social scientists of the day. What he was failing to produce was a corpus of alternative social sciences. This divergence between Plekhanov's philosophy of society and the social sciences had been growing through the 1890s, as the flourishing of rural-directed social research put Russia in the forefront of international achievements in this field. But by the end of the century Plekhanov acquired young champions to fight his battle within Economics *sensu strictu*. These were a new generation of Marxist students of rural society: Gurevich, Rumyantsev, Groman, Chernyshev and Vladimir Ulyanov – Lenin, whose political acumen and achievement were to make his views eventually dominant, whatever might be the finer points of the analytical disputation.

3 Lenin and Peasants: The Road to Revolution

Programme 1: Logical Consistency

Like every 'orthodox' Marxist from Russia, Lenin began as an orthodox Plekhanovite. Indeed, where grand theory was concerned he stayed a Plekhanovite through his life, ready to say so even when political struggle made the two into implacable enemies. This Plekhanovite layer in Lenin's thought was expressed in the way he integrated and argued his Marxism 'as a science', understood through its nineteenth-century models, and as an orthodoxy, which must be continuously defended. Challenges to it could only represent a conservative defence of class privileges or else reactionary cast of mind and the many ambivalences of a declining petty bourgeoisie. The harsh polemical edge and the pride at being merciless on behalf of the revolution – a Jacobin self-image – were common to Plekhanov and to Lenin. Lenin shared also in the 'orthodox' Marxist theory of progress through necessary stages, with the proletariat as the sole consistent agent of the revolutions to come.

Lenin's initial placement of Russia in this context followed directly

Plekhanov's 1885 book: the country was dominated by capitalism, it was in the process of rapid 'depeasantization' and at a stage at which the revolutionary removal of its autocracy became necessary for the full flourishing of capitalism.

The young Lenin entered the Russian Marxist scene in the dual capacity of an organizer and an analyst. This was to define his political profile to the end. As an organizer he began to make his mark in the 'Alliance for the Liberation of the Working Class', and, after arrest and a period of exile, by 1900 he engaged with his friends in the setting up of the Russian Social Democratic Workers Party (RSDWP). Eventually, at that party's congress of 1903, Lenin became this party's cofounder and a leader of one of its factions. By this time as a writer and an analyst he produced a sequence of polemical articles, some reviews and two books which represented well the dual focus of his concerns. The first of the books was devoted to systematic economic analysis of the development of capitalism in Russia. The second (*What Is To Be Done*) was devoted to the strategy of party organization, offering the image of a clandestine and highly disciplined cadre of professional revolutionaries.

Lenin's first book, *The Development of Capitalism in Russia*, related a systematic presentation of a Plekhanovian line of analysis to extensive economic data of the day (PSS, vol. 3). It made Lenin overnight into the central figure of Russia's Marxists' self-definition. A most significant ideological part of the book was its analysis of the agriculture. Rural Russia was presented as substantively capitalist and a treble index offered to substantiate it.[9] Firstly, the labour force engaged on the nobility's estates were increasingly being transferred from corvée (equated with pre-capitalism) to wage-labour (equated with capitalism). Anneskii, who concluded that by 1887 in the majority of Russian provinces wage-labour prevailed over corvée, was adopted to make this point (ibid., p. 198). Secondly, commodity economy had spread within Russian agriculture, subordinating it to capitalist market relations. Evidence presented had shown that indeed market-related rural production was on the increase in the Russian agriculture. Thirdly, commodity relations did combine with the 'separation of direct producers from the means of production', i.e. depeasantization – in Lenin's words:

The old peasantry is not only differentiating, it is being completely dissolved, it is ceasing to exist, it is being ousted by absolutely new types of rural inhabitants – types that are the basis of a society in which commodity economy and capitalist production prevail. These types are the rural bourgeoisie (chiefly petty bour-

9 For a brilliant Soviet criticism of Lenin's conclusion which proved very costly to the author, see A. Anfimov 'K voprosu o kharaktere agrarnogo stroya Rossii', *Istoricheskie zapiski*, 65 (1959).

geoisie) and the rural proletariat . . . Peasantry has been splitting up at enormous speed. (ibid., p. 177)

He also claimed that immigration, mostly of the middle strata of peasants, enhanced polarization. The peasant commune was mentioned only *en passant* as one of the 'remnants of the purely medieval past which continues to weigh upon peasantry' (ibid., pp. 329–30). The 'Kulaks', i.e. rural exploiters, were 'the true masters of the village'. It is not my brief to engage here in considering the major weaknesses and attractions of this book (see my *The Awkward Class* [Oxford 1972]). I shall proceed taking as given what Lenin believed to be the case as he shaped his political strategy.

In the same period Lenin engaged extensively in Plekhanov-like polemic against the populist writers and the Socialist Revolutionary Party, which he defined as representatives of petty bourgeoisie as well as the Russian version of German revisionism. In this argument Lenin presented the political conclusions of his 1899 study of the development of capitalism in agriculture. Russian villages were in this view undergoing a dual class war – the declining past-related struggle of peasantry as a whole versus the squires and the growing struggle of the rural proletariat against the rural bourgeoisie (PSS, vol. 4, pp. 432–4). By 1903 he addressed on this matter the second congress of the RSDWP, speaking on behalf of its dominant ISKRA group led by Plekhanov, Martov and himself. By that time Plekhanov and Lenin's personal relations were bad, each declaring the other to be inconsiderate, self-centered and crude. But the consistency of the deductive chain which led from the assumed laws of capitalist accumulation via the adopted characterization of rural Russia as capitalist to the party programme of orthodox Marxists secured their mutual support during the party congress. The ISKRAites agreed that as a transitional measure the extensive remainders of feudalism in Russia, supported by the state, still justified a specific programme for the Russian peasants. Yet, in view of the pre-eminence and advance of capitalism, Kautsky's main conclusion for Germany held true also for Russia – peasants could not be a truly revolutionary force. They had to be neutralized by the party of the revolutionary proletariat. The suggested agrarian programme of the RSDWP began with demands aiming to finalize the capitalist transformation of agriculture, through the abolition of the fiscal collective responsibility of peasant communes and the cancellation of laws restricting the freedom of peasants to sell their allotments and to leave their villages. This was expected to find support with the most active farmers and aimed 'to clear the way for free development of [capitalist] class war in the villages' (PSS, vol. 6, p. 347). To secure peasant goodwill towards the RSDWP some rectification of past injustices was also to be supported: the payments linked to the 1861 emancipation from serfdom were to be abolished. As to the peasant demands for land, the Russian Social Democrats were to support the return of the 'cut-off lands', i.e. the rather limited amounts of land some of the villages lost to local squires during the emancipation from serfdom. Peasants' committees were to be set up to preside over this process, the peasant commune not being considered able to carry out this task satisfactorily.

The 1903 Agrarian Programme had therefore expected little and offered little where peasants were concerned. A few years later Plekhanov explained the roots of this attitude as follows: 'Many of our comrades supported the [programme restricted to] "cut off" lands because they were afraid of a peasant agrarian revolution, as it would stop the development of capitalism in Russia' (GPS, vol. 15, p. 67). Yet already by 1902 first signs of peasant revolutionary militancy could be seen all through Russia.[10]

Programme 2: Revolution's Amendments and the Theory's Inertia

Within two years of the RSDWP's first agrarian programme, Russian peasants dramatically and massively refused to fit the 'orthodox' Marxists' models and theoretical considerations. In a spectacular display of class struggle, the peasants of Russia for the three years of 1905–7 fought the government and the squires, to be defeated only by a military operation, executions, prisons, exile and, eventually, by a *coup d' état* by the government itself, which dismantled its own constitution to get rid of a troublesome parliamentary bloc of peasant deputies. In this confrontation the peasant communes acted as the main units of peasant organization. Community-based national organizations, which peasants established overnight, as well as the peasant deputies, singled out by the Russian electoral system, made the peasantry's wishes very clear. They demanded all of Russia's land to be handed over to its peasants, to be divided by their communes on the basis of rough egalitarianism built into their structure. They demanded also amnesty for those arrested, free education for all and the election of officials, i.e. local power to peasant representatives.[11] In this struggle peasants refused all the efforts of conservative clergy and disciplinarian officialdom to bring them into line as their majority consistently allied with the radical wing of Russia's dissent. And the peasants proceeded to fight for two more bitter years after urban revolutionaries were defeated in their challenge to the

10 See T. Shanin, *Russia 1905–7: Revolution and a Moment of Truth* (London, 1985), chapters 1, 3.
11 ibid., chapters 3, 4.

autocratic rule. The period of 1917–20 was to show how little were their 1905–7 demands to be forgotten even after the 'forces of order' suppressed the peasant war and political challenge.

Lenin began to take stock of the unexpected behaviour of Russia's peasants as soon as early 1905. In the speed of his political adjustment he clearly left his friends and allies behind. He outran them to begin with by the enthusiastic and total nature of his support for the unfolding peasant struggle, while Russia's other Marxists of all factions moved toward such views slowly, ambivalently and with dark forebodings of backward-looking *Pugachevshchina* or 'another Vandée'.[12]

Lenin moved on rapidly to present a new ideological scheme for the future revolutionary regime. His explanation of peasant revolutionary *élan* lay now in rural Russia's still being, after all, pre-capitalist. 'Those who refuse to admit it cannot explain the recent broad and deep peasant revolutionary movement in Russia' (PSS, vol. 12, p. 249). The revolution was a bourgeois one aiming to remove a feudal state and a substantively feudal social structure. That was why peasants were still united as a class and revolutionary. At the same time the representatives of the Russian bourgeoisie were becoming increasingly scared of the revolutionary mood of Russia's workers and peasants. The bourgeoisie was looking accordingly for a compromise with and for protection by the tsardom. To succeed fully, Russia's bourgeois revolution must be taken out of the bourgeoisie's feeble hands. The proletarian forces in the towns and villages of Russia led by their separate organization were to play the major role in this bourgeois revolution. The new republic to be created by the popular majority would be a 'democratic dictatorship of workers and peasants'. A proletarian socialist revolution, the one in which peasants would necessarily appear divided, was still in the future. Accordingly, a new agrarian programme addressing peasantry's revolutionary capacity was urgently called for.

In April 1906 the fourth 'unificatory' congress of the Russian SDP met, with all of Russia's 'orthodox' Marxist factions in attendance. The issue of a new agrarian programme was in the centre of the agenda. All Russia's Marxists agreed now that peasant struggle should be supported and that the land of Russian squires was to be expropriated and handed over to the peasants. They debated the form this should take. By that time Lenin had advanced still farther in elaborating the new approach. A gap was opening not only between Lenin and the Mensheviks' wing of his party, more 'orthodox' by far, but also between him and the majority

---

12 The 'peasant war' led by Pugachev in 1773–4, arguably Russia's last great medieval popular upheaval and to many Russians a symbol of violence without prospects in defence of a golden past which never was. Vandée was the region of French peasants' royalist rising in 1793 against the French revolutionary government.

of his own Bolshevik adherents. Lenin spoke now not only of two stages but of two alternative roads of the unfolding capitalist transformation of agriculture. The bourgeois stage of the rural revolution could take different forms, a 'German' one and an 'American' one. In the first case capitalist transformation of feudal large estates would lead to the decline of the small-holders of the countryside. In the second case a revolutionary removal 'from below' of the large estates and a land redivision, together with a free market of land, labour and goods, would clear the ground for capitalism and for the rapid differentiation of ruralites into farmers – entrepreneurs and wage-workers. Marxists should not be indifferent to these choices: they should support the road which is more radical and more able to unleash the revolutionary creativity of 'the masses'. This is why they should support as progressive, i.e. as best facilitating capitalism, the nationalization of all land. (Endless explanations to the contrary, this was a simple rewording of the All Russian Peasant Union's demands and of the Socialist Revolutionary Party's programme of 'socialization of land', but on the understanding that this would not mean a socialist revolution, which was still to come.) Consequent on this view, Lenin spoke for alliance with the peasant movement and even for a political agreement with the Socialist Revolutionaries Party.

It was Plekhanov who led the attack on Lenin's new views. He was explicit as to the roots of his objections: 'Lenin looks at nationalization [of land] with the eye of an SR. He even begins to adopt their terminology. For example, he talks of popular creativity [of political forms]. It is nice to meet old acquaintances but unpleasant to see how Social Democrats adopt populist points of view'; and later 'Lenin lowers the level of revolutionary thought by bringing Utopian elements into our *Weltanschauung*' (GPS, vol. 15 pp. 68, 72). Plekhanov was supported by the leading Mensheviks, who formed a majority at the congress and whose agrarian programme of 'municipalization' was eventually adopted by it. ('Municipalization' assumed the sequestration of all lands belonging to the squires and the turning of them into an ownership of regional authorities, to be rented out to the family farmers. The peasant lands were to remain as they were, with the peasant communes.) Even the Bolshevik faction could not yet swallow Lenin's new turning. His 'land nationalization' programme was attacked in the Bolshevik press and refused by their faction at the congress. They suggested instead that land taken from the squires should be privatized, i.e. given to peasant farmers, with the aim of thereby advancing rural capitalism, well in line with the theory of necessary stages of progress they adhered to. It took time before Lenin had his view adopted as Bolshevik creed and, by that time, the revolution was coming to an end.

The conceptual structure of Lenin's new programme and strategy displayed some characteristics which were to colour for the next fifteen years his argument concerning peasantry. The general theory he adopted in the 1890s was kept intact as a necessary part of the 'science of society'. Any doubts as to that were treated as a schism and answered by abuse and excommunication. Yet the political strategy which until 1905 was but a deduction from the 'orthodox' science of society moved sharply, adjusting to new conditions as expressed by the new agrarian programme. The problem of an analytical gap which opened thereby was resolved by readjustment of the historical scale – a historiographic solution which kept the laws of political economy unchanged. In Lenin's own words, the reason for the mistake of 1903 was simply that 'while having defined correctly the direction of the development, we mistook *the point at which it was* . . . We assumed that the elements of capitalist agriculture were already in place in Russia' (PSS, vol. 16, pp. 268–9, italics added).

Programme 1½: The 'Point' as a Puzzlement

It was Lenin's 1905–7 historiographic resolution of the strategy/theory divide concerning rural Russia which imposed itself on the consequent developments of his thought. By the end of 1907 the revolution was defeated, its supporters suppressed or dispersed, its leaders mainly in prisons or exile. But the victorious monarchist chief minister Stolypin was not only an effective policeman. He matched heavy-handed repression by an effort at structural reforms.[13] In his view the revolution was facilitated by the collectivistic backwardness of the peasant communes and the inefficiencies of tsardom's administrative structure. To secure rural Russia from a new round of revolutionary upheaval he took steps, accordingly, to demolish the peasant communal structures through privatizing communal lands and giving them to the peasants. This was to advance the interest of the better-off and/or abler farmers. In face of the puzzling image of a minister acting radically on behalf of the tsardom (the main 'remainder of feudalism'), i.e. zealously carrying out a 'revolution from above' along lines which many liberals and Marxists prescribed as progressive, the Russian intellectual Left showed much disarray. Were his reforms good or bad, impossible or realistic? Stolypin was in confrontation with reactionary nobles, conservative merchants and corrupt princes, while fighting the revolutionaries at the same time. Which social class did he represent?

13 For Stolypin's reforms see A. Avrekh, *Tsarism; treteyunskaya sistema* (Moscow, 1966). See also Shanin, *Russia 1905–7*, chapter 6, section A.

Expressed in the ideological language of his convictions, Lenin's interpretation of Stolypin's regime was remarkably realistic. He defined Stolypin's rule as 'Bonapartism', using Marx's text concerning France in the middle of the nineteenth century, which spoke of a government as 'relatively autonomous' from the ruling class because of the fine balance of class forces locked in confrontation. As to Stolypin's vision of rural Russia, in Lenin's view it could work, for it was a policy facilitating and magnifying the natural process of the development of capitalism. To those who doubted the very possibility of Stolypin's reforms came Lenin's snappy 'to the contrary, it can' (*Net, mozhet*).

Rather than Stolypin's road towards capitalism Lenin preferred the 'American road' of revolutionary transformation from below. As the nationwide peasant organizations dissolved under the pressure of post-revolutionary repressions, Lenin still argued in 1909 that class alliance with peasants was possible even if they failed to establish a party of their own. He proceeded to watch with guarded empathy peasant deputies in the Russian Duma (PSS, vol. 21, pp. 268–71) and later compared Sun Yan Tse in the Chinese revolution to them – a progressive strategy in a backward society, to be supported by the revolutionary Marxists (PSS, vol. 23). But history was marching on and this meant that capitalism must be marching on in the Russian agriculture. The success of the Stolypin reforms, even partial success, would make it advance the faster. To Lenin capitalism spelt the necessary disappearance of peasantry as a social class, to be substituted by capitalist entrepreneurs and rural proletarians. The political scene added credence to this view for, when a new wave of industrial workers' militancy mounted in 1912–14, there was no equivalent to it in rural Russia. Was the 'historical point in time' assumed by the first agrarian programme of the SDP being reached after all?

Lenin proceeded with a consideration and an elucidation of the basic processes of rural political economy. He did so through the study of Germany and the USA Censuses of 1910 (PSS, vol. 27, pp. 131–338).[14] In his view those Censuses had documented the inevitable capitalist progress within agriculture. This was expressed in mechanization and the upswing in the use of wage-labour. The displacement of small units by large ones was in his view being concluded (when no concentration of land-ownership was actually recorded, Lenin assumed that an increased capital investment played a similar role). The general drop in numbers of farms was interpreted by Lenin accordingly. The view that in a capitalist industrial society small family units may actually expand their impact and share of agriculture was described as 'terribly wrong . . . the exact opposite of what is actually happening' (PSS, vol. 27, p. 134). To

14 The study of Germany was published only after Lenin's death in *Leninskii sbornik*, XIX (1939).

Lenin, the US Census defined by implication 'the past and the present of Russia' (PSS, vol. 27, p. 226).

Central to these conclusions was Lenin's assumptions that there could be only two dominant types of economy in the Europe and the US of the day, linked within necessary historical sequence and defining the nature of any economic form which did actually appear. It was either ('semi-'?) feudalism or capitalism. Family-farms within a fully fledged capitalist economy, national and international, were necessarily capitalist, if small.[15]

During the First World War nobody bothered to extrapolate considerations of political economy into a politically consistent Marxist strategy for rural Russia. Issues of war and peace dominated political debate. Lenin's second agrarian programme was still formally in place for the Bolsheviks but, as capitalism advanced, increasingly in doubt.

Post-revolutionary exile was Lenin's darkest hour. The revolution had failed, his party declined and divided, the war made the Second International collapse like a house of cards. He refused to be disheartened and used his exile to work his way through several libraries. But the mood was bleak. In a lecture delivered in January of 1917 he spoke longingly about the days of the 1905–7 revolution and said to his Swiss audience that those of them who were young would see the next revolution (PSS, vol. 23, p. 249). The next Russian revolution began within days of this speech.

4 Lenin and Peasants: The State of the Revolution

Russian Peasants, 1917: Deduction and Revolution

In his first response to the exhilarating news of the tsardom's collapse, Lenin drew mostly on his images from afar of Russian society and politics as established during the 1907–17 decade of 'Stolypinism' and of war. With Lenin's party organization badly disrupted by post-revolution repressions and decline, Lenin's direct contacts with Russia's extra-parliamentary politics were limited. He had practically none where rural Russia was concerned. He read extensively but second-hand knowledge made for a limited vision based mostly on deductions and on comparisons with the industrial West. The way his thoughts ran can be judged from his writings. The war economy would have made Russian capitalism more state-directed. The threshold of socialist economy was seemingly being reached – a capitalist yet centralized economic system could

15 For discussion see Shanin, *Russia 1905–7*, chapter 4.

be taken over with greater ease through political revolution by a revolutionary class. As to the political scene, the revolutionary fever of the industrial workers of Petersburg in 1912–14 and their return to strike action in 1915–16 found no equivalent in other social classes. Soldiers were not yet a socially defined composite of Lenin's political thoughts. It seemed that, as Plekhanov declared in 1889, social revolution was to come after all to Russia as a workers' revolution or not at all. Moreover, what was to Lenin an abominable sell-out to nationalist warmongers by the parties of the Second International disqualified them from speaking on behalf of a Marxist revolution. The single exception was Lenin's Bolsheviks. It was for them to form the vanguard of revolutions to come.

In Lenin's writings of February 1917, and on his return to Russia, in the 'April Thesis', he set as his party's immediate goal a proletarian dictatorship with Bolsheviks at the head, as the sole party pure of purpose and capable of understanding the new conditions and opportunities (PSS, vol. 31, pp. 7–110). This political formula was to be applied to Russia's most immediate social and political ills – the war which must be stopped, profiteering and shortage of foodstuffs which must be brought under control, the tsarist state apparatus which must be dismantled. As the next step Lenin called accordingly for an immediate effort by his comrades 'to deepen' the revolution. This included no support whatever of the new Provisional Government, no alliances with other political parties and the immediate setting up and arming of workers' militias. A structure of Soviets run on the lines of the Parisian Commune of 1871 was to replace the old machinery of the state.

How about the peasants? Could one, indeed, still talk of peasants at all in a country of developed capitalism where proletarian dictatorship was on the agenda? Lenin's initial conclusion was clear and, as deductions go, impeccable. The Bolsheviks were to focus their political effort on organizing rural wage labourers (*Batraki*) (PSS, vol. 31, pp. 24–5, 416–18; vol. 32, pp. 376–7). Soviets of rural wage labourers were to be set up as a matter of utmost urgency in all localities. As to agriculture, large production units were to be promoted under the authority of Soviets as the best solution to the issues of effective farming and sufficient food supplies. The socialist republic that was being fought for was to rest on the class power of the industrial workers supported by rural wage-workers as well as by the 'poorest of peasants' and poor urbanites. In line with this image of revolution's class content, the mushrooming Soviets of Peasants were to be split as a matter of urgency so that, in parallel with them, the separate Soviets of Rural Wage-Labourers and the once again separate Soviets of the 'poorest peasants' (i.e. the '*de facto* rural proletarians') were to be set up to express the class conflicts in the countryside (PSS, vol. 31, pp. 22, 38, 55–6). In May

1917 Lenin spoke of an alliance of workers with the 'half-proletarian peasants' only (PSS, vol. 31, pp. 24–5). The second 'agrarian programme' which aimed at a radical democracy of a pre-socialist type ('the democratic dictatorship of workers and peasants') was explicitly abandoned in view of the new 'point' on the necessary historiography's scale.

But while calling for these dramatic changes in strategy, urban as well as rural, Lenin had uncharacteristically expressed some doubts in so far as the peasants were concerned: 'What peasantry is we do not know; we have no statistics available; but we know that they are a power [in the land]' (PSS, vol. 31). By the end of 1917 there were in fact neither Soviets of Rural Wage-Labourers nor of the poorest peasants', while the impact of the Soviets of Peasants was large and magnified even more by the peasants in uniforms, i.e. the majority of soldiers who set up their own Soviets all through Russia. In autumn 1917, peasant 'direct action' was spreading in the countryside, the land of the nobility was being taken over and divided. Peasants on the move clashed with the government's forces. The Socialist Revolutionaries (PSR), the main peasant-supported party of Russia in 1917, refused to carry out promptly and fully the radical agrarian reform of the 'land to its tillers' type to which they had been committed since the 1905–7 revolution. Lenin's party adopted then on his advice the 'Integrated Instruction' based on 242 peasant briefs to their deputies as summed up by newspapers of the National Executive of the Peasant Soviets sympathetic to the PSR. With the Bolsheviks adopting peasants' basic demands, the peasants began to adopt the Bolsheviks as the party to support or, at least, to tolerate. That was particularly true when peasant-soldiers were concerned. In September 1917 (PSS, vol. 34, pp. 280, 287, etc.) Lenin spoke of mistakes in his earlier evaluation of how much fight is still left in the 'majority of peasants'. He was now also speaking about an alliance of 'workers and the *majority* of peasants' (italics added) against the bourgeoisie, the rich peasants, the foreign finance capital and the 'Bonapartist' state of the provisional government. What made for his new approach was that 'in a peasant country, with representative government, *a peasant uprising* is growing. As against that all the rest is unimportant . . . A proletarian–peasant revolution is coming' (PSS, vol. 34, pp. 388, 399; italics added).

Within weeks the Bolsheviks took power. The Provisional Government disappeared and the intermediate period of revolutionary transformation was over. A socialist revolution was formally declared.

The 'Second Stage': A Non-Programme for Non-Peasants

In full accordance with its view concerning the 'second stage' of revolution in the countryside, a new strategy was introduced by the party which freshly adopted the new self-designation as Communists. The transitional peasant unity of 1917, based on the Provisional Government's refusal to respect the majority wish for immediate peace and land redistribution, was now in their view over. The Provisional Government was overthrown, a peace agreement signed, peasant seizure of land legitimated. The land was being rapidly divided locally by the peasant communes. Soldiers were coming home to claim their share of land and to sink into the village communities – the mass of revolutionized soldiers (described by Lenin in late 1917 as one of 'progressive peasants') was being dissolved. The Socialist Revolutionaries paid for their failure to honour their commitments by split and decline, and the Bolsheviks and their government of People's Commissars became the only relevant representation of the revolution which was now spreading into the more backward parts of the country.

The 'dictatorship of the proletariat' was in place and this could mean only one thing. The workers and peasants-in-general alliance was now definitely over. Peasantry had to split into its class categories characteristic to a capitalist mode of production. A socialist revolution in the countryside was to begin.

At the Congress of Soviets in March 1918, the commencement of rural socialist transformation aiming at communist society was declared (PSS, vol. 35, pp. 44–56).[16] Indeed, one was not to speak now of 'peasantry' any more except as a woolly notion hiding the true class conditions. A class war between the bourgeoisie and the proletariat was now to take its course fully in the countryside. At the same time, one of the immediate problems the new government had to tackle was that of the food supply, which dwindled as the World War disorganization and the early steps of the civil war took their toll. (In early 1917, food shortages already underlay the demonstrations which triggered off the February revolution.) This issue of practical policy was now linked to the broad strategy of socialist revolution through the image of the rich peasant bourgeoisie commencing its class war against the proletariat revolution in the towns and the villages alike. The word *kulak* was selected (and extensively misused) as the description of a rich peasant class enemy in the countryside.[17] Their challenge was to be taken up and defeated through the 'food-supplies dictatorship' declared by the government on 8 May 1918. It aimed to suppress (*podavit'*) the rural enemies of the proletariat as well as of the socialist government and of

16 ibid.
17 V. Kabanov, *Krest'yanske khozyaistvo v usloviyalch 'voennogo kommunizma'* (Moscow, 1988).

the poorest population of towns and villages. Peasant opposition to the requisitioning of food was defined accordingly as 'a wave of kulaks' rebellions' (PSS, vol. 37, pp. 39–359) and the response to it summed up in Lenin's slogan – as ever, admirably clear: 'Death to them.' In August 1918 Committees of Rural Poor (*Kombedy*) were decreed for the purpose of class organization of the rural proletariat and the rural poor. Lenin declared this 'the most important problem of our internal development and even the most important problem of our revolution' and that 'from this moment our revolution becomes a proletarian revolution' (PSS, vol. 38, p. 413). The *Kombedy*'s task was to finalize the Russian socialist revolution by defeating its last major class enemy – the rural component of the bourgeoisie. They were to preside over the combined task of: (1) requisitioning, with the help of urban worker detachments, the food needed for the urban and rural workers and the rural poor as well as for the Red Army fighting the civil war; (2) rooting out market relations as unacceptable under socialism; (3) taking over capitalist means of production in the countryside; and (4) setting up a new socialist farming system. The peasants' wish to parcel land out into family units (and to run villages as traditional communes) was sheer stupidity. It was accepted in 1917 as a matter of expedience, not to clash with the peasantry despite its archaic images and its lack of ability to appreciate correctly what was best for the majority of them. Once the land was divided, most of them would have learnt that there was no real solution in it. 'The main enemy' was now the 'petty bourgeoisie', and especially 'its habits' (PSS, vol. 34, p. 376). And 'the only way out of it is the collective working of land' (PSS, vol. 37, p. 390). As class war spread in all villages the vast majority of peasants were assumed to support it.

This was the point where the new socialist farming system was to enter. In 1917, Bolsheviks advised the peasants not to parcel out the land of the squires, but they accepted parcelling-out when the bulk of peasants and peasant-soldiers insisted. The Bolsheviks legislated for parcelling out in November 1917 and February 1918, but also for the keeping together of the technologically advanced large estates to provide the exemplary farms of the future. The peasant localities disregarded the unacceptable part of these laws and carried out an almost total parcelling-out. By mid-1918 the new regime declared its further advance towards the only sensible way of farming, i.e. the larger-scale and thereby more effective socialist 'grain factories'. There was heated argument in government about the form these were to take, as state ownership, communes and some other types of collective farming were being considered.[18] What was not in question was, to quote *The Regula-*

18 ibid.

tions Concerning Land Administration of February 1919, that 'the agriculture based on family farms is transitory and obsolete.' Nor was there any need now for an agrarian programme to address peasants in a socialist revolution; indeed, the very notion of 'peasants' was 'unscientific' in the new context. Very much in line with Kautsky's 1899 prescriptions, the rural proletariat was to be mobilized for the socialist offensive and the 'middle peasants' were to be neutralized and led while the peasant entrepreneurs were to be fought tooth and nail. Or, more harshly still, as put in brutal language by the newspaper *Pravda* of 5 November 1918, 'the "middle peasants" will be made to accept socialist [i.e. large-scale] forms of economy and of thought and to go toward socialism even if growling and snapping [like a dog – *Ogryzayas*'].'

None of it happened. The established large units of production proved ineffective, unproductive and unpopular. The *Kombedy* – the assumed vanguard of rural socialist revolution – were abolished by the state itself by December 1918 after failing to perform effectively any of their tasks. In the confrontations of the civil war, peasant villages took part with remarkable uniformity – a village *vis-à-vis* the government, an army or else another village, rather than villages split along class lines. Yet the peasantry-rejecting legislation and the debate about 'which of the large is particularly beautiful?' were still in full bloom[19] when Lenin came publicly to recognize the lack of realism of the rural policies of 1918.

Lenin presented his argument while offering his third Agrarian Programme, addressing Russian peasants under a socialist regime. He introduced it at the eighth congress of the Bolshevik party in March 1919.[20] There was no opposition. Lenin's authority with his party was at its peak, but also, what he now had to say represented well the experience of the civil war and of the response to it by many of his more thoughtful comrades. Russian peasantry had on the whole preferred, or was more ready to tolerate, a Soviet regime than that of its enemies and secured thereby a Soviet victory. Peasantry was neither differentiating into classes nor was it ready to take to large farms. Yet it had to be admitted that 'in our country where the petty bourgeoisie controls all of the agriculture, without their support . . . we shall not survive for long' (PSS, vol. 38, p. 252). Therefore, while no political opposition was to be permitted, the 'middle peasantry' (i.e. peasants at large) were now to be treated differently from the way they had been treated when the final class offensive of proletariat against its enemies in the countryside was

19 *Vos'moi s'ezd* (Moscow, 1959), pp. 250–72, offered a sample of the views which were aired. See particularly the speeches by Milyatin and Mitrofanov.
20 *Vos'moi s'ezd*.

assumed to be taking place. In his call to rectify attitudes to peasantry, Lenin focused particularly on the bringing to an end of continuous use of force towards the peasants, 'which brings terrible harm'. Socialist revolution could still be carried out only by the proletariat, but one could not do it without 'the intermediate classes'. Lenin declared briskly that as to Marxist theory, it had no difficulties with the 'middle peasant'. 'Given 100,000 tractors', villages would become communist overnight: as long as this modern technology could not be offered, the Bolsheviks 'must learn from the peasants about ways to move forward to a better social and economic system' (PSS, vol. 38, p. 201). His new agrarian programme assumed state-managed family farming. The way the state management of the peasantry was to proceed now was summed up best in Lenin's sharp command to the cadres: 'do not dare to order people around.' What added significance to it was Lenin's admission in the same period that the rural party members were often simple rascals, the type of accidental human trash who turned the civil war to their own benefit. Peasants were to be left to their family farming and communal organization. These were to exist for a long time yet. An 'alliance' with 'the mass of the peasants' was called for. Yet, still, the socialist state was to direct agriculture.

There was a deep ambivalence in the new policies of befriending the bulk of peasantry and accepting its solutions and ways (or even 'learning from it') while the total control of state over the national economy was insisted on. This became even clearer as the civil war was coming to an end. In 1920 the government was decreeing the amounts of land and the crops to be farmed. It ordered into action farm-supporting technological units and set up arrangements for the army and the urban workers to be mobilized for the execution of these plans. Obligatory grain deliveries were to stay and food market was still being repressed by police action. What Lenin referred to as 'Our total control of the apparatus of cooperatives' was to provide a link in this system (PSS, vol. 40, p. 53). ('False autonomy' was taken away from rural cooperatives in 1918 and their structure centralized under state control.) This went hand in hand with the above, and so did the idea of supplying industrial goods by government plan and decree directly to the countryside. Large-scale state farms and rural communes were still to offer the lead, i.e. to help to transform family farming through the example of more effective agriculture. In Lenin's prediction the productivity was to increase by two or three times with the transfer to large units.

By late 1920, the unrealism of a totally centralized administration presiding over a majority of the country's producers on their family-farms became abundantly clear. Peasants refused to be run. Government decrees fell flat. The black market spread, with more than half of the actual urban foodstuffs now supplied in this way. The large 'exemplary' farms failed to 'offer the lead' to small producers; indeed, they performed on the whole much worse than the family farmers. A make-believe world expanded in government programmes and declarations had less and less to do with the realities of farming. Peasant opposition to the new regime mounted. With the Whites, who could spell the return of the squires, beaten and the civil war at its end, peasants saw no reason to work hard while their produce (the 'surplus') was being taken away. Armed rebellion was spreading through the countryside while demands for a 'true Soviet regime', for 'Soviets without Bolsheviks' and for a return to the goals of late 1917 got an increasingly sympathetic hearing even in the main centres of initial Bolshevik influence, inclusive of the workers of Petrograd and the sailors of Kronshtadt.

Half a century later a party ideologist of the Brezhnev era was to explain the 1919 turn in policies, i.e. the peasants' newly acquired friendly neutrality towards Bolshevik rule, as a 'political regrouping of the peasantry'. What happened in fact was the 'political regrouping' of the ruling party. It now admitted that in matters concerning peasants its up-to-date perceptions, predictions and tactics did not work. The failure of *Kombedy*, the regional rather than class-linked uniformities of peasant political behaviour, the peasantries' evident 'moral economy' and ability to resist dictates from above, led to a new programme. Peasantry was now to be tackled with new sensitivity and by new 'educational measures' (inclusive of the re-educating of the party cadres). But the basic strategy of state versus agriculture was to stay put. And, once again, it did not work, leading to a still sharper turnaround – Lenin's fourth Agrarian Programme, which formed the major element of the New Economic Policy (NEP).

Programme 4: Tactical Retreat and Ideological Turnaround

At the tenth congress of his party in March 1921, Lenin spoke of the need for a reorientation of political strategy in the light of new conditions: the revolutionary war which was won, the West European revolution which did not come, new Russia which had to be run on a new footing. The picture he painted was one of a country in total exhaustion, of an economy which had declined during the war and of growing anger among the peasants at the confiscation of agricultural 'surpluses' and at bureaucratic managers. There were peasant rebellions all over the country. Production of foodstuffs dropped to an all-time low.

The first and most urgent task was to calm peasant opposition and reverse the decline of agriculture. It was clear that the policies of

state-directed peasant economy had failed. One could fleece peasants
up to a point, but no way had been found to make them farm, and to do
so effectively. Government policy was still failing to prove the superiority of large-scale units of production and provide national needs with
their help (PSS, vol. 33, pp. 27–8). The solution Lenin suggested now
was to give way to peasants' major demands and do it at once: to abolish
requisition of farming produce and to introduce taxation instead, to
establish a free market in foodstuffs, to permit land renting and even
limited wage-labour. The actual extent of grain taken from the villages
without remuneration was to drop by half. Rural cooperatives, 'which
we kept up to now in strangulation' (PSS, vol. 43, p. 64), had to be
unchained and permitted to work outside of total control by the government. In one of his famous short phrases, due rapidly to turn into his
party's basic slogans-cum- 'words of wisdom', Lenin told his supporters
'not to try to be clever in a hurry' (*ne mudryt' naspekh*) – an extension of
his earlier call 'not to order people around' where peasants were
concerned. As against peasant culture one should not, he declared, use
confiscations but electrification. The new agrarian programme was to
form a major part of a comprehensive strategy entitled the New Economic Programme (NEP). Within two more months he declared its being
introduced 'with all seriousness and for a long time' (*vser'ez i nadolgo*)
(PSS, vol. 43, p. 140).

Rural policies of the NEP as defined in 1921 were supplemented by
stabilization of the value of currency and the Land Code, 1922, which
formalized peasants' rights to land and to produce as well as a measure
of local autonomy within the confines of the law.

Another dimension of the new strategy was the alert attention now
given to the monopoly of political power which the Bolsheviks/
Communists exercised. The fear of 'a Thermidor' – a political takeover
by new entrepreneurs linked to the new officialdom of the post-
revolutionary state – was felt acutely by Lenin and his circle. Accordingly, while the economy was being 'liberalized', the few shadow-like
parties of legal opposition were now finally suppressed, some of the
leading lights of the academic community were expelled from the
country by police orders, factions were banned within the Bolshevik
party itself. Lenin aimed at a peculiar combination of greater tolerance
towards peasants (inclusive of decision-making within local rural communities) and severe restriction or selective terror aimed at everybody
else operating outside the straight and narrow of the decisions made by
the ruling party's leadership. In his own words (in a memorandum 'for
the leadership's eyes only'), the policy now was to be one of 'increased
repressions against the political enemies of Soviet power . . . exemplary
legal procedures against scoundrels who misuse the new economic

policy . . . treble punishment to Communists when compared to those of non-party people' (PSS, vol. 43, pp. 306–7).

The first steps of the NEP were a considerable success. The peasant rebellions disappeared and agricultural production improved at considerable speed. Industry and transport moved towards their pre-revolutionary levels. The new political scheme accepted and institutionalized a dual system. In the economy, industry and finances were directly controlled by the government, while peasants exercised control of land and produce as well as of their own labour and environment. Political authority at the national level was completely in the hands of the Bolshevik government, but in the rural areas the day-to-day decisions resulted from the informal relations between the ruling party plenipotentiaries in the district executive committees (the *VIK*) and the general assemblies, and the officers of the peasant communes. The power of the communes lay as much in their legal status, recognized by the Land Code, as in patterns of peasant collective behaviour for which the commune provided a major focus.

With little doubt, the NEP was initially designed to meet the expediencies of post-war exhaustion, growing opposition by the majority of the population and the urgent need to offer some credible policies in conditions of peace. But there were deeper reasons and longer-term results to this move (or, as Lenin initially called it, 'temporary retreat'). Lenin recognized that at the roots of the crisis lay not only changing circumstances but also major mistakes in the past, and defined these as the belief in the possibility of direct transformation of the country to communism. Still greater loomed the question of the long-term strategy of constructing socialism in conditions which were unpredicted and indeed unpredictable within the context of 'orthodox' Marxist theory, i.e. under socialism within a 'backward' country with a massive peasant majority. The peasant dimension to it was expressed in the constant tension and the growing gap between 'orthodox' Marxism and the evolving rural strategy. At the end of 1922, as Lenin pondered the state of the revolution, he increasingly explored the possible ideological extensions and transformation of his 1921 policies. Only by 1988, in the new analytical universe opened up by the Gorbachevian revival, did the most radical of the Soviet historians come to debate a dramatically different late Lenin of 1922–3 as against his initial 1921 view of the NEP.[21]

---

21 See *Istoriki sporyat* (Moscow, 1988), especially the contribution by V. Lel'chuk, V. Danilov and Yu. Borisov.

Programme 4¹/₂: A Closing Gap?

Behind the ups and downs of the tactics of appeasement of the enraged peasantry, still aiming to achieve 1918's goals by different means (and with a different timetable dictated by the failure of West European revolution), a vaster subterranean shift of ground was beginning to take place in the defining of what was Russian socialism. To Lenin the shift came in late 1922–3, as the rapid improvement of the country's economic situation was making clear how effective the NEP proved to be. In this, he was still some steps ahead of his comrades, but even in his case the shift was mostly 'in the making', struggling as it were to find its shape. This is indeed why I choose to call it 'half a programme', fifth in order. There was much courage of imagination in what Lenin was now ready to admit and was trying to make his party adopt. There were also major limitations of understanding and anticipation concerning long-term development of the post-revolutionary state. The way Lenin's mind anxiously battled with the gap and the tension between his intellectual training and his experience, the Marxist 'orthodoxy' of the nineteenth century and the revolutionary practice of Russia 1905–22, gave a particular dramatic dimension to his 'last struggle'. We can judge this from six short texts and a record of his conversations with a man he tended to treat as a substitute son. The texts were dictated to his secretaries at his deathbed as a political message and last will to his inheritors within the Bolshevik party (PSS, vol. 45, pp. 343–406). He spoke also about these matters to Bukharin in Gorky, the place of rest to which the doctors ordered Lenin and where, far from daily politics, he was to contemplate for the last time his country, his party and his revolution.

Central to the new line of Lenin's thought was his changing approach to peasant cooperation. Assaulted by the 'orthodox' Marxists as a petit bourgeois Utopian scheme, 'state-ized' by the Bolsheviks in 1918, ordered to be 'de-strangled' by Lenin in 1921, but still not accepted as quite socialist even then, rural cooperation was now declared the crux of Russia's future socialist transformation. 'Cooperation is not to be adjusted to the NEP, but it is the NEP which must be adjusted to cooperation' (PSS, vol. 54, p. 195). In Lenin's presentation now, as long as 'power lay in the hands of the workers', i.e. his party ruled the country, cooperation would by itself lead to the construction of socialism there (PPS, vol. 45, p. 369). A multiplicity of cooperatives was seen now as 'the context in which *every peasant* can participate in the construction of socialism' (PPS, vol. 45, pp. 370–72). A whole historical epoch was said to be needed to achieve it, but 'a regime of civilised cooperators . . . is a socialist regime' (PPS, vol. 45, p. 273). Lenin was well aware of the depths of the ideological shift this view represented. In his words 'This is a fundamental change concerning socialism as its focus moves from the struggle for power to a cultural revolution aimed at peasantry and the transformation of state apparatus.'

But the 'fundamental change' in Lenin's mind seemed to spread still wider than the new policies concerning cooperation and the image of peasants building socialism at their own speed and in their own ways. He still accentuated the monopoly of power of the proletarian party but his definition of what 'proletarian' means was shifting. While suggesting the expansion of the parties' Central Committees through the drafting into them of workers (using this as an anti-bureaucratic device), he added 'I include here peasants also' (PSS, vol. 45, p. 347). The Central Commission of Control (due to supervise the government, the Central Committee and the Politburo directly) was, once again, to consist of workers *as well as* of peasants. Something quite incredible was being suggested to a party which still defined itself as an 'orthodox' Marxist, i.e. a 'petit bourgeois' membership from bottom to top of its ladder of organization and authority was now to be accepted and indeed encouraged.

The new view of peasantry and its place in Russia's socialist regime went together with a new vision of global revolutionary policies. The failure of West European revolution, which was confidently expected as late as 1920, led to growing direction of the Communist International's political efforts towards 'the East'. In Lenin's words, drawn once again from his last six documents, 'in the final result history is to be defined by the fact that Russia, China and India are the majority of mankind.' He had moved very far indeed from the times when the final result of history was to him defined by industrial progress, with the proletariat synonymous with revolution. The changing international perspective linked with the changing view concerning the peasantries of Russia.

Four years later, in 1926–7, as his own political life was drawing to its close, Bukharin first recorded and presented his 1922–3 conversations with Lenin. It was to be Bukharin's last shot in the defence of Lenin's heritage. As in the 1918 debate concerning the peace treaty with Germany and the policies of class war, Bukharin proceeded in the mid-1920s to develop to their full logical conclusion Lenin's own views, disclosing more fully their strengths as well as their weaknesses and contradictions. As the background, Bukharin stated that while peasantry is not homogeneous, neither is the Russian working class. The substance of the NEP, i.e. a mixed economy, integrated through the market and under state regulation, was not treated as a temporary expedient but as a system due to operate into the indefinite future. In the Russia of the 1920s, the Communists were to Bukharin the revolu-

tionary party of civil peace (BSR, p. 281). Central to these policies was
the need to bring peasantry peacefully and fully into the socialist camp.
To do so one had to overcome the sceptical attitude to peasantry of
some of the party members. They had to accept that peasantry's support
of socialism is a matter of struggle for allegiance, i.e. neither doomed
nor necessarily successful. Peasant cooperatives were at the axis of this
process. Different strata of peasantry would favour different types of
cooperatives (e.g. of supply for 'middle peasants', of credit for richer
ones, etc.). Even the 'kulaks' might become part of the process through
which peasantry 'grows into' socialism.

Within a year Bukharin was defeated and silenced. Then came
Stalin's collectivization, much murder, much destruction and many lies.
Half a century later, in a very different country – an urbanized and
industrialized superpower, the countryside of which failed to feed it
(and was rapidly turning into society's slum) – the rehabilitation of
Bukharin signified a return to Lenin's uncompleted Agrarian Programme 5 and to the late 1920s debate about the rural alternatives. The
issues Lenin tried to perceive and address in 1922–3 are, amazingly, still
there. So are many of the views, prejudices and legitimations which find
their roots in the Marxism of the Second International and in Stalin's
particular use of it. This explains why the old debate is once again alive
and acute in Gorbachev's USSR. Something new has been learned,
however, in the USSR and elsewhere, and a new post-industrial *Zeit-
geist* may offer new solutions which Lenin's generation would not accept
and could not even conceive. They have to do with the admission of new
dangers, new forms and new goals where socialism is concerned: the
dangers of an over-developed post-revolutionary state, the forms of
'expolary economy' (see item 6 above) and the goals of socialism with 'a
human face' – centred on 'the human factor'.

Brilliant political intuition and merciless political sense made Lenin's
political thought move farther and farther away from the deductive
simplicities of the Marxist orthodoxies of the 1890s. He learned from
experience, invented new political solutions, yet refused to be moved
from the 'science of society' of his youth as defined by the industrial
revolution of the nineteenth century. The consequent gap between
theory and policies set boundaries to Lenin's political imagination. By
1923 Lenin accepted the socialist (and revolutionary-for-socialism) potentials of the peasants – a dramatic ideological breakthrough which
paved the way to the Third World Marxisms and Third World revolutionary struggles still to come. He adopted in the last year of his life an
image of a socialist government presiding over a complexity of economic
forms which move along different if related parallel roads to socialism –
an idea of different socialisms is already there. Also, Lenin was increas-

ingly aware of the dangers of bureaucratization and the significance of organizations capable to restrain the new crystallizing class of planning-and-state controllers of power and privileges. The question as to what organizations can be brought into being to restrict the new hierarchy was certainly on his agenda, as it was to be on those of Khrushchev and Gorbachev. But a nineteenth-century mind was still not ready to accept anything but a nineteenth-century image of the future. This image of socialism came closest to the Utopia of Fourie: a world of communities which are large, clean, orderly, uniform, scientific, objective and re-plete. (Interestingly, this seemed also to be the preferred vision of the populist Chernyshevskii in the middle of the nineteenth century.) Together with the majority in his generation, Lenin adopted thereby an image of a future rooted in a romanticized model of the industrial revolution. The few realists of the day who knew better were dismissed by him as romantics. It took a different generation and the twentieth-century experience to be able to say what Einstein stated in the 1950s about his own vision of socialism, which one begins to grasp more fully only in the 1980s:

What to me constitutes the essence of the crisis of our time concerns the relationship of the individual to society. The individual has become more conscious than ever of his dependence upon society. But he does not experience this dependence as a positive asset, as an organic tie, as a protective force but rather as a threat to his natural rights or even to his economic existence.[22]

It is this dimension in which the regeneration of socialism must begin or socialism as a credo of moral supremacy must come to an end.

In his last days Lenin began to sense the dangers and unexpected depths of three major problems brought to light by the victory in the revolutionary war: that of the post-revolutionary state, that of ethnic divisions and that of peasants. His analytical and political effort to come to grips with those failed with his death. As to peasants, Lenin's last programme remained at its 'half-cock', '4½' point. The Moscovites waiting in the foodlines of a country which can put people on the moon and the leaders of a 'superpower' with a zero rate of major areas of agricultural growth for two decades[23] may well ponder the fate and the impact of, in Marx's words, the 'cleverly stupid anachronism . . . the undecipherable hieroglyphic for the understanding of the civilized' (MES, vol. 1, p. 326). They may even wish to learn something for their Second Socialist Revolution from 'the class which represents barbarism within civilization'.

22 A. Einstein, 'Why Socialism?', *Monthly Review* (February 1951), pp. 8–9.
23 ibid.

Let us leave the last word, sixty-five years after Lenin's death, to the official leader of Soviet Leninists. At the October 1988 conference concerning agriculture, Gorbachev declared 'from masters of their land we made day-labourers (*poden'shchiki*) . . . It happened because the majority of our senior administrators were indifferent to the fortunes of agriculture. We are paying now a heavy price.' He then reviewed the steps to be taken and proceeded to state the fundamental rural goals of the effort he leads, saying 'all this needs policy decisions. But such decisions can only be taken on the basis of new relations in the village, the return of the peasant as the master of land and of means of production. This would help to realize the human potentials. He concluded, 'The most central task today, Comrades, is to return people to the land as its full masters. This is the meaning of the restructuring (*perestroika*) of economic relations in the villages.'[24]

---

24 Gorbachev's address on 12 October 1988, written after *Izvestiya*, 14 October 1988, p. 1.

18

The Unrecognizable Marx and Russian Peasants: An Aside Concerning 'Deviations' (1881/1983)

The peculiar puzzle of late Marx, i.e. the massive intellectual effort and total publishing silence of the last twelve years of his life, the affinity he showed with the Russian revolutionary populists of the day, the changing focus of Marx's readings and notes to himself in 1875–81, all have a particular peasant and Russian dimension. My book Late Marx and the Russian Road *(London, 1983) explored this new stage in Marxist thought – an 'unrecognizable Marx'. What follows is a piece particularly relevant to the transformation of Marx's view concerning peasantry's political status* vis-à-vis *the socialist movement. There was a touch of genius there, when, defying the time-span and Marx's own earlier writings, came passages which can be read as a realistic critique of Stalin's collectivization or of peasantry's political response to socialist regimes in the 'developing societies' of today. The text to follow would be best read in relation to items 16 and 17.*

In 1881 Marx spent three weeks contemplating, one can say struggling with, an answer to a letter concerning the Russian peasant commune. It came from Vera Zasulich, made famous by her earlier attempt on the life of a particularly vicious tsarist dignitary, currently of the Black Repartition group and the future coeditor of the marxist *Iskra*. The four drafts of the reply Marx wrote testify to the immensity of work and thought which underlay it – as if the whole last decade of Marx's studies with its 30,000 pages of notes, but no new major text finalized, came together. The drafts are testimony of puzzlement but also of a growing consciousness of and the first approach to a new major problem. It is a veritable display of 'the kitchen' of Marx's thought at a frontier of knowledge at which he, once more, found himself a forerunner to his own generation and friends.

The discovery of the peasant commune by the Russian intelligentsia led to a sharp debate about its nature and historiography. To its detractors, the peasant commune was a creation of the tsarist state to police and tax the countryside, a device which conserved the backward ('archaic') characteristics of Russian agriculture and its political economy *in toto*.[1] To the populists and their academic allies, it was a survival of the social organization of primary communism, i.e. of the pre-class society, a remnant to be sure but a positive one, both in its present function and future potential. Behind the furious debate about the historiography of the commune stood fundamental political issues of strategy, of the class nature of the revolutionary camp, of its enemies and even of the nature of the future (post-revolutionary?) regime. To Marx the issue of the peasant commune, significant as it was for Russia, was also a point of entry to a variety of issues of much broader significance, theoretically and politically. These were the issues of peasantry within a capitalist (capitalism-centred?) world, and the type of sub-worlds and sub-economies such 'irregularity' is bound to produce. It was also that of the socialist revolutions in the world at large, i.e. of the 'peasant chorus' without which, he said once, the proletariat's 'solo song, becomes a swan song, in all peasant countries'.[2]

Already in the *Grundrisse* (1857) Marx had undertaken extensive comparative studies of peasant agriculture and of communal land-ownership within the major pre-capitalist modes of production. The peasant commune was not to him (or to the revolutionary populists) exceptional to Russia. It was simply the best preserved one in Europe – persisting for sound 'materialistic' reasons and by then increasingly placed in a new international and local context of advancing capitalism. Still, in 1868 in a letter to Engels he was clearly delighted with 'all that trash', i.e. the Russian peasant communal structure, 'coming now to its end'.[3] During the 1870s the works of Mourer and Morgan strengthened Marx's conviction, however, as to the positive qualities of the primary-tribal communities in their ethnocentricity (i.e. their concentration on human needs rather than on production for profits), and their inherent democracy as against capitalist alienation and hierarchies of privileges. The man of capitalism – the most progressive mode of production in

1 Central to that line of argument were the works and views of B. Chicherin adapted in Marx's time by A. Wagner and in later generations by P. Miliukov, K. Kocharovskii, etc., as well as by G. Plekhanov and I. Chernyshev in the marxist camp. This view was often referred to as the 'state school'. It was opposed by an equally impressive list of scholars and political theorists of whom N. Chernyshevskii and I. Belyaev were paramount to Marx's own generation. Marx himself spoke up sharply againts Chicherin.

2 Marx wrote the passage in *The Eighteenth Brumaire of Louis Bonaparte* (1852), referring to France, but deleted it in the reprint of 1869. The dates are significant for reasons discussed in my text.

3 Marx and Engels, *Sochineniya* (Moscow, 1961), vol. 32, p. 158. Relatedly in time, Marx had attacked Herzen's views in 1867 and spoken in absolute terms of the French

evidence – was not the ultimate man of human history up-to-date. The Iroquois 'red skin hunter' was, in some ways, more essentially human and liberated than a clerk in the City and in that sense closer to the man of the socialist future. Marx had no doubts about the limitations of the 'archaic' commune: material 'poverty', its parochiality and its weakness against external exploitive forces. Its decay under capitalism would be necessary. Yet that was clearly not the whole story. The experience and excitement of the Paris Commune – to Marx the first direct experiment in a new plebian democracy and revolutionary polity –were by now part of the picture. With the evidence of what appeared as the first post-capitalist experiment, Marx was more ready than before to consider the actual nature of social and political organization in the world he strived for. To all those steeped in Hegelian dialectics, children resembled their grandparents more than their parents. The 'primary' commune, dialectically restored on a new and higher level of material wealth and global interaction, entered Marx's images of the future communist society, one in which once more the 'individuals behave not as labourers but as owners – as members of a community which also labours.'[4]

Back from the past/future to the present, the consideration of coexistence and mutual dependence, of capitalist and non-capitalist (pre-capitalist?) social forms made Marx increasingly accept and consider 'uneven development' in all its complexity. New stress was also put on the regressive aspects of capitalism and on its link with the issue of the state in Russia. The acceptance of unilinear 'progress' was emphatically out. The extension of an essentially evolutionist model through the ideas of oriental despotism was by now insufficient. Specifically, Marx came to see the decline of the peasant commune in Western Europe and its crisis, in Russia, not as a law of the social sciences – spontaneous economic process – but as the result of an assault on the majority of the people, which could and should be fought. The consideration of the Russian commune in the drafts of the 'Letter of Zasulich' brought all this to the surface. It will be best to present the essence of the message in Marx's own words.[5]

To begin with, 'what threatens the life of the Russian commune is neither historical inevitability nor a theory but oppression by the State and exploitation by capitalist intruders whom the State made powerful at the peasant's expense'. The type of society in question was singled out by its international context, i.e. 'modern historical environment: it is contemporaneous with a higher culture and it is linked to a world

peasantry's conservatism (e.g. in the 1871 notes on the Paris Commune, ibid., vol. 17, pp. 554–7).
4 Marx, *Precapitalist Economic Formations*, (London, 1964), p. 68.
5 See T. Shanin, *Late Marx and the Russian Road* (New York, 1983), part 2.

market in which capitalist production is predominant', while the country 'is not, like the East Indies, the prey of a conquering foreign power'. The class-coalition of peasant-destroyers – the power-block in societies with peasant numerical predominance – was defined as 'the *state* . . . the *trade* . . . the *landowners* and . . . *from within* [the peasant commune] . . . the *user*' (italics added), i.e. state, merchant capitalists, squires and kulaks – in that order. The whole social system was referred to as a specific 'type of capitalism fostered by the state at the peasants' expense'.

To Marx the fact that the Russian commune was relatively advanced in type, being based not on kinship but on locality, and its 'dual nature' represented by 'individual' as well as 'communal land' ownership, offered the possibility of two different roads of development. The state and the specific variety of state-bred capitalism were assaulting, penetrating and destroying the commune. It could be destroyed, but there was no 'fatal necessity' for it. The corporate aspect of the commune's existence could prevail, once revolution had removed the anti-commune pressures and the advanced technology developed by Western capitalism was put to new use under the communal control of the producers. Such a solution would indeed be best for Russia's socialist future. The main limitation of the rural communes, i.e. their isolation, which facilitated a Russian edition of 'centralized despotism', could be overcome by popular insurrection and the consequent supplementing of the state-run *volost'* by 'assemblies elected by the communes – an economic and administrative body serving their own interest'. That is, shockingly, peasants running their own affairs, within and as a part of socialist society. Indeed, the Russian peasants' 'familiarity with corporate (*"artel"*) relations would greatly smooth their transition from small plot to collective farming'. But there is a condition to it all: 'Russian society having for so long lived at the expense of the rural commune owes it the initial resources required for such a change', i.e. the precise reverse of 'primitive accumulation' was now defined by Marx as the condition for successful collectivization of the Russian peasant agriculture. Also, it would be gradual change, '[in which] the first step would be to place the commune under normal conditions [i.e. in a non-exploitive context] on its present basis'.

In conclusion, to Marx, a timely revolutionary victory could turn the Russian commune into a major 'vehicle of social regeneration', a 'direct starting point of the system to which the contemporary society strives' and a grass-roots framework for 'large-scale cooperative labour' and the use of 'modern machinery'. Moreover, that might make some chiefly peasant countries 'supreme in that sense to the societies where capitalism rules'. That is, indeed, why 'the Western precedent would prove here nothing at all'. Moreover, 'the issue is not that of a problem to be solved but simply of an enemy, who had to be beaten . . . to save the Russian commune one needs a Russian revolution'. Note the expression *Russian* revolution, twice repeated within the text. Finally, to understand it all 'one must descend from pure theory to Russian reality' and not be frightened by the word 'archaic', for 'the new system to which the modern society is tending will be a revival in a superior form of an archaic social type.'

The issue of the peasant commune was used by Marx also as a major way to approach a set of fundamental problems, new to his generation, but which would be nowadays easily recognized as those of 'developing societies', be they 'modernization', 'dependency' or the 'combined and uneven' spread of global capitalism and its specifically 'peripheral' expression. There were several such components of Marx's new itinerary of topics for study and preliminary conclusions, none of which was worked out in full. At the centre lies the newly perceived notion of 'uneven development', interpreted not quantitatively (i.e. that 'some societies move faster than others') but as global interdependence of societal transformations. The 'Chronological Notes', i.e. a massive conspectus of Marx written in 1880–2, is directly relevant here. As rightly noticed in an interesting contribution by B. Porshnev (who refers it to the 'last 9–12 years period of Marx's life'), it shows Marx's attention turning to 'the problem of historical interdependence of people and countries in the different period of global history, i.e. the synchronic unity of history' (and one should add to dichronic intersocietal unity).[6] Marx comes now to assume for the future also a multiplicity of roads of social transformation, within the global framework of mutual and differential impact. In the *Grundrisse* he had already accepted it manifestly for the pre-capitalist past.) That is indeed why the generalized application of the discussion of 'primitive accumulation' in volume I of *Capital* is by 1877 so explicitly rejected. As is documented and argued by Wada, it meant also that Marx had begun to 'perceive the structure unique to backward capitalism'[7] – to say 'structures' would probably be to say it better. The idea of 'dependent development' is not yet there, but its foundation is laid. To sum it up bluntly, to Marx, the England he knew and 'that is more developed industrially' did not and indeed could not any longer 'show to the less developed' Russia the 'image of its own future'. By one of history's ironies, a century later we are still trying to shed the opposite claim of post-1917 Russia's monopoly over revolutionary imagination, the assumption that it is Russia which is to show to all of the Englands of our time the image of their socialist futures.

Marx's new turn of mind was unmistakably recognized and acknowl-

---

6 *Marx Istorik* (Moscow, 1968), p. 373.
7 Shanin, *Late Marx and the Russian Road*, p. 63.

edged after their fashion by doctrinaire Marxists. The 'Letter to the Editorial Board of *Otechestvennye Zapiski*' was left unpublished by the Emancipation of Labour group, despite promises to Engels who let them have it for publication. The 'Letter to Zasulich', written by explicit request to make Marx's views known, was not published by them either. (The first of these was initially published in 1887 by the *Messenger of the People's Will*, the second only in 1924.) Much psychologistic rubbish was written in Russia and in the West about how and why those writings were forgotten by Plekhanov, Zasulich, Axelrod, etc., and about the 'need for specialized psychologists to have it explained'.[8] It was probably simpler and cruder. In Marx's own generation there were already Marxists who knew better than Marx what Marxism is and were prepared to censor him on the sly, for his own sake.

The clearest salute to Marx's originality and to his new views was given a generation later by the most erudite of the Russian Marxists of his time, Ryazanov, the first director of the Marx–Engels Institute in Moscow, who first published in 1924 the four drafts of the 'Letter to Zasulich' (discovered by him in 1911). To him, the four drafts written during less than two weeks of intensive intellectual and political considerations indicated the decline of Marx's capacities.[9] On top of that hint he has added, quoting Edward Bernstein, an additional explanation for Marx's populist deviation: 'Marx and Engels have restricted the expression of their scepticism not to discourage too much the Russian revolutionaries.' Poor old Marx was clearly going senile at 63 or else engaging in little lies of civility and expedience, once he departed from the 'straight and narrow' of the Marxism of his epigones. An amusing affinity – during and after the 1905–7 Revolution, Lenin was accused of leaning toward populism by some of his Marxist adversaries and associates.[10] It seems that those two have had a peasant 'deviation' from Marxism in common.

---

8 Ibid., p. 129. How much all that still aches can be best exemplified by a short aside from P. Konyushaya, *Karl Marx i revolyutsionnaya rossiya* (Moscow, 1975), where after a stream of invectives against the multiplicity of 'falsifiers of Marx', i.e. everybody who discussed him outside the USSR, tells us that Plekhanov 'based his argument on the position formulated by Marx in his letter to "Otechestvennye Zapiski"' (p. 357). She forgets to inform us when, where and how.

9 David Ryazanov, see Shanin, *Late Marx and the Russian Road*, Part Two. For contemporary Western equivalents of that view see Marx and Engels. *The Russian Menace to Europe*, op. cit., p. 266, and on the left, J. Elster in K. Marx, *Verker i Utlag* (Oslo, 1970), p. 46.

10 Plekhanov's speech at the Fourth Congress of the Russian Social Democratic Workers' Party in 1906 stated it explicitly. On the other hand, the year 1905 also saw the appeals of the Saratov Bolsheviks and of Nikodim (A. Shestakov, the chief of the agrarian section of the Bolsheviks' Moscow committee) against Lenin's new agrarian programme, treated by them as 'capitulation' to the populist petty bourgeoisie.

19

Chayanov's Message: Illuminations, Miscomprehensions and the Contemporary 'Development Theory' (1986)

Item 1 of the book should help to place Chayanov's approach in the broad context of theoretical traditions concerning peasant economy. In this sense item 19 can be best read vis-à-vis *items 16 and 17 above (as well as contemporary works such as those by T.W. Schultz, A. de Janvry or A. Sen).*

This paper was written as an introduction to the second edition of Chayanov's The Theory of Peasant Economy. *Its new publishers agreed to my request not to strip the book of the excellent initial introductions by D. Thorner and B. Kerblay as well as the important glossary by R.E.F. Smith, with me confining my own contribution to Chayanov's twenty-years' impact on the Western scholarly literature. The extent of miscomprehension expressed in the debate concerning Chayanov's views gave particular edge to this intervention. The frustrations of the parallel twenty-years' fight of Soviet friends and of myself to bring Chayanov's work to light in the USSR and its outstanding relevance to the continuous crisis of Soviet agriculture made me finish the paper the way I did. Little did I expect then that within a year from its publication I should be delivering, in September 1987 in Moscow, the first public lecture about Chayanov's work at the Soviet Academy of Agricultural Sciences and be thanked by Chayanov's son for defending the honour of his father. More important, it was the president of the Academy who declared then and there the immense contemporary significance of Chayanov for the transformation of Soviet agriculture as the central component of* perestroika.

I finished my 1987 Moscow lecture about Chayanov by saying that those to whom matters of truth are their chosen occupation, the international community of scholars, celebrate with our Russian friends

Chayanov's homecoming – his return to his rightful place in Soviet scholarly discourse about both peasants and non-peasants. There is no need to add to it.

The first English edition of *The Theory of Peasant Economy* made history. The reactions following its publication in 1966 were remarkably strong. The book has been quoted right, left, and centre, by those who gave it considerable thought as much as by those who clearly received only a garbled version. The author was hailed by some as peasantry's new Marx, a hero-inventor of a radically new political economy. He was attacked with equal heat by the defenders of the intellectual old regimes. For a time Chayanov was high fashion but even since the swing of academic attention moved to new names and 'fads', many of his book's questions, insights, and even terms (e.g., 'self-exploitation') have remained as fundamental points of reference of the contemporary social sciences, economic and noneconomic. For that reason, the book made history also in the sense of acquiring a life of its own – an influence which shapes perception, focuses attention, defines plausibilities and modes of analysis, offers symbols, and often underlies political programmes, national as well as international.

The 1966 introductions and glossary by Thorner, Kerblay, and Smith did a fine job and their retention in the second edition makes unnecessary here any further summation of Chayanov's career and of the book's content and preliminary criticisms. I shall focus, therefore, on the book's own life and its place in the intellectual history of the dramatic two decades which followed 1966 and the subsequent scholarly as well as political attempts to come to grips with the so-called development theory. At the core lay the issue of general analytical approach and of attempts at conceptual re-tooling by the contemporary social sciences in the face of social reality of peasant economies which has proved most predictions consistently and dramatically wrong. This problem of theoretical inadequacies reflected in consistent failures of prediction and planned intervention has not gone away and, indeed, has since acquired new depth. Chayanov's theoretical contribution should be judged *vis-à-vis* experience and usage as well as in the face of the contemporary projections of the future, as a potentiality.

1 Usage, Experience, Meaning

The book's 'own life' meant necessarily that in encounter with its audiences the significance of its different elements varied from that attached to it by its author. Application centred mainly on the rural conditions within the contemporary 'developing societies'. The book was extensively used by analysts of different persuasions, countries, and academic disciplines. Its misconceptions were often as significant in effect as its illuminations. Despite the consequent variety there was a pattern to the ways Chayanov's insights and examples were perceived and selected for use.

The least utilized or accepted of Chayanov's main suggestions were his *consumption-needs/drudgery ratio*, relating the operation of family-farms to family consumption, labour, and demographic (or biological) regularities. Put in a rigorously scientific form and accordingly math-ematized, it was not substantiated by most of the available data drawn from the Russia of the early part of the century or else from the 'developing societies' of today. Nor was it particularly illuminating in an analytical sense. The reasons were partly spelled out by Chayanov himself. His formulas assumed the easy availability of farming inputs other than labour, especially of land (to which complex equipment, fertilizers, and credit should be added nowadays). This had seldom been the case; indeed, it was decreasingly so. Also, the demographic deter-minants act relatively slowly compared with the current trends of social transformations. The growing complexity, heterogeneity, and change-ability of contemporary agriculture and of the peasant ways to make ends meet would make this demographically related model very limited as against the factors which do not enter it: state policies and markets of goods and labour (by now worldwide), new agricultural techniques, the extra-village cartelization of supply, demand, and credit, or the social construction of new needs. What was to Chayanov 'not the sole deter-minant' shrank to barely a determinant at all, at least in the short term.

It is not surprising therefore that the major case when the discussed formula was put to use (and bore interesting fruits) was in a study by a leading anthropologist of the past within the present, expressed in the 'Stone Age Economics' of the gatherers and hunters.[1] A broadly paral-lel suggestion that Chayanov's needs/drudgery ratio may prove increas-ingly realistic as we proceed back along the history of rural Russia had indeed already been made by one of Chayanov's Marxist critics in the 1920s.[2] Following similar logic in introductions to the English and Spanish editions of *The Theory of Peasant Economy*, D. Thorner suggested a higher significance of Chayanov's 'ratio' for the thinly populated areas while E. Archetti assumed it for parts of Africa when compared to other 'developing societies' of today.

1 S. Sahlin, *Stone Age Economics* (Chicago, 1972), chapters 1–3. (The author disas-sociated himself, however, from the marginalist mode of Chayanov's explanation.)
2 G. Meerson, *Semeino-trudovaya teoriya i differentsiatsiya krest'yanstva v Rossii* (Moscow, 1926).

The general aspect of Chayanov's analysis which captured contemporary attention was the depiction of peasant family-farms as an economic form which differs from capitalist farming even in an environment clearly dominated by capitalism (and cannot be treated as feudal or 'semi-feudal' simply because it is non-capitalist). The analytical approach suggested was to begin the consideration of peasant agriculture 'from below', that is, from the operational logic of the family-farms rather than from the national and international flows of resources, goods, and demands. Of the two parallel specifications explored by Chayanov's book, the interpretation broadly adopted from his analysis of the particular economic structure and logic of the contemporary family-farms was not the demographic one (related to the needs/ drudgery ratio, with a possible autarkic extension of it). It was the one which defined a particular peasant economy by the *characteristics of family labour* and the relative autonomy of its usage at the roots of peasant survival strategies, which are systematically different from those of capitalist enterprises.[3] A diverse calculus of choices when production, land-renting, labour out-of-farm, etc., are concerned meant different patterns of operation of the farm enterprises as well as different extra-economic corollaries and different outflows into the political economy at the national and international levels. Evidence drawn from 'developing societies' substantiated this; indeed, there are difficulties in interpreting much of it in any other way. This evidence documented the capacity of peasants to out-compete the often well-capitalized farming enterprises based on wage labour, to buy out large land-holders, and to offer goods at the cheapest price. Peasant farms often work at a consistent negative profit yet survive – an impossibility for capitalist farming. Maximization of total income rather than of profit or of marginal product guides in many cases the production and employment strategies of peasant family-farms. And so on. The message is one of difference of operational logic, of output, and of outcome as well as of the possibility, at times, of actual retreat of the classical capitalist forms of production in the face of family farming. Chayanov's work offered an anticipation and analytical illumination of all these. The growing awareness of the significance of under-employment and employment patterns in the development of the contemporary rural economies facilitated the explicit as well as implicit popularity of this dimension of Chayanov's work.

Two recent sets of studies exemplify the relevance of peasant farm particularities and their interpretation in the light of the dominant usage

3 Kerblay stresses rightly the particular significance given to this position by B. Brutskus, but Chayanov has adopted it as well (if less exclusively), and it was through his work that this approach spread into the contemporary literature.

of family labour. Djurfeld, Taussig, Friedmann, and others have documented for different environments the tendency of agrobusiness to withdraw from the process of production in agriculture, focusing its profit-making activities on credit, supply of inputs, contracting, and selling, while leaving farming to the small-holders and 'skimming' them rather than replacing them.[4] Capitalist profit-accountancy prevailed over the capitalist form of production. Second are the recent studies of the paradoxical simultaneity of 'critical shortage of labor', said officially to be endangering or even demolishing the agriculture of Egypt, and of the parallel evidence of production figures directly contrary to it.[5] Once the data concerning capitalist farming are selected from those of the peasant sector the initial puzzle dissolves. It is the capitalist farming which folds up despite the efforts of its owners and the government's attempts to help them survive. The family-farms use family labour flexibly, draw on unwaged neighbours' help, and give priority to 'home' when deciding on the times of family members' departure to work elsewhere (e.g., the Gulf) or to return. As a result, family farmers advance their global production as well as their share of land held and produce compared with the capitalist farmers/employers. It means not a crisis of the agriculture of Egypt but its peasantization. (In so far as capitalism is defined by its classical formula as commodity production for profit based on the use of wage-labour, it is decapitalization as well.) One can multiply such examples.

This may be the place to refer to two standard misreadings of Chayanov linked to the issue discussed. First, his 'analysis from below' – that is, the building up of the understanding of the social economy which commences with the operational logic of family-farms – has often been treated as a substitution of the psychological and the subjective for the deterministic and the economic. This is wrong, for the material and structural determinants involved in the relations of production and exchange shape and restrict choices, even though more flexibility of possible and adopted strategies was built into Chayanov's explanatory scheme. What results is a combined explanation of some complexity, but the more realistic for it. In general terms there is little particularly 'Chayanovian' to it, for a combination of the 'objective' and the 'subjective' at the roots of human action has been assumed by a broad gamut of

4 J. Harriss (ed.), *Rural Development* (London, 1982). Also H. Friedmann, 'World Market, State and Family Farm', *Comparative Studies in Society and History* 20 (1978). The contemporary spread of the 'putting out' system outside agriculture broadened the conceptual issues involved.

5 B. Hansen and S. Radwan, *Employment Opportunities and Equity in Egypt* (Geneva, 1982); and E. Taylor, *The Egyptian Agricultural Labour Shortage: A Crisis for Whom?* (Manchester, 1985).

schools of thought (from Marx's 'men make their own history, but they do not make it as they please', etc.,[6] to the contemporary phenomeno-logical studies of intersubjectivity). The point is that an alternative general view, cross-cutting major conceptual divisions, adopts a differ-ent position. Within diverse schools of thought it assumed an arch-model of human action the determination of which is extrasubjective only – a puppet-theatre model of humans in society, associated with philosophical positivism. This view is necessarily misleading if applied to Chayanov's explanatory scheme.

Next, Chayanov's term 'self-exploitation' is often understood simply in its most direct sense of excruciating labour by underfed peasant families damaging their physical and mental selves for a return which is below that of the ordinary wages of labour power (equating it therefore with K. Kautsky's 'underconsumption' and Lenin's rural 'plunder of labour').[7] To Chayanov this is not the whole story, for it must be read together with his concept of 'differential optimums', that is, his con-clusion that in the different agrarian regions and sub-branches of farm-ing and at any given stage of technology, there are different optimal sizes of enterprise and that the decrease *as well as* increase from these will make productivity decline. To this the social context of peasant farming and especially the resulting availability of the family, kin, and neighbours' aid and unwaged labour should be added. Family economy is to Chayanov not simply the survival of the weak through their impoverishment, which serves super-profits elsewhere, but *also* the utilization of some characteristics of farming and of rural social life which may occasionally give an edge to non-capitalist economies over capitalist forms of production in a capitalist world.[8] The continuity and relative wellbeing of family farmers under capitalism can be therefore postulated as a possibility while self-exploitation (and indeed exploi-tation) takes place, even though *no* conclusion about a *necessary* sur-vival of such economic forms can be deduced or should be assumed within this line of thought.

To return to the utilization of Chayanov's insights in contemporary scholarship, the effect of Chayanov's general view of 'post-Euclidian' economics, which assumes the plurality of simultaneously operating

6 K. Marx and F. Engels, *Selected Works* (London, 1973), p. 398.

7 K. Kautsky, *The Agrarian Problem* (London, 1988), chapters 2c and 6b; and the study of US agriculture in V.I. Lenin, *Polnoe sobranie sochinenii* (Moscow, 1968), vol. 19, p. 343. See also item 16.

8 It has been pointed out by M. Harrison that selective preference for productivity of the small units does not explain on its own why capitalists do not react simply by decentralization of units owned by them. The answer seems to lie in the combination of economic or social patterns and effects as discussed.

economic systems and the need to match it by multiplicity of conceptual schemes, was characteristically ambivalent. It corresponded with the work of the more imaginative economic historians of pre-capitalism, especially K. Polanyi,[9] but those who were ready to quote Chayanov as their authority on contemporary rural economics usually treated it with more respect than application. Disciplinary languages and academic training tend to disregard the submerged assumptions on which they are based, with the conclusions drawn taken to be either universally true or universally false. In turn, eyes trained to universalist analysis of an ever-true *homo economicus* or of epochs which are uniformly capitalist or uniformly feudal tend to miss the centrepiece of Chayanov's assumptions, namely that family-farms are coincident with other economic 'systems', responding to and/or being penetrated and influenced by the dominant political economy without their particularity dissolved (indeed, remaining particular also in their response). The consequent issue is not only one of multiplicity of forms but also of what results from multiplicities of types of interdependence and of analytical categories engaged. Such a logic of composites was explored more recently in a debate between Marxists concerning the 'articulation of modes of production', but it carried there a significantly sharper stress on the hierarchy of socio-economic systems, on their domination and exploitation by each other (which Chayanov recognized but accentuated to a lesser degree). On the other hand, much of the 'articulation' debate was caught in the deadly trap of 'if not capitalist, then feudal', to peter out with little analytical consequence. An effort to introduce the concept of a particular Peasant Mode of Production, also made then, was a direct if not very successful attempt to incorporate theoretically the particular logic of peasant economy inserted into a dominant political economy.[10]

Finally, Chayanov's practical programme of agricultural transformation was made remarkably little of directly, considering the extent to which both its positive and its critical parts were validated by further experience. Once again Chayanov's views on these matters were often misunderstood (and at times rediscovered through experience and at considerable social cost, or else used while their authorship and background remained hidden).

Chayanov's actual programme for the advancement of Russian agriculture, presented fully in the book which followed *The Theory of*

9 K. Polyani, K. Arensberg and H.W. Pearson, *Trade and Market in the Early Empires* (Glencoe, Ill., 1971).

10 The concept of 'mode of production' loses much of its heuristic power without the in-built assumption of intra-mode class conflict at its core rather than on its frontiers. For further discussion see item 4.

Peasant Economy, consisted of three interdependent conceptual elements: rural cooperatives, differential optimums, and vertical cooperation.[11] The first adopted the experience of Europe, especially of Denmark at the turn of the century, while accentuating grass-roots democracy and a 'peasants are not stupid', antipaternalist and anti-bureaucratic view. The second element has already been mentioned. The third one concluded with a suggestion for a flexible combination, cooperative in form, of different sizes of units of production for different branches of farming. It had also shown that historically, while the concentration of land-ownership was insignificant, merchant capital penetrated and transformed peasant agriculture through 'vertical capitalist concentration', taking over selectively its extra-production elements and creaming off incomes (as in the US context, where 65 per cent of farmers' income from sales was then taken by railways, banks, traders, etc.). This process, however, is not a necessity. With the power of capital weakened by peasantry's organizations, and/or state policies, and/or internal contradictions between the capitalists, a different type of 'vertical concentration', which is cooperative and run by the peasants, can be established and even play a central role in the socialist transformation of society. Chayanov linked this to a powerful and remarkably realistic pre-critique of Stalin's type of collectivization, code-named 'horizontal cooperation', which substitutes maximization for the optimization of the sizes of units and bureaucratization for the suggested management 'from below'. The predicted result of such a 'horizontal' reform was the stagnation or decline of productivity of the agriculture. 'Horizontal' cooperation combined with the 'milking' of agriculture's resources for the sake of urban growth and the ordering about of peasants would prove as counterproductive as it would be antidemocratic. It would thus court peasant resistance or apathy and destroy the local store of irreplaceable agricultural knowledge and capacity for communal self-mobilization, for which bureaucratic pressure from above would prove a poor substitute. Shortage of resources would then be supplemented by their wastage, exploitive hierarchies by new ones as pernicious but less competent.

The typical misreading, especially by those who quoted Chayanov at second hand, tended to interpret his programme as a dream of archaic peasant bliss stretching into the future, a 'peasantism' from which no practical prescription for modern agriculture and rural change can be drawn. In fact the idea of peasant 'vertical cooperation' also included the need for large units of agricultural production and their further

11 Reproduced in B. Kerblay, *Oeuvres Choisies de A.V. Chayanov* (Paris, 1967), vol. 5; touched upon in short in the last chapter of *The Theory of Peasant Economy*.

extension as farming technology advances. It even accepted the 'grain factories' idea of the day, subject to the right technology. Outside his *Travels of My Brother Alexis* (a novella defined by him as 'a peasant Utopia'), there was no 'small is beautiful' message in Chayanov, only a sharp objection to a 'the larger, the necessarily more effective' assumption then prominent, and a functional suggestion for a combined development intended to 'optimize' (following the agronomists' best choice for any regional context of natural conditions and the available labour and technology), plus democratic decision-making 'from below'. A relatively slow pace of change can be deduced, related once again both to the wish to 'optimize' rather than to maximize and also to the characteristics of agriculture as understood. Agrarian reformers of different persuasion have encountered and documented ever since the dangers of excessive speed and bureaucratic zest when the transformation of agriculture is involved.

The peak of Chayanov's analytical work came in the 1920s, between the ages of 32 and 42, which for Russia will be mostly remembered as the years of the NEP – the New Economic Programme which followed the revolution, civil war, and the egalitarian redivision of all Russia's arable lands by its peasant communities. The main economic issues of the country were those of post-war recovery, industrialization, and increase of agricultural production, which in the conditions given meant the increase of agricultural productivity and partial transfer of the rural labour force into towns. The political context was one of a post-revolutionary state intertwined with a socialist, city-bound party facing a massive peasantry organized in rejuvenated peasant communes, in which 85 per cent of the country's population held more than 95 per cent of its arable land. This political economy was spoken of as one of 'state capitalism' and socialist control of the 'commanding heights of the economy', within a population most of whom were 'middle peasants'. Prognostication and planning by the rural specialists of Russia was defined by considerations which with hindsight are often referred to as the issue of the collectivization. Chayanov's treble alternative and his pre-critique are also relevant to agriculture and ruralites quite unrelated to Russia or to post-revolutionary states with Marxists in charge, but they can be tested most substantively *vis-à-vis* the collectivization debate and results.

The last twenty years have seen a considerable amount of soul-searching and policy change concerning collectivized agriculture, but nowhere more than in Hungary.[12] They first followed the Soviet 'horizontal' pattern, and after the 1956 revolution reorganized and tried it

---

12 N. Swain, *Collective Farms which Work* (Cambridge, 1985).

out again. What resulted was a decline or stagnation of agriculture and chronic shortages of food supplies (to which, before 1956, harsh repressions meted out to a resentful rural population should be added). Neither mechanization nor the deportation of 'kulaks' and the arrest of the 'saboteurs', nor bureaucratic orders and campaigns, solved the permanent agricultural crisis. Then the Hungarian leadership demonstrated the courage of retreat, made a clean sweep, and began in a totally new manner. Village-scale units were now combined with both multi-village and single-family ones. Those deported from their villages were permitted to come back and often to direct cooperative production. External controls declined, compulsory sales were abolished, and 'vertical' chains of mutually profitable production arrangements were set up and facilitated (e.g. a small-holder buying fodder at a price satisfactory to him from the large-scale collective enterprise of which he is a member, to produce within his family unit meat which is then sold on a 'free market' or under a contract). The agricultural results were dramatic, moving the country rapidly to the top of the European league where increase in agricultural production and incomes were concerned, not only resolving the problems of supplies but establishing Hungary as an exporter of food. The case of Hungarian agriculture and many other experiments with collectivization, positive and negative, in Europe as well as in Asia, Africa, and Latin America, acted as an important validation of Chayanov's suggestions for agricultural transformation, of his prognostication, and, up to a point, of his more general theoretical constructs and approaches. It was clearly not an issue of size or of collectivism or even of collectivization *per se*, but of the actual forms of rural transformation and of the new organization of production, as well as the way they combine with peasants-versus-bureaucrats relations, flow of resources, and the substantive issues of farming (and its peculiarities as a branch of production). In the face of all these issues, Chayanov's and his friends' superb understanding of agriculture, combined with that of rural society, made them unique. This makes his major project – what he called Social Agronomy – pertinent still. It is not that, on the whole, those who succeeded or failed have studied him directly in Hungary or elsewhere.[13] Such lines are seldom clear. But these people would (or will) benefit and could lessen some pains if they

13 The Hungarian scholarship had its own traditions of peasant studies, represented also on its Marxist wing, especially by the works of I. Markus. Its views were condemned by the Soviet-like collectivizers as anti-Marxist, but eventually won the day, and were expressed in the country's third (and successful) collectivization. The impact of the implicit cross-influences cannot be ascertained, but the views of Chayanov and his friends spread fairly broadly through Europe and Asia via the German professional literature of the 1920s.

would (or will) do so. The fact that this part of Chayanov's intellectual heritage is seldom considered or admitted has to do not with its content but with the nature of current ideological constraints, to which we shall return.

We still know far too little about Chayanov's most direct topic of concern: the Russian countryside in the face of Stalin's Collectivization. We do know that, contrary to the ideological myth to follow, it was not a natural deduction from Marxism or from Lenin but a fairly arbitrary result of the 1926–8 failure of rural policies and of inter-party factional struggle.[14] It was outstandingly destructive of resources and humans, facilitated the brutalization of the country's political system and contributed to the current inadequacies of Soviet agriculture and arguably to the demographic crisis and industrial slow-down of the last decades. The first post-Stalin steps of the Soviet studies of collectivization, relevant once again to the last two decades or so, indicated clearly that the flourishing of TOZ (that is, the self-help teams at its beginning 'vertical' rather than 'horizontal' in their implications) was effective and actually well supported by much of the Russian peasant population.[15] It was the decision of 'the Centre' to sweep aside practically overnight the TOZ as well as the socialist communes and every other regionally specific form of rural cooperation stemming from local initiative,[16] and to impose the one and only form of a village-size Kolkhoz directed from above, which defined the destructive trend of the 1930s.[17]

2 Methods and Labels

As stated, the misconceptions of Chayanov often played as important a conceptual role as the views he actually offered, and I have referred to a few of them. Two more, general in scope, will be considered to round

14 M. Lewin, *Russian Peasants and Soviet Power* (London, 1968). See also R.W. Davies, *The Soviet Collective Farm, 1929–1930* (London, 1980). The frequent use of Lenin's 1923 article 'On Cooperation' to legitimate the 1929–39 Collectivization is an open falsehood. The article does not focus on production cooperatives.

15 For example, see the item 'Kolektivizatsiya' in *Sovetskaya istoricheskaya entsiklopediya* (Moscow, 1961), and also M. Vyltsan, V. Danilov, V. Kabanov, and Yu. Moshkov, *Kolektivisatsiya sel'skogo khozyaistva v SSSR* (Moscow, 1982), especially chapters 1–3.

16 After the civil war there were a number of socialist communes which came to be considered 'too collectivized' and were dismantled in 1929–33 to provide for the homogeneity of the rural organization of production. There was also in 1928–30 some talk of gigantic-size Kolkhoz, but nothing came out of it.

17 See footnote 14. The productive successes during the last two decades of the family plots and of the experiments with the *zveno* system of multi-family units (autonomous within a general kolkhoz system) in the Soviet Union, and its current version under Gorbachev, offer an interesting reference to the issue of 'optimums' today.

out the picture: the status of conceptual models in Chayanov's works and his 'neo-populist' designation.

At the centre of Chayanov's method of theoretical analysis – indeed, what made him the leading theorist of his generation – lies systematic exploration of alternative models and typologies. Abstraction and purposeful simplification are systematically used to define and test causal links. As is usual when theoretical models are concerned, purposeful simplification means the overstatement of some characteristics. The totally non-waged family-farm and the eight pure 'economic systems' presented in the book discussed find their farther equivalents in his *Experiments in the Study of an Isolated State, the Nomographic Elements of Economic Geography*, and even in his 'science fiction' *Travels of My Brother Alexis* and the 1928 discussion of the 'farming in a bottle' of the future scientific production of foodstuffs.[18] Chayanov's mastery and extensive use of Russian empirical evidence (and its wealth for the rural scene of the day), as well as his pronounced practical interests as an agricultural reformer, make many of his cursory readers miss the fact that his was an endless and highly imaginative experimentation with the logic of analysis as a way to order the complexity of data in his grasp. He did not lack positive views of his own, made them clear, and can be criticized for them as well as for the methods he used to arrive at conclusions. This has been done by many, including the book's first editors and myself.[19] But Chayanov must be treated on his own terms; that is with understanding of the way his mode of exploration and actual conclusion differed from each other. This is why it is unhelpful and often plainly ridiculous to express surprise or dismay at Chayanov's disregard of market relations, wage-labour, or capital investment in the rural context. This 'disregard' is a method, an analytical suspension used to explore causal links through the media of a conceptual model (which can be more useful or less so). As to the issue of a conceptual model's realism, that is, its match with reality, it is important but provides only one element of theoretical thought. Chayanov experimented with a uni-causal demographic model, with a bi-causal model of agricultural development defined by population density and market relations intensity, and so on. Chayanov was also one of the leaders of the field of factual studies of market relations, monetization, and wage-labour, and was remarkably realistic when the day-to-day life of the Russian peasantry was concerned.[20] Recent studies by Soviet and other scholars have

18 Kerblay, *Oeuvres Choisies*. As in the case of *Travels of My Brother Alexis*, this was also defined as a 'Utopia', but this time a 'scientific-technical' one.

19 In a section devoted to 'biological determinism' in *The Awkward Class* (Oxford, 1972).

20 For example, his detailed Budget Study of the family-farms in the district (*uezd*) of Starobel'sk in Kerblay, *Oeuvres Choisies*, vol. 2.

indeed shown that he was right as to the low commodity production and very low use of wage-labour in rural Russia, 1900–14 and 1921–8.[21]

Every model is selective, and Chayanov made his own choices on what to focus his attention on and which causal links to 'bracket' or deaccentuate. These were relevant, of course, to his views as well as to his conclusions. For example, Chayanov stated in a 1927 debate that he was only then beginning his own studies of peasantry's socio-economic differentiation.[22] Considering what we know now about the relatively low class polarization of the rural Russia of 1912 and 1921–8, the focusing of attention on the rural cooperation and optimal use of labour made good sense to a leader of a trend committed to the advance of what was called Social Agronomy. But it limited the grasp of the exploitive potentials of simple cooperation, state/peasants interaction, and some other issues. (In parallel, the work by his major critic Kritzman and his assistants, who adopted from the young Lenin the model of peasantry's necessary polarization, overstated heavily their concern, arguably offering inducement to Stalin-type collectivization without sufficient awareness of its agrarian dangers and potential social pitfalls.) To recollect, one can criticize Chayanov for his priorities, or better still, consider their impact on his conclusions, but it is epistemologically naive to treat him as naive, blind to evidence, or overwhelmed by the ideo- logical aberrations of 'peasantism'.

The positioning of Chayanov within an ideological context and *vis-à-vis* analytical and ideological taxonomies suffered mostly from two miscomprehensions. The first was less prominent, less significant, and less literate, resulting from limited knowledge of Chayanov's back- ground and his range of publication, and from only cursory reading of Thorner and Kerblay's efforts to present its picture. It assumed Chaya- nov's singularity in inventing 'Chayanovism'. The other classified him as a *neopopulist* and derived his main characteristics from that.

The splendid tradition of Russian rural studies was rooted in the regional authorities' (*Zemstvo's*) 1860s to 1917 effort, introduced mostly by enlightened nobles and their employees within the 'rural intelligent- sia' to take account of and to improve the livelihood of the plebian populations in their charge, which were mostly rural and peasant.[23] Those studies reached maturity in late 1880 to 1906 (when Chayanov was being born or in school) to revive again after a failed revolution in 1909–14 (Chayanov began then, in 1912 and at the age of 23, his

21 See A.M. Antimov, *Krest'yanskoe khozyaistvo europeiskoi Rossii* (Moscow, 1980); V.P. Danilov, *Sovetskaya dokolkhoznaya dorevnya* (Moscow, 1979), vol. 2; T. Shanin, *Russia as a 'Developing Society'* (New Haven, 1975).

22 In a debate conducted by *Puti sel'skogo khozyaistva* (1927), nos. 4–9.

23 The best English source for coverage of those events is still G.T. Robinson, *Rural Russia under the Old Regime* (New York, 1949).

spectacular public career). As part of it, the conceptual family-farm focus can be traced back to A. Vasil'chakov's book of 1881, the Budget Studies development and initial usage to F. Shcherbina in the late 1890s, the Dynamic ('cohort') Studies to N. Chernenkov at the very beginning of the century, and the direct antecedents of Chayanov's assumption of structurally specific peasant economics to V. Kosinskii's book, published in 1906. The expression 'economics' is somewhat misleading, in fact, as was the usual occupational designation of most of those involved as 'rural statisticians of the *Zemstvo*'. What evolved were peasantry-focused social sciences in their broader sense, merging the contemporary Western disciplines of economics, history, anthropology, ethnography, sociology, demography, public medicine, agronomy, and ecology. Chayanov's originality is not in question. But his significance lay to a considerable degree in abilities of synthesis and presentation of the work of many others. In the best style of the Russian intelligentsia he was a very literate man: well read, fluent in a number of foreign languages, skilful in presentation, and besides an author of essays, five romantic novellas à la Hoffman, a guide to West European drawing, a local history of Moscow and a book of poetry.[24]

The description of Chayanov's work and of the views shared by the so-called Organization and Production School on social agronomy as neopopulist, especially when used as a synonym of programmatic 'peasantism' idealizing or hoping for a future peasant universe, is badly informed and misleading. A multi-stage miscomprehension is involved concerning populism, neopopulism, and Chayanov himself.

First, few bothered to work out the actual characteristics of Russian populism over and above its descriptions by political foes (especially Lenin's attack on the SRs, which, taken out of context, served its readers ill).[25] Russia's original socialism-for-developing-societies and its remarkable contemporaneous message which raised for the first time the issues of uneven development, state capitalism, party cadres, or social ecology is often being reduced to rural sentimentality. That it was they who created the first Russian socialist party of revolutionary type, its first urban trade unions and workers' press, or that their Geneva

---

24 Practically unknown, these novellas were recently published in Russian by Russica Publishers in the United States as A. Chayanov, *Istoriya parikmakherskoi kukly i drugie sochineniya Botanika X* (New York, 1982). An introduction by L. Chertkov offers insightful commentary on Chayanov's literary career, but in reference to his economics repeats some of the mistaken assumptions of his Soviet critics.

25 For discussion see T. Shanin, *Russia 1905–7: Revolution as a Moment of Truth* (New Haven, 1985). For studies available in English of Russian populism and its most manifest followers, the SRs party (the PSR), see F. Venturi, *Roots of Revolution* (London, 1960); I. Berlin, *Russian Thinkers* (Harmondsworth, 1979); and A. Walicki, *The Controversy over Capitalism* (Oxford, 1969).

branch permanent delegate to the General Council of the International was a man called Karl Marx, are simply left out of sight. The next stage in miscomprehension, the latter-day impact of populism – that is of its main theorists like Hertzen and Chernyshevskii and strategists like Zhelyabov or Kibal'chich of the People's Will – is treated as if it could be disassociated from the rest of Russian intellectual history. To exemplify, Lenin's *What Is To Be Done?*, manifestly modelled in context and in name on Chernyshevskii and the Peoples Will, loses its intellectual roots, becoming in turn the self-generated invention of a singular genius. The general interdependence of effects, the mutuality of borrowings, and the capacity to learn are 'streamlined' to appear as a set of dogmatisms, eternally diverse and absolutely pure (and totally right or totally wrong, of course). Chayanov, being neither 'a Marxist' nor a good bourgeois, must be assigned to one of the intellectual chains. A game for those not overburdened by knowledge of the actual context of Russian history asserts itself then, in a world divided into 'us' versus 'them', while everything else is put into a left-over category of populism due to trigger off images of sitting on the fence, sentimental attachment to obsolete archaism, Utopian dreams, and manure. As to Chayanov, the easiest way not to dismiss outright his genius or to surrender him to one's direct ideological enemies is to define him as a populist (with a prefix 'neo' added for the benefit of those prone to point out that his views differed substantively from those of the main theorists of Russian populism and from those who were defined in his generation as their most direct heirs, be it Chernov, Aksentev, or Gershuni). Chayanov took his cues from the declared Marxists V. Kosinskii, V. Groman, and I. Gurevich (I must disagree here with Thorner: it was Gurevich who first suggested 'demographic differentiation'), from the liberals N. Chernenkov and F. Shcherbina, as well as from the bona fide SR populist P. Vikhlyaev. His methods and conclusions paralleled in many ways those of the Bolshevik Central Committee member of 1905–7, P. Rumyantsev, and later work of similar persuasion by A. Khryashcheva. His tolerance of different ideas was known; in the 1920s he helped the careers of N. Kondratiev, the brilliant pioneer of the studies of global economic systems, as well as of the Marxist 'young Turks' like V. Anisimov. He also often disagreed with those of his own 'school', such as A. Chelintsev, but proceeded to work closely with them. There is no way to define his possible guilt by heritage or association.

The only way to resolve the question of Chayanov's populism is to consider his actual views *vis-à-vis* the contemporary Russian populists' main articles of faith concerning rural Russia. He did not accept the view of some right-wing populists in the 1890s that capitalism must fail to establish itself in poverty-ridden rural Russia. He did not adopt the most significant proposition-cum-programme of populism's left wing in 1906–22, the PSR, to turn peasant communes in control of all available land into the core structure of post-revolutionary rural Russia. He shared with the Russian populists, but not only with them, the wish to have Russia transformed along lines which would see autocracy abolished and democracy established (with much peasant colouring to it in a population which was 85 per cent peasants). The idea of 'service to the people' by the Russian intelligentsia was also 'populist', but by this time, not only so. Chayanov's political party *animus* was low. In the dramatic year of 1917 he was closest to the Popular Socialists, a mildly populist, markedly academic party of little following. He defined himself as non-party socialist. Throughout his life he was to stay the Muscovite intellectual at his best: erudite, hard-working, broad-minded, and deeply committed to humanitarian causes, scholarship, and aesthetics. This approach and those capacities were met in the 1920s by a remarkable laxity toward him by the authorities (said to be ordered by Lenin himself).[26] It was to cost him his life in the decade to follow and to end with his posthumous 'rehabilitation', for what it was worth.

As to their goals and predictions, Bolsheviks, SRs, and Chayanov shared hostility to rural capitalism, especially in its extra production forms (the 'kulaks'). In common with the SRs, Chayanov believed more in peasants' undifferentiated socio-economic advance or decline ('aggregate shifts') versus capitalist and/or state capitalist economy than in the significance of inter-peasant polarization processes. He was attacked because of that by many of the Russian 'orthodox Marxists', but some other 'orthodox' Marxists (for example, Kautsky) were far from sure on that score.[27] So were some of the Bolsheviks.[28] Chayanov's distrust of the 'large is beautiful' proposition accepted then by most adherents of Progress did not relate this to a peasantist dream *à la* Proudhon; in the hungry Moscow of War Communism he depicted a small-holder's universe in a text described as 'Utopia' (and a peasant one at that), but suggested something very different in the concluding chapter of the book he called in 1925 *The Theory of Peasant Economy*. One should best take as true Chayanov's own explanation of his views as rooted in the study of Russian agriculture, of which he had so superb a

26 Chertkov speaks of Lenin's order in 1921 to let Chayanov be 'because we need wise heads, we are left with too few of them' (Chayanov, *Istoriya parikmskherskoi kukly*, etc. pp. 23–5). The extensive publication of Chayanov's works, even then highly controversial, and his frequent travels to Europe in the 1920s substantiate the assumption of particular tolerance displayed toward him in those days.

27 See K. Kautsky, *The Agrarian Problem*, chapters 7, 9 and 10.

28 For N. Bucharin's place in this debate see M. Harrison in Harriss, *Rural Development*.

knowledge. On balance Chayanov was being defined as neopopulist mostly by default, a shorthand description which hides more than it reveals.

Why then the persistence of the neither-us-nor-them neopopulist designation in our own times? The reason lies in the ideological confrontations of our own generation to which the already discussed reductionism should be added. The admirers of the Green Revolution who believe in its anti-socialist potentials often interpreted the 'from below' approach as 'let it be as it is' for 'those above', and then used 'peasantism' as a handy ideological device to forget agrobusiness. Once one moves from the form to substance Chayanov is unacceptable to them: he is sharply anti-capitalist, with no trust in the benefit of 'free market' processes, and devoted to the cooperatives' warfare against the 'entrepreneurs'. Moreover he was clearly loyal to the Russian post-revolutionary state, refused to emigrate, and even prospered temporarily in his career under the new regime. For the orthodox Marxists of the 'developing societies' his method of analysis was equally unacceptable, for it challenged head-on Lenin's 1899 study, which had acquired the status of supra-model as to what peasant society is and/or is becoming. (Kautsky's position, definitely 'orthodox' and legitimated by Lenin's admiring references, yet in no necessary contradistinction with Chayanov's view of peasant economy's possible survival under capitalism, is still barely known.) But the crux of their 'need' to define Chayanov as neopopulist lay in the very assumption of the one and only, finite Marxism. As to Chayanov, he was neither 'a Marxist' nor a rich farmers' lover, but nor was he therefore simply a populist. He learned from many sources but stayed his own man.

Why then did not Chayanov become a contemporary guru, a patron saint of a new sect of admirers who would use his books to enforce and validate their own separateness and ideological purity? He has been quoted admiringly but nobody has claimed his mantle, while those called neo-populists have usually disclaimed such a designation. The answer lies partly in the ideological dualizations described above, but it was caused also by a fundamental limitation of Chayanov's mode of analysis, itself explicable in terms of the experience available when he wrote as against that of our own time. The most significant of the social transformations of the twentieth century was the advancing integration of increasingly complex social forms. Rural society and rural problems are inexplicable any longer only in their own terms, and must be understood in terms of labour and capital flows which are broader than agriculture. To understand the diversity of the results of collectivization, one must look at the countryside *as well as* at industry and at the political elites. And so on. Chayanov's analysis 'from below' is incomplete not only because its author was precluded from its completion. It cannot be completed by simply proceeding along the same road. Not accidentally, it was his most exclusively family-centred model, the demographic one, which first fell into disuse. The only way to handle effectively contemporary social reality is through models and theories in which peasant family-farms do not operate separately and where peasant economy does not merely accompany other economic forms, but is inserted into and usually subsumed under a dominant political economy, different in type. Also, peasant economies are being transformed (or even re-established) mostly by 'external' intervention, especially by the state and the multinational companies, intervention which outpaced by far Chayanov's experience as well as his theoretical schemes. This makes combined models 'from above' and 'from below' necessary for further exploratory advance. In this, Chayanov's analysis did play a major but restricted role. Some of his views were clearly mistaken (and invalidated by further evidence), but in the main his weakness lies in an analysis which was not incorrect but insufficient. For the increasingly complex rural world of today it has clear limits. Hence, no 'Chayanovism'; but there are many of Chayanov's illuminating insights, explicit and implicit, in the contemporary rural studies.

3 Historiography and the Future

At its 1966 beginnings the effect of Chayanov's book's first English edition was the direct result of a major crisis, of what was called the Third World and of its conceptualization within the Modernization Theory and its political corollaries, conclusions, and predictions.[29] The post-World War II rapid decolonization, the Cold War, and the expanding UN as a focus of new hopes, have redrawn maps as well as redefined and dramatized the problem of world inequality between 'The West' and what were then called 'the Backward Nations'. This global gap between states and societies became a fundamental issue of the day. A new terminology was coming into being, representing new concerns. The *global gap* was part of it. The confrontation of the 'world' led by the United States with the one led by the Soviet Union (extending its impact to the native revolutionaries elsewhere) made the issues of the *development* in the *Third World* into a matter of utmost political urgency. Fortunately the solution seemed at hand – *a take off* into the *self-sustained economic growth* along the lines tried out by the forerunners

---

29 For further discussion see H. Alavi and T. Shanin, *Introduction to Sociology of the 'Developing Societies'* (London, 1982).

of industrialization.[30] Western-style parliaments, markets, ideas, and education plus some aid or loans and investments were to facilitate it all. An assumed natural law of social equilibrium was to secure international equalization, stability, and homogeneity (the larger the discrepancy the more powerful its tendency for self-eradication).[31] Rationalization embodied in science was to help it along, for it is seemingly faster to import experts and expertise than to produce them first hand. The assumedly inevitable Progress was to close the First/Third Worlds gap, to eradicate poverty and to keep revolutionaries at bay.

By the turn of the 1950s the optimistic assumptions were proving shockingly wrong. The 'gap' was increasing. Pauperization advanced through much of the Third World. Post-colonial independence, economic spontaneity of local and international markets, literacy campaigns, and charitable aid did not resolve 'the problems of development'. The West and especially its slow-to-take-the-hint colonizers and budding neocolonizers clearly faced situations no longer describable as riots of despair, but massive popular wars and coalitions between the resentful governments of the 'backward' nations: the Algerian war and the Bandung Conference of the Nonaligned Nations, Congo, Vietnam, and a new UNESCO majority. On the intellectual scene Paul Baran, Gunnar Myrdal, and Paul Prebish savaged the Modernization Theory prescriptions and methods.[32] Against the old registers of correlates and determinants of *economic growth* came the new pessimism of focusing on the *bottlenecks* explaining the growing gap, in a catchy phrase which swept the world – *the development of underdevelopment*.[33] This was increasingly defined by the international dependency of the peripheries on the exploitive metropolitan centres. It was also defined intranationally by dependent plebeian populations which were structurally marginalized and excluded from the benefit of modernity – nowadays often called *the subaltern classes*. This conceptual box was increasingly being filled by peasants – the large majority then of the population of the *developing societies* (the 'backward nations' of yesterday). But peasants appeared now not only as victims or an object of development. The

30 W.W. Rostow, *Process of Economic Growth* (London, 1962).

31 A position advanced by the functionalist school in sociology and by the simpler versions of neoclassical economics particularly influential in the 1950s.

32 P. Baran, *The Political Economy of Growth* (New York, 1957); and G. Myrdal, *Economic Theory and Underdeveloped Regions* (London, 1967). The work of P. Prebish became known in the 1950s mostly through the Reports of UN ECLA he directed.

33 Introduced by A.G. Frank, *Capitalism and Underdevelopment in Latin America* (New York, 1969), to become for a moment arguably the most read book on theory of development.

dramatic impression of the victory of Mao's peasant revolutionary army
was spreading and being reinforced by guerrillas all through the Third
World. Also, the peasantry was increasingly being seen as a potential
political actor – a subject of history. In the 1960s peasants came to spell
new hopes of sweeping away oligarchy in Latin America, outfacing an
imperial army in Vietnam, helping to balance failures of industrialization or of the egalitarian programme attached to the Green Revolution.

Chayanov's emergence into the English-speaking world coincided
with a dramatic 'face to the peasants' realignment of attention which
took place in the 1960s. The World Bank officials and Marxist
revolutionaries, politicians and scholars, not forgetting the committed
student masses, rapidly turned peasantologists. From a piece of anthropological exotica, peasants have moved into the centre of debate about
the most significant contemporary issues. Overnight the discussion of
peasantry in books, theses, and programmes has shot up from next to
none to hundreds and then thousands of items. The very word 'peasant'
became 'hot' and 'with it'; like sex and crime it was by now selling
manuscripts to publishers and books to readers. The trouble was that
this academic avalanche was theoretically very thin. The freshly collected 'facts' about peasants, mostly localized, and the speculations
about them, mostly very grand and abstract, found themselves, like
Pirandello characters, searching for a conceptual framework which
could relate and transform them into a branch of systematic knowledge.
Of the available older writings of relevance only Lenin and Redfield
could be put to partial use,[34] while the more contemporary efforts to
make theoretical sense of the peasants were only then beginning to
come through.[35] Chayanov's 1966 book entered this void (together with
Marx's *Grundrisse*, presented first in English by Hobsbawm in 1964, and
a more conventional economics text by Schultz published in the same
year).[36] The richness of the data and the sophistication of the methodology put forward by Chayanov, the contemporaneity of his concerns,
and his broad theoretical sweep took the breath away from scores of

34 Translations of V.I. Lenin *Development of Capitalism in Russia* (initially 1899) were
particularly well known and used by the Marxists as the arch-model of analysis and of
conclusions concerning peasantry's demise. R. Redfield, *Peasant Society* (Chicago, 1956)
offered the usual starting point for many US anthropologists.

35 E.R. Wolf, *Peasants* (New York, 1966); T. Shanin, *Peasants and Peasant Societies*
(Harmondsworth, 1971); and B. Galeski, *Basic Concepts of Rural Sociology* (Manchester,
1972). Two early journals specifically devoted to peasantry began publication in the early
1970s in the United States and the United Kingdom: *Journal of Peasant Studies* and
Peasant Studies.

36 K. Marx, *Precapitalist Economic Formations* (London, 1964); and T. W. Schultz,
Transforming the Traditional Agriculture (New Haven, 1964).

peasantology beginners. Some declared allegiance, more used it to cut their teeth defending or re-establishing the orthodoxies of the past, but the most numerous simply utilized Chayanov's evidence and insights in their own analyses and schemes concerning peasants the world over.

It would seem that the very positioning of Chayanov as 'the man who knew about peasants', or his more literate designation as a social scientist who helped us see better the analysis of family farming as a particular form or element of economy, should lead to the gradual decline of his significance in the future. Peasants still form a major part of humanity, but their numbers are stationary and their share in the population of the 'developing societies' is rapidly in decline. They are also being 'incorporated', while the livelihoods of those who survive as rural small-holders increasingly include what have been considered as 'non-peasant' characteristics. A decline in the significance and the particularity of peasantries leading to a parallel depeasantization of the social sciences can be predicted, with Chayanov assigned eventually to the archives. Or can it?

The crisis of the 1960s has not been resolved but has actually broadened in its substance and its implications. The predicament of the Third World, made morally unacceptable and politically dangerous by the way the better-off have prospered, extended into a socio-economic crisis which includes 'us'. Structural unemployment at the lower pole of the First World has grown sharply and is increasingly being recognized as irreversible. A crisis of the Second World, both economic and moral, is visible and self-admitted, diminishing its ability to offer alternatives – the impact of a major model and determinant of development in the past generations is declining. All through the 1980s a parallel crisis of capitalism and of its actually existing alternatives has been growing, economically and politically but also conceptually; we face a reality we decreasingly know how to extrapolate or to grasp.

A central element of contemporary global society is the failure of capitalist economies, as well as of state economies, to advance unlimitedly and to secure general welfare in ways expected by the nineteenth-century theories of progress, liberal and socialist alike. Control and extent of profits by capitalist multinational companies is advancing side-by-side with the retreat of standard capitalist forms of production, and of social organization linked to the extension of unemployment and 'under-employment', of 'informal economies', and other networks of survival. Sluggish state economies are intertwined with the massive 'second' and 'third' (or 'black') economies, increasingly recognized as irreducible. While in the 'developing societies' islands of pre-capitalism disappear, what comes instead is mostly not the industrial proletariat of Europe's nineteenth century but strata of plebian survivors – a mixture of increasingly mobile, half-employed slum-dwellers, part-farmers, lumpen-traders, or pimps – another extra-capitalist pattern of social and economic existence under capitalism and/or Third-Worldish types of state economy. The populations involved in the informal and/or family-bound and/or 'black' and/or mixed economies are growing around the globe, and one cannot understand without reference to this either the way national economies work or the way people actually live. While exploitive relations are preserved and enhanced, the functional organiz-ation of economy changes, extending rather than concealing those elements of it which call for modes of analysis alternative to those ordinarily in use. By now a new 'green' radicalism has begun increas-ingly to respond politically to these experiences, new exploitive pat-terns, and conceptual insights. Theoretically the analysis of modes of incorporation by a dominant political economy is in increasing need of being supplemented by the parallel study of modes of non-incorporation operating in the worlds we live in.[37]

It is in this context that Chayanov's analysis of alternative and complementary economies, of family labour, of the non-monetized calculus of choices and of patterns of physical production (rather than their prices only), of differential optimums, of modes, and of utilities of cooperation – an analysis 'from below', attempting to relate structure to choice – will have to find its future possible echo and uses. So will the method of exploring models of alternative realities and rationales. In fact there are still hundreds of millions of peasants and as many may exist in the year 2000, but, paradoxically, Chayanov's fundamental methods and insights may prove particularly enriching for worlds of fewer peasants as well as of fewer 'classical' industrial proletarians, while the subject of his actual concern, the Russian peasantry, has all but disappeared, In no way would future theorizing be a simple repli-cation of Chayanov, but it might carry important elements of his achievements and that of the Russian rural analysis of 1880s–1928, as part of the body of new development theories aiming to understand more realistically our environments and to improve future worlds. Which will make a good epitaph for a memorial of a great scholar, when his countrymen remember to build him one.

---

37 For further discussion see item 6.

Index